Thomas McKean

Forgotten Leader of the Revolution

Thomas McKean

Forgotten Leader of the Revolution

by

John M. Coleman

AMERICAN FACULTY PRESS

44 Lake Shore Drive   Rockaway, New Jersey

ISBN 0–912834–07–2
LC card no. 74–19952

Designed by Chet Kadish/Cheshire Graphics, Inc.

To Agnes

Manufactured in the United States of America

Contents

Chronology

1734

March 19 (O.S.), THOMAS McKEAN b. New London, Chester Co., Pennsylvania, to William and Letitia Finney McKean.

1742

Letitia McKean dies; McKEAN enters Dr. Francis Alison's Academy.

1750

McKEAN studies law in office of David Finney, New Castle, Delaware.

1754

Admitted as attorney in courts of Delaware, including the Supreme Court.

1755

Admitted as attorney in courts of Chester Co., and those of Philadelphia.

1758

Admitted to bar of the Supreme Court of the Province of Pennsylvania.

1762

Elected to the Delaware House of Assembly from Newcastle Co.; re-elected for seventeen years, until 1779 when declines re-election.

1763

July 21, marries Mary Borden of Bordentown, New Jersey.

1765

As delegate from Delaware, with C. Rodney, McKEAN attends Stamp Act Congress, New York.

1766

Licensed to practice in all courts of Pennsylvania, also those of New Jersey.

1772

Unanimously elected Speaker of the Delaware Assembly; re-elected 1773, again in 1776.

1773

March 12, Mary Borden McKean dies at New Castle, leaving six children.

1774

McKEAN moves to Philadelphia, becomes member of the City Committee.

Sept. 3, marries Sarah Armitage of New Castle.

Sept. 6, as delegate from Delaware, McKEAN attends first Continental Congress; except for interim in 1777, serves as a Delaware delegate until 1783.

1776

June 18–25, Pennsylvania Provincial Conference, McKEAN elected chairman.

July 2 & 4, in Congress, McKEAN votes for independence.

July 15–18, commanding the 4th Battalion of the Associators, Col. McKEAN marches to Perth Amboy, N.J.; returns to Philadelphia the end of August.

September, McKEAN elected member for Newcastle Co., attends Constitutional Convention of Delaware.

1777

July, McKEAN becomes first Chief Justice of Pennsylvania Supreme Court under the constitution of 1776; re-appointed for twenty-two years, until elected Governor in 1799.

* * * * *

In 1781, McKean was elected President of Congress; in 1787 elected to the Pennsylvania Convention for ratification of the federal Constitution; in 1789 elected chairman of the Pennsylvania Constitutional Convention. In 1799 McKean was elected second Governor of Pennsylvania under new constitution, and was re-elected in 1802 and 1805, serving the constitutional limit of three terms. He was also twice elected a presidential elector, in 1792 and 1796. Elected to Pennsylvania's High Court of Errors and Appeals, when it was established in 1780, he served there until 1805. His last public position was as chairman of the Philadelphia "Committee of Defense," in 1814.

On June 24, 1817, the Hon. Thomas McKean died in Philadelphia, survived by his wife, five children, and thirty-four grandchildren.

List of Tables and Maps

Preface

Thomas McKean is remembered today, if he is remembered at all, only as a Signer of the Declaration of Independence. The best known episode in his life was his sending for Caesar Rodney, to break the tie in the Delaware delegation in time for the vote on independence in July, 1776. (The crucial vote was really on the second of July, but in the public mind it was the Fourth.) This dramatic episode is reenacted every year as part of the traditional Fourth of July ceremonies in Philadelphia and elsewhere, and is part of the sound and light displays in the summertime at Independence Hall, but even the actors would be hard pressed to tell you more about the characters they are representing.

In his lifetime, however, McKean was a man to be reckoned with. If you had wanted a political job in the American government when it was first being formed, if you were in trouble with the revolutionary committees and needed help, or were a prisoner of war and wanted to be exchanged—then a word from Thomas McKean might have done you as much good as a word from George Washington or Benjamin Franklin. In fact, he was one of the most powerful politicians of his generation, feared and respected by enemies of the revolution as much as any man in the revolutionary apparatus.

I first became interested in McKean's career almost twenty years ago when I was asked by a friend to look up the trial of a certain Ralph Morden for treason in Easton in 1780. This seemed a simple enough request—the records would all be in the Easton courthouse, I thought, and it would only take me a few hours to find them. Actually, it took several years, for the records had been scattered in every conceivable direction. The court dockets I found in the Philadelphia City Hall, not in Easton where the trial had been held, and Justice McKean's letters were in the Historical Society of Pennsylvania at 13th and Locust Streets. Records concerning the Mordens were in Hamilton, Ontario, where members of the family had fled, and in Toronto and Ottawa.

A few papers were in the National Archives or the Library of Congress, but British army records were in Ann Arbor, Michigan. Still more information I found in the New York Public Library, the New-York Historical Society, and scattered throughout Delaware—then in Colonial Williamsburg, the British Museum in London, and other places indicated in the Bibliography. In the course of looking up a single trial I had to visit a great number of libraries and archives, and as it turned out there was no one place where I could find the full story of this trial, or any of the other fascinating episodes in the legal history of the Revolution.

Everywhere I looked the name of Thomas McKean kept appearing. He was always there—sentencing people to death or assuring them of mercy. He apparently dominated the Congress for years, and seemed to be involved in everything. From a preoccupation with the Tories my interest shifted to this law-and-order man at the center of the storm. I became convinced that McKean's career was of vastly greater significance than had generally been recognized. Because of the scattering of the records the full extent of his contribution had not been understood even by specialists.

A notable condition that has frequently discouraged the study of judicial careers has been the inaccessibility of court records, but perhaps more important in McKean's case has been the dearth of information about the revolutionary activities of the middle colonies generally. Statesmen from distant places, such as Massachusetts or Virginia, were constantly writing letters to their families or constituents back home, but those in the revolutionary capital of Philadelphia or its vicinity—who were just as deeply involved, and more strategically placed—had fewer occasions to make written reports. They have thus been overlooked by historians, who have concentrated instead on diplomats like Franklin, who was overseas most of the time writing letters to his friends in the Continental Congress, or on Tories like Joseph Galloway, who was writing to his friends in the British government. Historians, after all, are primarily concerned with written records.

In the past few decades, with the publication of the complete papers of many of the Founding Fathers, there has been an increasing embarrassment of riches on this period of our history—but the surviving record, extensive as it is, is not balanced, and so far as McKean is concerned the facts can be found only in fragments. The result is that there is still no good biography of one of the most important of our Revolutionary leaders. The job has not even been attempted (except for Roberdeau Buchanan's genealogical work in 1890), and yet, if the Revolutionary era is to be properly understood, it should be. A synopsis of the most significant points in McKean's career will explain why.

First, Thomas McKean served in the Continental Congress longer than any other member. Indeed he was the only member who served in the Stamp Act

Congress, the First Continental Congress, and the Second Continental Congress nearly continuously "until the day [he] had assurance that the preliminaries of peace were signed." Of those who stayed with the Congress he was the most prominent. Washington left to join the military; Franklin, Adams, and Jefferson left for diplomatic posts; McKean was the most influential of those who remained.

Second, he held more public offices than any of his fellow-countrymen at that time—and it is hard to think of anyone who has ever exceeded his record. Of no one else in his generation can it be said that he served in both executive and judicial posts in two states and in the federal government, and in a legislative capacity both in one state and in the federal government. During most of the Revolution McKean was a member of the Continental Congress for the State of Delaware, and at the same time Chief Justice of Pennsylvania. He was President of the Continental Congress at the time of Cornwallis' surrender at Yorktown in 1781. As a result of his multiple office-holding he was able to make a most unusual contribution to the success of the American Revolution.

Third, and most important, he did more than anyone else to establish an independent judiciary in the United States. This honor is usually accorded to John Marshall, but it is my contention that the independence of the judiciary was established during the Revolution, and that Marshall merely used the tools that had been forged for him earlier, when the new American institutions were still taking shape. The separation of powers into the legislative, executive, and judicial branches was not achieved as a result of a theory. Power had to be gained by individuals, and McKean was the one—largely because of his plural office-holding —who was able to wrest power from the revolutionary committees which dominated all other institutions at the beginning of the war.

Fourth, as Chief Justice of Pennsylvania for twenty-two years, from 1777 to 1799, he maintained law and order at the nation's capital, and was responsible for the safety of the other revolutionary leaders. He presided over many bitterly contested treason trials during the war, and pioneered in several expanding fields of law in the post-war years. As presiding officer of the highest court in the new nation's first city, he developed a body of law which was set forth in *Dallas' Reports* as the original precedents for both federal and state jurisdictions, while at the same time (be it admitted) making a personal contribution to some of the negative connotations of the term "Philadelphia lawyer."

Fifth, he was the first "Jeffersonian" state governor in the nation, being elected in 1799, and "cleansed the Augean stables" by removing Federalists from office wholesale, thereby initiating in Pennsylvania the spoils system which for better or worse was to become characteristic of American politics, as each new party came to power in turn.

Sixth, he had one of the longest public careers of the Revolutionary generation. He was the last survivor of the Stamp Act Congress, and one of the last of the Signers of the Declaration of Independence—being outlived only by John Adams, Thomas Jefferson, and one or two others. Although just two years younger than Washington, he survived him by eighteen years. His three terms, the constitutional limit, as governor of Pennsylvania and his later services in a private and philanthropic capacity were all after Washington's death at the turn of the century.

To this list might be added the establishment of a large and distinguished family —always one of his primary interests— and a consideration of the members of his family as individuals will be brought into the story chronologically. Again, one is tempted to use superlatives. There were many ramifications to this family, as can be seen in the accompanying Genealogical Chart.

*   *   *   *

Since the subject of this study is so little known, I have not been at liberty to write or to quote freely, without giving sources. For the general reader I may have gone to the other extreme and documented too heavily, but my purpose has been to nail down each point, so that anyone who cares to can see where the general ideas come from.

In accomplishing this purpose I have had the stellar assistance of Gayle Read Chipman—kin of McKean's friend, George Read. Mrs. Chipman began as a research assistant, and ended as general editor; she prepared the chronologies, the genealogy, the bibliography, and the index. There is no part of the work that has not benefited from her eagle eye and her indefatigable researches.

I am also indebted to Tinker Vitelli who prepared the maps for this book, and gave me the benefit of several helpful suggestions. Map-making for eighteenth century terrain is a difficult and specialized activity, which like genealogy contains many pitfalls for an uninitiated historian like myself. I have been fortunate in having such a gifted neighbor.

The Pennsylvania Historical and Museum Commission did me the enormous favor of substantially subsidizing the publication of this volume, thereby assuring its appearance. Dr. Donald H. Kent of the Commission's staff has read the entire text, some of it in several forms, and from time to time has provided much needed help in the course of my research. Dr. S. K. Stevens, longtime Executive Director of the Commission, was slated to write an Introduction for this book, but died before he could complete the task.

I have likewise from time to time had the advantage of useful criticisms from such knowledgable scholars as John A. Munroe of the University of Delaware, Henry J. Young of Dickinson College, Nicholas B. Wainwright of the Historical Society of Pennsylvania, and Leon deValinger, Jr. of the Historical Society of Delaware.

The Supreme Court of Pennsylvania has been most cooperative in making its records available, and its Prothonotary, Patrick N. Bolsinger, and his staff have extended many courtesies to me over the years. Justice Samuel J. Roberts has several times allowed me to use his chambers for my work, when the Court was not in session at Philadelphia.

I have had pleasant associations with several members of the McKean, Read, Rodney, Borden, and other related families, who have provided me with information, encouragement, and family portraits, but not, alas, with previously undiscovered collections of family papers. The late Mrs. Thomas McKean Downs (better known to the reading public as Catherine Drinker Bowen) attempted to locate such collections for me but became convinced that they did not exist. Since her specialty was legal biographies, one of my first concerns in undertaking this work was to ascertain that she was not interested in doing a study of Thomas McKean herself!

Lafayette College has given me several research grants to facilitate my progress, and has been extremely patient with slow results. I am grateful also to Sharon Prime of Easton, who spent the better part of a year transcribing the manuscripts which form the basis for this account, and typing numerous drafts of the text. Someday, I hope, the transcriptions will see the light of day in volumes separate from this biography, for they cast much light on the hitherto unilluminated history of the middle states area, which has long been taken for granted but not in some respects understood. Marjorie Andrews and Hilda Cooper have typed various sections of the work with flawless accuracy, in spite of many office distractions.

To all of these people and to others who have not been named I express my profound gratitude. I would not want to impute to any of them, however, responsibility for errors of fact or interpretation which may have crept in, despite their best efforts.

JOHN M. COLEMAN

Easton, Pa.
January, 1975

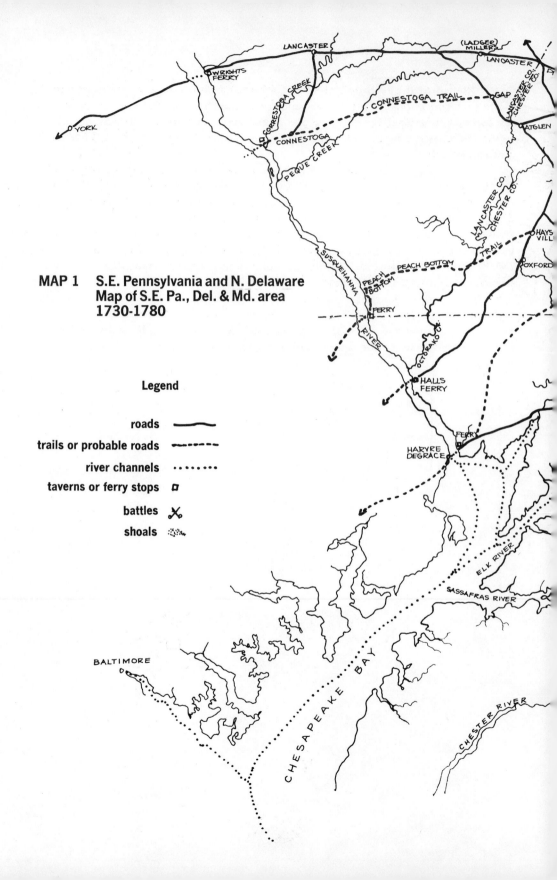

MAP 1   S.E. Pennsylvania and N. Delaware
Map of S.E. Pa., Del. & Md. area
1730-1780

Legend

roads	————
trails or probable roads	- - - -
river channels	· · · · ·
taverns or ferry stops	▢
battles	✗
shoals	⁑

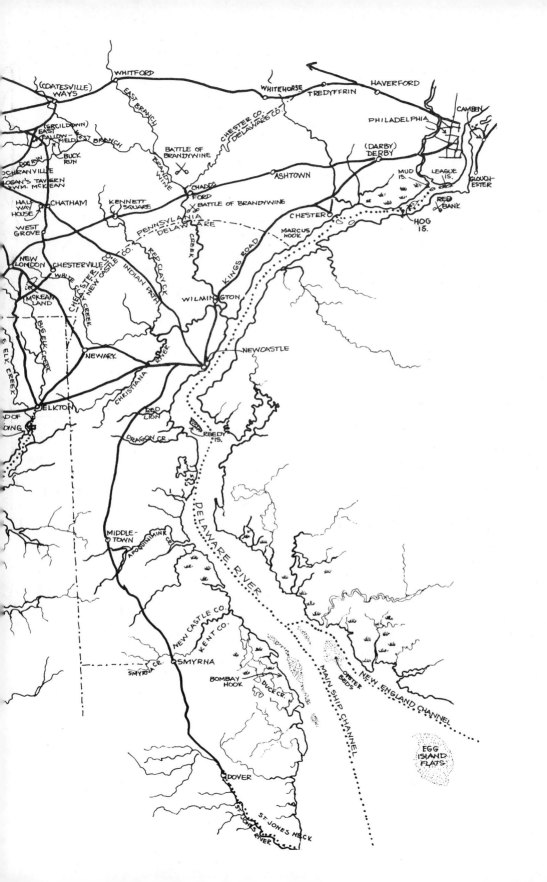

PART I

EARLY LIFE

Chapter I

Ancestors

"More than twenty-five years have passed, since I was without father or mother, sister or brother, Grandfather or Grandmother, Uncle or Aunt; and several of these connections departed this life from forty to sixty years ago." [1] Thomas Mc-Kean seldom mentioned his forebears or family; and this, his longest statement on the subject, revealed only that the author had suffered to an unusual degree the misfortunes that were common to his generation. When this letter was written, McKean was Governor of Pennsylvania, in the midst of a stormy second term, with little time for the careful editing of personal correspondence, but he had just received word of the death of his daughter, Anne.

This was a heavy blow, for Anne held a special place in McKean's usually veiled emotional life; shortly after her birth in 1773 his first wife, Mary Borden McKean, had died. Yet in writing to his bereaved son-in-law, Andrew Buchanan, he could neither express his own feelings, nor comfort the younger man. He could only resort wearily to a conventional faith. "Altho' therefore inured to such privations," his letter continued, "the last has made a deep impression, but God's will be done . . ."

At the Biblical age of threescore and ten, the former Chief Justice of Pennsylvania, and Signer of the Declaration of Independence, had little comprehension of the wellsprings of human emotion, or knowledge of the meaning of history—though few men had seen more of it enacted. No matter what he said, the tolling of these privations, a quarter or a half century gone, was not done by a man inured to them. Though he was hardened to the fact of death, and accustomed to making life-and-death decisions for others daily, he had never completely overcome his initial sense of bereavement. He reacted to each crisis with a stoic endurance, which he called Christianity, and learned to get along without sensibility or humor.

3

His first impressions remained: most of his immediate family had died before his birth, or during his early youth, and he, his brothers, and his sister had been left to make their way in the world with little except tolerably good health and clear minds as an inheritance. The omnipresence of death in those early years colored his thinking, and permanently conditioned his mood. His lifelong efforts to build up his family and defy fate by creating a dynasty were generally successful—notoriously so, in the press's view—and can only be understood in the light of this early struggle.

His mother, Letitia Finney McKean, had died when Thomas, her second son, was eight years old. His father, William McKean, far from being able to compensate for the mother's loss, was of little help to the children, and, in fact, had to be helped by them. An unsuccessful tavern-keeper, his life dwindled into a pattern of increasing failure and ended in obscurity. Robert, the oldest son, was cut off by disease in 1767 after a short but promising career, and Thomas provided an impressive monument for him, which must have wearied the man who chiseled it as much as it wearies the reader today; there was a distinct echo of political oratory in the eulogy.[2] On his father's headstone, by contrast, young Thomas provided only the laconic statement, "William McKean died November, 18, 1769, in the 65th year of his age." [3]

William's brother, the Signer's Uncle Thomas, was likewise a tavern-keeper—somewhat more successful than William perhaps, but ultimately involved in the same downward spiral. There were other brothers and sisters who left behind almost no trace. The parents of this generation, another William McKean and Susannah, died before the grandchildren were born. From the viewpoint of their grandson Thomas, the paternal line had come from and returned to nowhere. At the age of eighty, Thomas McKean wrote a short Autobiographical Sketch, in the third person as if composing his own obituary, which said nothing at all about his grandparents, and only this about his parents: "His father William McKean had married Letitia Finney of the same township [in Pennsylvania], 'tho both natives of Ireland." *

Apparently he knew little about his ancestors, and that modicum of evidence did not encourage further interest. In this situation, although learned in the law and admitted to its practice before his majority, he violated one of the basic tenets of the law: ignorant of the facts and without sufficient testimony, he tried and sentenced his paternal line to oblivion, assuming that the dismal records of his father and his uncle were due, logically, to a dismal beginning. On the contrary, genealogical research since his death has uncovered a great deal of information of which he and his contemporaries were unaware: the lives of his father and his uncle were reactions to the grandmother's personality, which was perhaps as overpowering as his own. Their downfall began with the loss of that support. Further, the paternal line closely paralled the eminently acceptable

---

* The original in Thomas McKean's handwriting, dated 1814, is to be found in the McKean Papers, IV, 43, HSP. Another copy in another hand, probably that of Joseph B. McKean, is in the Society Coll., HSP. It is identical with the original, except for minor changes in spelling. It is entitled "Biographical Sketch," but I prefer the term "Autobiographical Sketch."

maternal one. Although Thomas McKean never knew it, he had been endowed on his father's side as well as his mother's with a passion for individual liberty, and the fierce pride that turns desire into action.

The McKean [4] and Finney [5] families were both Scotch-Irish and arrived in Pennsylvania at about the same time, for much the same reasons. They were part of the same migrations from Scotland to Northern Ireland in the late seventeenth century, and from there in the early eighteenth to Penn's Province and Territories on the western bank of the Delaware. The McKean family claimed descent from Clan Donald, through the Clan MacDonald of the Isles—a rugged group noted for their quick resentment of any intrusion upon territory or rights, even in a country renowned for its unforgiving tribal feuds. Family connections were not matters of idle ancestor-boasting, but were tangible assets, for a clan's members acknowledged "kindred to forty degrees, fosterage to a hundred." [6] The name, incidentally, was always pronounced "McKane," as known not only from tradition, but from old records with alternate, phonetic spellings such as "McCain," "McCane," and "McKane."

There are numerous legends as to how and why these Scottish McKeans found themselves establishing a colony in the county of Ulster in Northern Ireland; the records show only that they went there under the auspices of the London Company, and were involved in the defense of Londonderry against the Catholic supporters of the Stuarts in 1688–89. Thomas McKean's great-great grandfather, according to a family history,[7] emigrated from Argylshire, Scotland, to Londonderry in search of asylum from religious and political persecution—a hope which soon faded. The London Company's Emerald Isle enterprise was ill-starred from the beginning; further embittered by punitive Parliamentary legislation, the settlers began a new exodus. Thomas's grandparents, William and Susannah McKean, with their children eagerly joined the general migration to America, a migration which caused a Quaker writer to exclaim, "It looks as if Ireland is to send all her inhabitants thither." [8] The Finneys and their seven children had preceded them by a year or so. Thus Thomas McKean's parents had only dim recollections of the old country, but *their* parents' sufferings, which had caused this voyage, had made an indelible impression.

A potent brew was being mixed in the character of these people: Scottish nationalism from Scotland, and Scotch-Irish frustrations from Ireland, were ready to be fermented with the growing resentments of colonial conditions in America. To a degree the Calvinistic preachers of that era were prophets, for in emotional terms the coming revolution had indeed been foreordained or predestined. It was not by accident that the Scotch-Irish Presbyterians of the middle colonies were to play such a leading role in the American Revolution. For generations they had been storing up dissatisfactions with their government.

The Finney family's experiences were similar to the McKeans'. A tradition to the effect that the McKean grandfather had been wounded and left for dead during the defense of Londonderry was matched by the story that Robert Finney, the maternal grandfather, had been left for dead at the Battle of the Boyne in 1690. Finney, moreover—and Thomas McKean must have heard this narrative from his own lips—"recovered, dreamed of the land he was to purchase, emigrated to America, and recognized it when he saw it." [9] In 1725 the Finneys settled in London Grove Township, adjoining New London, in Chester County, Pennsylvania.

Between 1715 and 1725 an ever increasing flood of Scotch-Irish refugees flowed into the southern part of Chester County. There they established new settlements, with names reminiscent of the towns in Northern Ireland, and before long these aggressive squatters had appropriated almost all the desirable lands in the area. The reception of the migrants was well described by a descendant of the Philadelphia Quakers, who beheld the influx with apprehension:

> The Scotch, of Ireland, saw in the New World a home. In New England they found the Puritans most intolerant [and] . . . moved to Long Island . . . while their application to Penn's Board of Proprietary Commissioners was being considered. The Welsh having taken up 30,000 As. in one allotment were claming for the right to set up their own separate jurisdiction in governmental affairs even to the establishment of a separate County. The Board of Commissioners saw the danger of the old tribal conditions being reestablished in the Pennsylvania Colony . . . They especially feared the Scotch, their years of unrest in the Old World, their centuries of warfare had made the Scotch contentious, and it was justly thought, since they could not adjust themselves even with the Puritans they would dominate the milder, non-resistant Quakers perhaps beyond endurance. So there was delay of action on the part of the Board with final decision to grant land on the "frontier."
>
> But while the Board was considering, the Scotch-Irish were coming . . . The "Irish," as Taylor the Quaker Surveyor called them in his reports, ceased to apply at Philadelphia. They got off at New Castle, drifted down the "peninsula" and filled the Counties of Kent and Sussex . . . establishing their Presbytery at New Castle. And "without your lief" drifted into the southern part of Chester County among the hills of the Elk and White Clay, much to the annoyance of the Board of Commrs.[10]

This comprehensive statement was a prelude to a careful report of the Chester County land-holdings of the McKean and allied families,[11] and it fits the pattern of these early migrations. There were Long Island and New England branches of several of these families, including the McKeans (or McKeens), but the records in most cases were not sufficiently complete to trace the connections with any degree of assurance. Because of the historic importance of clans, people of Scottish stock suffered from a shortage of surnames; it was not one, but several, families of the McKean and Finney lineages who migrated from Scotland to Ireland, and thence to the American colonies.

The member of the Pennsylvania community whose wanderings can most easily be followed was the Rev. Samuel Gelston, the first minister of the New London Presbyterian Church. Mr. Gelston was a friend and neighbor of the McKean and Finney families, and predecessor of the Rev. Francis Alison, who was to take over the education of Robert and Thomas McKean. He had been born in Northern Ireland and was educated and licensed to preach there. At the age of twenty-three he migrated to New England, and subsequently moved to Long

Island where he was ordained in 1717 and remained for upwards of ten years. From there he moved to the jurisdiction of the New Castle Presbytery, and was reprimanded by that body for accepting a call which had not been officially approved. Having acknowledged his transgression in this matter, and having promised never to do the like again, he was duly installed at New London in 1728—only to be removed in 1734 for immoral conduct.[12] The nature of his transgression was unspecified, but it was unusual for a minister to come to grief in this manner, and only in such a case would there be written records by which the comings and goings of these people might be traced.

The Finneys were strong Presbyterians, and Robert Finney (the Signer's grandfather) was a Ruling Elder in the Elk River congregation, later called the Rock Presbyterian Church, located on land which was claimed by both Maryland and Pennsylvania. This church was attended by people in the London Grove and New London districts until 1728, when the Presbytery of New Castle on the Delaware established a separate church at New London, with the Rev. Samuel Gelston as minister. Robert Finney was one of the chief founders of this church, and Gelston, and later Alison, were considered his protegés. In 1733 he bought a 900-acre tract called "Thunder Hill" in New London Township, where he lived as a neighbor of the McKeans for the rest of his life. Presumably this was the land he had dreamed of, while he was recovering from his wounds at the Battle of the Boyne.*

In 1720 Susannah McKean and her family arrived. Her husband may have been with her when they left Ireland, but in Pennsylvania she was always referred to as "the Widow McCain" (or "McCane").[13] Years later William Cobbett, one of Thomas McKean's bitterest enemies, wrote, "His grandfather was an Irishman who emigrated with the consent of his majesty and twelve good and true men." [14] In all likelihood, William McKean the grandfather's disappearance had a cause experienced by so many that the tragedy needed no explanation: a victim of the long voyage in over-crowded, under-fed conditions, he was one of that lost legion who died at sea, in mid-Atlantic, or within sight of the beckoning shore, like Charles Thomson's father, in that same exodus. The family first appeared in the local records when Susannah and six children applied for a survey in New London Township, Chester County, Pennsylvania.

Her application was for a survey of 300 acres about two miles south of the present village of New London on a tract which was crossed by a path from New Castle to the Indian town of Conestoga on the Susquehanna.[15] Her son by a previous marriage, John Craghton, and her nephew, William Waugh, applied for tracts adjoining hers, but after the survey, so far as is known, none of them

---

* The family legend is set forth in a number of places; see, for example, J. M. T. Finney, *A Surgeon's Life, the Autobiography of J. M. T. Finney* (New York, 1940), as follows: "It is related that Robert was one of the defenders of Londonderry and that he fought in the 'Battle of the Boyne,' during which he received a severe wound in the head and was left on the field for dead. However, he regained consciousness some hours later, caught a horse which he saw grazing near by, mounted and rode away. Eventually he made a good recovery, although he bore to his grave the scar of a fractured skull. The story is told that before leaving Ireland Robert dreamed he had gone to America and purchased land, and that after he came to America, he recognized in 'Thunder Hill' the land of his dreams."

formally registered the deeds to their holdings. This inattention to legal detail was thought by some to be characteristic of the Scotch-Irish, and was described by the authorities as pure stubbornness, and an unwillingness "to be holden" of English masters, but there may have been difficulties in finding the Land Office open at a time when they could complete the transaction. Another possibility is that the settlers were given informal licenses for land which was then claimed by the province of Maryland, until Pennsylvania had had time to secure title—and the time required was something over forty years, the debated boundary being finally fixed by Mason and Dixon in 1767.[16]

At any rate, Susannah Meacn [sic] was listed as a taxable for this land from 1725, and sometime before her death in 1731 she had managed to increase it to 400 acres. As witness of her prosperity, she had an indentured "servant maid Rachill." Like most of the Scotch-Irish, in her long struggle against adversity she had "kept the Sabbath and everything else she could lay her hands on." On August 5, 1726, James Logan, the Penn family's secretary, wrote to Isaac Taylor, the surveyor, "Widow McCane is here complaining heavily of a survey which is cutting her out of certain lands promised her." [17] And Taylor's reply on August 10 mentioned a piece of improved land which the Widow McKean had bought from one William Reynolds for ninety pounds. There is also a letter, dated "Ye 21 day of ye 3d mo. 1727," concerning a dispute with a man named Alexander, which indicates that the McKeans had faithful friends to back them up, and at least a semblance of legal justification for their claims: "Friend Abraham Emitt . . . I would have ye have a care of thy Proseding for I do no [know] yt Gabral nor his son Zacious Alexander hath no Grant for yt Land, but yt wido Mackean hath . . . ye biseness of Proporty is not to be triefeled with . . . Elisha Gatchell." [18]

In the last days of 1730 Susannah McKean wrote her will. She dictated it from her deathbed, knowing she was soon to die. She knew exactly what she wanted to have done, and how it was to be done; she would still advise the family that needed and depended on her guidance. The will, with its reminders of growing crops and wheat to be threshed, best describes the family circumstances:

> The last Will and Testament of Susannah McCain, now living Blessed be almighty God for the same in the Congregation of New London, this 28th day of December, 1730, in the name of God. Amen. Whereas I am conscious to myself of my own frailty . . . Do therefore first give, Resign and Bequeath my soul to God that gave it and my body to the Dust from whence it came in sure and certain hope of a future Glorious Reserection unto Etarnall life through the meritts of Jesus Christ our Lord.
>
> First—I leave to my sons William McCain & Thomas McCain as my heirs the four hundred Acres of land I now possess to each of them the equall half and to live together as long as they shall think fitt and when they Divide the land my son Thomas McCain is to have his half next to Mr. Saml Gelston's plantation . . . and I do leave to my son William McCain and Thomas McCain five horses and about twenty sheep and Eight cows and five calves and what wheat there is now in the mill, and what there is to thresh, and crop there is now growing on the Ground at present and all the house hold Goods and furnishing Except what belongs to my Daughter

Barbara. My son William McCain the one half & Thomas McCain the other half. and I do leave to my William McCain Ten pounds, and to my son Thomas Ten pounds, and I do leave to my daughter Barbara Murrah Thirty pounds / Thomas McCain to pay the one half of it and William McCain the other half. and I do leave to my son John Craghton two ewes. William to give one ewe and Thomas McCain the other ewe. and to keep them till they have two lambs. and I do leave my son-in-law John Henderson one shilling and to my daughter Margt Henderson one shilling to be paid by Wm and Thomas McCain and I doe leave to Mr. Saml Gelston Twenty shillings to be paid against the first of April next. Wm. McCain to pay the one half & Thos McCain the other half, and I do leave my servant maid Rachill the last year of her time, and I do leave my son John Craghton and my son William McCain & Thomas McCain my lawful Exer of this my last Will and Testament.

As witness my hand and seal this 28th day of December, Anno Dom. 1730.

Signed, sealed and Delivered in the presence of

Jo Ross   Susannah McCain [19]
Wm Waugh

In a few weeks she was dead. Her habit of control and her calm acceptance of the inevitable were clear in every line. Between the lines was a realistic appraisal of her heirs, and an admonition to remember those needier than themselves, exemplified in the charitable, perhaps formal, contribution of twenty shillings to the minister of the New London Presbyterian Church. If the next generation of the family was gradually to lose its way, deprived of her commanding presence, it should not come altogether as a surprise.

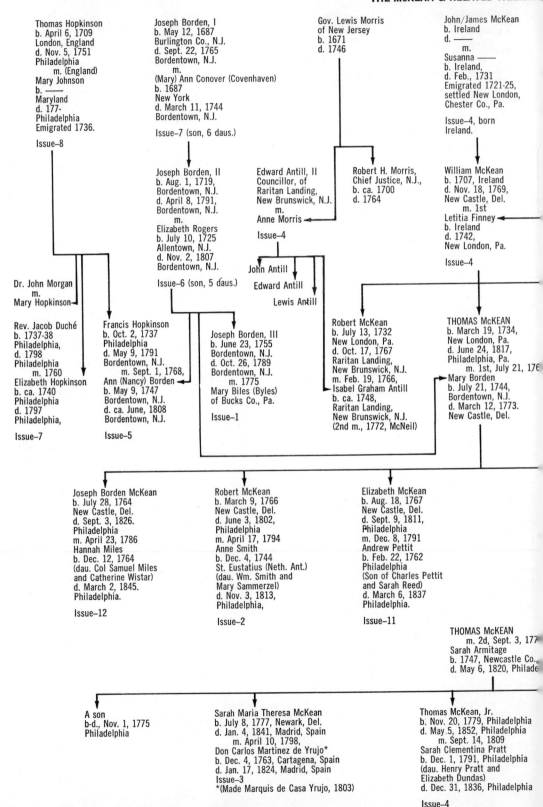

Thomas Hopkinson
b. April 6, 1709
London, England
d. Nov. 5, 1751
Philadelphia
    m. (England)
Mary Johnson
b. ——
Maryland
d. 177-
Philadelphia
Emigrated 1736.

Issue–8

Joseph Borden, I
b. May 12, 1687
Burlington Co., N.J.
d. Sept. 22, 1765
Bordentown, N.J.
    m.
(Mary) Ann Conover (Covenhaven)
b. 1687
New York
d. March 11, 1744
Bordentown, N.J.

Issue–7 (son, 6 daus.)

Gov. Lewis Morris
of New Jersey
b. 1671
d. 1746

John/James McKean
b. Ireland
d. ——
    m.
Susanna ——
b. Ireland,
d. Feb., 1731
Emigrated 1721-25,
settled New London,
Chester Co., Pa.

Issue–4, born
Ireland.

Joseph Borden, II
b. Aug. 1, 1719,
Bordentown, N.J.
d. April 8, 1791,
Bordentown, N.J.
    m.
Elizabeth Rogers
b. July 10, 1725
Allentown, N.J.
d. Nov. 2, 1807
Bordentown, N.J.

Issue–6 (son, 5 daus.)

Edward Antill, II
Councillor, of
Raritan Landing,
New Brunswick, N.J.
    m.
Anne Morris

Issue–4

John Antill
Edward Antill
Lewis Antill

Robert H. Morris,
Chief Justice, N.J.,
b. ca. 1700
d. 1764

William McKean
b. 1707, Ireland
d. Nov. 18, 1769,
New Castle, Del.
    m. 1st
Letitia Finney
b. Ireland
d. 1742,
New London, Pa.

Issue–4

Dr. John Morgan
    m.
Mary Hopkinson

Rev. Jacob Duché
b. 1737-38
Philadelphia,
d. 1798
Philadelphia
    m. 1760
Elizabeth Hopkinson
b. ca. 1740
Philadelphia
d. 1797
Philadelphia,

Issue–7

Francis Hopkinson
b. Oct. 2, 1737
Philadelphia
d. May 9, 1791
Bordentown, N.J.
    m. Sept. 1, 1768,
Ann (Nancy) Borden
b. May 9, 1747
Bordentown, N.J.
d. ca. June, 1808
Bordentown, N.J.

Issue–5

Joseph Borden, III
b. June 23, 1755
Bordentown, N.J.
d. Oct. 26, 1789
Bordentown, N.J.
    m. 1775
Mary Biles (Byles)
of Bucks Co., Pa.

Issue–1

Robert McKean
b. July 13, 1732
New London, Pa.
d. Oct. 17, 1767
Raritan Landing,
New Brunswick, N.J.
m. Feb. 19, 1766,
Isabel Graham Antill
b. ca. 1748,
Raritan Landing,
New Brunswick, N.J.
(2nd m., 1772, McNeil)

THOMAS McKEAN
b. March 19, 1734,
New London, Pa.
d. June 24, 1817,
Philadelphia, Pa.
    m. 1st, July 21, 176
Mary Borden
b. July 21, 1744,
Bordentown, N.J.
d. March 12, 1773.
New Castle, Del.

Joseph Borden McKean
b. July 28, 1764
New Castle, Del.
d. Sept. 3, 1826.
Philadelphia
m. April 23, 1786
Hannah Miles
b. Dec. 12, 1764
(dau. Col Samuel Miles
and Catherine Wistar)
d. March 2, 1845.
Philadelphia.

Issue–12

Robert McKean
b. March 9, 1766
New Castle, Del.
d. June 3, 1802,
Philadelphia
m. April 17, 1794
Anne Smith
b. Dec. 4, 1744
St. Eustatius (Neth. Ant.)
(dau. Wm. Smith and
Mary Sammerzel)
d. Nov. 3, 1813,
Philadelphia,

Issue–2

Elizabeth McKean
b. Aug. 18, 1767
New Castle, Del.
d. Sept. 9, 1811,
Philadelphia
m. Dec. 8, 1791
Andrew Pettit
b. Feb. 22, 1762
Philadelphia
(Son of Charles Pettit
and Sarah Reed)
d. March 6, 1837.
Philadelphia.

Issue–11

THOMAS McKEAN
    m. 2d, Sept. 3, 177
Sarah Armitage
b. 1747, Newcastle Co.,
d. May 6, 1820, Philade

A son
b-d., Nov. 1, 1775
Philadelphia

Sarah Maria Theresa McKean
b. July 8, 1777, Newark, Del.
d. Jan. 4, 1841, Madrid, Spain
    m. April 10, 1798,
Don Carlos Martinez de Yrujo*
b. Dec. 4, 1763, Cartagena, Spain
d. Jan. 17, 1824, Madrid, Spain
Issue–3
*(Made Marquis de Casa Yrujo, 1803)

Thomas McKean, Jr.
b. Nov. 20, 1779, Philadelphia
d. May.5, 1852, Philadelphia
    m. Sept. 14, 1809
Sarah Clementina Pratt
b. Dec. 1, 1791, Philadelphia
(dau. Henry Pratt and
Elizabeth Dundas)
d. Dec. 31, 1836, Philadelphia

Issue–4

SELECTIVE GENEALOGY

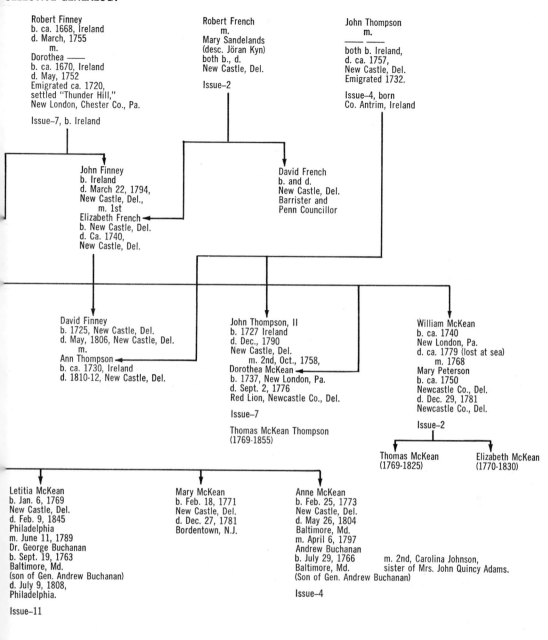

Robert Finney
b. ca. 1668, Ireland
d. March, 1755
m.
Dorothea ——
b. ca. 1670, Ireland
d. May, 1752
Emigrated ca. 1720,
settled "Thunder Hill,"
New London, Chester Co., Pa.

Issue–7, b. Ireland

Robert French
m.
Mary Sandelands
(desc. Jöran Kyn)
both b., d.
New Castle, Del.

Issue–2

John Thompson
m.
————
both b. Ireland,
d. ca. 1757,
New Castle, Del.
Emigrated 1732.

Issue–4, born
Co. Antrim, Ireland

John Finney
b. Ireland
d. March 22, 1794,
New Castle, Del.,
m. 1st
Elizabeth French
b. New Castle, Del.
d. Ca. 1740,
New Castle, Del.

David French
b. and d.
New Castle, Del.
Barrister and
Penn Councillor

David Finney
b. 1725, New Castle, Del.
d. May, 1806, New Castle, Del.
m.
Ann Thompson
b. ca. 1730, Ireland
d. 1810-12, New Castle, Del.

John Thompson, II
b. 1727 Ireland
d. Dec., 1790
New Castle, Del.
m. 2nd, Oct., 1758,
Dorothea McKean
b. 1737, New London, Pa.
d. Sept. 2, 1776
Red Lion, Newcastle Co., Del.

Issue–7

Thomas McKean Thompson
(1769-1855)

William McKean
b. ca. 1740
New London, Pa.
d. ca. 1779 (lost at sea)
m. 1768
Mary Peterson
b. ca. 1750
Newcastle Co., Del.
d. Dec. 29, 1781
Newcastle Co., Del.

Issue–2

Thomas McKean
(1769-1825)

Elizabeth McKean
(1770-1830)

Letitia McKean
b. Jan. 6, 1769
New Castle, Del.
d. Feb. 9, 1845
Philadelphia
m. June 11, 1789
Dr. George Buchanan
b. Sept. 19, 1763
Baltimore, Md.
(son of Gen. Andrew Buchanan)
d. July 9, 1808,
Philadelphia.

Issue–11

Mary McKean
b. Feb. 18, 1771
New Castle, Del.
d. Dec. 27, 1781
Bordentown, N.J.

Anne McKean
b. Feb. 25, 1773
New Castle, Del.
d. May 26, 1804
Baltimore, Md.
m. April 6, 1797
Andrew Buchanan
b. July 29, 1766
Baltimore, Md.
(Son of Gen. Andrew Buchanan)

Issue–4

m. 2nd, Carolina Johnson,
sister of Mrs. John Quincy Adams.

Sophia Dorothea McKean
b. April 14, 1783, Philadelphia
d. Dec. 27, 1819, Philadelphia

Maria Louisa McKean
b. Sept. 28, 1785, Philadelphia
d. Oct. 21, 1788, Philadelphia

Chapter 2

His Father's Failure

Susannah McCain's oldest son was named John Craghton, and his will was dated Dec. 24, 1731. He signed it by making a mark, for he was illiterate, and he chose his "Trusty Bruther Thomas McKane" as his sole executor. He mentioned his sister Barbara Murry, his sister Margaret [Henderson], his brothers William and Thomas "McKane," his cousin William Waugh, and "Mr. Gellston"—but his total estate was much less than his mother's had been. Since neither he nor his mother had completed title to their lands, they were leaving only their "rights" to these lands, for whatever they might be worth.[20]

Craghton like his mother died shortly after executing his will, and the family property was divided as directed in these two documents. From 1732 to 1742 William and Thomas McKean (the father and uncle of the Signer) were listed as taxables in New London Township. The property which they held was located two miles south of the village on both sides of the road from New Castle to Conestoga. William lived in his mother's house, some distance southwest of the road, near a spring, and Thomas lived in another house northeast of the road. William married Letitia Finney within a year or two after Susannah's death, and the young couple lived in this house during most of the short decade of married life that Letitia was to enjoy, and presumably the children were all born there.

Letitia Finney's brother Lazarus in 1729 had petitioned the Court of Quarter Sessions at Chester for a license to keep a tavern at the New London crossroad, and had been the first member of the community to receive such a license. For him it had proved a prosperous enterprise, and was well known as a local inn (the term "hotel" did not come into fashion until later); and this action may have been the inspiration for the moves which the McKean brothers subsequently made. It should be noted that as long as the McKeans remained at New London they were living near the senior Finneys of the Thunder Hill Tract, and

12

close to Mr. Gelston, whose place was taken by the Rev. Francis Alison in 1737.

In 1741, the two brothers became restless, and in that year or the following they moved. Thomas obtained a license to keep a house of entertainment at Tredyffrin "at the sign of ye Blue Ball," and William petitioned for a similar license at a place that was later called Chatham in London Grove Township. For the first year, however, he was granted only a license to sell "beer and syder," as this was a conservative community. He then rented a property called "the Half Way House" from the Pennsylvania Land Company of London, patented to John Fothergill, "Doctor of Physick," *et al.*, and in some way misrepresented the facts as to the ownership of this establishment, with the result that his subterfuge was detected and the application was rejected. Fortunately, from his viewpoint, the rightful owners neglected to press their claim, and he was able, through great persistence, to obtain the desired license. In this newly acquired establishment Letitia Finney McKean died in August, 1742, leaving four small children.

During the emergency William McKean returned to New London. He buried his wife in the graveyard of the Presbyterian Church there,[21] and arranged to leave Robert, aged 10, and Thomas, aged 8, as more or less permanent boarders with the Rev. Francis Alison, who had begun to take in students at his farmhouse manse during the previous year.[22] He left the younger children, Dorothea and William, in the care of the Finneys, and they remained in the Finney family's orbit, at New London and later at New Castle. Having done the best he could with his limited means, he returned to his tavern, and the family was never reunited under his roof again.

His plight was too common for comment in that day, but it deserved and received sympathy. He probably wanted to have the children with him, but the Rev. Francis Alison was an excellent school-master and, indeed, was to become one of the most distinguished educators on the North American continent. Obviously a mere tavern-keeper could not provide comparable opportunities for the two older boys, and the little children were too young to be deprived of some sort of maternal care. So back he went to his tavern in London Grove Township—and in less than a year there was trouble. This was a Quaker neighborhood, and the residents drew up a "Contra Petition" to the Justices of the Quarter Sessions at Chester, in the August term of 1743, as follows:

> that William McCane of the township of London Grove aforesaid having obtained for some years past a license to keep a public house, the said McCane hath in & for some time past kept or permitted a very ill conduct & Practice in and about his aforesaid house, permitting or suffering people to swear, curs, fight, and to be drunk, which practices must woodsbe very afruntive & pervoaking to Almighty God & against the pease & laws of our King and agrivol and truble to all sober & well inclined people to see such un Christian Like practices given without Remedy . . .[23]

The petition was signed by some twenty-five persons, with names like Pennock, Taylor, Morton, Bryan, and Willson, and was backed, "The Petitioners passed by offense of McKean [sic], he promising to behave better for time to come." The Court suggested compassion for a man so recently bereaved.

The situation at the Half Way House was not permanent, however, and when a certain James Logan, tavern-keeper in Cochranville in the township of Londonderry, died in 1744, William McKean moved there and the next year he married the widow Anne Logan (who had six children of her own), and petitioned for the transfer of his license from London Grove to Cochranville. Robert and Thomas McKean were still boarding with the Rev. Francis Alison; Thomas was then eleven years old. William and Anne McKean kept the tavern at Cochranville, which had a favorable location on the road from New Castle to Lancaster from 1746 to 1751, but at that point Anne died and William lost his license. There were numerous rivals for the franchise, including some of Anne's children, who were now full-grown and claiming their inheritance. By this time Robert and Thomas had left Dr. Alison's school and had launched forth on careers of their own. Robert went to Philadelphia to study "physick" with Dr. Thomas Cadwalader, an uncle of John Dickinson's, and Thomas went to New Castle to read law with his cousin, David Finney.

There has long been a legend that Thomas McKean was born at Cochranville, but the truth is that his father was there only during the years from 1744–5 to 1751–2—when Thomas was in his teens, from approximately eleven to eighteen years of age. Young Thomas may have visited his father during vacations in this period, but the only evidence that has survived is another sarcastic remark, made long afterwards by the uncharitable William Cobbett: "This vile old wretch who now disgraces the courts of the unfortunate State of Pennsylvania was formerly a stable-man at a tavern in Chester county." * Presumably Thomas occasionally did stay with his father, helping out, though he never mentioned it himself in any of his writings.

The winner in the contest for the franchise at Cochranville was James Cochran, the chief landowner in those parts, who had previously supported the licenses of Logan and McKean, but who now desired to have the privilege himself. William McKean was not listed as a taxable in Londonderry township in 1752, or in any subsequent year, and it is not at all clear what he did from this point on. He purchased a small tract at a Sheriff's sale, in East Nottingham township on the road from New London to Lewisville, and at the same time attempted to rent land again in London Grove near the original Half Way House. The tenant who had occupied these premises during the previous year, Thomas Nichols, refused to vacate, and an unpleasant squabble ensued, which so disgusted the Justices at Chester that they "Settled by rejecting both Nichols and McKean" and thereupon granted the right to Andrew Caldwell, an employee of the Pennsylvania Land Company of London.

Caldwell ran the taven until 1760, when he died, and his widow put the property up for sale or rental. William McKean once again petitioned for the franchise, but his petition was not granted. Meanwhile, the Pennsylvania Land

---

* William Cobbett, *Porcupine's Works*, VII, 300. Cobbett adds a few other charges in this pleasant little verse:

>   OLD TOPER to *currying* horses was bred,
>   But tir'd of so humble a life,
>   To *currying favor* he turned his head
>   And's now *curried* himself by his wife.

Company of London had been producing little or no income in this area for its investors, and thus decided to have a public sale in Philadelphia in 1763, for a general liquidation of its assets. Many persons who had been tenants of the company became purchasers of their previously rented land, and speculators appeared from miles around to take advantage of the opportunity. Thomas McKean, who was "aggrieved at the treatment his father was receiving in response to his petitions for a license to keep a Public House in London Grove Township," attended the sale and bought two plantations, attempting to secure his father's position against the Caldwell heirs, or other potential rivals.[24] He was not entirely successful, however, as the Caldwells had built a new house "which they could not afford to do," and finally William McKean withdrew from the contest and went to live with his son Thomas in 1763.[25]

Thomas had married Mary Borden of Bordentown, New Jersey, on July 21, 1763, and his father moved in with them (or, at least, into a house owned by his son) almost immediately. The only source of information for this period of Thomas and Mary's life gives their place of residence as Wilmington.[26] However, Thomas McKean always described himself as an Attorney at New Castle, which was then a more important community than Wilmington, since it was the legislative headquarters for the "Three Lower Counties on the Delaware" and a county seat. McKean owned various properties, at various times, in this area, and their home may have been located in the farmland outside of New Castle, on land that was considered part of Wilmington.[27] In any case, the father had nowhere else to go, and there is no other record of him, except for a scrap of paper dating from 1758 indicating that his son Thomas was solving some of his financial problems at that time.[28]

Uncle Thomas dropped from the property lists at Tredyffrin in 1753, and was living at Easttown, renting or working in a tavern there.[29] He lived until 1779, but was never in a position to help his brother or his nephew. The other members of the family had disappeared from sight altogether, so far as records were concerned, except for the Hendersons who were to reappear in a later generation. Probably, therefore, William McKean lived with (or near) Thomas and Mary all through the 1760's while his son was starting his political career, participating in the Stamp Act Congress, and increasing his practice and family. Only the end of his story was recorded. In the year 1769 William McKean was buried in the graveyard of the New London Presbyterian Church, by the side of Letitia, his first wife, and the line on the headstone over his grave was his only obituary.[30]

Chapter 3

Education under the
Rev. Francis Alison

When Letitia Finney McKean died in 1742, her sons Robert and Thomas had already learned "reading, writing, and arithmetic." [31] Even as children they were better educated than most, if not all, of their McKean aunts and uncles, and they must have received much of this training from their mother. The Finneys had always stressed the importance of education, and had been prime movers in the formation of the New London Presbyterian Church, and afterwards of the New London Academy. The plight of the McKean children, when they were left motherless and without the possibility of continuing their education, had been an important factor in the decision of the Rev. Francis Alison to start a school in his parsonage.

Such a school had been suggested by the Presbytery of Lewes as early as 1738, and the Synod of Philadelphia had appointed committees to raise money for it, both locally and in England and in Scotland, in 1739. The fund-raising began just before the alarms of the War of Jenkins' Ear; consequently, the efforts were unsuccessful. However, by 1743 there was sufficient support for Dr. Alison to open the school near "Thunder Hill" in New London, and thereafter the academy's career was interrupted but once, by the British invasion after the school had been removed to Newark, Delaware.[32] In 1744 the Synod of Philadelphia officially adopted the new institution, and provided that "all persons who pleased might send their children and have them instructed *gratis* in the languages, philosophy, and divinity." The McKean boys were among the first pupils, and at the end of the first six months there were twelve students in attendance.[33]

Dr. Alison was then in his late thirties, having been born in 1705 in County Donegal, Ireland. He had received an excellent education at an academy under the supervision of the Bishop of Raphoe, and had subsequently been a student for several years at the University of Glasgow. He had come to American in 1735, and served first as a tutor in the family of Samuel Dickinson of Talbot County, Maryland. It is doubtful that he remained there long enough to teach John Dickinson (who was born in 1732), but he had numerous contacts with him in later years.[34] In 1737 he was ordained by the Presbytery of New Castle on the Delaware, and was assigned to the New London Presbyterian Church to take the place of Mr. Gelston. Here he purchased a farm adjoining the tract of Robert Finney, the leading Elder in his church.[35]

Dr. Alison's wife was the former Hannah Armitage, daughter of James Armitage, an Englishman who had moved to New Castle and become Justice of the Court of Common Pleas and the Court of Oyer and Terminer in the Three Lower Counties.[36] She was ten years younger than her husband, and was the oldest of a large family of children born (to two wives) over a thirty-one year period. The brother closest to Hannah in age, whose name was Enoch Armitage, was later one of Thomas McKean's first clients at the beginning of his legal career in New Castle,[37] and the youngest sister (thirty-one years younger) was Sarah Armitage who became McKean's second wife, in a marriage that lasted for almost fifty years.[38]

Students from Philadelphia, such as Jacob Duché, or George Read from Delaware, lived with the Alisons, as did boys whose homes were closer, but were motherless, as were the McKean brothers and Charles Thomson. The association of the boys with Mrs. Alison, as well as with her husband, was a close one over a long period; her influence on them in these formative years must have been deep and welcome, and less forbidding than her husband's. In his brief Autobiographical Sketch Thomas McKean wrote only that at the time he entered the school he was

> in his ninth year, and although he was a year and nine months younger than Robert, they both learned the Latin and Greek languages in the same class and boarded together for near seven years. When they had acquired a knowledge of the languages, the practical branches of the mathematics, rhetoric, logic, moral philosophy and of everything taught in that institution (then the most celebrated in the Province) the two brothers quit it and separated.[39]

How much Greek they learned from this experience is dubious. Robert may have had some use for it in later years, expounding the New Testament as a clergyman, but Thomas never used or quoted from it, except in translation. He frequently used Latin, however, and incorporated long passages of classical as well as lawyer's Latin in legal opinions written without the aid of dictionaries or other references. It was characteristic of him that he said nothing about the people at the school, except for his brother (with whom he was competing), and that he made no mention of art, music, sports, or recreation of any kind. He was interested only in what he called "learning" and in making his way in the world. There was an absence of leisure or play in his boyhood—if he can be said to have had a boyhood—and his feelings or emotions were rigorously suppressed.

His brother Robert was ambitious and practical in the same way; when the opportunity arose to further his true calling as a physician through the vocation of the ministry, he switched from the Presbyterian to the Anglican Church, as the latter required training in England. There, not incidentally, he obtained medical training as well.[40] With equal unconcern and realism, Thomas switched from one political faction to another—without deviating from his basic goal.

Dr. Alison's methods of teaching have been described by several of his students, and were obviously effective. Every weekday morning, during the eight years that the school remained in New London, he heard recitations and commented on his pupils' efforts. He continued his direct, personal supervision of their work even after the Synod of Philadelphia added an "usher" (or teaching assistant) to his staff. One of his first students, Matthew Wilson of Lewes, later an usher himself, after the school had moved to Newark, Delaware, and Dr. Alison had become Vice Provost of the College of Philadelphia, wrote this rather cumbersome but vivid description of the early days at New London:

> while Latin and Greek were in teaching, we were not only taught the English grammar by comparing it with the Latin, with the principles, difficulties, beauties and defects of our mother tongue; but also we were taught to write and speak correct English. Nay, while the English, Latin, and Greek grammars were accurately taught and exemplified in every lesson in our classes, every part of the Belles Lettres, as the Pantheon of heathen mythology, rhetoric, and figures, geography and maps, chronology and Grey's *Memoria Tribunica,* Kennent's *Roman* and Potter's *Greek Antiquities* and ancient customs; Vertot's *Roman Revolutions* and other history (which we were not only obliged to read, but answer any questions out of them he chose to interrogate); and besides all these, characters, actions, morals, and events were taught and explained by him in every lesson.
>
> As knowledge and composition, or writing and speaking, are the two greatest ends of a liberal education, we received the greatest advantage from his critical examination every morning of our themes, English and Latin, epistles, English and Latin, descriptions in verse, and especially our abstracts or abridgements of a paper from the *Spectator* or *Guardian* (the best standards of our language), substantially contracted into one of our exercises . . .
>
> When we came to read *Juvenal,* our declamations began, which we wrote and delivered from memory. And after *logic,* our syllogistic disputations.[41]

The school was supported by the Presbyteries at Lewes, New Castle, and Donegal, and by the Synod of Philadelphia. Accounts prepared for the Synod in 1748 contain such entries as: "November, 1743, Elk River, £1 10 0. White Clay Creek, £1 15 0. Pencader, £1 7 6," etc. Dr. Alison was paid £20 per annum, and when he was provided with an usher, the latter received £15 per annum. These salaries were not large, even by the frugal standards of the day. Dr. Alison expressed his attitude in a letter to President Stiles of Yale, during a correspondence which began in the 1750's [42] as follows: "These sums could not bear expenses to a man in a public station; but I thank God, I have ever lived above pinching poverty since I settled in America; and can leave a small matter to my children, which will be enough with honest industry; and without this, no estate is sufficient." [43]

Here was Puritan character-building in its most strenuous and Spartan form. No pupil of Dr. Alison's was to grow accustomed to idleness or luxury. Decades later Charles Thomson, reminiscing with Dr. Benjamin Rush who had attended a similar academy, recalled clearly the four or five years he had lived "as a Scholar in the house of the Revd. Dr. Alison when a young man, and that he never saw him smile, nor in a good humor during that time." He also recalled that he had walked more than forty-five miles, to Philadelphia, "to buy a set of the *Spectators,* which were read with great pleasure by himself and Schoolmates." Another student's liveliest recollection of the school was of Dr. Alison's "proneness to anger." [44]

It was a matter of principle with Dr. Alison that students should not "live above their abilities & future incomes," and he was willing to set an example of plain living and high thinking himself. As he wrote to President Stiles, "few farmers are or will ever be able to give their sons a learned education in . . . cities . . . And farmers' sons must furnish ministers and magistrates for all our frontier inhabitants; or they must sink into ignorance, licentiousness, & all their hurtful consequences." [45]

Dr. Alison's conservative leanings made him a natural leader of the Old Side element in the Presbyterian Church. In 1741 he had played a leading role in expelling the New Brunswick Presbytery from the Synod of Philadelphia—an action which precipitated a schism in the Church that lasted until 1758.[46] The issues in this dispute had grown out of the Great Awakening of 1740, and were complicated, but the Old Side leaders felt that they were upholding the principle of an educated clergy, and of sound doctrine, as against mere enthusiasm or emotionalism. The Synod of Philadelphia became the stronghold of the Old Sides, and Dr. Alison's school was a practical expression of the theological viewpoint which he and his colleagues maintained.

The New Sides supported educational institutions, too, partly because of the pressure exerted on them by leaders like Dr. Alison. The nucleus for their efforts was the famous Log College which had been founded at Neshaminy in Bucks County, Pennsylvania, in 1726, by the Rev. William Tennent. This school had originally been opened under the auspices of the Synod of Philadelphia, but had trained many of the leaders of the Presbytery of New Brunswick, which was ousted from that Synod when the split began in 1741. The Presbytery of New Brunswick then combined with another Presbytery in New York, and since the Log College had always had a limited curriculum and inadequate resources, and was only twenty miles from Philadelphia, they arranged to have its successor opened at Elizabeth, New Jersey, in 1747—subsequently at Newark, New Jersey, in 1748, and eventually at Princeton in the early 1750's.[47]

In 1752 Dr. Alison was called to Philadelphia by Benjamin Franklin to join the faculty of the new academy there, and three years later, when the name was changed to the "College, Academy, and Charitable School of Philadelphia," he became the Vice Provost. Gradually reconciled with his former opponents of the New Side persuasion, he cooperated with several of their educational projects, and helped to heal the split between the two groups in 1758. The New Side leaders turned out to be more aggressive and successful in the promoting of educational institutions than the Old Side leaders had been, and the College of New Jersey at Princeton was particularly fortunate in sending a delegation to England for financial support at a favorable moment, when political disputes between the mother country and the colonies were relatively quiet.

The New London School, like the College at Princeton, moved several times before reaching its final location at Newark, Delaware, in 1767. Officially incorporated as the Newark Academy by John and Richard Penn in 1769, at that time it had about sixty students; but by then the political climate was not favorable. Overseas financial support dwindled, and the school's growth was slow. After the Revolution, the school's future was assured, however, as it became the College of Delaware. Among the thirteen trustees named in the original charter of 1769 were Dr. Alison and several of his former students from New London days, including Thomas McKean and Charles Thomson.[48] They had all retained a certain partiality for their Old Side, Presbyterian *alma mater* in its new little country town, which they called the "Athens of Delaware." * This feeling was undoubtedly increased as the College of New Jersey grew larger, and as the College of Philadelphia more Anglican. Temporarily, Dr. Alison despaired, and was ready "to resign [his] place in the College, & retire to the County meerly thru Chagrine—The College is artfully got into ye hands of Episcopal Trustees."[49] Thomas McKean's instinctive conservatism was first expressed in this early period when he was a dedicated supporter of Francis Alison's Old Side efforts on behalf of sound education.

One of the issues which brought the Presbyterian factions together was the effort by the Quaker political machine in Pennsylvania, under the leadership of Benjamin Franklin and Joseph Galloway, who were political if not practicing Quakers, to do away with the Penn family's proprietorship and establish a royal government in Pennsylvania. This effort included the Three Lower Counties, which, however, were reluctant to cooperate, being wary of losing the independence they enjoyed, due to their unique, semi-detached position in the province.[50]

The Quakers in the Pennsylvania Assembly, who dominated the politics of that province, and had caused trouble even for William Penn, the Founder, were annoyed when the latter's sons, Thomas and Richard Penn, deserted the Quaker faith and became Anglicans. They now began to outdo themselves in thinking of reasons for taxing the Proprietors' estates and limiting their powers. The Presbyterians, thereupon, took alarm at the possibility of losing their rights under the existing, and very favorable, Charter, and Francis Alison joined other Presbyterian leaders such as Gilbert Tennent and John Ewing in circulating a letter to the effect that "Presbyterians here . . . are of the opinion that . . . our privileges by these means may be greatly *abridged*."[51] In this effort Dr. Alison had the support of religiously oriented laymen such as George Bryan, a prominent member of his new church in Philadelphia, and John Dickinson, an ex-Quaker—

---

* Newark, Delaware, was finally chosen for this institution, as a conveniently located village which could be easily reached from Philadelphia, the Delmarva Peninsula, or the South. Much later, in 1828, a second New London Academy was organized.

both of whom would be associated thenceforth not only with Dr. Alison, but also with Thomas McKean.

The Presbyterians' struggle against the establishment of a royal government in Pennsylvania soon merged with the conflict over the policies of the British Prime Minister, George Grenville—the Revenue Act of 1764 and the Stamp Act of 1765—but by that time the denomination had formed a solid front. Contentious though they were, they came together to oppose the Quakers and the Anglican Church,[52] and to press constantly for the defense of the frontier, during the French and Indian War and afterwards.[53] In common, too, were their memories of the impoverished conditions their forebears had endured in Northern Ireland. With emotional issues like these they had no doubts whatever as to the righteousness of their political activities, or the unrighteousness of their opponents. Benjamin Franklin, who was later to unite with them in the coming struggle against the British, had been utterly repelled by their attitude at the time they were opposing his appointment as Agent to London, and had lashed out at them as "religious bigots who are of all savages the most brutish." [54]

A more hopeful and constructive cause the Presbyterians joined in was their effort to build schools and colleges for their children. In 1766 the Presbyterian leaders in the middle colonies held several meetings for the purpose of focusing their efforts on a single institution, preferably the College of New Jersey. They were also looking for new teachers and a new president. Committees were formed to make recommendations, and Doctors Alison and Ewing were among those considered for the key positions: president and professor of moral philosophy. Suddenly, in the midst of this activity, the trustees announced that they had chosen John Witherspoon of Scotland as the new president. Dr. Alison was annoyed that the committees had not been consulted, and was worried that Witherspoon might not be sufficiently versatile for his new position. His skepticism was expressed in a letter to Ezra Stiles at Yale, dated December 4, 1766, "They have chosen one Wetherspoons, a minister in Paisly in Scotland; he is esteemed as a keen satirical writer, but they know nothing of his academic abilities . . . they have voted him two hundred sterling per ann. but whether he can teach any thing but Divinity is hard to say." [55]

He need not have worried—John Witherspoon would measure up. Dr. Alison himself soon came to esteem him as a man of parts, worthy of his position, and a most forceful spokesman for the causes they both believed in.[56] In religion, politics, and economics the two leaders stood for the same idealistic principles, though Alison, as the older man, on the scene for more than twenty years, represented the views of an older generation. As often noted, John Witherspoon was to be the only clergyman to sign the Declaration of Independence. The College at Princeton would train more leaders of the American Revolution than any other institution, except possibly Harvard or William and Mary.

As an individual, however, Dr. Alison probably trained more leaders of the Revolutionary years than anyone. Among his pupils at the New London academy, and then at the Philadelphia school, were three Signers of the Declaration of Independence—Thomas McKean and George Read for Delaware, Francis Hopkinson for New Jersey and also Charles Thomson, who was to be Secretary to the Continental Congress throughout its existence. Jacob Duché, another of his students, served as Chaplain to the Continental Congress until in a fit of eccentricity he confused independence and sin. John Ewing became Provost of the University of Pennsylvania, a distinguished scientist as well as scholar. Hugh Williamson moved to North Carolina, but returned as a zealous delegate to the Federal Convention from that state, on whose behalf he signed the Constitution.

Dr. Alison's successor in New London, Dr. Alexander McDowell, maintained these high standards, and among his pupils were James Smith, a Signer of the Declaration for Pennsylvania; John Cochran, surgeon-general of the Continental Army; George Duffield, an outstanding New Side Presbyterian and Chaplain of the Pennsylvania militia and the Continental Congress; also David Ramsay, delegate from South Carolina to the Continental Congress, and the first major historian of the war. Nor were these all; the roster of the Continental Congress over the years included many alumni of the New London/Newark Academy.[57]

The political views of Dr. Alison have been preserved in several papers, including an interesting undated discourse entitled "Of the Rights of ye Supreame Power, & ye Methods of Acquiring It." They were in the mainstream of Protestant and Radical Whig thinking, and this was the philosophy his students were imbued with. "The divine right of Governors [is] a dream of court flatterers. In one sense every right is divine yt [that] is constituted by ye law of God & nature. Ye rights of ye people are divine as well as those of Princes. Nay, more divine as princes were constituted for ye good of ye people. A good Subject should bear many private injuries rather than take arms against a prince who was in the main good and useful to ye State, but if ye attempt is made against him for a precedent to hurt ye community, then the Prince evidences his disregard to ye publick welfare & forfeits ye power committed to him." [58]

There was more in the same vein, remarkably prescient. Although the following passage was written about the time of the Stamp Act, it was without a doubt the sort of thinking that animated Dr. Alison's students when they became constitution-makers in later decades: "Upon dethroning a Tyrant, or ye extinction of a Royal family, or on ye death of an Elective King, there arises an Interregnum; in which time ye political union of a State is not dissolved; they seem to be for this time in a sort of a simple democracy; & they may determine by a plurality of votes. Of those at least who used to be concerned in Civil affairs, what shall be their future plan of Government, & who shall govern them? & unless ye Majority are setting up a destructive form of polity, a smaller part ought not to break off, without ye consent of ye majority." [59]

His reasoning was conservative, yet revolutionary in the tradition of the Glorious Revolution of England. The contrast between his moods can be seen in two somewhat conflicting letters to Dr. Stiles written in the year 1766. In October he inveighed at length against a pamphlet by Joseph Galloway, supporting the Stamp Act, "in which [Galloway] used all his art to persuade the people to submit to that enslaving Statute."[60] Yet in December he wrote hopefully of "our design of an union . . . a Plan of Union to comprehend all the associated Congregational & Presbyterian Churches in North America, & *in Great Britain.*[61] Would God give wisdom to form such a plan, how great a blessing would it be to our churches." [62]

It would be too much to expect that American independence was visible in 1766, even to this prophet, but the spirit of freedom was there, and a deep concern for political affairs. Not all of Dr. Alison's students were to support independence consistently, but most would, and George Read, who voted against the proposed Declaration on July 1, 1776, nonetheless soon became a Signer and supported the American cause diligently thereafter. As for the Rev. Jacob Duché, who had apparently wedded himself to the cause of independence by marrying Elizabeth Hopkinson, sister of the Signer-to-be, his sudden and surprising defection can be explained charitably as the effect of imprisonment and mistreatment by the British on an erratic and egotistical mind. The enthusiasm of Thomas McKean, Charles Thomson, and their fellow alumni never waned, from the beginning to the end of the struggle, nor indeed beyond. Dr. Alison laid the groundwork for much that was to happen in the Revolutionary era not only through the subjects he taught, but by the manner in which he taught his students to think.

Chapter 4

Early Career in New Castle

New Castle was named by Col. Richard Nicholls, who captured the town from the Dutch in 1664, on orders from the Duke of York. No one knows whether Col. Nicholls was thinking optimistically of Newcastle-on-Tyne, or, diplomatically, of William Cavendish, then Earl of Newcastle. Having assisted in the preparation of the "Duke's Laws," Nicholls supervised their adoption in the new possession, but with tact and patience, so that the change-over in government was notably smooth and lasting.[63] The residents, then and later, seemed to waver in their designation of the place—New Castle and Newcastle being used interchangeably for the town and county. The customary and most convenient form, however, was to use New Castle for the town and Newcastle for the county.

The area was unique in a number of respects, and deserves a brief description. Although laid out as "Fort Casimir" by Peter Stuyvesant, governor of the Dutch possessions in these parts, the town had been known as "New Amstel," and in its early days was occupied by Swedes, Finns, and Dutch, in addition to the omnipresent English. The port could be reached by ocean-going vessels, but normally was safe from privateers, for navigation in the Delaware required a pilot familiar with the constantly shifting shoals. Shortly before the arrival of William Penn the location was described by two Dutch travellers, as follows:

> New Castle is about eight miles from the falls [Trenton], and the same distance from the mouth of the river or the sea [Lewes]. The water in the river at New Castle, at ordinary flood tide is fresh, but when it is high spring tide, or the wind blows hard from the south or southeast, it is brackish, and if the wind continues long, or it is hard weather it becomes a little saltish.[64]

Here, at the main port of call on the Delaware River, William Penn first landed in 1682, and the farsighted Proprietor soon realized that the eastern shore

24

of the peninsula was an essential corridor to his new province, lying at the head of the bay. The following year Penn's Second Frame of Government was agreed upon by the colonists, and he succeeded in adding to his jurisdiction the "Three Lower Counties," purchased from the Duke of York. Unfortunately, their precise boundaries were somewhat obscured in flourishing verbiage, and certain areas were alternately or simultaneously claimed by Pennsylvania and Maryland for many years. The three counties in Pennsylvania were Philadelphia, Chester, and Bucks; the Lower Counties were Newcastle, Kent, and Sussex.

The Assembly and Council organized under the Second Frame of Government spent themselves in arguing and contradicting each other, and although a united Council had been formed, with eighteen Councillors (three from each of the six counties), the Councillors from the Lower Counties withdrew to form a separate body in 1691. They then high-handedly proceeded to reinstate their old laws and draw up new ones, making their first statement on the rights of self-government at this time. *Amor patriae* seems to intensify in inverse ratio to the area of *patria*. Penn reluctantly acknowledged this separate legislative body, and appointed William Markham Deputy Governor for the Lower Counties and Thomas Lloyd for Pennsylvania proper.

Penn's troubles in England were even greater than they were in America, and for two years, after 1692, he lost his American possessions altogether and they were placed under the authority of New York's colonial governor, Benjamin Fletcher. Reinstated to his proprietorship, Penn found that the Lower Counties had their own Supreme Court and were insisting on their own legislature. He was still in a weak position and his efforts at compromise were to no avail. In 1703/04, the first General Assembly of the Lower Counties met at New Castle; it was organized as a unicameral body as a slight concession to the Proprietor, and it continued to meet there until 1777. More by way of wisdom than courtesy, the Lower Counties agreed to accept Pennsylvania's governor as their own.

Thus New Castle had the unique advantage of being the only place on the continent where there was a popular assembly, but no governor in residence to oppose its Whig leanings. The Governor of Pennsylvania and the "Territories," as they were sometimes called, had his hands fully occupied in Philadelphia, and was primarily a spokesman for the Proprietors, rather than the British Crown. Thereby the Lower Counties normally enjoyed a degree of political freedom, or "salutary neglect," as Edmund Burke termed it, that was much envied by the larger colonies. For this same reason restless elements such as the Scotch-Irish immigrants, preferred to disembark at New Castle and avoid the complications of life in the provincial capital, Philadelphia.

There were other advantages to the singular status of the Lower Counties. Although bifurcated below the gubernatorial level, Penn's original grant and these purchased counties were legally one province. Citizens of one portion were also citizens of the other, while retaining the rights and obligations of the first—a technicality which proved very useful to those of sufficient stamina and ambition, two qualities with which McKean and some of his friends were notably endowed. This arrangement provided an even wider opportunity than the English procedure, familiar and more or less in use in the colonies, by which a candidate for election was not required to be a resident in his constituency. This oddity gave McKean an unimpeachable position later, when opponents and critics could not believe that the multiplicity of offices which he held could really be legal.

The semi-detached status of the Lower Counties also provided an opportunity for the Assembly, which was enjoyed to the full, but carefully not called to public attention. Penn's charter contained the proviso, applicable to all the colonies, that the laws passed by the colonial assemblies must be sent to the Privy Council in England within five years of enactment; if that body did not annul them within six months after receiving them, the legislation would remain in force. Yet there is no record that any law passed by this small Assembly was ever disallowed by the Crown, for the simple and startling reason that none was ever sent.[65] Others elsewhere were aware of this omission, but apparently kept their thoughts to themselves. In a rare moment of irritation, Benjamin Franklin, in England, writing to Charles Thomson, remarked, "What you mention of the Lower Counties is undoubtedly right. Had they ever sent their Laws home as they ought to have done . . ." [66]

Thus, from its founding New Castle was a court town, and a center of political activity. There was a Swedish settlement upstream on Christiana Creek, which became Wilmington, and there were a number of Dutch settlements such as Fort Nassau, near the present Gloucester, New Jersey, but otherwise Penn's settlers beheld a wild valley. The wolves in the neighborhood were so numerous and dangerous that the inhabitants had to dig pits as traps to safeguard themselves—the more direct extermination required too much valuable ammunition. However, the growth of the newly and carefully laid out Philadelphia was extremely rapid, and other towns such as Chester, once the tiny settlement of Upland under the Swedes, expanded as well, and others began to spring up along the river.

New Castle continued to be an important center, not only as the capital of the Lower Counties, but also as a transportation center. Travellers from Philadelphia southward would drop down the Delaware River to New Castle, then continue their journey by water or cross the peninsula to board ship again on the Chesapeake Bay. New Castle enjoyed this favorable situation throughout the eighteenth century, and received more traffic in the nineteenth, when the national capital was moved to Washington. Not until the coming of the railroad, when the north-south route was shifted to the west, through Wilmington, did New Castle lose its importance. Even in the eighteenth century, however, New Castle lacked the protected docking facilities which would have enabled it to compete with Philadelphia as a port, and had no streams adequate to produce water power as had the Brandywine Creek, for instance, where small industries began to appear in the 1740's.[67] So New Castle remained a stop-over point, with excellent taverns, and a legislative and judicial center, but never became a metropolis.

The most prosperous activity was river traffic, with coastwise craft called shallops, light open boats propelled by sails and oars, sailing up and down the river daily, and ocean-going trade with the British Isles, Southern Europe, the Madeiras, and the West Indies. The larger ships, of necessity, originated from

Philadelphia or Wilmington, but usually they put in at this little port on their way through. Produce from the Delmarva Peninsula, such as flour, corn meal, or lumber, was brought on board, and imported goods for the region were unloaded here. In 1764 a lighthouse to guide ships through the Delaware Capes, before picking up the river pilot, was erected near Cape Henlopen.

With a population of about 1,000 then—and, in fact, through the Revolution—New Castle offered McKean many opportunities in addition to the special advantages mentioned. Above all, there was the chance for professional training and advancement and, more immediately, a livelihood and the means to secure his future. In 1750, at sixteen years of age, Thomas McKean left Dr. Alison's school at New London, and came to the capital of the Lower Counties, some twenty miles distant, to read law with his cousin, David Finney. From that date, and for the next sixty years, he would be making money and acquiring offices and power, first at New Castle and then in Philadelphia, without let-up or stint. There was no limit to his energy or ambition, and his rapid rise might well have been due to, rather than despite, the lively competition.

In person he was "tall, erect, and well proportioned. His countenance displayed, in a remarkable manner the firmness and intelligence for which he was distinguished. His manners were impressive and dignified." [68] A contemporary described him as a "veritable Anak," and he was, in fact, by the standards of his generation, a giant, standing well over six feet, spare and long-limbed, with the straight-arrow posture essential to, and derived from, constant riding. Proof of his great physical strength is found in several courtroom accounts, possibly apocryphal, but all agreeing upon a man ready and able to swoop down upon a timorous posse and indiscriminately knock heads together, without fear or hesitation.

His superb horsemanship was no minor asset during the early, hectic days of the Revolution. McKean often had to cover incredible distances, and sometimes did so at a speed which seemed to result in his appearance at two places simultaneously. Nor did this skill and endurance diminish in later days, when the judicial circuit covered a roadless wilderness and mountains, and his colleagues seemed subject to assorted gouty pains, necessitating carriages, or at least, a much slower pace. In all his life McKean never had a serious accident with a horse.

The long nose in his portraits makes the comparison too obvious, perhaps, but in the high, broad forehead and the pronounced bone structure there is an unavoidable resemblance to the stern Senators of an earlier republic. The set of the jaw, the somewhat compressed lips, marked conscious efforts at self-control—not always successful for McKean. The same features appear in portraits of the older John Calvin, who, incidentally, was also trained as a lawyer and likewise enjoyed his wine. The awe caused by the appearance of the "gigantic Chief Justice" must sometimes have been caused by assets congenital, as well as those he had achieved.

The material rewards of success, the visible signs of power, were to be essential to McKean throughout his life, and he began to obtain them as soon as he had perceived his most direct route to do so. His motivation was not entirely materialistic, however, and the later deliberate choice of the revolutionary's course was equally characteristic; perhaps his excessive self-confidence blinded him to the possibility of defeat. Towards the end of his life this self-confidence had aged into egotism. In retrospect he felt his accomplishments had been entirely his own, and all unassisted. Witness the Autobiographical Sketch, written in his old age, wherein he described his apprenticeship at New Castle:

> [He] went to the once city, then town, of Newcastle to read law with a cousin, David Finney, who was a practicing lawyer and had a good law-library: he was there but a few months when he engaged as a clerk to the Prothonotary of the court of common pleas to perform the duties of that office. He by this situation, at the same time he was studying the theory, learned the practice of the law.
>
> In about two years after this by his assiduity and conduct he was approved by the county court deputy Prothonotary and Register for the probate of wills &c for the county, and acted in that character until he was twenty years of age (his Principal residing on his estate in the county of Sussex near eighty miles from Newcastle.) Such was his industry and reputation that before he was twenty-one years of age he was admitted an Attorney at Law in the courts of common pleas for the counties of New-castle, Kent, and Sussex upon Delaware, and also in the supreme court. In a year he was in considerable practice, and the year ensuing he was admitted as a Lawyer by the court of his native county of Chester, and soon after in the city and county of Philadelphia.[69]

One would think that the Finneys had had nothing whatever to do with his achievements. In fact, three generations of Finneys were actively helping him: his grandfather, Robert Finney of Thunder Hill, who lived until 1755, when young McKean was admitted to practice in Chester County; his uncle, Dr. John Finney, "the wealthiest owner of real estate in the vicinity [of New Castle];" [70] and his cousin, David Finney, who was soon to be "the wealthiest citizen of Delaware." [71] McKean, of course, had to give satisfaction in the various positions offered him, in order to advance in his profession, but without the Finney influence and prestige he would never have had so many opportune offers.

Since McKean never gave David Finney his due—in any of his surviving papers —the memoirs of Thomas McKean Thompson may supply an adequate description of this generous benefactor. T. McKean Thompson was a nephew to both Thomas McKean and David Finney. For the benefit of his children, years later, he wrote reminiscences concerning those members of the family he had known. According to Thompson, his aunt Ann Thompson

> a sensible and accomplished woman, married, when young, David Finney, Esq., of New Castle, on the West bank of the Delaware River, the only son of Dr. Finney, an eminent and wealthy physician of that town. His mother was Miss French, the sister of David French, Esq., a distinguished English barrister, a companion, and probably, one of the counselors of the proprietary Penn family and a man of great wealth.* Dr. Finney bestowed on his son a liberal education. He studied law, not with a view to its emoluments, for at the time of his marriage to my aunt, he was heir apparent to two of the finest estates in the Province of Pennsylvania, and the

---

* This association with the Penns, remote as it was, should be noted in connection with McKean's subsequent appointment as attorney for the Penns in Delaware.

chief part of which on the death of his father and Uncle French (who never married) he afterwards actually inherited. He therefore, as I believe, never became a practicing member of the bar, but was advanced to a seat on the Supreme Court. [So far as his character was concerned] I have already told you his education was liberal, his bodily health was uninterrupted through life. I have no recollection of his ever having had a disease, till that which resulted in his death. His understanding was sound, his general deportment kind and cheerful, and his benevolence unbounded. As a husband, he was uniformly affectionate, kind, and respectful; in his eyes his wife was hardly capable of doing wrong; and as a father he was affectionate and indulgent, it may be to a fault.[72]

Although McKean described Finney as a "practicing lawyer," he did not consider that he practiced very diligently; Thompson was not sure that Finney practiced at all, but was "advanced to the Supreme Court." Lists of members of the bench and bar, prior to the Revolution, are sparse, and were then also. All evidence makes it plain, however, that most members of the bench were neither learned in the law, nor expected to be learned in the law, far less required to practice it.[73] David Finney's abrupt advancement, therefore, was not unusual at the time; the prime requisites he had in plenty. His appointment to the Supreme Court of Delaware was not made until 1778, a year after his former pupil had risen to a higher rank.

Finney's name appears, prior to the Revolution, on certain lists of members of the Supreme Court of the Lower Counties, but this was not the Supreme Court per se. Detailed lists produce a peculiarity: from time to time, when required, special commissions were issued to certain persons to act as judges for the trial of blacks, the court to sit for certain sessions, and for those only. This court was styled the Supreme Court and apparently had the like authority, brief though it was; appeal from its verdicts lay only to the Crown. David Finney was twice thus commissioned, on January 25, 1771, with Evans Rice, and again on December 9, 1775, with John Jones, all of Newcastle County.[74]

David Finney inherited properties not only from his father, but even more from his mother and her brother, David French, who was connected with the Penn family. He had lands across the Pennsylvania line, in Chester County, as well. When McKean arrived in New Castle to read law with him, his wealthy cousin might have been living in what was later the Booth house, across from the Court House Square, or (when the south wind brought brackish water and mosquitoes) at his country estate, the Hermitage.[75] Thomas McKean Thompson remembered the Finney households thus:

He sold one large farm in New Castle County, called Muscle Cripple for $20,000.00 . . . The property was worth that sum in hard money. It was one of the finest farms in the State of Delaware, some five hundred or more acres of excellent land, with convenient buildings, well watered, etc., and within convenient distance of New Castle . . . I remember Muscle Cripple well . . . My Aunt [David Finney's wife], accostomed to a plentiful table, kept a large poultry yard of turkeys, several kinds of ducks, and common fowls, to the feeding of which she daily attended herself . . . Mr. Finney with his family removed thence to their mansion house in New Castle, and subsequently to his farm adjacent to that town, where he departed this life at an advanced age . . . Mrs. Finney was an estimable woman. Besides the advantage of a good education, she had a large share of practical knowledge, what we call "common sense," was cheerful, kind, benevolent, and I trust and believe a sincere Christian. having become a member of the Presbyterian Church in early life, and continued a consistent member until her death.[76]

McKean's uncle, Dr. John Finney, had settled in New Castle about the same time the grandfather, Robert Finney, had settled in Chester County. A doctor of medicine and a surgeon, he was also a Justice of the Peace for Newcastle County, and Judge of the Orphans' Court for many years. He owned half a dozen of the principal houses in the town and "about thirty tracts of land, comprising several thousand acres in New Castle, St. George's, and Appoquinimink Hundreds in Newcastle County." [77] With such a multitude of residences, his precise home at a given time is a matter for guessing, but the likeliest at the time of McKean's arrival would be the now misleadingly called Amstel House. He had bought it in 1738 for a hundred and ten pounds, and later added what became the main section. He continued adding to his real estate as he prospered; in 1751 and again in 1761 he bought land in Londonderry Township, Chester County, Pennsylvania. His sense of responsibility as a leading citizen of the community was not lost in all these acquisitions, and from time to time he would also accept political and military positions. Several times his name appeared in the local records in conjunction with those of his son David, and his nephew, Thomas McKean.[78]

As a poor relation in such homes, McKean was expected to work at all times, and he did. As Thompson's memoirs describe him, "His patrimony not being large, from a sort of necessity he early contracted the habit of industry, which stuck by him through life. When I first became acquainted with him . . . he was remarkable for his industry and preciseness . . . I have heard him say he made four hundred pounds, or Pennsylvania currency, about $2,000 the first year of his practice." [79] By comparison William Livingstone, a typical New York lawyer earned £70 in 1748–1749, the first years of his practice. In 1749–50 he made about £145—with his relatives supplying the bulk of his commissions. Livingstone's income did not reach £400 until 1754, after which it increased rapidly. It was by no means rare that lawyers less fortunate in kin or talent had to supplement their legal fees by manual labor.[80] McKean, in that first year of practice, was just coming of age. Only four years earlier he had been living with Dr. Alison, who had been contented with, or resigned to, an annual salary of twenty pounds.

One of the first things the young McKean did upon arrival was to become, officially, a member of the Presbyterian Church of New Castle. After a seven-years' exposure to Dr. Alison, a commitment of this sort on his part was almost inevitable. In the records of the church there is a subscription list, dated 1750, with the sixteen-year-old Thomas McKean listed as making four payments of two shillings, four pence, each. He was included in the alphabetical list of members of this church as late as 1772, but these two references are the only ones.[81] His piety over the years became increasingly a matter of form and was not entirely satisfactory to his observant nephew, who commented cryptically, "He had no other proof of attachment to religion than what is often given by men in high places: outward respect, such as going to church on the forenoon of the Lord's day, etc." [82]

During his years of apprenticeship he became "by habit and inclination [a] man of business." [83] He perfected a precise, legible handwriting that was a pleasure to read, and developed the logical and orderly procedures whereby he accomplished and recorded the multifarious transactions of an increasingly busy life. He saved rough drafts of important letters, and the drafts were as neat and polished, from salutation to formal close, as the finished copies. Letters to friends and family were as carefully composed as legal briefs; in fact, it was taken for granted that anything he wrote would be clear and accurate, in both penmanship and content. This habitual precision "some years afterwards used to challenge [his nephew's] patience when occasionally calling him to his meals, as it was utterly inconsistent with his established usage to quit his employment whether reading or writing until the paragraph was finished." [84]

The fact that David Finney, who had no need of a profession, had chosen law, whether or not he practiced it, marked the changed status of the legal profession in the colonies. Once so distrusted that attempts had been made to dispense with it, the profession had risen to éclat and power. The complications of rising prosperity, expanding commerce, and above all, matters having to do with the ownership of land had transformed lawyers into a necessity which the ordinary citizen could no longer do without. In remote settlements the justice of the peace, the plaintiff, and the defendant might all argue from their own copies of Jacob's *Every Man His Own Lawyer*. First published about 1730 in England, this legal handyman's guide went through at least seven editions in the colonies. But the seaboard was rapidly becoming too sophisticated and competitive for such do-it-yourself jurisprudence.

Without even the *pro forma* law schools of England, the accepted legal training was simply a matter of study with an admitted attorney, and watching the judicial process in action, when possible; in fact, this was the English procedure, although William Blackstone, disgusted with the system's inadequacies, was soon to reorganize it. In isolated areas the legal preceptor might have such a small practice that his apprentice's duties were largely devoted to overseeing quills and sand-sprinklers, and dusting off the green bag which was the symbol of the profession. Nor was such a lawyer's library likely to afford much reading matter for study. Patrick Henry, McKean's junior by two years, grew up to become a farmer, then a merchant, in a backwoods community in Virginia, with only one professional attainment—he had been taught a little Latin by his father—and yet, when these ventures failed, he decided upon law. After borrowing two other requisites, Coke's *Commentary upon Littleton,* and a *Digest of the Virginia Statutes,* and two months' study, he proceeded to Williamsburg, where he applied for, and received, a license to practice the profession. [85]

The admitted scarcity, if not absence, of David Finney's legal practice for his young apprentice's observation was outweighed by certain great advantages, especially the opportunity for observing the judicial process in the capital of the

Lower Counties, and Finney's law library, which was undoubtedly augmented by that of his uncle, Col. David French, the "distinguished English barrister . . . of great wealth." Although the *Duke of York's Book of Laws* (1676–1682) and the collections of statutes passed by the assemblies of Pennsylvania and the Lower Counties, and probably those of neighboring colonies, were at hand, law libraries such as these were handicapped in a particularly important area. There were no collections of provincial opinions, and thus no American precedents. Trial records did not have to be kept; their Honors regarded their notes as personal memoirs, or mere memoranda. A. J. Dallas, attempting one of the first such collections, his *Reports,* which appeared in 1790, wrote many a desperate note, hoping to refresh an honorable recollection. In the colonial era there was, therefore, little alternative to the study of English law reports and guides. This had "a prodigious effect in making American law imitative of the English, by making English cases and legal treatises the measure of competence, the fount of inspiration, and the precedent for emulation." [86]

In widespread use in the colonies were Michael Dalton's *The Countrey Justice* . . . first published in London, 1618; Edward Coke's *The First Part of the Institues of the Laws of England, or a Commentary upon Littleton,* London, 1628, which went through many editions; and William Hawkins' *A Treatise of the Pleas of the Crown,* London 1716. Another highly esteemed work that was studied by young McKean was *The Security of Englishman's Lives, or the Trust, Power and Duty of the Grand Juries of England* by John Somers, reprinted in Boston in 1720, and later. Others considered of such value and practical application that they endured not only through many English editions, but American as well, up to the Revolution, included *English Liberties or the Free-Born Subject's Inheritance* by Henry Care and William Nelson; Edward Wingate's *Maxims of Reason: or the Reason of the Common Law of England,* London, 1658; and Matthew Bacon's *A New Abridgement of the Law,* Savoy, England, 1731–59.

The more controversial books, perhaps not incidentally, were mainly translations. Montesquieu's *The Spirit of the Laws,* translated and published in London in 1750, reflected the viewpoint of the philosophe rather than the jurist, and aroused relatively little debate. But Puffendorf's *The Law and Nature of Nations,* translated in 1720, and Burlamqui's *Principles of Natural Law,* translated in 1748, were read by many older members of the bar and bench only in order to be denounced. Blackstone's monumental *Commentaries on the Law of England* was still a-building, to be published in 1765—the cornerstone, *An Analysis of the Laws of England,* having been placed in 1756.[87] By 1754 the new apprentice had been admitted to practice in all courts in the Lower Counties.

In 1756 the Justices of the Supreme Court of the Lower Counties appointed McKean "not only without any solicitation but without any previous knowledge on his part" to prosecute the pleas of the Crown in Sussex County. The appointment was confirmed in 1757 by the Attorney General of the Province and Lower Counties, John Ross, who lived in Philadelphia and needed a local attorney to act in his place. He further directed young McKean, "You are to sign all Indictments in & with my name." [88] The following year, at the age of twenty-three, McKean was elected Clerk of the House of Assembly at New Castle "of which he was unapprised until informed by the Speaker, Benjamin Chew, Esquire." He accepted and was reelected in 1758, but "after that declined it." The first time he was elected by a majority vote; the second time the vote was unanimous.[89] Concurrently, his legal practice was expanding, as were his friendships.

Meanwhile, studying law in London, John Dickinson had met Robert McKean, who was studying both theology and medicine, and shortly after Dickinson's return he met Robert's younger brother, to the instant and lasting pleasure of both. The first letter that Thomas McKean received from John Dickinson, with whom he corresponded regularly thereafter for half a century, was dated October 20, 1757:

> As I flatter myself that we are to look upon ourselves as friends to each other throughout Life, I hope you will not expect any declaration of my Esteem, but will be convinced by all my actions & the unaffected freedom of my Behaviour towards you, that it is very great . . .
>
> I hope your house [in the Lower Counties] will treat the Governor with more respect than ours, & show the world you have at least more good manners, if not more Christianity than the peaceable people.
>
> Please to present my Compliments to Miss McKean [his sister, Dorothea] & believe me Your sincere friend . . .[90]

In the spring term of the year 1758 McKean was admitted to practice before the Supreme Court of Pennsylvania, the highest honor to which a lawyer could aspire in the colonies at that time. Only twenty or twenty-five lawyers were then included in this elite, without comparison the most prestigious group in the colonial legal profession. Many of the best-known lawyers were not yet members: Francis Hopkinson, Edward Biddle, Andrew Allen, Jasper Yeates, Joseph Reed, Elias Boudinot—to mention only a few. John Dickinson's name does not appear in the "List of Attornies of the Supreme Court of the Province of Pennsylvania," written by Edward Burd, who had been admitted in 1774, and again post-Revolution in 1778, and was Prothonotary of the court from 1778 to 1806.[91] Dickinson had been admitted to the New Castle bar in 1753, a year before Thomas McKean, and also in the city and county courts of Philadelphia.* The fact that he was not a fully-recognized lawyer in Philadelphia might have been one reason why he entitled his most famous work *Letters from a Farmer in Pennsylvania* . . .[92] McKean's recognition, as he himself wrote, "considering his youth, occasioned a little envy not only among the Juniors, but also some of the Seniors of the profession." The envy of others, far from embarrassing him, was "an additional spur to his industry, and he was indefatigable in acquiring legal knowledge." [93]

---

* Dickinson went to England shortly after his admission to the Philadelphia lower courts, and returned in 1757. He does not appear to have actively practiced law for some time thereafter in Pennsylvania, and it may be that he never found time, or did not care to fulfill the necessary two years' requirement. A perusal of Dallas' volumes appears to confirm this conclusion. In April, 1773, Dickinson appeared before the Supreme Court, but "with Tilghman," i.e., not in his own right.

  There is some evidence that a lawyer having completed the requirements of the Inns of Court and being there admitted to the bar, was *ipso facto* admitted to the highest courts of province or colony upon his return, in the early part of the eighteenth century. But if this is true in the case of Dickinson, no supporting evidence has so far been found.

The French and Indian War, raging during these years both along the frontier and on the high seas, had relatively little effect on the Lower Counties. McKean and several of his associates enrolled in Captain Richard McWilliam's Company of Foot in 1757, and drilled from time to time, but that was the extent of their activity. David Finney, John Thompson, who was soon to marry McKean's sister Dorothea, and George Read, his classmate at Dr. Alison's academy, were also members of McWilliam's company.[94] This experience strengthened friendships and cemented political and legal alliances, but induced little enthusiasm for the army in this group—all remained strong believers in civilian control over the military. During this emergency, McKean's uncle, John Finney, a Colonel as well as Judge and Doctor, was commissioned to equip three companies from the Lower Counties by William Denny, Governor of the Province.[95]

In this same year, 1758, McKean was admitted to the Society of the Middle Temple in London. He did not go to England, however, as several writers have claimed on the evidence of the certificate and a bookplate which noted his membership in the society, but was admitted *in absentia* as a special student, *admissus est in Societatem Medii Templi Londoni—specialiter,* and was required to pay £4 14 6 for fees and the printing of his certificate.[96] Admission *specialiter* was an extension of the older custom of admission *per favor,* a shortcut to the rank of barrister by which a number of Americans had avoided the necessity for residence and examinations at the Inns of Court.[97]

In fact, by the early 18th century, the Inns of Court and Chancery had atrophied to little more than gentlemen's clubs, some forfeiting even that status; Clement's Inn was occupied by local brewers and actors from the Drury Lane Theatre. Law students actually in search of legal training were simply registered at one of the Inns of Court, then articled to London attorneys, special pleaders, or conveyancers for serious study. By 1753, Blackstone was urging that such studies be transferred to the supervision of the universities. To emphasize the point, he began his famed lectures and continued them at Oxford. Recognizing their parlous state, the Inns of Court in 1762 changed their regulations and requirements, and began to recover their earlier eminence.*

---

* "Gentlemen from all over England sent their sons to be articled to London attorneys, just as they had once sent them to the Inns of Court . . . For the Inns of Court and Chancery were more decayed even than the eighteenth-century universities. New chambers were still being built, but Clement's Inn was accommodating local brewers . . . comedians from Drury Lane . . . The inns were used as clubs by the gentlemen of all sorts . . . Serious law students, such as Mansfield, made private arrangements for instruction with special pleaders and conveyancers."

William Blackstone wrote that the interpretation of the law, in both Inns and universities, was being left to "obscure and illiterate men." He therefore "concluded that the universities were the places where future judges and administrators must thenceforth be taught," and began lecturing at Oxford in 1753, "on Mansfield's urging . . ." Alan Harding, *A Social History of English Law* (London; Penguin, 1966), 288–89.

Chancellor Samuel Dickson, in an address to the Law Association, noted, "It is true that no corporate or official instruction was at that time [1750–60] given under the authority of the Inns of Court, and that until Blackstone began his lectures [as an established course] in 1758 no course of study was presented and no public instruction furnished, even in the universities, for students preparing for admission to the English bar. It was customary, however, to read in the office of a preceptor . . . to enjoy the advantage of his supervision and instruction . . ." *The Law Association of Philadelphia. Addresses Delivered March 13, 1902 . . . To Commemorate the Centennial . . . of the Law Association* (Philadelphia, 1906), 3–4.

This honor came to McKean just a month after his admission to the bar of the Supreme Court of Pennsylvania, and the two distinctions greatly increased his professional prestige. As a matter of course, therefore, when the new King came to the throne in 1760, Thomas McKean was among the prominent subjects of the Crown in the Lower Counties to join in the provincial proclamation of George III.[98] At such times all the colonies, and in some cases mere factions, made haste to accept and welcome a new regime.

During 1758 McKean's cousin and recent teacher, David Finney, retained him as counsel to have a writ of entry for some lands in Kent County, formerly belonging to Robert French, consisting of many thousands of acres, "put into its original state, it being unduly 'allowed" [to someone else] by a writ of error issued by the Supreme Court of the Lower Counties.[99] Robert French's oldest son, the barrister David French, had died without issue, and despite the expressed wishes of both father and son, the properties had then gone to the family of Ann French, who had married Nicholas Ridgely and died in the lifetime of her brother David, instead of to the family of Elizabeth French, wife of Dr. John Finney, the father of the plaintiff.

David Finney and Thomas McKean, as his counsel, endeavored for several years to persuade the Supreme Court to reverse its order to the Court of Common Pleas of Kent County, as a matter of equity, but the court denied its power to do this, largely—plaintiff and counsel believed—because of Ridgely's great influence in that locality. After more than a decade of legal maneuvering, they appealed to the King in Council, reciting their peculiar difficulties, "At the time of bringing the writ of error John Vining, Esquire, [step-son of Nicholas Ridgely] who held a seventh part of the lands in question, was Prothonotary of the Common Pleas, and one of the justices of the Supreme Court, and for many years after was the chief-justice of the said court; Charles Ridgely, Esquire, who with his sisters, &c [children of Nicholas Ridgely by a second marriage] held all the rest, was President of the Court of Common Pleas, so that the current of favor ran violently against the Plaintiffs in error in both courts . . ."

Still persevering in 1774, Finney and McKean sent their appeal to Benjamin Franklin in London for his "care and management," confident that the friendship which had formerly subsisted between Franklin and David French, and also with Dr. John Finney, who sent his regards in a postscript, would incline Franklin to use his influence in England on their behalf. They assured him that their mutual friend, John Dickinson, considered their case properly founded in both law and equity, since the courts in the Lower Counties had equitable as well as legal powers, and were thus more powerful "than any single court in England." The Supreme Court of the Lower Counties, they maintained, could grant a remedy without recourse to the legislature—on appeal against their own writ of error, in this case. "A conveyance not properly executed is no conveyance at all," they said. They enclosed a bill of exchange for £50, and promised fifty or sixty pounds more, when Franklin had obtained the best advice possible in London, which he did. This was the last appeal of record from the American colonies to the British Privy Council, and unfortunately for Finney and McKean, the case was never finally determined.[100]

McKean's career as a politician began in October, 1762, when at the age of twenty-eight he was elected a member of the Assembly of the Lower Counties, for Newcastle County. Now "he for the first time ventured on the stormy sea of politics, which he encountered and stemmed afterwards for forty-six years." [101] This position he held for seventeen years, until October, 1779, despite the fact that he moved to Philadelphia in the summer of 1774, as one the delegates from the Lower Counties—soon to become Delaware—in the Continental Congress, and also despite the fact that he simultaneously occupied positions of importance in Pennsylvania. The political situation in the Lower Counties, as the newly-elected member described it, resulted from a split between the Court Party and the County Party. McKean was a favorite of the County Party, in Newcastle County, but neither faction was "violent." His group "wished an independence in the Judges and impartiality in the laws," and felt that the administration of justice was "under an undue influence" when dominated entirely by the Governor, or a lawyer who might be one of the Governor's henchmen, as all held their commissions "during the pleasure of the governor . . ." [102]

Caesar Rodney, who had an estate near Dover, the county seat of Kent County, and who represented an element increasingly opposed to the group led by Nicholas Ridgely,* was appointed with Thomas McKean to revise and print the laws then in force—"which they speadily executed." [103] Viewing their task, John Dickinson gave his friend some good advice: "I desire you would not take too much care of your Business in Newcastle. Iff [sic] you write with such application you will make yourself too weak to receive any Benefit from your [vacation]—Moderation in everything is the source of Happiness—too much writing—too much Reading—too much Eating—too much Drinking—too much Exercise—too much Idleness—too much loving—too much continence—too much of Law —Physic—or Religion—all equally throw us from the Ballance of real Pleasure. This has been said a thousand time—always believed & practiced against—It is still true." [104]

Moderation itself can be practiced to excess, appearing something less than admirable, and following this wise counsel would later cost Dickinson his balance and his reputation. For the pleasures and temptations of the body such advice was well-taken; in certain other respects it was perhaps questionable. As for McKean, he chafed at moderation. His application to his labors daunted other men; he was neither weakened nor winded by such feats. Setting the pattern for the future, he completed his assignment with dispatch. Rodney and McKean together more than justified the Assembly's selection. In the same manner McKean unfailingly satisfied his constituents, despite the forbidding qualities which worried his friends and provoked his enemies, while he continued unwearyingly on his steady course. Somewhat baffled, his nephew attempted summing up:

> Although always popular in public office from twenty-one or twenty-two years of age till near the close of his life, his manner of obtaining public favor was anomolous

* Rodney's estate on St. Jones's Neck, a few miles southeast of Dover, was adjacent to an estate of John Dickinson's, which is now a museum open to the public. The Rodneys, Dickinsons, and McKean were early Whigs in the Revolutionary period, and subsequently Jeffersonians.

[*sic*]. I used myself to be surprised that he was popular, and have heard friends, his contemporaries, say that they were utterly surprised at his popularity. When quite a young lawyer with his numerous clients, his manner of sifting out the facts of the cases submitted to him especially if there were any appearances of juggling, being so pointed and severe. The secret to be developed must be referred to the selfish principal [*sic*] that rules the human heart: the people had confidence in his integrity, industry and talents, and were willing to submit their interests into such hands.[105]

EXPANDING
INTERESTS

Chapter 5

Family Beginnings

For twenty-four years, from 1750 to 1774, Thomas McKean kept his residence in Newcastle County. He practiced law, entered politics, married, started a family, and began taking care of his relatives in or near the busy little capital of the Three Lower Counties. From the beginning, however, his interests expanded, up and down the Delaware River, beyond the confines of a single province. His connections with Philadelphia also began in 1750, when he was sixteen years old, through the simple process of keeping in touch with his brother Robert, who had gone there to "study physic" with the eminent Dr. Thomas Cadwalader, who was "one of the Proprietary and Governor's council for the province." [1] He had boarded with his brother for seven years at Dr. Alison's school in New London, and was closer to him than to anyone else in his youth; further, Robert seems to have been equally competent and successful in a variety of activities, and perhaps more amiable than his younger brother.

Dr. Cadwalader was famous for making dissections for the benefit of young doctors who had not been abroad for a proper medical training, and for conducting the first autopsy in the colonies; in addition, he was one of the few Philadelphia physicians who dared to inoculate for small-pox in the 1730's.[2] Evidently, a good teacher, he was reputed to have correctly diagnosed the "West Indian dry gripes" as lead poisoning from the pipes used in distilling rum. Some twenty years earlier, he had been associated with Benjamin Franklin in the founding of the Philadelphia Library. He married Hannah, daughter of Thomas Lambert, Jr., who owned most of the land in Trenton, New Jersey, and remained in that area for a number of years. Before returning to Philadelphia in 1750, he donated £500 for the establishment of a library in Trenton, similar to the one that he and Franklin had founded earlier. Dr. Cadwalader's many connections with prominent people proved useful to the McKean brothers in later years. While in New

Jersey, he was physician to Governor Belcher; his sister, Mary Cadwalader, was the mother of John and Philemon Dickinson.[3] It was under his tutelage, apparently, that Robert McKean, on October 11, 1752, read a paper entitled "A Discourse of a Vacuum" to the "Honorable Half-Dozen Clubb" in Philadelphia.[4]

John Dickinson was born in 1732 on the Eastern Shore of Maryland, but during the years 1750 to 1753, he read law in the office of John Moland of Philadelphia. Afterwards, enrolled for three years in the Middle Temple, he studied law in London. During his sojourn there, he associated frequently with Robert McKean, who was then studying medicine and theology. He became acquainted with Thomas McKean after his return to America, and the long correspondence between John Dickinson and Thomas McKean began in 1757. "From the year 1757 until his death," McKean wrote, "I was [Dickinson's] constant and confidential correspondent; few months passed for fifty years without a letter from each other. I know everything respecting his public and private conduct from 1756 till his death; and ever esteemed him as a sensible and virtuous gentleman, and a true Patriot: his letters to me and now in my possession will prove it to every worthy and good character." [5]

Wealthy land-owners of this period tended to spread their families over three or four provinces in a single lifetime. The ties between the Lower Counties and Philadelphia were especially close—so much so that a modern historian has coined the term "Philadelawareans" to apply to them.[6] Thomas McKean and John Dickinson, as well as Benjamin Chew and several others, were to be Philadelawareans, and plural office holders of the first order. Many of Philadelphia's most prominent families, such as the Dickinsons, the Chews, the Galloways and the Reads, had come to the city via the Lower Counties from Maryland, or points south; others, like the Rodneys and the Whartons, originated in the Lower Counties. The natural avenues of transportation for all such travellers were the navigable rivers; in the case of the Delaware River, the ultimate destination might be on either side, in Pennsylvania or New Jersey, but Philadelphia was the magnet which attracted the greatest number.

Prosperous people were not the only ones who spread out geographically. Slaves, indentured servants, laborers, preachers, and many others traveled extensively, though not in equal comfort or style. A distressing example was described in an advertisement which mentioned Thomas McKean, dated from Perth Amboy, New Jersey:

> Run-away from the subscriber, in the month of October, 1762, a Mulatto Woman Slave, named Violet, about thirty-five years of age; she is very active and rather tall. Some time afterwards she was seen in company with one James Lock, somewhere on the Susquehanna, and by information was apprehenhended and committed to gaol, in the year 1764, in Frederickstown, in Maryland . . . From that gaol she was reported to have made an escape, and about two months ago was discovered about fifteen miles from Ball-Fryer's Ferry, in Frederick county afsd, where she had three children. Edward Bonnel, of Monmouth county in the province of New Jersey, was formerly her owner, and after his decease she was sold by his executors to the subscriber. Any person who may take her up must secure her strictly, or she will cer-

tainly escape again, being remarkably artful. Whoever delivers her and her children to the subscriber or THOMAS McKEAN, Esq. in New Castle on Delaware, shall receive [FIFTEEN POUNDS], or TEN POUNDS for the wench only, and reasonable charges from

PHILIP KEARNEY [7]

Benjamin Chew was a Philadelawarean who, although brought up as a Quaker, subsequently became an Anglican—as did Thomas and Richard Penn, the sons of the Founder, and a number of others, such as Dr. Thomas Cadwalader. Chew, as Speaker of the Assembly of the Lower Counties in 1757, informed Thomas McKean of his election as Clerk of the Assembly, and at about the same time McKean was appointed to prosecute the pleas of the Crown in Sussex County, this time by the Attorney General of the Lower Counties, John Ross.[8] Chew had attracted more than local notice at the Albany Conference in 1754; in 1755 he became Attorney General of Pennsylvania, serving until 1769, while also serving as Speaker of the Assembly of the Lower Counties for several years, beginning in 1756. As spokesman for the Proprietors, he was present at the Easton Conference with the Indians in 1758.[9]

While Chew was holding these various positions, specifically from 1757 to 1761, a young man named Francis Hopkinson, another alumnus of Dr. Alison's, was reading law in his office. Hopkinson and Thomas McKean were later to marry sisters, and for several years they were close, though eventually the friendship soured.[10] Hopkinson, a devout and active Anglican, may have been one of those who persuaded the older McKean brother to become an Anglican and to study theology in England, as well as medicine. There was also a practical advantage for Robert McKean in this conversion; the Society for the Propagation of the Gospel in Foreign Parts often paid the transportation costs of young Americans seeking ordination in the Church of England.

Hopkinson's preceptor, Benjamin Chew, had extensive land-holdings and business connections to the southward, especially in Kent County,[11] and for years had been in close touch with the McKeans' uncle, among others in New Castle, by virtue of his official positions. A letter from Colonel John Finney and Thomas Gooch to Chew, from New Castle, May 23rd, 1758, indicates a fairly constant contact during the French and Indian War:

> We are much obliged to you for the pains you have taken with the General to relieve us from the heavy burden of supporting our new raised forces . . . His Honor [Governor Denny] signified as his opinion (when at New Castle) that each Captain should pay his own men . . . We shall be obliged to you if you will take the charge of ordering Drums and Colours to be sent to Lancaster. We doubt not that you will use your best offices with the General and the Governor in behalf of this small Government.[12]

Whether by the influence of Chew, Dr. Cadwalader, or for some other reason, Robert McKean decided to emulate St. Luke by combining the science of divinity with medicine, and thereupon went to England for ordination, as required by the Anglican Church. He took advantage of the double opportunity so offered to further his medical studies [13] by taking advanced courses in anatomy with Dr. Hunter, and midwifery with Dr. Smellie. William Hunter had conducted a school of anatomy for many years in his London home; especially admired were his winter lectures when "the weather is cold enough to admit of bringing dead bodies into the theater." His skill and knowledge were royally as well as generally approved, and he was appointed Physician Extraordinary to Her Majesty, the Queen. Dr. Smellie was one of the first scientific "man midwives." Until then, obstetrics had been practiced solely by women, "who were usually conceited in proportion to their ignorance," according to their male successors.[14]

In 1757 the Rev. Robert McKean returned to America with an appointment by the Society for the Propagation of the Gospel in Foreign Parts, better and more briefly known as the "Venerable Society," as a missionary to New Brunswick, New Jersey, with responsibility also for Piscataway, Spotswood, Woodbridge, and more distant settlements in the central parts of the province. On January 8, 1758, he wrote to the Society that he had "arrived at New Brunswick the 16th December, 1757, and was kindly received." [15]

The long trip to London which preceded this happy conclusion had been a trial; his transportation may have been paid by the Society, but he had had limited funds while he was there. His "experience of the hardship laid upon young Americans who were obliged to go to England for ordination made him an ardent and perhaps intemperate advocate of the plan of appointing American Bishops, a cause so ably urged by [other Anglican clergymen]." [16] On this issue, at least, his combative manner resembled that of his brother Thomas, though he was taking a tack which normally led to the opposite side of the debate, for the dissenting churches (such as the Congregational and Presbyterian) could not tolerate the thought of an American episcopacy, with the consequent importation of English ecclesiastical law.

Whether Robert McKean would indeed have become a Tory, if he had lived until the Revolution, obviously cannot be determined now. Most Anglican clergymen, especially if supported by the Venerable Society, were inclined that way, and the missionaries were required to take an oath of allegiance *both* to the Bishop of London and to King, and to repeat these oaths whenever there was a new accession.[17] Thus, Robert McKean joined other colonial missionaries in congratulatory messages to Richard Terrick in England, when Terrick was translated from a lesser see to become the 100th Bishop of London:

MAY IT PLEASE YOUR LORDSHIP,

> To permit us with the most sincere congratulations to express the deep sense we have of the goodness of Divine providence in advancing your Lordship to the see of London . . . We flatter ourselves that the countenance and protection that the clergy in these remote parts have hitherto happily experienced from your Lordships worthy predecessors will be continued to us and that we shall soon feel the salutary effects of your influence and paternal affection . . .[18]

In 1760 Robert McKean was one of three Anglican clergymen appointed to greet a new royal governor on his arrival in New Jersey, and this he did in similarly fulsome language. The address, directed to "His Excellency Thomas Boone, Esq., Captain General and Governor in Chief in and over His Majesty's Province of Nova Caesaria, or New Jersey and Territories Thereupon Depending in America, Chancellor, and Vice Admiral of the same, etc." expressed not only the clergy's congratulations to the new governor on his appointment, but their sense of obligation to contribute in every way possible to the tranquility and harmony of the state; and in return, they continued, "We are encouraged to believe that we shall receive the same Favour, Countenance, and Protection [as in the past]." [19]

This was a far cry from the principle of separation of church and state, implicit in the Presbyterian doctrine of the Rev. Francis Alison, on which he had been brought up. But Robert McKean was now a member of the Established Church, playing a role which had been prescribed most exactly. The following year, as one of six Anglican clergymen selected to welcome another royal governor, he signed his name to this all-too-clear statement of his position:

> The church of england, always faithful and steady in their attachments to our admirable form of government, cannot fail of your excellency's protection, and support in all her privileges: And we presume to engage to your Excellency, that we will on our part, agreeably to our sacred obligations, constantly inculcate loyalty to our good and glorious sovereign, and the most ardent affection for our happy constitution, while at the same time we shall do everything in our power to contribute to the ease and honour of your Excellency's administration.[20]

During the six years from 1757 to 1763, the Rev. Dr. Robert McKean served as a medical missionary in New Brunswick and surrounding communities, combining medicine with his parochial duties for the purpose, primarily, of winning people for the church. He was also active in ecclesiastical affairs in a wider area; from April 30 to May 5, 1760, he participated in a convention of clergymen at Philadelphia, and "was regular and faithful in his attendance," overseeing the activities of the Church of England in both Pennsylvania and the Lower Counties.[21] On May 5, 1760, he was one of two New Jersey missionaries to join ten Pennsylvania clergymen in a memorial to the Proprietors,[22] and on the 15th of the same month, at the commencement of the College of Philadelphia, less than three years after his return from England, he received an honorary degree of Master of Arts, in the company of the Rev. Samuel Davies, President of the College of New Jersey; Rev. Philip Reading, at Apoquiniminck; Rev. Thomas Barton, at Lancaster; Rev. Samuel Cooke, at Shrewsbury; Rev. Samson Smith, at Chestnut-Level; and Rev. Matthew Wilson, in Kent County.[23]

In a letter to the Venerable Society on April 15, 1761, McKean included a quaint personal note, "One circumstance respecting myself, though perhaps foreign to the nature of this letter I can not resist an inclination I have of telling you. I have, Sir, changed my condition in life, being happily married about two months ago to the daughter of one of my parishioners." [24] The bride was Isabel Graham Antill, and the wedding had taken place on February 19th at Christ Church in Shrewsbury. She was the daughter of Edward Antill II, of Raritan

Landing near New Brunswick, and his wife, the former Anne Morris, who was the daughter of the Governor, Lewis Morris; [25] thereby Isabel was also the niece of the Chief Justice of New Jersey, Robert Hunter Morris, who held that office unchallenged from 1738 to 1764, despite absences caused by other activities such as serving as Governor of Pennsylvania from 1754 to 1756.[26]

Governor Lewis Morris had been the friend and protector of John Peter Zenger, the printer, and Antill, McKean's father-in-law, had served as a Provincial Councillor in the Jersies for both Governor Morris and Governor Belcher. Seven years earlier, Antill had contributed the munificent sum of £1800 towards the founding of King's (later Columbia) College, in the interest of the Anglican Church. McKean described him as "a man of most exemplary life and singular piety," who undertook to read prayers and a sermon every Sunday at churches without a priest." [27] His daughter, however, was described by a malicious critic as "a young lady of very gay and independent spirit, not calculated to enhance the domestic happiness of the missionary." [28]

Later in the same year, Robert McKean received a call from the congregation of St. Peter's Church in Perth Amboy, New Jersey, who "had so much their heart set on Mr. McKean" that they would neither consider nor accept the minister chosen for them—a most unusual proceeding in a church where higher authorities ordinarily decided such matters.[29] Perth Amboy at that time was the capital of the province of East Jersey, and the Governor's parish, sharing with Burlington in West Jersey the prestige of being capital of both parts of New Jersey in alternate years.[30] The wife of William Franklin, the last of the royal governors, was said to have presented to St. Peter's the surplice used by its minister; and Robert McKean's pastorate coincided with the "golden age" in the history of Perth Amboy.[31]

During this period, the young rector's services were at first "restricted to that parish exclusively, at the request of the vestry"; nonetheless he practiced medicine, started a school, administered a library, founded the New Jersey Medical Society (about which more later), and inevitably became involved in activities outside his parish, for Trinity Church at Woodbridge, "a branch of [his] former mission," also came under his care.[32] There was as yet no indication that he had such a short time to live.

Meanwhile, the McKeans' sister Dorothea was growing up under the protection of the Finney family, and in October, 1758, she was married in Philadelphia by the family's constant and respected friend, the Rev. Francis Alison, to John Thompson of New Castle.[33] Thompson was the oldest of four children, of whom one, Anne, was the wife of David Finney, the cousin who had taken Thomas McKean as a law apprentice when he left Dr. Alison's school. Dorothea McKean was Thompson's second wife; by his first wife, Mary Sands, he had a son, David, who studied medicine with Dr. Thomas Cadwalader in Philadelphia a number of years after his new Uncle Robert. John Thompson and Dorothea McKean were themselves the parents of four children who lived to maturity: Elizabeth Thompson, who later married Colonel William McKennan; John Thompson, Jr., who married his first cousin, Letitia Elizabeth McKean[34] (the daughter of Thomas's younger brother, William); Thomas McKean Thompson, whose "Thompson Register" has been frequently quoted above; and Robert Thompson, who remained a farmer, the only member of the clan who never went into public life.[35]

These relations and connections gradually disappeared from McKean's circle; there is little mention of them during the revolution or in the years he spent as Pennsylvania's first Chief Justice. But they were not forgotten, and when at last McKean was Governor of Pennsylvania, and had the authority and opportunity to help them, they were all remembered, to their profit and possibly to that of the state as well. If none added notably to the luster of the positions provided, neither did they discredit or abuse these positions. The clamor over such thorough-going nepotism in fact contradicted the charges made by the same sources, and since repeated, of McKean's snobbery and deference to aristocracy. McKean must have had much cause for amusement when he heard references to his self-created "Royal Family," as the *Aurora* christened them.[36]

The Thompsons were Scotch-Irish, like the McKeans and the Finneys, and a close-knit group. When John Thompson died, "it was the wonder and talk of the neighborhood that the children (the eldest of them a half-brother, and by the then law of inheritance in the State of Delaware, entitled to two shares) should have divided his property among themselves without a lawsuit, or even calling in a friend or neighbor to assist them in doing so . . ."[37] Thomas McKean Thompson recalled his father:

> I knew him to be a ready scribe, well versed in arithmetic, surveying, and the other branches of mathematics. He wrote an excellent hand, and was master of bookkeeping, which proved of great advantage to him as for the greater period of his life he was engaged in public business. In early life for a short period, he taught school, then embraced the mercantile business, was afterwards elected Sheriff of New Castle County, the most populous and wealthy in the State, in which office (as I understood) he served nine years, or three constitutional terms of three years each. Subsequently he removed from the county seat to a large farm ten miles distant from it, and but a few miles from the Delaware River, on which he continued to reside until his death . . .
>
> [He] having a number of slaves, farmed on a large scale compared with farmers in this vicinity, although a proportionately small scale compared with many parts of Maryland and Virginia. His annual average crop of wheat might have brought him $1000 to $1500., according to the price for the time being . . .[38]

Dorothea's life was rather a hard one, despite a devoted husband and moderate prosperity; she lost several children as infants, and suffered constantly from ill health herself. Her brother Thomas was evidently close to her, for she named one of her children after him, the son just quoted. When Thomas's first wife, Mary, died in 1773, Dorothea took some of his children into her care: the two-weeks' old baby, Anne, and her two-year-old sister, possibly the other two girls also— the older boys were taken in charge by their maternal grandparents in Bordentown. Dorothea had several small children of her own at the time, and although she was helped by her husband and brother, they were both active politicians, and thus frequently absent. Her sense of duty to her family prevented any questioning of his added burden.

Two years after Thomas had acquired a second wife, in 1776, Dorothea was still looking out for some of his children, including the oldest boy, Joseph Borden McKean. Suddenly, while the men were away at the crucial Constitutional Convention of Delaware, she and her son, Thomas McKean Thompson, and her nephew, Joseph Borden McKean, fell critically ill of a "marshy or remittant fever," an illness which became epidemic some years later, and was better known as yellow-fever.* John Thompson and Thomas McKean came at once, having requested leave of absence from the Convention, and remained as long as they could be useful, McKean writing his wife that he had "little hopes of [Joseph's] recovery, but a day or two will determine his fate . . ." Two days later he wrote again: Dorothea had died, but the boys were improving.[39] Young Thomas McKean Thompson could not remember anything about his mother's death, although he was then eight years old and clearly recollected how often he had seen her as an invalid. From this he assumed he had been sent away to visit relatives, to be spared the gloomy scene.[40] Rather, he was too sick to be conscious of the scene—but he and Dorothea's other children lived to realize that his Uncle Thomas's feelings of duty and gratitude were also deep.

Thomas McKean's younger brother, William, was a sea captain who "it is supposed, was lost at sea" during the Revolution.[41] Little is known about him, except that he lived in New Castle, was married, and had two children. He did not have as liberal an education as his older brothers, but worked along the river-front as a boy, and yielded to the lure of the sea when he was fully grown. Thomas McKean kept in touch with him and included him in his correspondence; writing to Sally McKean at New Castle, on July 12, 1779, he sent his "affectionate regard" to "his brother & his wife," who lived farther down-river at St. George's Hundred. About three months later the Captain set sail on the voyage from which he never returned.[42]

When William's widow, Mary Peterson McKean, died leaving his children without a guardian—some two years after his disappearance—Thomas McKean was sent for to make the necessary arrangements for their education and future. This he did promptly and efficiently, and if perhaps he was too brief with the young boy, another orphaned namesake, his simultaneous obligations to the Continental Congress and the Pennsylvania Supreme Court, as well as the peripatetic condition of his own family, left little time for sentimental pause. Within a fortnight of his sister-in-law's death, McKean wrote to Matthew Irwin, to whom the lad had already been apprenticed, "as I expect him up this week, I must request your decisive answer, whether you can lodge him or not in your own house, for he

---

* The "marshy or remittant fever" described by McKean had been known for some time along the coastal areas; it appeared in mid-summer, reaching its height in August and September. By the early 1790's, when the great epidemics began in the area, some of its causes were suspected; the cures were not, but rather rivalled the disease in risk. Dr. Benjamin Rush's *An Account of the Bilious Remitting Yellow Fever . . .* (Philadelphia, 1794) was one of the first to identify it specifically, and name it. See *The Autobiography of Benjamin Rush,* ed. George W. Corner (Princeton, 1948), 95–102; *The Papers of Benjamin Franklin,* Vol. VI, 338–39. ed. Labaree (New Haven, 1963).

is too young to be intrusted to his own management . . . If you had not agreed to this when you took him, no consideration should have induced me to put him Apprentice." [43] The other child, Letitia Elizabeth, eventually married her first cousin, Dorothea's son, John Thompson, Jr., a Presbyterian minister.[44]

But from 1754, when he was twenty, until just before the Revolution, Thomas McKean's attention, uninterrupted by personal sorrows or claims, was concentrated upon his increasingly lucrative law practice in New Castle. His cases involved the usual problems of a rural society, with an expanding proportion of commercial or maritime suits.[45] Conflicts over wills and land, suits for personal injury and damages, non-fulfillment of contracts, slander cases, and cases involving run-away slaves were the mainstay of his practice. The members of the bar, although often appearing against each other, were in fact close friends who cooperated politically, and in the promotion of various public-spirited enterprises. There are records of cases with John Dickinson and McKean on opposite sides, though their friendship was never broken.[46]

A case typical of this early period, although it actually occurred somewhat later, was a routine slander case which was remembered for generations, because it brought the participants into sharp focus. A certain Mr. Buncom had described a neighbor in most scurrilous terms, and Miers Fisher, a Philadelphia lawyer who was not one to overlook public contumely, had made out the defamation in the Chester County Court in terms that could hardly be denied. McKean undertook the defense and promptly called "some scores of witnesses, not to deny the slander, but to show that his client was such a notorious liar that no man in the county believed anything he said, and that therefore no damages could possibly have been sustained by the plaintiff. *And so the jury found.*" [47] His forensic prowess was attained as much by an ability to influence juries as by legal learning.

McKean's success in the pre-Revolutionary period gave him the financial independence necessary to sustain him through long years of war and public service. It gave him entrée into the ranks of the select few who in effect governed the Lower Counties, and provided him with the wherewithal to become a substantial landowner; in 1763 he started acquiring land, in Pennsylvania as well as in the Lower Counties, and continued to do so for the rest of his life. He was never to command the resources of a Finney, or a Dickinson, or a Rodney, and was perhaps regarded as the working member in his contracts with such people. But, as time went on, his ability and his energy put him into positions of power, so that he could associate on equal terms, or even as the senior partner, with persons who were wealthier than he. Wealth for him was merely a means to an end, not the end itself; for the better part of his life he was dedicated to public service.

As early as June 14, 1762, John Dickinson wrote to McKean from Philadelphia:

I should be extremely glad if you would turn your horse's head to Easton—you will see a glorious country—the celebrated Bethlehem & Nazareth & Gnadenhutten—a thousand Indians—Sir William Johnson, etc. etc. In short I think we may spend a Week there with great Pleasure, & after that you may transport me off to the Jersies, "To Thebes, to Athens, or the Lord knows where."

> I desire you would come up, & I will give you a better Reason than any I have mentioned. But not now—I hope you will be very much pleased with in many circumstances uniting to make a Trip to the most remarkable Parts of our Province agreeable—& it will not break in upon our larger scheme at all . . .[48]

The arch tone of this letter is surprising, and more so the suggestion that Mc-Kean should make a trip for the sole purpose of pleasure. Dickinson assumed that McKean would prefer to take him "off to the Jersies," and there were indeed some well known vacation spots in that province, such as the Great Falls of the Passaic, near the center of modern Paterson; this was regarded as one of the country's greatest natural wonders until Alexander Hamilton, in 1791, turned a banker's eye on the seventy-foot falls and harnessed them for industrial water power.[49] A likelier explanation lies in the fact that New Jersey had a specific aesthetic attraction in Bordentown, a beautiful young lady, Mary Borden, whom McKean was most probably courting at that time.

They might easily have met her through her father, Joseph Borden, who among other enterprises owned the stage-boat line connecting Philadelphia and Bordentown, and the stagecoach from Bordentown to Perth Amboy via the Lowrey Road, then the best overland route to the vicinity of New York. By this route, according to Borden's advertisements, travellers enjoyed "the quickest 30 or 40 hours, the cheapest and fastest way that has yet been made use of . . ." * A canny and successful businessman, whose lack of interest in the less commercial aspects of education was no handicap to a subsequent judicial career, Borden made a point of knowing everyone in the area who travelled, and either loaned money or extended credit to a great many of them.[50] Further, on the death of *his* father, Joseph Borden I, he became one of the wealthiest men in the Jersies. Of the seven children of Joseph and Elizabeth Rogers Borden, four survived infancy: Mary, Letitia, "Nancy" (Ann), and a son, Joseph Borden III, an attractive young man of promise—who became a cavalry officer early in the Revolution, was wounded at Germantown, and never fully recovering, died a few years later.[51]

---

* The *Pennsylvania Gazette,* April 4, 1751, ran the following advertisement: "This is to give notice to all persons that shall have occasions of transporting themselves, goods, wares, or merchandize from Philadelphia to New York or from the latter place to the former that by Joseph Borden there is a stage boat well fitted and kept for that purpose and if the wind and weather permit will attend at the crooked-billet wharf in Philadelphia every Tuesday in every week and proceed up to Bordentown on Wednesday and on Thursday morning a stage waggon with a good Arning kept by Joseph Richardson will be ready to receive them and proceed directly to John Clucks opposite the city of Perth Amboy who keeps a house of good entertainment and on Friday morning a stage boat well fitted and kept by Daniel O. bryant, will be ready to receive them and proceed directly to New York and give her attendance at the White Hall slip near the half moon tavern, if people be ready at the stage days and places tis believed they may pass the quickest 30 or 40 hours, the cheapest and fastest way that has yet been made use of . . . also people living on or near the road may have business done by letter or otherwise due care will be taken in the delivery of letters verbile message & cr. by us.
>
> Joseph Borden
> Joseph Richardson
> Daniel Obryant"

Quoted in E. M. Woodward and John Hageman, *History of Burlington and Mercer Counties N. J., with Biographical Sketches of Many of their Pioneers and Prominent Men* (Phila., 1883), 485.

Rev. Robert McKean had moved to Perth Amboy in 1761, and when Thomas visited his brother, he would certainly have taken the "fastest way"—inevitably meeting its owner. In 1765 Borden and McKean were to serve together in the Stamp Act Congress at New York City, but they had many interests in common before that. McKean's rapidly growing law practice involved commercial activities up and down the Delaware River, and frequent visits to New Jersey. In 1765, he was formally admitted as an Attorney at Law in New Jersey, and in 1766 he was promoted to "Solliciter and Councellor at law in all His Majesty's courts of law and equity in the said province" by His Excellency, William Franklin, the Royal Governor.[52]

He received the latter honor on the recommendation of Frederick Smyth, Esq., the Chief Justice succeeding Robert Hunter Morris (his sister-in-law's uncle), and of Charles Read, Esq., Second Justice. Read, who, if remotely kin to the Read family of the Lower Counties, would have been disowned by them for his Tory proclivities in a few years, had been a commissioner at the Indian Conference of 1758, in Easton,[53] and was often in Philadelphia where his friends, for a while to come, included the Hopkinsons and the Chews. In fact, officials of the two adjacent provinces often travelled to and through New Castle, where the splendid little taverns encouraged friendship as well as politics.

On July 21, 1763, her nineteenth birthday, Mary Borden married Thomas McKean, who was twenty-nine.[54] No portrait of the bride, none of her letters, survive. There is only a graceful shadow, tenderly outlined by others. Mary and her younger sister, "Nancy," who married Francis Hopkinson five years later, were reputed to be "great beauties." Hopkinson's memorial poem to his sister-in-law, which McKean so admired that he had it carved on her tombstone, paid affectionate tribute to a quiet, thoughtful, and devout person whose memory was cherished:

> Fair was her form, serene her mind,
> Her heart and hopes were fix'd on high:
> . . . Meekness perfum'd each rising pray'r . . .[55]

McKean was an eligible, acceptable match, though hardly as affluent as his father-in-law. He could well afford to take a wife; his careers in law and politics flourished side by side, and seemed to nourish each other. In June, a month before the wedding, he had received the honorary degree of A.M. from the College of Philadelphia, in recognition of professional competence justifying his early admission to practice before the Supreme Court.[56] His brother Robert had been similarly recognized in another profession. He knew not only the rich and powerful, who accepted him because of his ability, but also the lesser gentry and country people—who would come forward with the Revolution—and these people accepted him as one of their own. He was not, in strict truth, one who had achieved success entirely alone, and his fondness for the trappings of the public offices he sought was an admitted weakness, but his high self-evaluation was in fact largely justified—though doubly abrasive for that reason.

At the wedding the groom towered over the bride, as he did over nearly every-one. His presence was imposing, even intimidating; his voice commanded attention. He was a natural leader, who would preside over and dominate mass meetings with obvious ease; throughout his life positions of leadership came to him unsought. He was known as a "speaker rather than a writer," one of the leading orators of his generation, and a lawyer destined from his first case to become a judge.[57] His craggy features, somewhat beak-like nose, and piercing blue eyes, together with his tremendous build and matching vitality, made him not merely handsome, but something more—a memorable, challenging man.

Mary Borden was no match for such a man. Physically or in stamina, few were, male or female, and Mary was fine-boned and delicate; none of the Borden children inherited their father's robust health. Her training and character fitted her for the expected role of submissive wife and devoted mother, but as McKean's wife she would soon be called on to play other, equally demanding roles as well. She would need to be head of the household during his frequent, often prolonged, absences; she would be required, not just to entertain, but to be an ever-prepared hostess for the numerous meetings of friends and clients, produced by her husband's dual careers. When emergencies, such as childbirth, occurred during his absence, she would have to be self-sufficient or rely on friends in the neighborhood, not on her own, distant family. The tragedy of her early death was almost inevitable.

But the future cast no shadow on that July of 1763. Weddings crowded with guests and prolonged festivity were celebrated mainly on the frontier, where a reason for a rare, boisterous gathering was welcome. Mary Borden, a quiet and devout Anglican, would more likely have had a decorous wedding in her home, at candle-lighting time, with friends calling after the ceremony. Public accounts of who attended, far less what they or the bride wore, were not the custom, although such reserve was sometimes broken in a startling manner by a comment on what the bride's financial attractions or expectations might be. A simple announcement of the event might, or might not, appear in a local gazette. There was no newspaper in the province of New Jersey then, or for some years to come, so Mary Borden's wedding was not announced. Her younger sister's wedding was noted in September, 1768, in the *Pennsylvania Chronicle* by an enthusiastic correspondent in Bordentown, "On Thursday last Francis Hopkinson, Esq., of Philadelphia, was joined in the Velvet Bands of HYMEN to Miss Nancy [Ann] Borden, of this place, a lady amiable both for her internal as well as external Accomplishments . . ."[58]

The minister was not required to be of the communicant's parish, and there was one nearby who would certainly have attended, possibly bringing with him his wife and a distinguished in-law. The groom's brother, the Rev. Robert McKean, would surely have been requested to officiate, but because he was a nonresident, no record would appear in the local parish. The bonds between the brothers were close, and Mary must have valued them, for it was her brother-in-law, not her husband, who shared her Anglican faith. Their second child, named after his uncle, and his god-son, was the special favorite among the nieces and nephews, and it was he who was remembered in the Rev. Robert McKean's will.[59]

Honeymoons were not customary in those days,* and less than three weeks after his marriage, McKean was buying land in West Fallowfield township, Chester County, Pennsylvania, near the site of his Uncle Thomas' tavern.[60] Moreover, both of his weddings were marked by feverish bursts of political activity. His marriage to Mary Borden occurred between the first and second of his terms in the Assembly of the Lower Counties. During his first term he and Caesar Rodney had revised and published the laws of the Assembly which had been passed up to that date.[61] During his second term he was actively involved in two new, time-consuming but interesting projects, separate from his legislative duties.[62] He was one of the original Trustees of the New Castle Common, and he was one of the three Trustees of the Loan Office of Newcastle County, an appointment which was renewed in 1768 and 1772. The birth of his first child, Joseph Borden McKean, on July 28, 1764—a year before McKean and his father-in-law, for whom the child was named, attended the Stamp Act Congress—occurred in New Castle at a time when the young legislator was greatly preoccupied by the responsibilities of these new offices.

The New Castle Common was a significant institution, an unusual experiment in municipal government which was so successful that it has lasted until the present day. A tourists' guidebook describes it in these terms:

> The lands known as the New Castle Common must not be confused with the Green. The Green, being a broad central square, corresponds with what many New England towns know as "the Common." But here in New Castle the Common comprises other lands quite separate and distinct. They lie beyond the northwestern bounds of the present town and are mainly in the open country . . .
>
> The Trustees of New Castle Common own the land in trust "for the use, benefit and behoof of the inhabitants of the town." The beneficiaries are "the inhabitants"— not the town as a political body, for its government has no hand in the trust.[63]

This land had been used as common property from the time of the earliest Dutch settlement. Following William Penn's arrival, he ordered a survey of 1,000 acres "thus delimiting the previously vague area of the common tract," but this survey had been inaccurate and had set aside 1,068 acres, according to later measurements. By 1764 there were complaints about encroachments on the tract, and the new Proprietors, Thomas and Richard Penn, ordered the establishment of the trusteeship described above, which was done by a deed naming the original

---

* Thomas Colley Grattan, *Civilized America* (2 vols., London, 1859), chap. entitled "The Women of America" 64–5, provides this acid description: "the shrinking from observation which is universal in Old England is here nearly unknown. A couple rarely seeks to escape from the crowd when they leave the altar . . . Married tonight, they see friends to-morrow, and appear in the visiting circle at their own home, at the common table of the boarding house, or in the public room of the hotel, with amazing *nonchalence* . . . the honeymoon of a Yankee must be passed in his hive. He never thinks of flying to rural shades, to hum among the flowers. He sticks fast to the cells where his treasures are hoarded. The wedding day once over, he hastens to his countinghouse, and begins to work double tides, to make up for the four-and-twenty hours he has lost. And the young creature [the bride] . . . is left to stare and be stared at." This was a Victorian reaction to an old American practice. Written long afterwards, it nevertheless described both of McKean's weddings exactly.

trustees: thirteen in number, of whom the first five were John Finney, Richard McWilliam, David Finney, Thomas McKean, and George Read.[64]

These were lifetime appointments, and as the various trustees died the towns-people were to elect successors, also to serve for life, usually men whose families had been identified with New Castle's history for a long time. This arrangement, with but minor adjustments, survived the Revolution and all the subsequent vicissitudes of American history. In addition, there were the Trustees of Market Square and Court House Square (the Green), and McKean was named to this body also, established some years later. In the latter case the Assembly designated the first five trustees, who were to serve for life, with the provision that the last survivor of the group should name his successors.

Serving as Trustee for the Loan Office of Newcastle County involved heavy responsibilities, for the Loan Office prepared and printed bills of credit, received applications from borrowers, examined titles before making loans, and extended loans to deserving persons.[65] The shortage of gold and silver was the reason given for the establishment of this agency. The purpose was not only to assist those who were having difficulty in meeting their obligations, but to encourage the develop-ment of new lands and increase the general prosperity of the area by expanding the amount of circulating currency. Certainly, this was the opinion of the ma-jority of voters in the community, with whom the Loan Office was very popular. The Loan Office likewise issued "draughts for the Governor's support," and was thus the agency by which the power of the purse was exercised on behalf of the legislature. For McKean this position meant the performance of numerous chores, but it was good training for the perplexities of later years, especially for the financing of the Revolution. An effective system of extending credit, and raising money, it would always be useful in times of emergency. In 1775, for example, the trustees prepared and printed £30,000 in bills of credit, because of the short-ages "due to frequent remittances to Great Britain in discharge of debts incurred for merchandise, etc."

On July 10, 1765, Governor John Penn appointed McKean the sole notary, and tabellion public, for the Lower Counties [66]—another position requiring de-tailed work—and on the same day McKean became Justice of the Peace, and Justice of the Court of Common Pleas and Quarter Sessions, and of the Orphans' Court, for the County of Newcastle.[67] Since the famous Stamp Act, which had been passed by the British Parliament on March 22, 1765, made the use of stamped paper for legal documents mandatory, McKean quickly found himself in a position where he either would, or would not, comply with its provisions. He could not remain neutral.

Chapter 6

Interruption—the Stamp Act Congress

Legislatures in both England and America had been appointing corresponding secretaries, or committees of correspondence, for many years before 1764. The American committees were originally set up to conduct correspondence with colonial agents in London, but at this time they began to be used, quite tentatively, as parts of an incipient revolutionary apparatus.[68] There was at first nothing subversive about appointing such committees, but when the legislatures in America began to correspond with each other in an effort to uphold their rights and privileges, as against the British government, their activities became increasingly revolutionary.

The initial step was taken by the legislature of Massachusetts-Bay, when a five-man committee was chosen to write to the legislatures of the other colonies to ask their help in obtaining the repeal of the Revenue Act of 1764, and to prevent the passage of the proposed Stamp Act.[69] At the same time, they instructed a six-man committee to write to their agent in London, who had not spoken out vigorously enough, objecting to his willingness to accept on their behalf taxation of "a people who are not represented in the House of Commons."[70] James Otis was to be a leading figure in both committees. These fateful steps were taken during the temporary absence from Boston of leading conservatives, such as Chief Justice Thomas Hutchinson, who quickly denounced the legislature's program as "the most injudicious conduct [he] ever knew the House of Representatives guilty of."[71]

Pennsylvania and the Lower Counties responded by appointing committees, as requested, but their respective legislatures had reasons of their own for this move, and were at first little interested in protesting the Acts of the British Parliament.[72] The Pennsylvania Assembly, or rather its dominant faction at the moment, was deeply involved in an effort to terminate the proprietorship of the

55

Penns, and to convert the province into a royal colony. Franklin and Galloway were the leaders of this effort, and their immediate concern was to avoid ill-timed protests that would antagonize the Britsh government, and jeopardize the Quakers' complicated maneuvers.

The Proprietary Party, under the leadership of the Attorney General, Benjamin Chew, and the Chief Justice, William Allen, saw what seemed an unusually favorable opportunity to weaken the Quaker coalition and, taking advantage of it, they succeeded in the next election in removing Franklin and Galloway from the Assembly. The Quaker faction retained control of the Assembly, however, and sent Franklin to England to try to reform, or eliminate, the proprietorship, and after the *next* election, when Galloway was returned to the Assembly, they made him Speaker.[73] The following year they supported the Assembly's decision to send delegates to the Stamp Act Congress. The Proprietors' chief support at this juncture came from the Scotch-Irish Presbyterians and the frontiersmen, who thus came forward on the ground-swell of anti-British opinion that was slowly rising in most segments of the population, as the implications of the Sugar Act and the Stamp Act were publicized throughout the colony.

The Assembly of the Lower Counties appoined a committee of correspondence, consisting of Thomas McKean, John Caton, and Benjamin Burton, and this committee on October 30, 1764, forwarded a petition to Henry Wilmot, Esq., in London, secretary to the Penns, and Member of Parliament, with the request that he "present their Petition as soon as [he learns] that the Petition of the Assembly of Pennsylvania . . . has been laid before His Majesty, but not before, the propriety of which conduct [he] will readily perceive." [74] The reason for this curious directive was that the political leaders of the Lower Counties were anxious, above all, to dissociate themselves from the legislature of Pennsylvania, and to win favor with the Proprietors and with the Crown. Their petition was not a protest—the language was obsequious to a degree rare even in an earlier generation, in the days of divine-right monarchy:

> We will not presume, dread Sir, to say what Motives may have actuated the Assembly of Pennsylvania on this occasion, but Justice and common Gratitude to our Proprietors demand of us to declare to your Majesty, that this Government hath enjoy'd the most perfect Happiness & Tranquility under [the Proprietors'] Administration, that our Charter Rights and Liberties have been inviolably preserved to us, which hath been an Encouragement to great Numbers of industrious People from various parts to come & settle among us, and hath enabled us the better to contribute to the Aids demanded of us by Your Majesty in the late War, which we have cheerfully granted to the Utmost of our Abilities . . .
>
> As therefore we Your Majesty's most humble Petitioners have not hitherto experienced any Mischiefs or Inconveniences to arise from the nature of a Proprietary Government, but on the contrary are sensible that the publick hath derived many Advantages from it, and the Proprietors have never been guilty of any Act of Oppression or Injustice towards us, we could never join in any Complaints against them, and most humbly beseech Your Majesty not to consider us as involved with the Assembly of Pennsylvania in their said Petition or the Consequences which may ensue from it.

> Permit us, Royal Sir, with the most profound submission, and with Hearts over-flowing with duty and gratitude, to take this opportunity of thanking Your Majesty for the manifold instances of Your Paternal Tenderness & Regard to us and Your other Loyal Subjects in this distant Quarter of the World, and in a more particular manner for your most gracious Care & Protection of us in the late War, and to offer up our fervent Prayers to Heaven to bless & preserve Your sacred Person, and continue the British Sceptre in Your Royal Line to the latest Generations.[75]

This petition was signed by Jacob Kollock, Speaker of the House, and transmitted with a letter in McKean's handwriting, signed by all three members of the committee of correspondence. It is hard to believe that the 30-year-old Mc-Kean, who was soon to become one of the staunchest of revolutionaries, would lend himself to such a servile address. But these were the views of the Assembly to which he had been elected just two years earlier, and in future years, when he was attending intercolonial congresses, this Assembly would still be the authority to whom he reported. He was serving people who were sincerely loyal to the British Crown, and even more to the heritage of idealism bequeathed by William Penn. His performance at the Stamp Act Congress was thus especially remarkable in the light of the persistent conservatism of his political confrères. The secret of his success was that he was in touch, as always, with people outside of politics, and the whole province was beginning to feel the pinch in British policies. He was playing a waiting game—for much higher stakes.

The strategy that was being followed by the Assembly of the Lower Counties was not as simple as it seemed, nor was it directed by junior members like Mc-Kean. It was the strategy of the Proprietors, whose leaders were supporting one Assembly against the other, in an effort to retain control of both, in behalf of the Penn family. The man in charge was Benjamin Chew, Attorney General of Pennsylvania, and formerly Speaker of the Assembly of the Lower Counties, ably assisted by William Allen, Chief Justice of Pennsylvania, and John Dickinson. McKean was willing to go along, because he had connections with the Penns, and also with Chew, whom he had represented in court.[76] At the moment his attitude appeared to be one of loyalty and gratitude, both to the Proprietors and to the Crown, but the basic purpose of the Proprietary strategy was to frustrate the conversion of Pennsylvania into a royal province, and McKean was aware that this policy was ultimately one of opposition to the Crown, no matter how humbly presented.

Benjamin Chew explained the reasoning behind this subtle maneuver in a letter to Thomas Penn in London, dated November 5, 1764:

> I have the pleasure of inclosing you an address to the King in Council from the Assembly of the Lower Counties at their last meeting, the principal design of which was first to manifest their affection for you and your family and to do justice to your characters; and secondly, by a side wind to counteract the petition from the Assembly of this Province. The members to a man acceded to the proposal I made to them to address the King on the occasion, provided it could be framed so as to be free from several objections they started about the propriety of their intermeddling with a matter done by this Assembly, which was independent of them. This required

a good deal of nicety; but I was happy enough to fall on the enclosed draft, with which they were much pleased and it passed nemine contra. As they have no standing agent, there, by my advice, they have enclosed it under cover to Mr. Wilmot; but have left his letter open, that if you judge it improper for him to present it—as he is your agent—you may get Mr. David Barclay, Jr., or any other person you please to present it. On the whole I have authority from the House to desire you either to present it or suppress it, as you think may or may not answer the end proposed by them—it being impossible for any one at this distance to form so good a judgment in the matter as you can who are upon the spot.[77]

Neither of the Penns' Assemblies, in Pennsylvania or in the Lower Counties, had been foresighted enough to be concerned about the Revenue Act (or Sugar Act) of 1764, until the act actually became effective. Both had been more interested in the struggle against the proprietorship. The effects of the act were significant, however, and they began to be felt at just the time when the proposed Stamp Act was being debated. The terms of the Revenue Act included a 3d-per-gallon tax on molasses, wine duties aimed at the favored Madeira wines, the elimination of drawbacks, or rebates, on foreign textiles,* and restrictions on the exportation of lumber—this provision affected the Lower Counties directly. The measures were not drastic in themselves, but attached to them were provisions for strict enforcement, and this was something new. Since the Lower Counties on the Delaware were exposed to British sea power along their entire length, and the city of Philadelphia itself could be reached by the British navy, these provisions were quickly felt.

The manner in which the act was enforced came to be more important, politically, than the specific taxes imposed. Edmund and Helen Morgan, in their comprehensive study, *The Stamp Act Crisis,* observe: "Most annoying, perhaps, was the literal-mindedness of naval officers . . . when the commanders of ships in American waters received instructions to assist in collecting the customs, they went about the business with no regard whatever for the facts of economic life. It is not likely that Parliament intended the new restrictions to apply to every dory that crossed an American river, but the Navy thought it necessary to exact the full measure of obedience from everything that floated, especially since the officers claimed a share of the prize money on every seizure they made." [78]

Up the river, Chief Justice William Allen, the patronage boss of the Proprietary faction in Pennsylvania, complained that the policy of strict enforcement was having a similarly disastrous effect in the Philadelphia area. Writing to business correspondents in London on November 20, 1764, just two weeks after Benjamin Chew had written to Thomas Penn, Chief Justice Allen objected specifically:

even the intercourse between here and New Jersey is, in a great Measure, interrupted, which was carried on in Flats and small Boats, and the produce of the Western part of that Colony shipped off from this City, but now, one of those poor fellows can-

* This provision would raise the price of *foreign* textiles, then considered a luxury. The idea was to restrict the colonists to British textiles. Foreign meant European—not British or American.

not take in a few Staves, or Pig Iron, or Bar Iron, or Tar, &c, but they must go thirty or forty Miles, or more to give Bond, the Charge of which and his travelling, make the Burthen intollerable. It never was the intention of the Legislature at home to destroy this little River-Trade, which is carried on in a kind of Market Boats, but their Regulations were only for Sea Vessels. This is the general Complaint all over the Continent.[79]

In a situation of this sort the point at which protest becomes disloyal is difficult to determine, but the complaints and evasion in the case of the Revenue Act soon became mob violence in the case of the Stamp Act. At this point some Americans were guilty of riot, if not treason. Again, the distinction was hard to discern in individual cases. But just as it was difficult to decide when the Americans became subversive, so it was debatable when the British government became consciously repressive. The reaction of the Americans, after all, was based on a deep-seated conviction that there was some sort of threat, still formless, to American liberties in the "encroaching power of Parliament." [80]

The Revenue Act of 1764 had been designed primarily to meet a problem of financing, though it might have produced dangerous results. Similarly, the decision to maintain a large standing army in America, after the French and Indian War, was a pragmatic decision to meet local problems, taken without adequate consideration of its political implications.[81] Even the Stamp Act, which was to produce such an explosion, was considered by most Englishmen as a reasonable and necessary extension of Parliamentary sovereignty. Without a broad-based tax, how could they support the government of the vast areas in North America which they had won in the recent war?

In England, Benjamin Franklin was out of touch with American public opinion, and in the beginning of the crisis sent back a series of unrealistic messages: urging compliance with the Sugar Act and the Stamp Act, appointing several of his friends as distributors under the Stamp Act, and even apparently acquiescing in the use of force to support the acts by his son, William Franklin, the Royal Governor of New Jersey.* If some of the most astute Americans, including Benjamin Franklin, failed to anticipate the violence of the American reaction, how could the British be blamed for similar failure?

At the time of the passage of the Stamp Act, however, the ministry of George Grenville had received a number of warnings as to the extent of opposition in America, and had decided to exert their authority nonetheless. Perhaps wishfully, they ignored the storm signals, and thought that with adroit management they could pass the bill and see that it was enforced.[82] Grenville's decision to warn the colonies by a Parliamentary resolution that a Stamp Act would be passed in another year, if the colonies could not suggest a more equitable method

---

* Fortunately, Franklin readjusted his thinking in time to help bring about the repeal of the Stamp Act, and save his reputation. His friend Joseph Galloway assisted in the publication of his famous "Examination before a Committee of the House of Commons." Dennys de Berdt's unflattering analysis was that Franklin "stood entirely neuter till he saw which way the cause would be carried, and then broke out fiercely on the side of America." William B. Reed, *The Life of Esther de Berdt, aftrwards Esther Reed of Pennsylvania* (Philadelphia, 1853), 107. Galloway never underwent the same conversion.

of taxation, has often been criticised in that it gave the Americans time to form an opposition. But Grenville thought that his gambit had been highly successful; he had got the Parliament to agree in principle to a controversial bill, without distracting them with details, and had made it appear that the Americans had failed to do their part in supporting the Empire, or even in paying for their own defense. He never expected that a satisfactory alternative would be proposed, and when several of the colonies actually expressed a willingness to meet their obligations, he gave them no indication as to how much money was expected. He intended to pass a Stamp Act, and was manipulating the political machinery skillfully—or so he imagined.[83]

In addition to considerations of power politics, there were practical causes for the delay in passing the Stamp Act, such as the fact that no one in England knew "the details of American judicial procedures well enough to name and describe the documents upon which a tax should be collected." [84] To remedy this embarrassing ignorance several inquiries were sent to private individuals, and on August 11, 1764, the Earl of Halifax, Secretary of State for the Southern Department, sent out a circular letter to the colonial governors asking for "a list of all instruments made use of in public transactions, law proceedings, grants, conveyances, securities of land or money within your government, with proper and sufficient descriptions of the same . . ." [85]

Various sizes of paper would be required for the documents in question, and all this paper was to be "stamped" or embossed in England, and sent to the colonies in the amounts and sizes needed, according to estimates made from the answers to these inquiries. But not only did Halifax not allude to the ministry's specific plan; Franklin himself, in London, was not aware of this feature of the Stamp Act, and at the time assumed that a heavy seal for embossing the paper would be given to the stamp distributors, with which they could "stamp" paper made in the colonies. He suffered a considerable financial loss due to his misconception, in that he sent to his partner in Philadelphia a large quantity of double demy, which could not be used.[86] Not the least of the complaints against the Stamp Act was that the British Board of Stamp Commissioners, and its colonial distributors, were given a "virtual monopoly of the sale of much of the paper used in the colonies." [87]

Meanwhile, the indiscriminate and unexplained inquiries were bound to perturb merchants, land speculators, and others in the colonies, but most especially lawyers and legislators.[88] Thomas McKean's opposition to the legal aspects of this measure was demonstrably sincere; upholding an untaxed and unregulated judiciary was always to be of primary importance for him. The Stamp Act was not the first, and certainly not the last, of many threats to this concept which he would vigorously resist. The act also placed a tax on newspapers, almanacs, pamphlets, broadsides, insurance policies, ships' papers, dice, and playing cards, as well as legal documents. There was even a double duty "where the instrument, proceedings &c. [were] in any other than the English language"—which was very unpopular among the Pennsylvania Germans.

William Gordon, a contemporary historian,[89] believed that the idea of holding an intercolonial Congress at New York in 1765, to meet the growing emergency, "was hatched [in Massachusetts] at the Warren household during a conference of the Warrens and Otises," [90] but opposition to the Stamp Act was spontaneous almost everywhere. Of the thirteen colonies which eventually participated in the Revolution, nine responded to Massachusetts-Bay's suggestion, and two others officially indicated that they approved of the protest. The New Hampshire Assembly, though it did not send delegates, formally approved of the Congress's resolutions afterwards. In North Carolina the Assembly, frustrated by the Governor's unwillingness to call them into session, rebuked the Governor later.

Several of the colonies represented at New York experienced difficulties in appointing delegates, but were not deterred. Delaware and New Jersey were faced with the same problem as North Carolina, but in these provinces the legislators were daring enough to act illegally, on their own responsibility.[91] The New York Assembly's committee of correspondence simply nominated themselves as delegates—which was considerate of them, because New York was to be the host colony.[92]

The Assembly of the Lower Counties consisted of eighteen men "fifteen of whom appointed the other three": Jacob Kollock, the Speaker, from Sussex County; Caesar Rodney, from Kent County; and Thomas McKean, from Newcastle.[93] Their instructions were to join with the committees from the other provinces "in one united and loyal petition to his majesty, and a remonstrance to the honorable house of Commons of Great Britain against the Acts of Parliament, and therein dutifully yet most firmly to assert the colonies right of exclusion from taxation by Parliament, and pray that they might not in any instance be stripped of the ancient and most valuable privilege of a trial by their peers . . ." [94]

Jacob Kollock, the Speaker, failed to attend, possibly because the Assembly was expected to be in session at the same time, but the colony was adequately represented by Rodney and McKean.[95] Rodney was favorably impressed by the quality of the delegates from the other provinces: "an Assembly of the greatest ability I ever yet saw," he called it.[96] McKean, on the other hand, was to remark (with the benefit of hindsight, to be sure), "There was less fortitude in that Body than in the succeeding congress of 1774: indeed some of the members appeared as timid as if engaged in a traiterous conspiracy." [97]

Altogether twenty-seven delegates representing nine colonies answered the roll call at New York on October 7, 1765, as follows:

Massachusetts: James Otis, Oliver Partridge, Timothy Ruggles
Rhode Island: Metcalf Bowler, Henry Ward
Connecticut: Eliphalet Dyer, David Rowland, William Samuel Johnson
New York: Robert R. Livingston, John Crugar, Philip Livingston, William Bayard, Leonard Lispenard
New Jersey: Robert Ogden, Hendrick Fisher, Joseph Borden
Pennsylvania: John Dickinson, John Morton, George Bryan
Delaware: Thomas McKean, Caesar Rodney
Maryland: William Murdock, Edward Tilghman, Thomas Ringgold
South Carolina: Thomas Lynch, Christopher Gadsden, John Rutledge.[98]

McKean and many others wanted to elect James Otis as Chairman, but the Congress chose the more conservative Timothy Ruggles. Actually Otis had changed his tune recently; the "great incendiary" was on his good behaviour, so the selection of someone else made little difference, except symbolically.[99] Otis impressed one observer from New York as "not riotous at all, despite his radical reputation." [100] In Massachusetts there were ugly rumors that he had sold out. Two of the South Carolina delegates, Gadsden and Lynch, tried to persuade Congress simply to ignore the authority of Parliament, but again the delegates decided to adopt a more moderate and humble stance.[101]

As for the Lower Counties (soon to be known as Delaware), being one of the smallest of the colonies, it was interested in having an equal vote for each colony. Long afterwards McKean wrote a letter to Timothy Pickering in which he said, "a vote by States was by me made a *sine qua non* in the first Congress held at New-York in 1765 . . . and also in that at Philadelphia . . . in 1774." [102] He had seen the test vote on the chairmanship lost by one vote, because of the number of delegates from New York, which was not the largest colony, merely the host colony, so the significance of an equal vote for each colony was clear from the beginning. Also, the fact was not lost on him that granting an equal vote to each colony was an excellent way for the radical faction to pick up support, and give the appearance of being stronger than their numbers might justify. This proved to be one of the most important decisions of the Stamp Act Congress.

The Congress chose separate committees for addressing the King, the House of Lords, and the House of Commons. McKean served on the committee to address the House of Commons with James Otis and Thomas Lynch, for both of whom he had the highest respect, and was partly responsible for the classic statement; "these colonies are not, and from their local circumstances, cannot be represented in the House of Commons in Great Britain." He also joined Livingston and Rutledge on a committee to revise the minutes of the proceedings. On October 26, when the work of the Congress had been completed and the delegates were getting ready to go home, Caesar Rodney wrote to his brother Thomas describing their labors: "You, and many others, perhaps are surprised to think that we should set so long when the business of our meeting seemed only to be the petitioning of the King, and . . . addressing that august body, the great legislative of the empire, for redress of grievances . . . it was likewise necessary to set forth the liberty we have, and ought to enjoy (as freeborn Englishmen) . . . This was one of the most difficult tasks I ever yet see undertaken, as we had carefully to avoid any infringement of the prerogatives of the Crown, and the power of Parliament, and yet in duty bound fully to assert the rights and privileges of the colonies." [103]

Almost fifty years later John Adams, who had *not* been a member of this early gathering, wrote to McKean: "Your Name among the Members of Congress in New York in October, 1765, is and has long been a singular distinction. I wish you would commit to writing your observations on the Characters who composed that Assembly and the objects of your Meeting. Otis and Ruggles are particularly interesting to me; and everything that passed on that important occasion is and

will be more and more demanded (and it is to be feared in vain) by our Posterity." [104]

Astonishingly enough, written records were not available to McKean in Philadelphia, and it took him more than a year to obtain the documents that he
needed to make an adequate reply.[105] Then on August 20, 1813, he wrote: "I
can at length furnish you with a copy of the proceedings of the Congress held
at New York in 1765; it is inclosed herewith. After diligent enquiry I had not
been able to procure a single copy either in manuscript or print, done in the
United States, but fortunately met one, published by J. Almon in London, in
1767, with a collection of American tracts in four octavo volumes, from which I
caused the present one to be printed: it may be of some use to the historian at
least." [106]

He then proceeded to give his recollections in considerable detail, and in much
the same form that he would use again in his Autobiographical Sketch in 1814.
In his letter to Adams he confirmed the view that "there were several conspicuous
characters," but "Mr. James Otis appeared to me to be the boldest and best
speaker. I voted for him as our president, but Brigadier Ruggles succeeded by one
vote, owing to the number of the committee from New-York, as we voted indi-
vidually . . ."

His further comments on Ruggles should be read as they appeared in his
Autobiographical Sketch. Since the Stamp Act Congress was the one episode in
McKean's life that he himself described—in the way in which he wanted it to
be recorded in history—and since his words have been borrowed and paraphrased
by many writers, as if they came from an account written at the time, the entire
passage should be considered verbatim. McKean was eighty years old when he
wrote this account, and knew that he was then the last survivor of the Stamp Act
Congress. His memory was still excellent, and his powers of succinct expression
unimpaired. Nevertheless, forty-nine years had gone by, and the patriotic tone
was strictly post-revolutionary. The reader should be warned.

> In the war between Great Britain and France, that terminated in the year 1763,
> the colonies of the former had made such exertions, that the Parliament made a
> grant to them severally of many thousand pounds sterling to relieve them; and yet
> in less than two years after the peace of Paris, they made an act imposing stamp
> duties on them, which if it had gone into operation would have extorted some hun-
> dreds of thousands annually from the colonies, and subjected their property to the
> absolute disposal of men over whom they had no control, and who benefited them-
> selves in proportion to the taxes they imposed thus arbitrarily on their fellow subjects
> in America.
>
> To avert this dreadful condition a proposition was made in 1765 by the Assembly
> of Massachusetts Bay to the other Assemblies of the British colonies on the continent
> to have a Congress of committees from every legislative assembly convened at New
> York in October of that year. This measure was adopted in every province where
> the Governors could not prevent it. So publicly did the rulers of the British Isles use
> official power to prevent conventions of the people even for the purpose of petition-
> ing the King and Parliament to consider and redress their intolerable grievances.
> Thomas McKean was a member of this Congress from Delaware; they met at New

York in October, formed a declaration of the rights of the colonists and of the violations of the same which they transmitted to the King, Lords, and Commons, with petitions to every one of them for a repeal of the Act of Parliament commonly called the Stamp Act &c. Owing to a change of Ministers in Great Britain or the apprehension of a very serious opposition in the colonies, the stamp act was repealed, but at the same time an act was passed declaring that the British Parliament had a right to bind the colonies *by law in all cases whatsoever.*

In this Congress, a few members were suspected to be inimical to their proceedings, or acted as if they wished to recommend themselves to the British Ministry, of whom the President was one, some others were timid, and refused to sign their proceedings. Mr. McKean on the [last] day of the session, addressed the President and said, that he had not heard a single objection to anything which had been finally agreed to, nor an observation from him of disapprobation; he requested therefore that he would now assign his reasons for refusing to sign the petitions. To this he answered that he did not concieve himself bound to give any reason; on which the other told him, the Gentlemen present had met to endeavour obtaining the repeal of an unconstitutional and oppresive act of the British Parliament, and a redress of other grievances, and as unanimity and sociability had hitherto prevailed among them, it appeared to him strange to find any one decline to sign his name to what he had at least apparently approved, without any excuse or observation on the occasion; that if there was any thing treasonable, offensive or indecent in their proceedings he thought it an act of comity nay of duty to inform his brethren of it: some others spoke briefly to the same purpose.

After a considerable pause, he said it was against his conscience; upon which Mr. McKean rang the changes on conscience, and the president apparently much displeased said, "young gentleman, you shall hear from me to morrow"; he was instantly answered, he would not only wait 'til tomorrow, but for ten days to oblige him. The Congress then adjourned sine die; and the President quit New York next morning before the dawn of day.

The Speaker of the Assembly of New Jersey [Robert Ogden] had refused to sign, and requested his colleague Joseph Borden, Esquire, not to mention the circumstances on his return home for some time, and to use his influence with Mr. McKean to conform to the like, but he could be prevailed upon only not to mention it in New Jersey as he passed through it, unless the question was put to him; he was asked in two or three different towns, the names of the Gentlemen, who had not signed the petitions, and gave them without hesitation. In a few days afterwards the speaker was burned in effigy in the town where he resided as well as in several others, and when the General Assembly was next convened at the city of Burlington a new Speaker was chosen. The resentment of the degraded Gentleman and his friends was pointed at Mr. McKean, and threats uttered, of which he was speadily informed, and without delay he went to Burlington, where he waited on the Governor, the new Speaker &c, and tarried two nights, without hearing any menaces whatsoever.

When Messieurs Rodney and McKean made their report of the proceedings of the Congress at New York to the Assembly of Delaware, the House was pleased to return them their unanimous thanks.[107]

McKean's letters to John Adams, in these later years, were considered "ostensibles"—an apt term to describe letters which might be shown to others, but were not intended for actual publication. In writing about the Stamp Act Congress, however, McKean may have had in mind the "delineation of the historic pen," mentioned in the Autobiographical Sketch, quoted above, especially since no one else had published an authoritative account of the momentous event. A year or so before the Autobiographical Sketch he had described the scene to Adams in sharper, more personal, detail. President Ruggles would not sign, and

> peremptorily refused to assign any reasons, until I pressed him so hard that he at last said, "it was against his *conscience*," on which word I rung the change so loud, that a plain challenge was given by him and accepted, in the presence of the whole corps; but he departed the next morning before day without an adieu to any of his brethren. He seemed to accord with what was done during the session so fully and heartily, that Mr. Otis told me frequently it gave him surprise, as he confessed he suspected his sincerity . . . Mr. Ogden . . . following the example of the President, declined to sign the petitions, tho' warmly solicited by myself in private and also by my father-in-law Colo. Borden, his colleague: the consequence of my mentioning this fact as I returned to Newcastle thro' New-Jersey, was to Mr. Ogden a burning in effigy in several of the counties . . . to me, menaces of another challenge. The great mass of the people were at that time zealous in the cause of America . . .[108]

McKean was a large, strong man who prided himself on his physical courage, so when he went to Burlington to face down his enemies, he was not greatly worried. Furthermore, if there were to be violence, McKean had the mob on his side, for he and his group were supporting the popular cause. As for influence, his father-in-law was one of the most prominent politicians in New Jersey, and his older brother was an Anglican minister who was highly regarded there, and had married into one of the leading families. He himself was an attorney·with a widespread clientele in New Jersey, who had just been admitted to practice and was about to be promoted to "Sollicitor and Councellor at Law" by the Royal Governor, William Franklin.

The Stamp Act had been passed on March 22, to be effective on November 1, 1765, but by that date no stamped paper could be purchased anywhere in the middle colonies.[109] William Cox, who had been appointed stamp distributor for New Jersey by Benjamin Franklin, had been persuaded to resign early in September. Although New Jersey and Delaware had had less violence than most of the provinces, the smell of violence was in the air, and Cox was taking no chances.[110] It would seem that Mr. Ogden likewise felt that discretion would be the better part of valor, since he had been burned in effigy in several towns already, and was about to lose his position as Speaker of the Assembly of New Jersey.[111]

McKean's allies and opponents were to have widely varying experiences. In May, 1766, James Otis was elected Speaker of the Massachusetts Assembly (with Sam Adams as Clerk)—from which position he was promptly ousted by Governor Bernard, who was acting within his rights, but was just as promptly frustrated by the Assembly, who substituted Thomas Cushing, a strong Otis supporter. John Adams crowed, "What a Change! . . . the Triumph of Otis and his Party are compleat." [112] To this triumph was added another, reported by New Jersey's Governor William Franklin to his father in July, "the Assembly [of Massachusetts], by the Influence of that Firebrand Otis, has imprudently turn'd out all the Crown and other Officers out of the Council." [113] Thus, Otis continued in political prominence for about nine more years, despite his growing eccentricity, until he gradually sank into tragic insanity.

McKean's suspicions of President Timothy Ruggles were well-founded; he later became a Brigadier in the British army and fought against the Americans. McKean kept an eye on him throughout the war, and his papers contain a communication carefully endorsed: "Intercepted Lre of J. Wentworth, Esqre, late Governor of New Hampshire to Brigadr. Timothy Ruggles, London, June 7th, 1780." Meanwhile, the "degraded gentleman," Mr. Ogden, wisely confined himself to but one public statement, and that somewhat of a recantation. In November, 1765, in a special session called by Governor Franklin at the request of the Assembly, Speaker Ogden explained that he had refused signing the petitions of the Stamp Act Congress as he thought individual addresses from the colonies would be more effective, but as he had become "the object of too general a resentment," he offered his resignation, which was immediately accepted.[114]

McKean also mentioned in his Autobiographical Sketch that he had earlier been made a justice of the peace "and of the court of Common pleas, quarter sessions of the peace and Orphans court for the county of Newcastle." He went on to say that "In the November [1765] and February [1766] terms following he sat on the Bench, which ordered all the officers of the court to proceed in their several vocations as usual on unstamped paper. This was done accordingly and was perhaps the only court that did so in any of the colonies or provinces on the Continent." * In this statement he was clearly in error. His court may have been the first, or one of the first, but it was not the only court on the continent to proceed in that manner. For example, the justices of the Frederick county court in Maryland opened without stamped paper in December, 1765, and the common pleas court in Northampton county in Pennsylvania did likewise in January, 1766.[115]

The lawyers in several cities, including New York and Philadelphia, found themselves under great pressure from the populace, and issued numerous public statements condemning the Stamp Act and urging the courts to ignore the provisions of the law. In New Jersey there was a large meeting of lawyers at New Brunswick in February, 1766, which was overwhelmed by hundreds of Sons of Liberty who came uninvited.† Merchants and traders, as well as retailers, were also active in opposing the unpopular measure. The act was effectively nullified

---

* In an autobiographical letter to George Washington, dated April 27, 1789, McKean wrote, "In 1766 I first took a seat on the Bench at Newcastle, having before been in the commission of the peace & a Justice of the common pleas for that county, and had influence enough to have justice administered upon unstamped paper."
    In 1799 an anonymous pamphleteer wrote, "His boasts of weight of influence, and services in [the Stamp Act Congress] are well known to all who have heard him for the last twenty years, spout out his own praise." *To the Electors of Pennsylvania* by a Pennsylvanian, 1799 (John Carter Brown Library, Providence).

† Col. Isaac Barré had used the expression Sons of Liberty in a speech before the House of Commons. The term was generally applied to resistance groups who opposed the Stamp Act in 1765. In the period from 1766 to 1774 the activities of these groups gradually changed, and they became less significant. Sometimes they continued to issue propaganda, but their coercive function was taken over by the committees of inspection or safety. See Philip Davidson, *Propaganda and the American Revolution,* chap. on "Merchant and Mechanic Organizations."

in a number of ways; for example, ships' clearances were approved en masse, and hurriedly, before the act went into effect, or filled out later and issued anyhow, in anticipation of repeal.[116]

The Stamp Act remained on the books for less than five months, and even during that period it was a dead letter everywhere except in Georgia. Most courts, it is true, avoided meeting the issue squarely, and postponed their meetings and delayed action until after the expected repeal. Finally, on the 18th of March, 1766, Parliament passed the Declaratory Act (in the same terms as the Irish Declaratory Act of 1719), asserting that Parliament had full authority to bind the colonies "in all cases whatsoever," and then repealed the Stamp Act.[117] Americans tended to ignore the Declaratory Act, and give undue credit to the aging and ailing William Pitt for the repeal of the Stamp Act. Pitt had spoken eloquently several times against the taxing of the colonies, and in secret session he had pointed out, even more effectively, that the government was unable to enforce the law because most of its troops were at frontier out-posts; but he was a strong believer in Parliamentary sovereignty, and not so much of a "friend of America" as many Americans believed.[118] In the new ministry, which was nominally under Pitt's direction, Charles Townshend would emerge as the dominant force, and the issue of taxation would rise again.

The news of the repeal was brought to Philadelphia by a Captain Wise, who was immediately invited to the London Coffee House, and together with his crew was given presents and punch. Many of the "first men played hob-and-nob over their glasses with sailers and common people" [119] at this joyous celebration, and the city was illuminated at night for a gigantic beer party—much to the disgust of Joseph Galloway and other conservative subjects of the Crown, who felt that the general enthusiasm was being artificially stimulated. At a feast the next day at the State House gallery "it was unanimously resolved by those present to dress themselves, at the approaching birthday of the king, in new suits of English manufacture, and to give their homespun garments to the poor." [120] Similar events occurred from one end of America to the other, as soon as the good news arrived. At New York the mansion of General Gage himself "was gorgeously illuminated," and the town of New Castle on the Delaware was brightly lighted "on the joyful occasion . . . and really made a pretty appearance from the water," according to young Francis Hopkinson, who was in a ship going down river on his way to Ireland.[121]

The significance of the Stamp Act Congress was that it provided a precedent for united action, and a widespread awareness of the constitutional problems of the empire. There had been virtual unanimity throughout the continent as to the undesirability of the Act—disagreement only as to the proper course that resistance should take. When public opinion was again aroused, and the need for concerted action was more generally understood, the precedent of the Congress would not be forgotten. Moreover, the Sons of Liberty were now organized in many of the colonies, and courageous leaders had emerged who were known to the leaders of the other colonies. The committees of correspondence, which had hitherto dealt mainly with colonial agents in England, would soon be writing more frequently to each other.[122]

In the domain of the Penns, no one was more clearly identified with the patriotic cause than Thomas McKean. When New Englanders or Southerners got into trouble with the mother country (and, more immediately, when the New York Assembly was suspended in 1767), the record of Thomas McKean at the Stamp Act Congress would quickly come to mind. Others might become famous in other ways: his friend John Dickinson for his skillful pamphleteering; his father-in-law, Joseph Borden, and his associates, Caesar Rodney of the Lower Counties, and George Bryan of Pennsylvania, for their organizing abilities; but Thomas McKean would be remembered for his imposing personality, his determination, and his sheer nerve at the Stamp Act Congress. These were inherent qualities which would cause people to turn to him instinctively in moments of indecision and danger.

Chapter 7

Robert McKean and the New Jersey Medical Society

While his brother Thomas was rising to prominence in the Stamp Act Congress in New York, Robert McKean was experiencing unmistakable intimations of mortality. The illness which would destroy him in two years (consumption, or tuberculosis) first appeared about the 25th of October, 1765, when he "was seized with a very tedious and dangerous sickness that rendered [him] entirely incapable of any business for about three months." [123] For the time being he arranged to have his pulpit supplied by the Chaplain of the 28th Regiment,[124] and pushed forward with his other activities as well as he could, but the disease steadily progressed.[125] As late as April 27, 1767, he could still write: "For more than a year past no kind of public worship has been maintained in Amboy except that of the Church of England in consequence of which several persons of other denominations regularly attend our service." [126]

During his term as pastor, St. Peter's Church had been enlarged, a spire had been added to its steeple, and its graveyard was improved. He had also maintained the library which was supported in Perth Amboy, as at other Venerable Society churches, by the Society for the Promotion of Christian Knowledge, and had started a school in order to make proper use of the library. A few days before his death, his colleague, the Rev. Dr. Thomas Chandler of St. John's Church in Elizabeth, noted: "Wasted away with a tedious disorder, the worthy, the eminently useful and amiable Dr. McKean is judged by his physicians to be at present at the point of death. A better man was never in the Society's service." [127]

His greatest contributions during his last years, however, were to the medical profession, as organizer and first president of the New Jersey Medical Society. This was the first organization of its kind in the American colonies,[128] and it

69

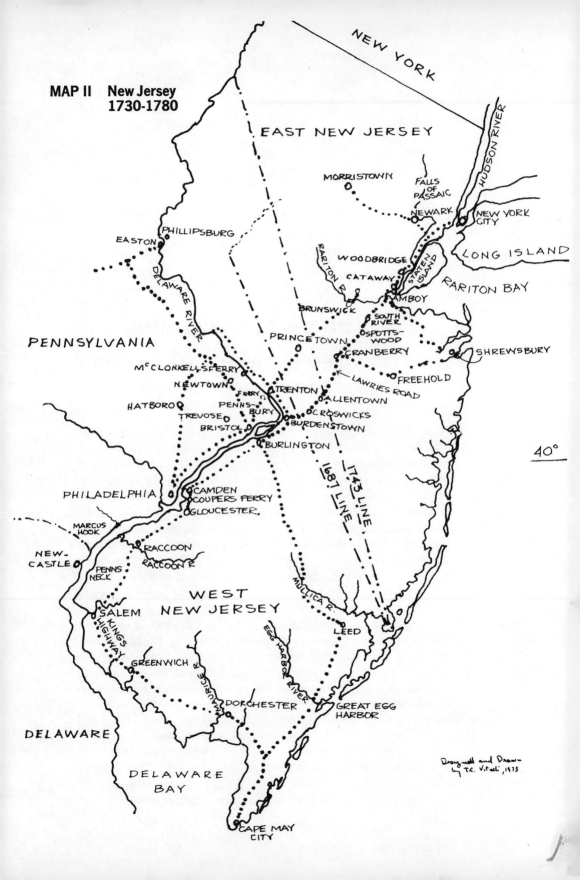

formulated the principles and ideals of the medical profession, and separated the functions of the doctor from those of the priest, the druggist, or the family friend.[129] This group also distinguished between well-trained practitioners and the "peripatetic quacks who set themselves up as 'doctors of medicine,' charged what the traffic could bear, and remained long enough only to be found out by patients who had come—often too late—to a legitimate physician." [130]

On June 27, and again on July 14, 1766, the *New York Mercury* carried a notice which read as follows:

> A Considerable Number of the Practitioners of Physic and Surgery, in East New-Jersey, having agreed to form a Society for their mutual Improvement, the Advancement of the Profession, and the Promotion of the Public Good:—And desirous of extending as much as possible, the Usefulness of their Scheme, and of cultivating the utmost Harmony and Friendship with their Brethren, hereby request and invite every Gentleman of the Profession in the Province, that may approve of their Design, to attend their first Meeting, which will be held at Mr. Duff's, in the City of New-Brunswick, on Wednesday the 23d of July, at which Time and Place the Constitutions, and Regulations of the Society are to be settled and subscribed.[131]

Seventeen doctors met at Duff's Tavern, at the northeast corner of Albany and Peace Streets in New Brunswick, in response to this notice. The Rev. Dr. Robert McKean was elected President, and Dr. Christopher Manlove was elected Secretary; probably it was he who had had the foresight to bring the little book (sixteen inches long and six inches wide) in which the minutes of the society were permanently recorded. Some of the doctors, particularly the clerical physicians, were formally dressed with "white cravat, ruffled shirt, silk hat and even a wig." [132] This combination of minister and doctor in the same person was not unusual; seven of the thirty-six members of the Society in its first decade combined the two roles.[133] Most members, however, had no such pretensions to elegance, and dressed "as befitted those constantly in the saddle: dun-colored kerseys, blue broadcloth coat, linen homespun shirt, wool or yarn stockings, felt hat, plain silver buckle at shoe and knee, and shoulder-length hair loose or gathered at the nape with a deer thong." [134]

The business of the first meeting was to draw up Instruments of Association, and to pool the members' knowledge so that they could draft a suggested Table of Fees and Rates. The former project had been the subject of much thought before the meeting, and was a conspicuous success; the latter was written hastily in a single afternoon by a committee appointed by President McKean, and gave "the wrong impression" to the public. Some of the principles that were to guide the members of the Society—principles that have had a permanent value—were the following:

> 1stly. That we will never enter any house in quality of our profession, nor undertake any case, either in physic or surgery, but with the purest intention of giving the utmost relief . . .
>
> 2dly. That we will at all times when desired, be ready to consult or to be consulted by any of our brethren . . .

3dly. That we will not pretend to or keep secret any nostrum or specific medicine of any kind, as being inconsistent with the generous spirit of the profession . . .

4thly. That we will on all occasions treat one another as becomes the medical character . . .

5thly. That as we have separated ourselves to an office of benevolence and charity, we will always most readily and cheerfully, when applied to, assist gratis, by all means in our power, the distressed poor and indigent in our respective neighborhoods . . .

6thly. That we will hold meetings twice every year [and other organizational matters] . . .

14thly. That this Society shall not be dissolved but by the concurrence of seven-eighths of the whole body.

Lastly. that this Society will do all in their power to discourage and discountenance all quacks, mountebancks, imposters, or other ignorant pretenders to medicine . . .[135]

The Table of Fees and Rates was intended to provide approved charges, with the proviso that members could abate bills "on account of poverty, friendship, or other laudable motives, but on no other consideration whatever, under pain of expulsion." The problem of unpaid bills was to be resolved by limiting credit to three months after the patient's recovery, except that "foul" diseases were to be paid for immediately, and strangers were to pay at once. Visits in town "where the physician can readily attend without riding" were to be free, unless several such visits were required. The rates were set forth in pounds, shillings, and pence, and were thought to be reasonable; they included a surprising variety of treatments, considering the limited knowledge of the day:

	£	s	d
An ordinary call, up to a mile and a half	–	1	6
Each additional mile	–	1	–
Simple fracture	2	–	–
Amputation of a leg or thigh	3	–	–
Operation for cataract	3	–	–
Extirpation of the tonsils	1	–	–
Extirpation of large cancerous tumors	1	10	–
Extirpation of small cancerous tumors	–	15	–
Extracting a tooth	–	1	6
For delivering a woman in a natural case	1	10	–
Laborious case, requiring forceps or crotchet	3	–	–

Rates for medicines
    [Elexirs, essences, etc. in great detail, exclusive of visiting
    and traveling fees] [136]

It should be remembered that the germ theory of disease had not yet been advanced, and Galen's four fluid humors—the sanguine, the phlegmatic, and choleric, and the melancholic—dominated the scientific thinking of the profession.* Whiskey and biting a bullet were still the most reliable pain-killers, with opium available only occasionally. Patients put their lives on the line when they submitted to an operation, but the doctors felt that they took risks more frequently, exposing themselves day after day to diseases for which there was no known cure. Thus, the rates which the Society proposed were not "an unjust scheme for bringing the public to terms," but an honest effort to evaluate the services which they rendered.[137]

Nevertheless, there was a tremendous clamor against the Society, and the second meeting, on November 4, 1766, at Elizabethtown, was devoted to correcting the public's "misapprehensions." Dr. Manlove, the Secretary, was instructed to send copies of the Instruments of Association to the newspapers, and to explain the many problems, affecting the public as well as the medical profession, which the new Society was attempting to solve. He was also to announce that the Table of Rates would be suspended, pending further study, except that doctors who were members of the Society would not exceed the rates that were listed. He was likewise to set forth the desirability of legislation on medical subjects, but at the same time to assure the public that until the Assembly acted, the Society would do its best to avoid abuses by voluntary regulation.

Dr. McKean was not able to attend this meeting because of failing health, but he sent a message in which he passed along a prescription he had received from a Dr. Ayres of Newport, Rhode Island. Dr. Ayres had received the nostrum in turn from Dr. Jared Elliott of Connecticut, with whom he had studied: it consisted of a formula with ground glass as the chief ingredient, which "would immediately cause a very severe pungent pain, and an universal shock, something like an electric stroke," useful for dropsies and hysteric cases. Dr. McKean made it clear that he knew nothing of the effects of this remedy himself, but he had been assured that it had often been used successfully. The Society considered the prescription and "judged it not prudent to recommend the use of it, without more authentic proofs of its success"—a decision which probably spared a number of New Jerseyites considerable agony.[138]

The third meeting of the Society was held in Perth Amboy on May 5, 1767. Dr. McKean presided this time and was reelected President, in spite of the fact that his illness was increasingly evident.[139] The Society considered several applications for admission, and accepted a few applicants who were known to at least some of the members, and were well recommended. It tabled the application of a man who "was a stranger to all the members, lacked testimonials, and had not previously informed the Society of his intentions." Presumably they made the right decision in this case, for the candidate did not reappear at the next meeting.

* Catherine Drinker Bowen, *John Adams and the American Revolution*, 643. "[John Adams']
  classmates at Harvard debated the truth of Copernicus's theory. The narrowing of one's
  mind to this strange constriction is a struggle painful, almost impossible; the Age of En-
  lightenment has tales to tell that wash our world away. Gone are Pasteur, Lister, and the
  germ theory of disease. Gone is Darwin. Special creation, spontaneous generation rule the
  universe."

In order to ensure high standards of education (in the absence of governmental action), the members next agreed that they would not accept apprentices who lacked proficiency in Latin "and some Greek," and that they would train their apprentices for four years, "of which three shall be spent with [the] master, and the other may (with his master's consent) be spent in some school of physic in Europe or America." The apprentice's fee was set at £100. These regulations were intended to weed out superstitious or credulous practitioners, but there were a few critics, both then and since, who were churlish enough to suggest that they were really based on little more than snobbishness, or class prejudice.

In August, 1767, Robert McKean consulted Dr. John Morgan of Philadelphia about his weakening condition, describing his symptoms with clinical frankness, and receiving in reply a letter which was a model of its kind.[140] Dr. Morgan had served for four years as surgeon to the Pennsylvania troops in the French and Indian War, and had then studied medicine in Edinburgh; in the spring of 1765 he returned to found the first medical school in America at the College of Philadelphia. He had recently married Mary Hopkinson, the sister of Francis Hopkinson, and was therefore indirectly a connection of McKean's by marriage. Morgan's diagnosis was *phthisis pulmonalis,* and it confirmed McKean's worst suspicions. His letter was dated September 3d, 1767:

> Last night I received your obliging favour of the 20th Instant. & now set down to answer it with that attention which I think it deserves. Little should I merit that confidence you are pleased to repose in me if I was not to deliberate very seriously of your case, or were I to procrastinate giving my advice when asked in a matter of so much consequence.
>
> My sentiments therefore shall be delivered with that candour & punctuality I should hope for myself in like circumstances.
>
> The clearness with which you deliver your history of the disease leaves no ambiguity with me as to the nature & extent of it. That your life is in danger if the utmost management is not made use of I apprehend must be your own opinion. For my part I am persuaded that all the attention of your friends & your own will are indispensably necessary for your relief, and under God nothing less can prove effectual to give a happy issue to the disorder.
>
> I doubt not but every thing that hath been done is right, but as you do not relate what plan of cure you observ'd till you ask'd my advice, I think it proper to write as if it were not a case which has been already under the care of any physician, by which I mean to deliver my opinion as in a consultation of several call'd together, & as the younger giving my advice first.
>
> That your disorder is a true *phthisis pulmonalis* appears evident to me, but I think it is not yet so far advanced but that it may admit a radical cure; if we are so happy as to agree upon a proper plan of treatment, which is the thing now to be considered. Let us then take our Indications from the present state of your lungs & strength of body. The fever & pain with the night sweats & difficult respiration, together with the violence & duration of the disease, the troublesome cough & the present ulceration of the Lungs are to give us light in this matter. These declare a very general & hitherto a very fixed obstruction in that viscus. The sweats arise from the adsorption of Pus into the Blood, as is plain from the decrease of this symptom since an expectorate came on.

That these are Tubercles in the Lungs is highly probable from that constant irritation to cough, & from this consideration that inspection has invariably demonstrated the existence of the tubercles in every similar complaint so violent & so long continued. The strength of body must be greatly impaired from every concurring circumstance . . . [Several technical paragraphs omitted.]

. . . As to palliatives, the Elixir paregoric is the most effectual with sugar candy & the like to still & quiet the cough.

. . . Tinctures of the Bark to begin with, then bitters & Elixir vitrioli may come in—& lastly Bark in substance, gentle exercise, etc.

But above all a free & temperate Air is necessary throughout the whole of the disorder, therefore get out as often as you can.—If you or other gentlemen who may be advised in the case approve of the above, it will be easy to improve these hints into proper formula.

JOHN MORGAN, M.D.[141]

Shortly after receiving this letter Robert McKean wrote his will—as well he might. He described himself as Clerk and Missionary for the Society for the Propagation of the Gospel in Foreign Parts, and dated the will September 13, 1767.[142] Witnesses were Gannetta Harrison, his brother-in-law Lewis Antill,[143] and his brother Thomas McKean. He mentioned his father William McKean (who was still alive), his wife Isabella,[144] his brothers Thomas and William, his sister Dorothea the wife of John Thompson, and his nephew Robert, his namesake and the second son of Thomas McKean who was always included in the New Jersey documents.[145] He did not include any children of his own, and presumably had none.

On October 17, 1767, he died at Raritan Landing near New Brunswick, while visiting his father-in-law Edward Antill. He was buried in St. Peter's Churchyard in Perth Amboy, where there is a monument to him as the "founder and First President of the Medical Society of New Jersey," and also a monument erected to his honor by his brother Thomas McKean:

In Memory of
The Rev. Robert McKean, M.A.
Practitioner in Physic, &c
And Missionary from the Society
For the Propagation of the Gospel
in foreign Parts
To the City of Perth Amboy,
Who was born
July 13th, 1732, N.S.
And died October 17th, 1767.
An unshaken Friend,
An agreeable Companion
A rational Divine
A skillful Physician,
And in every Relation of Life

A truly Benevolent and
Honest Man,
Fraternal Love hath erected
This monument.

Some thirty years later, on June 24, 1798, McKean wrote to his friend, John Dickinson: "The expression of your affectionate regard for my brother [Robert] so long since deceased is very grateful to me. I know his friendship for you was reciprocal. May I die as good a man." [146]

Chapter 8

Hare or Hound?

Question: At the beginning of the present rebellion, when the inhabitants first took up arms, had the people, in general, independence in view?

Answer: I do not believe . . . at that time, that one-fifth of the people had independence in view . . . The progress of the spirit of independence was very gradual. So early as the year 1754, there were men in America, I may say in the towns of Boston, New York, Philadelphia, and Williamsburg, who held independence in prospect, and who were determined to seize any opportunity that offered to promote it . . . These men, when the Stamp Act was passed, made a stalking-horse, or screen, of the gentlemen of the law in every part of America, to cover their designs, and to sound the trumpet of opposition against Government; but avowed, that their conduct was on the ground of obtaining a redress of American grievances, and not with a design to separate the two countries . . .

When the Tea Act was passed, they made the same use of the merchants who were smugglers in America, as they had done of the lawyers before, still declaring that they meant not independence . . . So late as the sitting of the Congress in 1774, the same men, when charged with it in Congress, and whilst they held it tenaciously and religiously in their hearts, they almost to a degree of profanity denied it with their tongues—and all this was done on their knowledge, that the great bulk of the people of North America was averse to independence . . . If we look at the resolves of Congress, down almost to the very period of their declaration of independence, we shall find the same language, the same pretense of obtaining a redress of grievances held out to the people . . .[147]

This memorable exchange took place during the examination of Joseph Galloway before a committee of the House of Commons in London on March 19, 1779. Galloway, of course, was a Loyalist who by this time had lost everything in the Revolution, and was prejudiced, perhaps bitter. But his description has the ring of truth, and is supported by much evidence. Furthermore, he had been in as favorable a position to observe the politics of the period as any man in America, for he had been Speaker of the Assembly of Pennsylvania from 1765 to 1774, and chairman of the host delegation to the First Continental Congress in Philadelphia in the latter year—still participating himself, it might be added, in the deception he so vividly described.[148] He was thoroughly out of sympathy with the Congress, however, and in 1775 he refused election to the Second Continental Congress, and by the end of the following year fled to the protection of the British Army.

During the British occupation of Philadelphia in 1777–1778 (the Valley Forge Winter), Galloway was General Howe's right-hand man, striving valiantly to establish a civil government, instead of martial law, in the occupied territory.[149] Again, he was in an excellent position to observe, although his hopes and plans for a restoration of British control collapsed when the British army abandoned Philadelphia, and he himself went into permanent exile. Nevertheless, his understanding of the period should be given due weight because of his experience.

In any case, it is almost impossible to find a better description of what happened, for the Patriots, who were playing an increasingly dangerous game, systematically destroyed letters or messages which might betray their activities, or convict them of treason. The evidence is therefore mostly negative. McKean and his confederates saved a great deal of correspondence *before* the Stamp Act in 1765, and *after* the success of the revolution was assured (say, from the French entrance into the war, and the British evacuation of Philadelphia). Yet for the period of greatest tension, from 1765 to 1774, the remarkable lack of revealing correspondence is revealing in itself, and there is no frank and open analysis of political strategy or tactics. Propaganda, yes, brilliant and enduring. But cold-blooded, hard-headed, cynical analysis (of the sort Galloway offered from the Loyalist viewpoint)—this was a luxury the Patriots could not afford. They had ropes around their necks, if they were caught, and they developed the habit of caution. Many of the letters they wrote were unsigned, or contained mystifying references, guarded by obscure language that only the recipient would understand.[150]

Even in their old age these men refused to write histories of the revolution. One of them, Charles Thomson, with a vast collection of information, which he had accumulated for many years as permanent Secretary of the Congress, started to write a history, only to think better of it and destroy what he had written.* Men who were constant letter-writers, and who lived long after the danger had passed, like Adams, Jefferson, or McKean, although they wrote about other sub-

---

* John F. Watson, *Annals of Philadelphia* . . . (Phila., 1830), 546. "[Thomson] was after the peace much urged to write a history of the Revolution, and after the year 1789, when he first settled at Harriton, actually gathered many curious and valuable papers, and wrote many pages of the work; but at length, as his nephew told me, he resolved to destroy the whole, giving as his chief reason, that he was unwilling to blast the reputation of families rising into repute, whose progenitors must have had a bad character in such a work. A letter from John Jay, which I saw, stimulated him to execute [the history] 'as the best qualified man in the country.'"

REV. FRANCIS ALISON, D.D.
(Courtesy: Presbyterian Minister's Fund.)

JOHN DICKINSON, by Charles Willson Peale, 1770.
(Courtesy: Historical Society of Pennsylvania.)

FRANCIS HOPKINSON, by Robert Edge Pine, 1785.
(Courtesy: Historical Society of Pennsylvania.)

GEORGE READ.
(Courtesy: Historical Society of Pennsylvania.)

JACOB DUCHÉ, by Francis Hopkinson, ca. 1770.
(Courtesy: Historical Society of Pennsylvania.)

CHARLES THOMSON.
(Courtesy: Historical Society of Pennsylvania.)

RESIDENCE OF CHARLES THOMSON.
(Courtesy: Historical Society of Pennsylvania.)

RESIDENCE OF JOSEPH BORDEN.
(Courtesy: Bordentown Library Association. Photo by Earl Loretangeli.)

THOMAS McKEAN AND SON, THOMAS McKEAN, JR.,
by Charles Willson Peale.
(Courtesy: Mrs. Rowland Evans, Bryn Mawr, Pa. Photo by Peter Dechert.)

SARAH ARMITAGE McKEAN AND DAUGHTER, SOPHIA DOROTHEA,
by Charles Willson Peale.
(Courtesy: Mrs. Rowland Evans, Bryn Mawr, Pa. Photo by Peter Dechert.)

DUCHÉ'S HOUSE, RESIDENCE OF GOV. THOMAS McKEAN.
(Courtesy: Historical Society of Pennsylvania.)

jects almost daily, for some reason never undertook a factual and detailed description of the greatest of their political achievements.

In McKean's case there is a curious over-supply of documents concerning his appointments and promotions in this period, all of which were carefully preserved, including such items as the following:

> Appointment as Attorney at Law in the Province of New Jersey, signed by Charles Read, June 1765 [151]
>
> Appointment as Notary and Tabellion Publick in the Government of the Counties of Newcastle, Kent and Sussex on Delaware, signed by John Penn, July 10, 1765 [152]
>
> Appointment as Justice of the Peace in the County of Newcastle, signed by John Penn, July 10, 1765 [153]
>
> Appointment as Sollicitor and Counsellor at Law in New Jersey, signed by William Franklin, Oct. 31, 1766 [154]
>
> Detailed letter (two copies) by Thomas McKean to John Penn concerning the latter's land-holdings and potential income in the Lower Counties, Novr. 10, 1770 [155]
>
> Appointment as Collector of His Majesty's Customs for the Port of New-Castle, signed by James Hamilton, Sept. 10, 1771 [156]
>
> Oath to be true and faithful in the service of His Majesty's Customs, before George Read, Sept. 13, 1771 [157]
>
> Appointment and Instructions for the Collection of the Customs for the Royal Hospital at Greenwich, signed by Henry Hulton, dated at the Custom-House at Boston, Oct. 1, 1771 [158]
>
> Some correspondence by Francis Hopkinson to Lord and Lady North concerning the above position, by which he received the appointment "to be exercised by deputy" and informed McKean of the same, Feb. 28, 1772 [159]
>
> Entries in Joseph Shippen's Letterbooks for May 28, 1772, and March 25, 1773, informing McKean as Speaker that the Governor, John Penn, "begs you will be pleased to inform the House as soon as they meet, that he will, with the utmost Readiness attend them . . ." [160]

Yet, at the same time, his revolutionary correspondence cannot be found. In other words, his *safe* activities were fully documented, with almost no indication in the written record except circumstantial evidence, and glimpses here and there, that he was ever involved in any kind of opposition to the British government, and certainly not in the organization of illegal or treasonable resistance. Nevertheless, towards the end of his incomplete Autobiographical Sketch, in discussing the Townshend taxes in 1767, on tea, paper, painters' colors, and glass, McKean implied that he had indeed taken an active part: "The impost was so small that it was concluded no opposition would be made; but there were Gentlemen in these colonies who remembered their Stamp Act, and reflected on the consequences of a submission: 'that it would be established as a precedent, and many an error by the same example would creep into the state.' A correspondence ensued in consequence between a few Gentlemen, who had known each other at the Congress held at New York in 1765 . . ." [161]

It must be remembered that some of the alarms that were sounded at the time of the Stamp Act, such as Patrick Henry's famous resolutions in Virginia, sounded so much like treason that they "were handed about with great privacy" in Philadelphia and New York.[162] A few of the surviving letters of Sam Adams in Massachusetts contain the request that the recipient not let the letter or a copy get out of his hands, "but return it by the first opporunity." [163] The official report that McKean and Rodney submitted to the Delaware Assembly, in May 1766, explained the secrecy of their subsequent transactions in this manner: "It was recommended by the Congress to the several Colonies, to appoint special Agents for solliciting Relief from the present Grievances, and to unite their utmost Interests and Endeavours for that Purpose. It was also recommended by the Congress, that the greatest Precaution be used to prevent any of the Addresses being printed before they were presented, lest they might be considered as an Appeal to the People rather than as Application to our Sovereign and the British Parliament." [164]

The minutes of McKean's and Rodney's report to the Assembly conclude with the statement: "They also beg Leave to lay before the House two Letters which they have received from Dennys De Berdt, Esq; a Gentleman in London appointed special Agent for the Province of Massachusetts-Bay . . ." This was on May 27, 1766. On the 30th McKean moved that an Address be sent "to the King's most Excellent Majesty" thanking the King for the repeal of the Stamp Act, and when this motion was passed he, Rodney, and Read were appointed a committee for the preparation of the Address.

On June 5th it was moved "That Dennys De Berdt, of the City of London, Esq; be, and he is appointed, Agent for this Government, to present the Address to the King's most Excellent Majesty from this House" and also "That Thomas M'Kean, Caesar Rodney, and George Read, Esquires, be the Committee of Correspondence for the current Year, and that they transmit the said Address to Mr. De Berdt." [165] In this way was created the Delaware triumvirate, which dominated the committee of correspondence for many years, and would eventually represent the state in the Continental Congress.*

---

* George Read (1733–1798) was born in Maryland, studied law in Philadelphia, and settled in New Castle where he practiced law after 1754. He was Attorney General for the Lower Counties, 1763–74, during which time he also served in the Assembly. Member of the Continental Congress, 1774–77, he refused to vote for the resolution of independence on July 2, 1776, but signed it subsequently. From November, 1777, to March, 1778, he was acting president of Delaware; he was delegate to the federal Constitutional Convention, 1787, and U. S. Senator, 1789–93, thereafter Chief Justice of Delaware. At about the same time as McKean's first marriage Read married Gertrude Ross Till, the widow of Thomas, son of the late Chief Justice of the Lower Counties, William Till. See DAB and Charles P. Keith, The Provincial Councillors of Pennsylvania (Philadelphia, 1883), 194–5.

Caesar Rodney (1728–1784) was born and died near Dover, Delaware. Except for a brief period he was a member of the Delaware Assembly from Kent County, 1761–76. A delegate to the Continental Congress, 1774–76, he voted for and signed the Declaration of Independence. He was not re-elected in 1776, but did return to Congress in 1777; from 1778–81 he served as president of Delaware.

His father having died when he was sixteen, he chose Nicholas Ridgely in open court as his guardian. Ridgely was married to Ann French, sister of Elizabeth French, the wife of Dr. John Finney, McKean's uncle. Rodney suffered from a facial cancer, which began to bother him in the early 1760's and eventually caused his death. For that reason he never had his portrait painted, and tragically, being a warm man who enjoyed companionship and life, for the same reason he never married.

His sister, Lavinia, is often mentioned in the McKean Papers, and his younger brother Thomas, as well. Thomas was also, later, a delegate to the Continental Congress, briefly a judge of the Delaware Supreme Court, and finally, through McKean's intercession, ap-

While waiting to hear from their Agent in London, the Assembly continued its routine business, consisting of applications for swamp-draining projects, and other such improvements for the public benefit, as well as numerous purely private petitions. For example, on June 3rd there had been a petition from a prisoner in the "Gaol of New-Castle," named Robert Chalfant, "setting forth his utter Incapacity of discharging those Debts for which he is confined . . ." and on June 9th, following three separate readings, he was elegantly released by "An ACT for the Relief of Robert Chalfant, a languishing Prisoner in the Gaol of New-Castle, with respect to the Imprisonment of his Person." [166] The relationship of the Assembly with the Governor, John Penn, one of William Penn's grandsons, was friendlier than most such relationships, but formal. The Assembly's insistence on putting first things first was illustrated on June 9th by a typical notation:

> The Door-keeper informed the House, that Mr. Secretary waited at the Door.
>
> Ordered,
>
> That he be admitted.
>
> And he was admitted, and informed the House, that his Honor, the Governor, had by him returned the several Bills which he had under Consideration, to which his Honor agreed, and was ready to enact them into Laws.
>
> Then the House took into Consideration the Governor's Support.
>
> Resolved,
>
> That One Hundred Pounds be given to His Honor.[167]

On November 1, 1766, the triumvirate of McKean, Rodney, and Read "were continued a Committee of Correspondence for the present Year," to keep in touch with Dennys de Berdt in London, and later in the same session of the legislature Rodney and McKean brought up the matter of land records for the Lower Counties, for the period before 1682. These had been moved to New York, and were no longer available to the local residents or their lawyers without considerable trouble and expense. Their absence could hardly be called an emergency, but the House "being informed by Messirs. Mc'Kean [sic] and Rodney, that the same are now greatly defaced, and will very soon become unintelligible, to the great Injury and Grievance of divers Owners of Lands within this Government," immediately resolved that a committee consisting of Rodney and McKean should be sent to New York to consult with the Secretary of that province, and obtain copies of such records as pertained to the Lower Counties.[168]

A legitimate project it was, and entirely acceptable to the more conservative

---

pointed U. S. Judge for the Mississippi Territory, 1803–11. His generally unsuccessful career was marked by instability of character and mind, in sharp contrast to that of his brother, Caesar, for whom he named his son, Caesar Augustus. The ties between the Rodney and McKean families were close for several generations. Caesar Augustus Rodney had a son named Thomas McKean Rodney, born 1800. See DAB and George H. Ryden, ed., *Letters to and from Caesar Rodney, 1756–1784* (Philadelphia, 1933) which includes a biography.

members, but one wonders why the two delegates to the Stamp Act Congress, who had returned from New York less than a year before, were anxious to go back. There is no evidence as to the underlying motives, if there were any, for their arranging to have themselves sent, but the record shows that the initiative was theirs, and the stated justification. Perhaps it just happened that the committee (McKean only, for Rodney was unable to go) [169] was to be in New York at the critical moment when the official news of the Townshend Acts arrived, and the New York Assembly was suspended. If so, why was no mention made of this curious coincidence?

McKean's report, as recorded in the minutes of the Delaware Assembly for October 26, 1767, contained no hint of the turmoil he had seen, which legislators in all the American assemblies were watching with the closest attention. Anyone having access to these minutes, if he wished to ignore controversy, was free to do so.

> In Pursuance of certain Resolutions of the late Honorable House of Assembly of this Government (Copies whereof are herewith laid before you) I proceeded to New-York in the Province of New-York, in June last, and there carefully perused all the Orders of Governors, Minutes of Council, Surveys, Patents, Wills, Records, and original Papers, dated before the Year 1682, and now remaining in the Secretary's Office for said Province, and caused such Parts of them to be transcribed, as, in my Opinion, in any wise related to the Titles of Lands in this Government; which, being carefully compared with the Originals, properly authenticated, and bound up in one Book in Folio (together with divers Letters, &c. respecting my Proceedings on this Service) I beg Leave to present to this Honorable House, humbly hoping my Conduct in the Premises will meet with your favorable Acceptance.
>
> I am also to inform the House from the Committee of Correspondence for the last Year, that they received a Letter, since the last Adjournment, from Dennys De Berdt, Esq.; Agent for this Government, acknowledging the receipt of the Address to the King's most excellent Majesty on his gracious repeal of the Stamp-Act, and also the Piece of Plate with which he was complimented by the House; [170] and giving an Account, that he obtained the Favor of Lord Shelburn, the then Secretary of State for the Southern Department, to deliver the said Address to his Majesty, who very graciously received the same, and was so well pleased with it *that he read it over twice*. The Agent's letter on this Occasion is now laid before you.[171]

How misleading can the written record be? The extraordinarily disturbed state of affairs in New York, while McKean was there, can only be understood if one recalls that New York was the headquarters of General Gage, but that the General had been unable to deploy his British troops against civil disorders at the time of the Stamp Act because they were too widely dispersed along the frontier.[172] The Quartering Act of 1765 [173] (to quarter troops on the population) had called for enabling legislation by the New York Assembly, but the Assembly had defied it. When the Assembly met in May, 1766, General Gage was in the process of concentrating his forces in order to compel the New York government to yield. The Assembly resorted to delaying tactics in July, 1766, and the General in a fury reported their misdeeds in detail to the home government. Everyone knew that strong measures would soon be taken, and in England even the "friends of America," such as Lord Shelburne, agreed that the New York legislature must be forced "to obey the Quartering Act to the Letter and without quibbling." [174]

Meanwhile, the trouble was spreading, for the New Jersey Council declared that the Quartering Act was another form of "taxation without representation," and even more unfair than the Stamp Act, for it taxed only those colonies where there were troops. In December, 1766, the New Jersey legislature, as did New York's, complied with the Act partially and grudgingly, thereby creating another crisis. New York had provided bedding, firewood, candles, and kitchen utensils for two battalions—but not salt, vinegar, cider, beer, or rum. According to General Gage, New Jersey likewise provided some supplies and not others. The colony of Massachusetts Bay, not to be outdone, joined New York in evading a Parlimentary resolution which called for compensation for the victims of the Stamp Act riots.

By January, 1767, the British government was faced with the continued refusal of the New York Assembly to obey the letter of the Quartering Act, or to compensate Governor Cadwalader Colden for the losses he had sustained. To make matters worse some 240 New York merchants publicly petitioned for freer trade, and brusquely criticised the Revenue Acts of 1764 and 1766, which had set up vice-admiralty courts. Pitt, by this time, was in semi-retirement at Bath, and apparently demented. The "Great Commoner," had accepted a title as the Earl of Chatham, and was now a member of the House of Lords. His middle-class constituents, disillusioned, began to call him "Lord Cheetem," and because of a painful gout, or perhaps disillusioned himself, he cut himself off from his former friends and even from the members of his cabinet.[175] The ministry was increasingly dominated by Charles Townshend, Chancellor of the Exchequer.

The blow fell in June, 1767, when Parliament passed a series of measures, known as the Townshend Acts, suspending the New York Assembly (until it complied with the Quartering Act), creating an American board of customs commissioners, and providing for a revenue. The suspension of the New York Assembly was by all odds the most serious of these measures, for it was a constitutional challenge to the Crown, which in the past had had the sole prerogative of approving or vetoing the acts of colonial legislatures. Now it was Parliament that forbade the Governor of New York to approve legislation after October 1, 1767, and it was Parliament that declared the acts of the Assembly null and void in advance. There was even talk of requiring an oath to uphold the Declaratory Act, to be taken by colonial governors, councilors, and assemblymen, but this failed to pass.[176]

The complaint about taxes (on tea, paper, painters' colors, glass, and sundries) was an effort to make the common people feel the blow, and as propaganda it was supremely successful. Even just laws may meet implacable opposition, if it can be shown that they will cost money, and from that day to this the Townshend Acts have been associated in the public mind with taxes. To thinking men the other parts of the Townshend program represented potentially a far greater threat to their liberties, and the leaders knew that these measures precipitated a constitutional crisis which affected the mother country as well as the colonies. McKean, in a 1778 charge to a grand jury at Lancaster, in which he explained the coming of the Revolution—although he did not ignore the propaganda value of the taxation issue—dwelt equally on constitutional questions:

> . . . When absolute domination took possession of [the King's] soul; he by the advice and assistance of a corrupt, profligate and abandoned ministry, meditated a plan of subjugating and enslaving his subjects abroad, concluding that it would be easily effected, and that in consequence thereof he might rule at home, without the expence of bribing, or the trouble of going through forms even with the shadow of a parliament . . .
>
> All freedom of debate and determination were taken from the Assemblies of this country, by the act of the 7th George 3, ch. 59, for suspending the legislative power of New-York . . .
>
> A standing army in time of profound peace without the consent of our legislatures, and above the controul of all civil authority, were then quartered in America, to dragoon us into a submission to these tyrannical measures . . .*

As shown in the *Minutes of the House of Representatives* [of the Lower Counties], McKean was in New York in June, 1767. The land-records project, which he completed and reported on at New Castle in October, must have required several months, and explains his presence in New York in July, when the news of the Townshend program arrived. More than routine search would have been required to locate these ancient legal documents, and the project would also have demanded extreme care in reading and in legible copying, followed by comparison with the originals and authentication; a tedious, time-consuming task which resulted in "281 sides, or pages . . . bound up in one book in folio . . ." [177]

What else he did, besides causing the records to be transcribed, or how long he stayed, can only be determined by an event private and sorrowful—qualities which always silenced McKean. His brother Robert was reaching the last stages of his illness at Perth Amboy at this time: he was soon to die at Antill's home at Raritan Landing, near New Brunswick. Robert's will was dated September 13, 1767, Thomas McKean being one of the witnesses, and he died on October 17, 1767, and was buried at Perth Amboy shortly afterwards. [178] It is reasonable to assume that Thomas was with Robert at the signing of the will, and at his death or burial, and that he ordered the monument in his brother's honor in St. Peter's Churchyard soon after his death.

Since Perth Amboy is just across the river from Staten Island, McKean may have remained in the New York area from June until October, and had just returned to the Lower Counties when he made his report on October 26th. Politics being always his major interest, he had undoubtedly followed the political

---

* *Charge Delivered to the Grand-Jury by the Honorable Thomas M'Kean, Esquire* (Lancaster, printed by Francis Bailey, 1778), in The Library Company, Phila. McKean was here echoing the famous speech of William Pitt in Parliament: "I rejoice that America has resisted. Three millions of people, so dead to all feelings of liberty, as voluntarily to submit to be slaves, would have been fit instruments to make slaves of the rest." However, McKean was going beyond Pitt, as most Americans did by this time, and expressing a deep opposition to the principle of monarchy.

events in New York during this period, and thus it is doubly amazing that there is no surviving correspondence, since he later stated explicitly that there had been correspondence "between a few Gentlemen, who had known each other at the Congress held at New York in 1765 . . ." [179]

One glimpse of the intensity of political activity immediately after the Stamp Act comes through a report by Governor Francis Bernard of Massachusetts to General Henry S. Conway, Secretary of State for the Southern Department in London. This report indicates that there *was* revolutionary activity as early as 1765–66, and that New York was then the center of it. Governor Bernard quoted from a narrative which he said he took "from the mouth of a Gentleman who was present at the time and place."

> On the 31st day of Decemr 1765, two persons came to New London [Connecticut] and went to a Tavern there: they said they came from New York; one of them called himself Hughes and said he [Hugh] was brother to Mr. [John] Hughes of Philadelphia appointed Distributor of Stamps there, the other called himself Mott. They sent for 6 or 7 inhabitants of New London who were known to be the most violent against the Stamp Act, and produced to them a letter from one [Isaac] Sears of New York, a noted Captain of the Mob there, recommending them and their business of the people of Connecticut. They said they were sent by the People of New York to inform the People of Connecticut that it was expected troops would be sent from England to enforce their Submission to the Stamp Act; that it was necessary for them to unite in opposition to the English Forces upon this occasion; that most probably New York would be attacked first, and therefore Connecticut ought to march in defence of New York; that they were therefore sent to learn what Number of Men from Connecticut might be depended upon to assist the People of New York . . . [180]

Governor Bernard added that a "professed Agent from Connecticut" came to Massachusetts to consult about the business of opposing the Stamp Act, but "he was so open and unreserved in his negotiation, that I cannot believe he was charged with so dangerous a commission as conserting [sic] the raising Men." [181] Revolutionary activities of this sort, he thought, came from the lower sort of people, but they were of a dangerous tendency. As might be expected, the popular leaders in Massachusetts were increasingly hostile to Governor Bernard, and by fall of 1766 the *Boston Gazette* was printing stories to the effect that the Governor was privately advocating the payment of officials' salaries from Royal funds, thereby removing them completely from American control. In May, 1767, the Massachusetts Speaker, Thomas Cushing, warned Dennys de Berdt in England that if the new taxes were to be used to collect money to pay such salaries, "the people would declare them unconstitutional." [182]

On August 14, 1767, some of the populace in Massachusetts celebrated the anniversary of the day in 1765 when they had staged a riot, and the Sons of Liberty had adopted resolutions that were reprinted as far away as Virginia. Governor Bernard at this point became convinced that the Boston "desperadoes" were working for independence, and that the instigators of the movement were "Otis and his gang." True or not, the leaders in Boston now launched a campaign against the Townshend Acts, criticising particularly the suspension of the New

York legislature. As Professor Jensen describes it, "Governor Bernard believed that there was an agreement between the 'factions' in Boston and New York whereby the Boston leaders were to lead the protest movement, using their newspaper, the *Boston Gazette,* with the New York papers reprinting the materials from it. This was in fact what happened. The popular newspaper in New York, Holt's *Journal,* faithfully copied propaganda from the *Boston Gazette* during the winter of 1767–68." [183]

John Dickinson's *Letters From a Farmer in Pennsylvania to the Inhabitants of the British Colonies,* twelve in number, appeared anonymously in the *Pennsylvania Chronicle* late in 1767. They were widely reprinted in all the colonies, and earned Dickinson the reputation of being the "Penman of the American Revolution." In 1768 Franklin had the *Farmer's Letters* reprinted in London, and in 1769 they were translated into French and published in Paris.* Dickinson and McKean were in substantial agreement during this period. At the same time the colonial newspapers were becoming increasingly important vehicles of propaganda for the patriotic cause. There were about two dozen of them, and they "teemed with essays upon colonial rights." [184] It was in September, 1768, that units of the British army were sent to Boston, to help the customs commissioners there and for other reasons, and from that moment Boston moved to the center of the political stage. Sam Adams, the most effective organizer and propagandist of Otis's "gang," had been active for a long time, but he now became the very symbol of the revolutionary movement, looked to for leadership by resistance groups everywhere.

Many of the colonies adopted non-importation agreements during this period, in spite of the reluctance of some of the merchants in the seaport cities. Philadelphia refused to join the movement until February, 1769, and Delaware was slower, because, as George Read explained, "it seemed unnecessary for the people of this government to enter into resolutions of non-importation . . . as we had no traders among us who imported goods from Great Britain, except in very small quantities, and in vessels belonging to Philadelphia, which was sufficiently guarded by the agreement of her own citizens." By August 17, however, local sentiment had been sufficiently mobilized to bring about an informal agreement among the merchants not to import from the mother country, on pain of having the violators' names published in the public newspapers.

In the course of the next year, as the initial tide of patriotism ebbed, a number of storekeepers "forfeited their word, their honor, and their Christian faith" by breaking the agreement, and stronger sanctions had to be devised. George

---

* Moses Coit Tyler, *The Literary History of the American Revolution* (2 vols., New York, 1897), I, 234–240. "Though published without the author's name, they were instantly recognized as the work of John Dickinson . . . Of [the] ominous events in Boston, John Dickinson was an observer from his distant home in Delaware . . . so stirred . . . he wrote 'A Song for American Freedom' . . . a bit of versification obviously the work of a man neither born nor bred to that business. With some natural tremors of maidenly coyness, Dickinson at once sent the manuscript of his poem to his friend James Otis, in Boston; and by Otis, who knew real poetry when he saw it, the demerits of this song in that regard were freely pardoned for its practical value in giving sonorous voice to the emotion then beating in all hearts." It was first published in the *Boston Gazette* for July 18, 1768, and then widely reprinted.

Read was chairman of a general committee under which a system of spies was set up in each town in Newcastle County. In June, 1770, he reported, "They met lately at Christiana, and were unanimously of opinion that the Philadelphia agreement should be supported; and for this purpose, two persons were appointed, in each town, a committee of inspection to *watch the trade.*" [185] These committees had no legal powers, and kept no records, but they were remarkably effective in accomplishing their purpose.

Non-importation agreements naturally created a demand for domestic manufactures, and a small beginning was made along these lines in the early 1770's. Glass was manufactured near Lancaster, china in Philadelphia, and broadcloth fabrics at a number of locations. Most of these efforts failed when trade with the British was resumed, but a few survived and were expanded in later years, when trade for one reason or another was again cut off. The normally sedate Watson, in his *Annals,* referring to a long row of wooden houses built for industrial purposes in 1770 near the area which later became the Philadelphia Navy Yard, noted that it "afterwards became famous as a sailor's brothel and riot house on a large scale." Then, carried away by his own wit, the author added, "The former frail ware [china] proved an abortive scheme."

Alexander Graydon's contemporary *Memoirs of His Own Time,* on a more sober note, described the political situation in Pennsylvania as follows:

> I speak of the early stages of the contest . . . [There was] a great diversity of opinion; many sincere whigs considered a separation from the mother country as the greatest evil that could befall us. The merchants were on the whig side, with few exceptions; and the lawyers, who, from the bent of their studies, as well as their habit of speaking in public, were best qualified to take a lead in the various assemblies that became necessary, were little less unanimous in the same cause . . .
>
> On the whig side of the question, Mr. John Dickinson, always in the political antipodes of Mr. Galloway, was, at this time, most prominent and distinguished . . . Next in conspicuousness to Mr. Dickinson, among the members of the city bar, were Mr. [Joseph] Reed and Mr. McKean . . .[186]

In London Joseph Reed on May 31, 1770, married Esther de Berdt, daughter of Dennys de Berdt (who had died on April 11th), and shortly afterwards returned to Philadelphia with his wife and mother-in-law, the widow of the colonial agent.* He thereupon became one of Sam Adams' links with both London and

---

* Joseph Reed and Esther de Berdt had first met in London in 1763, but the romance had been discouraged by Dennys de Berdt, who did not think the young American a suitable match for his daughter. Reed returned to America in 1765, and began to practice law. He kept in touch with the de Berdts, however, and gradually Dennys de Berdt relented. In 1767, Reed was appointed deputy secretary for the province of New Jersey, largely through his future father-in-law's influence. By 1769, de Berdt (who was 75 and in ill health) asked Reed to come to London to be his assistant, and suggested that he go first to Boston to meet Sam Adams, James Otis, and others—to prepare himself to represent Massachusetts. Reed did as directed, and made a favorable impression, but before he could get to London Dennys de Berdt died, leaving his financial affairs in great confusion. Reed married Esther, as he had long wanted to do, but he found himself to his surprise responsible for her family. See John F. Roche, *Joseph Reed, a Moderate in the American Revolution* (New York, 1957), 13–32. Also see William Reed, *The Life of Esther de Berdt, afterwards Esther Reed* (Philadelphia, 1853).

Philadelphia—it was frequently a triangular correspondence—and at the same time cooperated with John Wilkes' efforts on behalf of the Americans. Reed had earlier suggested to Sam Adams that Arthur Lee of Virginia, whom he had known in London, would be a good replacement for de Berdt, when the latter died.[187] This suggestion had led to the beginning of a regular correspondence between Adams and the Lees, often including McKean, which matured as the Adams-Lee junto of the Continental Congress.

From the time of his return to Philadelphia, Reed also remained in touch with his brother-in-law, Dennis [sic] de Berdt, who was nearly his contemporary, and helped him establish contact with the Lower Counties; in 1775 he succeeded in having Dennis de Berdt named as New Jersey's representative in London, to take the place then being vacated by Benjamin Franklin.[188] The Reed-de Berdt family, which was a prolific one, grew up on both sides of the Atlantic (mostly in London and Philadelphia), and became acquainted with numerous political sympathizers, who were to prove significant in the Revolutionary era. Moreover, Reed was able to combine a trans-Atlantic correspondence with Lord Dartmouth, who, incidentally, was step-brother to the Prime Minister, Lord North, with membership in a colonial committee of correspondence—but like McKean, he was careful to cover his tracks.[189]

Sam Adams naturally sought a correspondence with the Pennsylvania Farmer as soon as he could, quoted his opinions, and when he met him in Philadelphia in 1774 pronounced him a "true Bostonian." [190] He wrote to many others, whether he knew them or not, urging them to get in touch with their friends in other colonies for the good of the cause. Occasionally he let slip the word "independence," as he did in a letter to Richard Henry Lee of Virginia, dated April 10, 1773, when he said, "I have often thought it a Misfortune, or rather a Fault in the Friends of American Independence and Freedom their not taking Care to open every Channel of Communication." [191]

During that same year both Thomas Mifflin and George Clymer of Philadelphia visited Sam Adams in Boston. When a tea ship came up the Delaware River in December, 1773, it was Mifflin and Clymer who wrote to Adams on behalf of the committee in Philadelphia concerning methods of resistance.[192] When Paul Revere rode to Philadelphia with news of the Boston Tea Party, he singled out Mifflin, Reed, and Charles Thomson for the delivery of the letters he was carrying. A few months earlier Reed had entertained Josiah Quincy, Jr. at his home, as an unofficial good-will ambassador from the Boston group.[193]

One of the most interesting of the links between Boston and the middle colonies was Dr. Thomas Young, who had first been active in Boston from 1766 to 1773, then moved temporarily to Newport, Rhode Island, in 1774–5, and finally established himself at Philadelphia as Secretary of the Whig Society. While Young was still at Newport, Sam Adams, attending the Continental Congress in Philadelphia, wrote to him, "I regretted your Removal from Boston when you first informed me of it, but I trust it will be for the publick Advantage . . ." [194] Young was one of the most effective of the non-Philadelphians who were deployed in the Quaker City, to help bring it into the revolution. In 1772 he had been a dedicated worker on a committee of twenty-one in Massachusetts.[195] In 1775 and 1776 he was equally active in Pennsylvania, drumming up support for the movement in the Philadelphia area. As serious about his scientific interests as he was about politics, in the midst of his various activities in 1775 he "found time to communicate to the *Gazette* a paper on 'the billious and putrid fevers prevalent in hot weather,' wherein for the good of the public, he opposed the traditional method of sweating and 'the still more cruel method of blistering from crown to ancle,' recommending instead a calomel purge and a diet of mild acids." [196]

So far as formal organization was concerned, it has usually been said that the occasion for the establishment of intercolonial committees of correspondence arose from the *Gaspée* affair in Rhode Island in 1772,* but elsewhere the committees had been active long before.[197] Certain individuals, such as Sam Adams and Benjamin Franklin, had also developed networks of supporters that were as extensive as those of any of the committees. They had repeatedly sought contacts with both private individuals and official agencies, in England and in the other colonies. Moreover, as James Miller Leake has pointed out, in *The Virginia Committee System and the American Revolution,* there was a "continuity of personnel" in several of the committees of correspondence, as they evolved from committees dealing with colonial agents in London to inter-colonial committees, and as the various Assemblies assumed control over their activities—until the final step, when some of the committees assumed control over the Assemblies.[198] Leake emphasizes the development in New York where "in 1748 the Assembly appointed an agent, placing him under the direction of a committee of correspondence chosen exclusively from the Lower House . . . In 1765 the New York Assembly was represented at the Stamp Act Congress by its standing committee of correspondence . . ." [199]

Without entering the controversy as to whether Massachusetts or Virginia should be given credit for intensifying the activities of the committees of correspondence, it can be stated simply that the middle colonies had been engaged in this business as long as any,[200] and that in Delaware the committee which was appointed in 1766, in connection with the Stamp Act, provided "continuity of personnel" in the famous triumvirate of McKean, Rodney, and Read, until the War of the Revolution was well on its way to being won. On October 21, 1768, for example, it was

On Motion of Mr. M'Kean

Resolved,

That the House take into Consideration the State of the Government, and particularly how far the Inhabitants thereof are affected, by the Operation of some late Acts of the British Parliament [the Townshend Acts] . . .[201]

* The customs schooner *Gaspée* ran aground near Providence on June 9, 1772, while pursuing another vessel. After dark the ship was boarded and set on fire, and the commanding officer wounded. When news of the incident reached England, a commission was appointed to investigate the matter, consisting of the Chief Justices of New York, New Jersey, and Massachusetts, the Governor of Rhode Island, and the Judge of the Vice-Admiralty Court in Boston, but they were unable to find witnesses who would cooperate. Instead, the legislature of Virginia suggested the formation of "committees of correspondence and enquiry" to look into the procedures that were being introduced by the British.

On the 24th it was resolved that the usual triumvirate be a committee to draw up an address to His Majesty on the subject, and on the same day the Speaker, John Vining, "laid a Letter of the Table, to him directed, from the Honorable Peyton Randolph, Speaker of the Honorable House of Burgesses of the Colony and Dominion of Virginia, representing the Hardships the Colonies in General sustain by some late Acts of the British Parliament . . . and hoping that this House will concur with them and the other Colonies on this important Subject." [202] McKean and others like him deeply resented the necessity for these humble supplications, comparing themselves with Moses and Aaron in Egypt, pleading for their people.*

However, in accordance with this directive, the commitee acted expeditiously in preparing its report and in having Dennys de Berdt reappointed as their agent in London—and on the 27th the address was approved by the Assembly and sent, in the form of a three-and-a-half page document, the gist of which is contained in these two paragraphs:

> But permit us, Royal Sir, as Lovers of Britain and our excellent Constitution, as solicitous to enjoy the Rights and Liberties of Freemen and Englishmen, and to transmit them to our Posterity, as your faithful and loyal Subjects, to prostrate ourselves at your Royal Feet, and humbly to implore your gracious Attention to the following particulars, which strike us, and all the good People we represent, with the most dreadful Apprenhension and Affliction.

> With the most humileating Sorrow we have beheld your Majesty's ancient Colony of New-York, deprived of her Legislative Authority by an Act of the late British Parliament, and with equal concern we observe, that Duties for the sole and express Purpose of raising a Revenue in America, have been lately imposed by other Acts of the same Parliament, upon several Articles of Commerce imported into these Colonies, which we are obliged to purchase.[203]

In replying to the Speaker of the House of Burgesses in Virginia, the Delaware Assembly expressed its complete approval of the actions of Virginia, enclosed the substance of their own communications with the King, and noted that they had not made application to either of the Houses of Parliament, "in which we have followed the Steps of the Provinces of Massachusett's Bay, Connecticut, New-Jersey, Maryland, and some others." [204] Obviously, the colonies were already in close touch. The Delaware communication also demonstrated the subtlety with which they could turn the tables on the British, vigorously opposing taxation by "their Fellow-Subjects of Great Britain . . . to whom they will not yield in Loyalty and affection to their Sovereign"—thereby carefully shielding themselves against charges of treason.

The argument which they used was ingenious, yet historically accurate: "That they conceive it to be an inherent Right in his Majesty's Subjects, derived from God and Nature, handed down from their Ancestors, and confirmed by his Royal

---

* "But Pharaoh's heart was hardened," as McKean said in his *Charge to the Grand Jury at Lancaster* in 1778 (Library Company, Phila.) Along the same lines Jefferson wrote, "We have supplicated our king at various times in terms almost disgraceful to freedom." (Quoted in Dumas Malone, *Jefferson,* I, 206.)

Predecessors and the Constitution, that they should, in Person, or by their Representatives, give and grant to their Sovereign those things which their own Labors and Cares have acquired and saved [i.e. taxes] . . . and that they cannot now but with the greatest Uneasiness and Distress of Mind part with the Power of demonstrating their Loyalty." [205]

An early attempt to alleviate the conditions of slavery also occurred in Delaware in 1767, when Caesar Rodney and others proposed a clause "totally prohibiting the Importation of Slaves into this government." Many of the wealthier landowners of the area were in favor of this reform, but the measure lost by a close vote. McKean was absent; the debate occurred a few days after his return from New York, and his brother's death and funeral. During his absence, his first daughter, Elizabeth, had been born, on August 18, 1767; McKean might well have been, for once, exhausted and anxious to be at home.

His presence would not have changed the result, however, for he had always been conservative on property matters, and he looked on slavery in that light. Having voted to continue the slave trade, the House with unconscious irony added a clause to the bill "for the Regulation of Slaves," punishing the blacks *for profane Swearing, &c.*[206] While debating such everyday subjects, the House also considered a bill "against Ring-hunting of Deer with Dogs, whereby many of the Hogs and Sheep of the said Inhabitants have been killed . . ." [207]

Whatever one may think of the wisdom of the measures they passed, their procedures were orderly and decorous. From time to time they brought their rules up to date, and they were excellent rules, which made a deep impression on the members, who did their best to continue them during the revolutionary times that followed. Indeed, the Continental Congress, which at first considered itself above such petty matters of protocol, eventually had to impose nearly identical rules of order and procedure.

> First, That all Members of this House shall appear at the Calling over their respective Names at every Adjournment on Penalty of a Check from the Speaker . . .
> Secondly, That no Member of this House shall presume to speak or interrupt any other Member of the same whilst he is speaking . . .
> Thirdly, That no Member of this House shall be suffered or allowed to speak to any one Matter or Thing above three Times . . .
> Fourthly, That no Member of this House go out of the same after Adjournment, before the Speaker . . . [or] during the Sitting thereof and continue thereout above the Space of half an Hour . . . [208]

In June, 1769, the House responded to a communication from the Speaker of the House of Burgesses in Virginia by approving a communication (prepared by the usual committee of correspondence) containing an eloquent protest against trials overseas.[209] The committee in this matter was acting as spokesman for the House, during its sitting, and not merely as an interim body during a recess. The original of the communication was sent to the colonial agent in London, to be transmitted to the King, but copies were sent by the Speaker of the House to other provincial Speakers.

In 1770, similarly, there was a communication from Robert Lloyd, Speaker of the Assembly of the province of Maryland, which received the same sort of response.[210] Again, the issue was the right of trial by a jury from the vicinity, and the liberty to summon and produce witnesses for the defense. On a number of occasions the committee reported to the legislature that it had received and sent *several* communications, which were apparently available to the members at that time, but were not incorporated in the minutes.[211] The omission must have been deliberate; matters of much less moment and interest were meticulously included in the minutes.

The official establishment of a legislative committee of correspondence in 1773, following the *Gaspée* incident at Rhode Island the previous year, thus made little difference in Delaware. Such a committee had been in existence for a long time, and had already taken the initiative in formulating policy. The appointment of a five-man committee on October 23—adding John McKinly and Thomas Robinson to the triumvirate—was actually a step backwards for this colony, as the two new men were much more cautious than the original three. The way in which this committee was created was preserved in the *Rhode Island Colonial Records,* and not in the Delaware minutes, because the crucial action was taken in a committee of the whole house. Also, the matter was of particular concern to Rhode Island.

In this instance, as in others, the triumvirate of Read, Rodney, and McKean was clearly in control, directing the actions of the Assembly. True, this was a small legislature of only eighteen men, but some of them, particularly from the more distant and isolated sections, were frequently recalcitrant. On a motion by Mr. Read the letters from Virginia, Rhode Island, and Massachusetts were read.

And the House, taking the same into consideration, resolved itself into a grand committee of the Whole House.

The Speaker [Mr. Rodney] left the chair.

Mr. M'Kean took the chair of the committee [and presided over the debate].

Mr. Speaker resumed the chair.

Mr. M'Kean reported from the committee, that they had directed him to make the following report to the House, viz.:

Whereas, the Speaker of the late Assembly, presented to the House several letters, which he received during the recess of the House; one, from the truly patriotic House of Burgesses . . . enclosing a copy of certain resolutions entered into by them, on the 12th of March last; one, from the honorable House of Deputies, of the colony of Rhode Island and Providence Plantations . . . 7th of May last; and one, from the free and spirited House of Representatives, of the province of Massachusetts-Bay . . . 28th of May last; and requesting that a committee of this House may be appointed, to communicate, from time to time, with the corresponding committees, appointed by the said Assemblies, and named in the said respective resolves . . .

Resolved, that a standing committee of correspondence and inquiry, be appointed, to consist of five members, any three of whom to be a quorum; whose business it shall be, to obtain the most early and authentic intelligence of all such acts and resolutions of the British Parliament, or proceedings of the administration, as may relate to, or affect the British colonies in America; and to keep up and maintain a correspondence and communication with our sister colonies . . .

Resolved, that it be an instruction to the said committee, that they do, without delay, inform themselves particularly of the principles and authority on which was constituted a court of inquiry, held in Rhode Island, said to be vested with powers to transport persons accused of offenses committed in America, to places beyond the seas, to be tried . . .

To which said resolves, the House agreed, *nemine contradicente.**

Delaware was now often in advance of Pennsylvania, where Joseph Galloway, the conservative Speaker, was delaying action as long as he could, without alienating himself from the radicals altogether. He agreed, he said, that it was "of the greatest importance to cooperate with the representatives of the other colonies in every wise and prudent measure," but since the present Assembly was about to be dissolved, the best he could do was to earnestly recommend a consideration of the *Gaspée* incident to the succeeding Assembly.[212] Galloway was not cut from the same cloth as Caesar Rodney; Pennsylvania, under his leadership, would always be reluctant to support the revolution. By the end of 1773, ten of the thirteen colonies had established legislative committees of correspondence—in some cases this step was *not* a significant change—and by February, 1774, two more, New York and New Jersey, had established committees. When Pennsylvania finally joined the movement, their committee had to be appointed by the Philadelphia citizens, in a mass meeting called to consider the Boston Port Bill.[213]

It was in 1769 that Thomas McKean became one of the original trustees of the Academy at Newark, Delaware, the continuation of Dr. Alison's old school in New London.[214] He was also to participate in the founding of the Wilmington Academy in 1773,[215] and still later to play an active role in the reorganization of the University of Pennsylvania.[216] It was fitting that a man with so many children and, later, grandchildren should devote his time and energy to education, but in McKean's case the effort came not merely from a sense of duty but from a love of learning, at least in fields for which he had an aptitude.

In March, 1768, he was chosen as a member of the American Philosophical Society, in a group which included the Rev. Jacob Duché (who was soon to marry a Hopkinson), Edward Shippen of Lancaster, and Governor William Franklin of New Jersey. At this same meeting the Society established six organic committees for the systematic investigation of subjects of a scientific nature which might from time to time be brought before it. For the rest of his life McKean was to retain an active interest in the affairs of the Society.[217]

Since no letters have survived from the period of McKean's first marriage, to shed light on his everyday life, the best contemporary source we have is a poem by Francis Hopkinson in the form of a letter "To T _____ M _____," written sometime between Hopkinson's marriage to Nancy Borden in 1768, and Mary

---

* *Rhode Island Colonial Records, 1770–1776,* VII, 235–7. In such phrases as "the truly patriotic House of Burgesses" and "the free and spirited House . . . of Massachusetts-Bay" one catches over-tones of the rhetoric of latter-day American political conventions.

Borden McKean's death in 1773. The two brothers-in-law were still on friendly terms, and the poem was sent to McKean for his amusement, but it portrayed a quality in McKean that must have grated on Hopkinson, and possibly contributed in later years to the cooling of their relationship.

'Tis true I have nothing material to say,
But will mention what incidents fell in my way;
Our leaving *Newcastle,* and how we got hither,
Half tir'd to death, thro' wind and foul weather.
I mounted at nine, and set off on my journey,
along with my brother-in-law the attorney;
Who took with him papers, so many and bulky,
He found it convenient to ride in his sulky.
We travell'd and chatted, and made ourselves merry,
And who should we meet a few miles from the ferry,
But the great little man: the justice I mean,
Rever'd and belov'd by the swains of *Christeen.*
You know that at present, however, he labours
Beneath a sad quarrel with one of his neighbors;
But then to *Newcastle* was going to show
What homage the vulgar to justices owe.
He stopp'd us, and while we stood still in our places,
Related his story, and cited some cases,
To prove how exceeding important the trust is,
And what veneration is due to a justice.
My brother assented, or seem'd to assent,
To all that was urg'd—away then he went,
Whilst we on our journey pursued as before,
Till we came to the ferryman's house on the shore.
Now this ferryman happen'd to be the vile brute
Who affronted his worship, and rais'd this dispute;
He likewise related his case to the lawyer
In such agitation, he work'd like a sawyer;
Whilst I stood impatient, unable to stir,
For his story was tedious, and caus'd a demur:
At length I exclaimed—as I am a sinner,
We've no time to lose, we shall miss of our dinner:
But the man fully bent to wipe off his attainer,
Stept into the boat, and there told the remainder;
The lawyer assented, or seem'd to assent,
To all that was said—then forward we went.

*   *   *   *   *

For this was the time when the lawyers resort,
From all quarters round to attend *Chester* court:
Attornies and clients here lovingly meet,
The one to be cheated, the other to cheat.[218]

In 1771 an incident occurred which may have caused tension between the two brothers-in-law, but the surviving documents fail to explain the significance of what happened. For more than a year Hopkinson had travelled in England, cultivating friends and relations, seeking an appointment to a public position in America, but when the appointment came, it was as Collector of His Majesty's Customs at New Castle, with the option (at his own request) that the position could be held *by deputy*. News of the appointment arrived in February, 1772, and Hopkinson immediately informed McKean, apparently intending that the latter should be his deputy.* Meanwhile, McKean had already obtained the appointment from James Hamilton in Philadelphia, on September 10, 1771, and from Henry Hulton in Boston, on October 1st. Hulton was the "Principal Receiver in America, of the Duty collected out of Seamen's Wages, for the Use of the Royal Hospital at Greenwich," [219] and the oaths McKean took (before George Read), were variously dated September 12 (and 13), 1771.

The incident is puzzling for many reasons. Why did Hopkinson who needed the job, and the cash that went with it, arrange to get the position for his brother-in-law, who needed neither? How did McKean succeed in getting the job first, when Hopkinson had obtained it by the direct intervention of his relations, Lord and Lady North? Was McKean using the job as a cover for his more revolutionary activities,[220] and could this be the reason (since Hopkinson later became as staunch a patriot as McKean) that Hopkinson swallowed his disappointment at the way things turned out? Why *did* McKean take the job from the hated Customs Commissioners in Boston: was he merely helping the Royal Hospital at Greenwich, or was he intending to use the enormous powers of the office "by night as by day to enter and go on board any Ship . . . [or] to go into any house, shop, cellar, or any other place where any goods wares, or merchandizes lie concealed, or are *suspected* to lie concealed, whereof the customer & other duties have not been, or shall not be, duly paid"? [221]

In 1799, when McKean was running for Governor of Pennsylvania, and this incident was brought up by his opponents, an anonymous "Pennsylvanian" wrote an indignant pamphlet addressed "to the Electors of Pennsylvania," which contained a damning indictment of McKean's conduct in these years, based on a detailed knowledge, and carrying a degree of conviction on every point, except one—the inexplicable action of Francis Hopkinson in obtaining a position

---

* On Nov. 8, 1771, a Mr. Warren in London wrote to Lady North that he had received a letter from Francis Hopkinson "dated Sept. 9th" informing him that the previous day the collector of Customs for Newcastle had "died by having drank to Excess." He applied for the job on Hopkinson's behalf, writing the latter, "I doubt not but you may easily depute your Brother in Law to act for you." When Hopkinson received this message, he wrote McKean, on Jan. 16, 1772, "If the Patent sh. be obtained for me you then have a good Plea for repairing any Injuries your Pos[ition] may have suffer'd by representing that you held the office pro Tempore upon my Account—if your Name should be substituted, you will be at Liberty either to keep the Office or throw it up again as you may judge most prudent . . . Love to Sister & the little Gentry." (Public Archives Commission, Dover, Del.)

On Feb. 28, 1772, Hopkinson wrote to McKean again, saying he had received "Letters from Mr. Warren informing that he had succeeded in his Applications for my Appointment to the Collectorship of your Port. He encloses me a Card from Lady North to him assuring him of the Appointment. The Packet we hear is arrived, but the Post not yet come in, so that my Commission is not come to Hand. As soon as I am properly authorized, I shall pay you a Visit in Order to converse upon the Subject, & settle our Plan respecting the Office." (Huntington Library, San Marino, Calif.)

to be held by deputy. (Hopkinson himself was long since dead.) The writer of this pamphlet was convinced that McKean had always changed with every political wind and was unworthy of further confidence. He had been a Whig in 1765, a Tory in 1766, a Whig again in 1767, and was prepared at that point to make another switch whenever it would be to his advantage. According to this writer, the facts were as follows:

> in 1772 [sic] the collector of the customs of the port of New Castle died, and Mr. M'Kean saw an office vacant worth from 100 £ to 150 £ sterl. a-year, which he conceived only waited his asking for it. It was in the gift of the governor of the Delaware counties in the first instance, of the board of commissioners of the customs at Boston in the second, and lastly, of the King, or rather of the minister of Great Britain. Mr. M'Kean was lawyer enough to know that if he accepted this office, he must take an oath to carry the revenue laws of Great Britain into execution in their fullest extent, according to their form and effect. This however, did not prevent him from studying his own emolument; immediately on the death of the collector, he sent a messenger to Philadelphia, requesting from Mr. James Hamilton, (then governing as president of the counsel *ad interim* between the departure of John Penn, and the arrival of governor Richard Penn,) a commission, as collector of the Customs of the port of New Castle on Delaware: Mr. president Hamilton, exercising authority under the crown, no doubt, thought he could recommend himself to his superiors by purchasing off a flaming patriot with an office, whose salary paid by the King, was but 90 £ a-year, and therefore immediately granted the commission, and under it Mr. M'Kean took an oath of office: By this he became a complete tory, that is, a person sworn to carry into effect the odious duty of enforcing revenue from the colonies by acts of a parliament, in which they were not represented. This is not all, Mr. M'Kean received a second commission from the commissioners of the customs at Boston, who had the general superintendance of the collection of the British revenue of the colonies, and whom Mr. M'Kean had often, while he was a Whig, branded as an unconstitutional board; under this second commission, he again took the oath, and was installed collector of the hated duties; and in all probability, he would have been obliged to have packed up his awls and gone off, with the other revenue officers of the crown, on or before the declaration of independence, if the king's pleasure notified through Lord North, had not superceded him by the appointment of another collector of the customs for the port of New Castle, and taken away his salary of 90 £ a-year and the contingent perquisites of 50 £ or 60 £ more. This converted him, and he became again a whig . . .[222]

Nevertheless, the relationship of Francis Hopkinson and his brother-in-law remains unexplained, since Hopkinson sought the post for McKean, and not for himself, as claimed above. The only reply that McKean gave to the charges against him was to deny that he had ever served as Collector of His Majesty's Customs.[223] Beyond that the questions remain unanswered, and Hopkinson's relationship with McKean continues to be a mystery. Without doubt it was ambivalent; he usually agreed with McKean's politics, but temperamentally he found him uncongenial. Furthermore, there was always the problem of determining where McKean *really* stood. Hopkinson had a flexible and subtle mind, but his emotions were steadfast; with McKean it was the other way around; the mind was clear and steady, but the emotions were unpredictable. He could "hold with the hare and run with the hounds" without compromising his larger purposes, but for Hopkinson this was duplicity.*

* Bergen Evans, *Dictionary of Quotation* (1969), cites Humphrey Robert's *Complaint for the Reformation* (1572), and says the expression was already at that time a proverb for duplicity.

PART III

THE COMING
OF THE
REVOLUTION

Chapter 9

The First Continental Congress

It was particularly mortifying to us to see the whole system of civil authority in the province, yielding to this most dangerous power; and at the very time when the interposition of the civil magistrate was of the most pressing necessity, to check the wanton and bloody career of the military, the Lieutenant-Governor [Hutchinson] himself declared, as Governor Bernard had before, that "he had no authority over the King's troops in the province," and his Majesty's representative in Council became an humble supplicant for their removal out of the town of Boston! What would be the feelings of our fellow subjects in Britain, if contrary to their Bill of Rights, and indeed to every principle of civil government, soldiers were posted even in their capital, without the consent of their Parliament? And yet the subjects of the same Prince in America who are entitled to the same freedom, are compelled to submit to as great a military power as administration shall please to order to be posted among them in a time of profound peace, without the consent of their assemblies! . . .[1]

This eloquent statement of the House of Representatives of Massachusetts-Bay, was attributed by Governor Hutchinson to Sam Adams, and was dated Nov. 1, 1770. It came after the Boston Massacre on March 5th of that year, but before the *Gaspée* incident at Providence in 1772, and the Boston Tea Party the evening of Dec. 16, 1773. The solidarity of the colonies was by no means certain at this time, for on the very day of the Boston Massacre the British government under the leadership of the new Prime Minister, Lord North, had moved to repeal the Townshend Acts (except for the tax on tea), thereby adopting a conciliatory policy which soon led to the crumbling of the common front among the merchants of the American cities.[2] Adams and his "gang" were continuing their propaganda, but for the moment with little effect.

In a year or two actions, not words, would be required; in the meantime arguments and explanations were necessary to build support for the American cause. Not only in the other colonies but in the mother country itself an American party had to be formed, and every "friend of America" would be welcomed, and might prove helpful in ways as yet unforeseen. "To be an American or a friend of America," Miss de Berdt had written from England to her future fiancé in Philadelphia in 1769, "is a great disadvantage," for in "this melancholy situation of things it is impossible for anyone to stem the tide against America." [3] Nevertheless, on both sides of the Atlantic strong-minded people were urging their friends to stand firm. "Your only safety lies in Union" was advice that came from England as often as from America. Dennys de Berdt wrote frequently in this vein, adding helpful hints, such as the remark that "the manufacturers [in England] are ripe for tumult, and that is really the most favorable circumstance that could happen." [4]

A typical letter was written by John Norton, the London agent of the Virginia committee of correspondence, concerning the duties on tea in 1773: "Our present Parliament who are just prorogued have made such Strides towards Despotism for sometime past, with respect to the East Indian Company as well as America, that we have too much Reason to dread bad Consequence from such Proceedings. Some of my Friends in the India Direction tell me that they have Thoughts of sending a Quantity of Tea to Boston, New York, Philadelphia, Virginia & South Carolina, which Government seems to approve, but they suspect their Motives are to make a Cat's Paw of the Company, and force them to establish the 3 [pence] American Duty." [5]

The celebrated Boston Tea Party had its counterpart along the shores of the Delaware, and the Sam Adams Papers contain a letter from the Philadelphia committee, signed by George Clymer and Thomas Mifflin, written in the utmost haste and dated Dec. 27, 1773:

> Late on Saturday night our Committee was informed that our Tea Ship was at Anchor within 15 miles of this City. They then agreed to meet yesterday morning at 9 o'clock in order to prepare Matters for a general Meeting of the Town and to prevent the Entry of the Ship at the Customs House.
>
> The committee having met . . . nominated three of their Body to proceed to Chester where the Ship was supposed to be; and directed them to prevail if possible on the Captain to leave his Ship at Chester; to come up to Town himself, and settle the Matter with the Inhabitants of the Town who would meet at 10 o'clock this Day.
>
> The Gentlemen appointed to go to Chester had but just left the Town, when Advice was received that the Ship had left Chester, and was on her way to this place. A very considerable Body immediately sett off to prevent her coming up; and meeting with her about 4 miles from Town brought her to Anchor; and conducted the Captain to the Coffee House where the Committee were sitting.
>
> The Committee readily obtained from Captain Ayres a solemn Promise not to enter his Ship until the Sentiments of the People could be known respecting her.
>
> We are this Minute (Monday, 12 o'clock) returned from a Meeting of the Town which consisted of at least 5,000 who collected in One Hour after Notice was given of what was intended. We have not time to insert the Resolves; but we can assure

you that the Ship is to be sent immediately to Reedy Island, 60 miles from Philada; the Captain is allowed to stay in Town until 2 o'clock tomorrow to provide Necessaries for a Voyage to London; and a Committee was named to see the Ship and Captain off at the time appointed.[6]

The meeting was concluded with an unanimous Vote of Approbation to the Town of Boston for their spirited Conduct in destroying their Tea rather than suffering it to be landed.[7]

They added a breathless postscript, "We forgot to mention that one of the Consignees who came from London with the Ship resigned without hesitation." [8] A point of honor with Mifflin, in particular, was that the tea agents should be given the same treatment as had been accorded to the Stamp Act distributors some eight years earlier. For weeks the Philadelphia committee had been working to bring public opinion in this area to a new peak of excitement, and obviously they had succeeded. Philadelphia, in fact, was in the unusual position, momentarily, of being in the revolutionary vanguard, and on October 16 the city held a mass meeting which approved a set of resolves on the Tea Act, which was used as a model by other colonies, including Massachusetts.

When the ship arrived, the Philadelphians behaved more mildly than the Bostonians had, and were proud of having avoided violence, but clearly they had been willing to use whatever measures the occasion demanded. George Clymer expressed this willingness in a letter to Josiah Quincy, Jr. in 1774, approving the boisterous conduct of the Boston mobs in stilted but ominous language: "Those among us of the most enlarged sentiments, and who have elevated ideas of liberty, are unwilling to censure any irregularities, or even extravagances, which a zeal for her cause may have produced; But narrow minds can scarcely in any case be brought to approve, where domestic economy and good order seem to be disturbed." [9] In a word, Clymer was ready for blood.

For McKean the year 1773 had been a particularly difficult one. On February 25 his sixth child, Anne, was born, and in little more than two weeks her mother was dead. Mary Borden McKean was only twenty-eight, and his grief at her loss must have been deeper, knowing that she might have been saved by his brother Robert, one of the few colonial doctors trained in obstetrics, if he had not died also. How well he remembered that a similar crisis had overwhelmed his father! His bitterness and sorrow, however, did not prevent him from determining to hold the family together, and to continue his public course as well. The necessary, but temporary, arrangements were made accordingly. The oldest, "Josie," was not quite nine, almost exactly the age he had been when his mother had died, but "Josie" would not be turned over to the impersonal care of a school; he and the older children would find a kindly refuge with McKean's sister, Dorothea Thompson, whose children were about the same age. The Borden grandparents, mourning the loss of one daughter and dreading the loss of another, Letitia—who died in June—welcomed the baby Anne and her two-year-old sister, Mary, into their large home.

Mary Borden McKean was buried close to the side door of Emmanuel Episcopal Church in New Castle, and for once McKean openly acknowledged private emotion, though spoken for him by another. Here it was not the vital statistics alone, nor the conventional and politic praise engraved for his brother, but in this case the graceful eulogy to Mary, written by Francis Hopkinson, was carved in full upon her tombstone:

> Fair was her form, serene her mind,
>   Her heart and hopes were fix'd on high:
> Her hand beneficent and kind
>   Oft wip'd the tear from sorrow's eye.
> The sweets of friendship soften'd care;
>   Love, peace, and joy, her soul possest:
> Meekness perfum'd each rising pray'r,
>   And ev'ry rising pray'r was blest.
>
> In heav'n we trust, her sainted spirit sings
> Glad *Hallelujahs* to the *King of Kings*.[10]

The letters he wrote and received in this period were not kept, not even the expressions of sympathy and offers of help from such close friends as John Dickinson. McKean did not like to be reminded of difficulties, or the possibility of failure, and consequently destroyed every record of personal crisis. Yet the obligations he accumulated at this time would not be forgotten. They would be paid in full during the coming years of civil strife, when favors to certain persons could only be performed at great personal risk. Inevitably his law practice was neglected during these months, but of all his public commitments only one appeared to daunt him. He had been elected Speaker of the Delaware Assembly the previous October; this March, when the Assembly was in session, his friend Caesar Rodney quietly took up again the responsibilities of the speakership, which he had held before.

Determined to re-unite his family, McKean knew that the sooner he remarried the sooner this would be accomplished, but now he also knew that he required more of a wife than that she be a loving mother. A second marriage was expected of a widower with children; no man would want to take over the constant, tedious duties of mother and housewife, and certainly not a man as active in public affairs as McKean. Under the circumstances he was not hasty; indeed, he mourned somewhat beyond the customary time. From the viewpoint of a hopeful bride with a calculating eye he was still a catch, successful and obviously headed for greater things, physically in the prime of life—and six children were no alarming or unusual number, particularly since their maternal grandparents appeared both affectionate and affluent.

In May, 1774, McKean took lodgings in Philadelphia, but he retained his New Castle residence. Property and residence requirements were not yet such that this move was necessary for him politically, but a re-united family would need a home in the city as well as a mistress to preside over it. By late summer he had chosen an eminently suitable new wife. A year and a half after Mary's death, he married Sally Armitage of New Castle, and if his choice was made by head not heart, it was a wise one; he was fortunate indeed to have persuaded a beautiful, intelligent woman, who was much sought after, to accept such great responsibilities.

The daughter of James Armitage and his second wife, Mary Land, Sally was the youngest in a family of nine children.* James Armitage, born in Yorkshire, had been a successful emigrant, becoming a large landowner; several times he was appointed a judge in Newcastle County. Through marriage, Sally Armitage was related to the Van Leuvenighs, Gillespies, Montgomerys, and the Cooches— families prominent in the Lower Counties and Maryland, many of whom were McKean's political colleagues. But another connection by marriage, through whom Sally and Thomas McKean must have been long acquainted, may have had a guiding hand in this happy affair; Sally's oldest sister, Hannah, had married Dr. Francis Alison, and had provided a home for the motherless young Thomas—then her husband's pupil and now his devoted friend. While Sally's financial expectations or attractions were not those of a Borden, she had inherited some real estate and a keen understanding of business and property matters.[11]

There is evidence enough, however, that McKean's choice was made by heart as well as by head, and that Sally reciprocated his feelings. Unlike many conjugal letters of the day, which had formal, stilted terms of affection, and in sharp contrast to his public image, McKean rarely wrote his wife without sending love and kisses, to his children and to her. "Love me and pray for me, as I shall do for you whilst Tho M:Kean." [12] Stationed in New Jersey with his battalion, he was preoccupied with her safety and health, "Your indisposition gives me great pain . . ." By way of cure he recommended that she take rides; for that purpose he had purchased a pair of horses for her, and she was to engage a coachman; if none could be found, Col. McKean would send his servant Sam. Nor did Sally fail to attend "so very minutely to every article that I could want . . ." [13]

* In the Genealogical Section, HSD, there is information concerning several generations of Armitages. James Armitage, the father, was born in Yorkshire, England, about 1688, and died in White Clay Creek Hundred, Newcastle County, Delaware, about 1753. He was a Justice of the Peace and a Justice of Common Pleas. In the McKean family Bible (McKean Papers, HSP), in Sarah Armitage McKean's handwriting, appears the following notation:

Births of the Children of James Armitage, who were alive at his Decease—

By his first wife the two first	Hannah	Born November 6th 1715	[m. Alison]
	Enoch	January 22d 1725.6	
	Samuel	January 26th 1730.1	
	Mary	October 17th 1732	[m. Dunn]
These the children of James and Mary Armitage	John	January 3d 1734.5	
	Ann	May 19th 1737	[m. Van Leuvenigh]
	Dorcas	March 7th 1741.2	[m. Montgomery]
	Nathan	September 20th 1744	
	Sarah	December 19th 1746	[m. McKean]

Mary Armitage's husband was Thomas Dunn. Ann's husband, Zachariah Van Leuvenigh, was a client of McKean's in a run-away slave case (William Brodie, Admr. of Robert Allen, junr. v. Zachariah Van Leuvenigh, no date, John Carter Brown Library, Providence.)

Another interesting fragment of information appears in a letter from Caesar Rodney to his brother Thomas, Philadelphia, June 20, 1770 (*Delaware History*, III, 112): "A few days ago a Veshell arrived here, on board of whom Robert Montgomery (who married Dorcas Armitage) died. They were in the harbour of Gibraltar when he died; they carried him ashore, buried him and then proceeded on their Voige here. He was on his Return from Leghorn and intended to take a passage from Gibraltar to Lisborn where he left his wife."

Her husband's letters—every one of which she carefully preserved—and the comments of friends and critics have made a clear mirror for the second Mrs. McKean. When an appealingly vivacious and pretty girl was also the youngest of a large family, she was bound to be somewhat over-indulged, and more so without the corrective hand of a father, for James Armitage had died when Sally was seven. Thus, Sally dismissed her maid, an impudent "little hussey," [14] and for three months, on circuit, the Chief Justice made inquiries and endeavored to procure another, even to the point of buying one of Mrs. James Wilson.[15] In the midst of Congressional affairs he tried again, but in vain, "I offered 20/ a week, but the Jades won't leave town." [16]

Briefly, when the pressures of Court and Congress seemed too much, McKean considered exchanging them for the country, "whereon I may live cheap, and spend the remainder of my days in comfort . . ." [17] Sally would have none of it, and McKean replied, "I thought you loved a Country life, but you seem now to prefer the Town—Agreed; we will continue in one. The general character of the Ladies is, that they are fickle, ever changing, &c. and never satisfied, but I flattered myself you were an exception." But a paragraph or two later he changed his tack, and desired her to come home for "you have stayed rather too long in the country." [18] Sally was sometimes dissatisfied, but she was neither fickle nor changing; she well understood her husband of but a few years and knew that "the remainder of [his] days" would be far longer in the busy life of the town than in the dull comfort of the country.

If Sally Armitage was somewhat spoiled, that trait was far outweighed by intelligence and a strength of character that was nearly equal to her husband's. Influenced by the Alisons and the other members of her family and its circle, her convictions and interests were strong and active, and thoroughly in sympathy with the revolutionary cause, as were those of her close friend Caesar Rodney, who could never, handicapped as he was by illness, be a suitor.[19] She may well have been wary of domesticity in her youth, for she was already twenty-eight when she accepted marriage with Thomas McKean.

Written as he rode circuit, McKean's correspondence was unique and revealing, almost a continuation of private conversations. In her first letters Sally sent political news, which pleased him. McKean sent detailed instructions on the household and other matters, but broke off, "Thus I have planned this whole business, but I know you can do it better." [20] Casually, with obvious confidence that she could cope with the matter, McKean on his way to Yorktown (York, Pennsylvania), added in a letter to Sally, who was not at home due to the awkward proximity of the British, but in temporary residence at Paxton, that in about a week "half a dozen Gentlemen will probably dine with you, but I will send Sam from Carlisle (if nothing particular prevents) a day before hand. A good rock-fish would be acceptable." [21]

Newspapers and copies of articles were sent back and forth constantly; few wives would have cared to receive "the King of G. Bs. speech, which I have sent you . . . [in which] he appears to be frightened." [22] But McKean paid her a higher, rarer compliment, unspoken, in these letters; he never doubted her ability to keep a secret, or her discretion. He did not break the Congressional oath of secrecy, nor the oath implicit in the privileged communications of a lawyer; but whatever informed persons might be saying "out of doors," and his own speculations and opinions were included in his letters to Sally, and plainly some of his more interesting comments were written in answer to her inquiries. Unfortunately, neither of the McKeans considered it important to save *her* letters, all of which have disappeared.

Both the bride and groom were Presbyterians, and McKean and Dr. Francis Alison, the bride's brother-in-law, were working together in various educational, religious, and civic activities in Philadelphia.[23] However, the minister of the Presbyterian church in New Castle was also closely kin to the bride, so it was the Rev. Joseph Montgomery of that place who performed the ceremony. In a non-clerical, non-familial way Rev. Montgomery derived extra pleasure from this wedding. He himself was married to a woman of an independent nature, much like Sally's—Rachel, the sister of another budding revolutionary, Dr. Benjamin Rush. A year later the Rev. Montgomery made his political views public, in a sermon which stated that "a defensive war is lawful," and Americans must not "submit [their] necks to the yoke"—stronger statements than the Continental Congress was then making.[24] The acquaintance became friendship, and may have been discreetly helpful to both the Rush and Montgomery families in later years. In 1780 the Rev. Montgomery, having moved to Pennsylvania, was elected to the Congress.

This second marriage, marred by no matrimonial disagreements greater than occasional brief criticisms, survived forty-three years of personal and national tragedies, and the ups and downs of McKean's turbulent careers. A few rare flashes indicated that Sally had as much of a temper as he had; yet because his was only too well known and feared, Sally exerted a special degree of self-control. Ambitious for her husband, she was too intelligent to indulge herself in personal quarrels. Those historians who have blamed the feud with the Bordens on McKean's second wife have done Sally Armitage McKean an obvious injustice. Nor was the simple fact of his customary, and expected, re-marriage the cause. Joseph Borden, renowned for a practical and realistic attitude towards life, would have been more astounded had McKean chosen to remain a widower.

Two years after their marriage, writing from Perth Amboy, McKean suggested that Sally might best send him the saddle and bridle he wanted by the Bordentown stage, with a covering note to Mr. Borden.[25] A month later, contemplating a possible visit by Sally to his army post at Perth Amboy, he directed her to "Send all the children to Bordentown until you return . . ."[26] In June, 1778, from York, Pennsylvania, he wrote Sally, in Paxton, sending her a lengthy account of the British Commissioners' propositions, and in closing added, incidentally, that he had "rec^d a very affectionate Letter today from Mr. Borden, all well except Mrs. Borden. No more news."[27] As late as 1786 Joseph Borden drew up articles of agreement concerning real estate between himself and Mc-

Kean's second son, Robert, "in Consideration of the Natural Love and Affection He hath and beareth unto his said Grandson Robert McKean . . ." [28] Even then McKean's relations with the Bordens were still good.

The matter of the Customs appointment, and its attendant misunderstandings, in 1772, had somewhat strained the friendship between McKean and his brother-in-law, Francis Hopkinson, however, with mutual accusations of duplicity. Hopkinson may have had the more obvious reasons for his opinion, but by 1774 he himself stood on questionable ground. In that year McKean opted for the First Continental Congress, and Hopkinson for the Royal Council of New Jersey; the family was divided.[29] This was a clear and deep political divergence, and Hopkinson was not appointed to the Continental Congress until June 22, 1776—well after Richard Henry Lee's resolution concerning independence and, indeed, just in time to become a Signer. McKean thus regarded Hopkinson as too recent a convert, with motives sincere perhaps, but not quite as unsullied as they might have been. Hopkinson, whose many talents did not include an aptitude for business matters, had moved to Bordentown, and temporarily disengaged, was assisting in the management of the Borden estate and businesses.

Early in 1774 the Bordens became involved in a bitter, though ludicrous, letter-to-the-editor controversy with a certain Nathaniel Lewis, who hid behind the inadequate pen-name of "Siwel Leinahtan." The battle began over the alleged opening of the latter's letters by "Joseph Borden, a New Jersey stage master," and Hopkinson promptly took up the pen in defense of his wife's father.[30] Numerous obscure characters such as "Retsnup" (Punster) participated. On Borden's side was a "pretty little musical poetical witling, who lately emigrated from this city into New-Jersey, in quest of the robe and full-bottomed wig" [recognizable as Francis Hopkinson] and on the other, directing the Lewis attack, was someone described as a "petty-fogging scavenger of the bar, who [shows you] how to throw as much dirt as you can, and shows his skill in the law, by securing you from action for slander . . ."

In one "Dear Natty" letter, Hopkinson came perilously close to identifying the foe's "head-work man . . . so learned in the law . . . When I see him in a morning strutting his pavement in red slippers, plaid gown and starched cap, I am struck with a certain awe in fear of him. I always do as the poor man did when he saw the Devil—take off my hat and say *How do you do, Sir?* You might have hunted the whole city and not found his equal." [31]

Hopkinson's barbed prose was to attack the Chief Justice in later years in strangely identical phrases. But if the "musical poetical witling" was indeed referring to McKean, no evidence existed besides their mutual suspicions, and plainly the Bordens did not share Hopkinson's feelings at that time. The controversy became, though semi-anonymous, increasingly personal and nasty until it vanished from the press. McKean was not always above such sniping engagements, but, intensely busy at this period, he would hardly have wasted precious time on this one. Far less, so recently bereaved, would he have stooped to an irrational attack, no matter how camouflaged, upon his former father-in-law, in whose affectionate care his youngest children still remained. Nevertheless, he rightly suspected that he was Hopkinson's intended target.*

The feud with the Bordens still lay in the future, as did Hopkinson's open and direct involvement in it—likewise the contributing stresses and disruptions of the revolution. The friction between McKean and Hopkinson was basic, inherent in deeply antagonistic personalities, and not in any way attributable to Sally. As McKean's authority, and indeed his inquisitorial powers, increased in the coming years, they inevitably touched upon family ties. McKean was aware of family loyalties and obligations, and worked faithfully to fulfill them, but he could never bring himself to express gratitude with any degree of graciousness—and did not allow the weight of his obligations to be added when balancing the scales of legal justice.

Throughout the difficult year of his first wife's death, and in the year following, McKean's responsibilities in civic matters continued, and even increased. He was Trustee of the Loan Office, of the New Castle Common, the New Castle Market Square, the Newark Academy, and a member of the American Philosophical Society, whose interests were turning to more practical, immediate problems. At the time of its chartering by John and Thomas Penn, on April 10, 1773, he also became a Trustee of the Wilmington Academy; [32] on the same day he was re-appointed Justice of the Peace of the Province of Pennsylvania.

Early in 1773, the British Parliament had granted the East India Company a monopoly on the tea trade with the American colonies, and by late summer efforts were being made everywhere to renew and increase the resistance. Not only was McKean active in these efforts; other present and future members of his family were also. McKean was appointed, on October 23, 1773, to the official committee of correspondence for the Lower Counties, a committee now consisting of the original dedicated trio with two dubious additions; the following February his late wife's father, Col. Joseph Borden, was appointed to the committee of correspondence for Burlington County, New Jersey, and later in the year was a member of the first New Jersey Convention, held at New Brunswick, at which meeting he was appointed to the committee of correspondence for the entire province.[33] Hopkinson was not as yet in the patriot ranks.

On May 27, Andrew Buchanan of Baltimore, Maryland, chaired a meeting there which named him to a position comparable to Borden's. In Baltimore the committee became one of observation as well, and further, assumed "a general supervision of the public morals," although more by persuasion than by coercion. They recommended that out-door fairs be discontinued as "serving no other purpose than debauching the morals of their children and servants," and disapproved such sports as racing, cock-fighting and like extravagance, "not only as

* George Everett Hastings, *The Life and Works of Francis Hopkinson* (Chicago, 1926), 321–2, cites with approval the opinion of Burton Alva Konkle that "the quarrel began in 1776, when Pennsylvania adopted a new constitution, which was championed by Judges George Bryan and Thomas McKean and was opposed by Benjamin Franklin, Robert Morris, James Wilson, and Francis Hopkinson." As indicated above, I believe the friction began much earlier; the two men were on opposite sides, politically, in 1774, and the trouble had begun before that.

wrong, but as derogatory to the character of the patriots at that solemn hour." [34] Buchanan was the father of two young men who would later marry two of Mc-Kean's daughters, Letitia and Anne, whose birth had caused Mary Borden McKean's death at just this hectic time.

In the fall of 1773 Dr. John Finney resigned as Naval Officer for the Port and District of New Castle, perhaps because of his nephew's position as a ringleader of the Delaware Assembly, and on March 22, 1774, he died. His wife, Sarah Rich-ardson Finney, died about the same time, leaving their son, David Finney, Mc-Kean's cousin and preceptor, one of the wealthiest inhabitants of the Lower Counties.[35] McKean continued to serve as attorney for his cousin, and made efforts to help him obtain his inheritance, but in May, 1774, he moved to Phila-delphia—while retaining his New Castle residence and likewise his membership in the Delaware Assembly. Transportation between New Castle and Philadelphia was still primarily by shallop, or by ocean-going vessel, though travel by land was possible with arduous exertions.*

McKean's first residence in Philadelphia was probably one of the inns of High (later Market) Street, near Second. There were three well-known taverns in that vicinity: the Royal Standard, which was on the corner of Second Street; the In-dian King, where the Masons met, near Third Street; and the Indian Queen, near Fourth.[36] Probably he stayed at one time or another at all three of these establishments, as a widower, but when he re-married, he and his wife received guests most frequently at the Indian King, or at Clarke's Inn, located in a grove of walnut trees opposite the State House. At the time of the First Continental Congress, John Adams mentioned in his *Diary* that he dined "in Market Street" with Mr. McKean, Reed, Rodney, and others.[37] Adams was not yet acquainted with the Philadelphians and often confused the spelling of their names, but here he must have been referring to George Read, of the well-known trio, not Joseph Reed of Pennsylvania.

Moving to Philadelphia a few months before the convening of the First Con-tinental Congress, McKean joined a growing number of future revolutionaries who were drawn to the city, either as a result of changes in their own plans, or by invitation from such far-seeing leaders as Benjamin Franklin or Sam Adams. Some of McKean's fellow Philadelawareans, such as John Dickinson and Charles Thomson, already had dual establishments. Joseph Reed had returned from Lon-don with his English bride, Esther de Berdt, and settled in the metropolis as early as 1770, rather than in Trenton, whence he had departed. Tom Paine ar-rived in the fall of 1774, with letters from Franklin, and was put to work editing the *Pennsylvania Magazine.*

Thomson, like McKean, married a second wife in the beginning of September, 1774, and cut short whatever holiday he might have planned, in order to settle

---

* John A. Munroe, *Federalist Delaware*, 33, notes that "In 1774, Samuel Bush, of Wilmington, who had commanded a brig in the West India trade, bought a sloop of about thirty tons and inaugurated a weekly service between Wilmington and Philadelphia. This new project was successful from the first and a freight service between these two ports was maintained by the Bush family for more than a century." Two of George Read's brothers, and Mc-Kean's brother William became involved in this river traffic, and eventually in overseas commerce.

down to the Congressional grind a few days after the wedding. Dr. Thomas Young, who had been a participant in the Boston Tea Party and other patriotic activities in that area before his departure for Newport, Rhode Island, was summoned by Sam Adams, then attending the Congress at Philadelphia, and in 1775 he, also, moved to Philadelphia. Still later, in 1777, Jonathan Dickinson Sergeant, who had been a member of the Congress from New Jersey,[38] settled finally in Philadelphia and became Attorney General—serving under McKean, who was then Chief Justice of the state's Supreme Court.

The Boston Tea Party was followed by retaliatory measures on the part of the British ministry and Parliament in the spring of 1774. The "Coercive" or "Intollerable" Acts were passed, and under the terms of the first of these acts, the Boston Port Bill, the harbor of that city was to be closed on June 1. The mood of the British government was angry, and their ignorance concerning American affairs was abysmal, according to Josiah Quincy, Jr., who visited several of the pro-American leaders in London at this time, and reported his findings to his American friends prior to his return to Boston and pre-mature death within sight of land in April, 1775, at the age of thirty-one years.* Mass meetings were held throughout America, as the deadline drew near, to consider ways and means of aiding Boston, and nowhere were the patriotic efforts more carefully coordinated than in the Three Lower Counties of Delaware. The similarity of the resolutions passed in the three county seats indicated clearly that the committee of correspondence, which had been guiding the resistance activities of that area for eight or nine years, was functioning smoothly.

McKean was the main speaker at two important meetings, on June 29 at New Castle and on July 23 at Lewes,[39] but he attended other meetings, probably including the large one on May 20th in the city of Philadelphia.[40] The purpose of the Philadelphia meeting was to persuade John Dickinson to take an active part in the movement, to assure that *some* action would be taken for the relief of Boston. Paul Revere had arrived in the city with news of the Boston Port Bill the previous day, and Charles Thomson, Thomas Mifflin, and Joseph Reed had spent most of the 20th trying to overcome Dickinson's hesitations. According to Joseph Reed's "Narrative," "At this time Mr. Dickinson was in the highest point of reputation and possessed a vast influence, not only with the Public at large but among the Quakers in particular, in consequence of his marriage into that sect. No person in Pennsylvania approached him as a rival in personal influence.

---

* Benjamin J. Lossing, *The Pictorial Field-Book of the Revolution*, I, 498, n. gives this quick sketch: "Mr. Quincy was associated with John Adams in the defense of the perpetrators of the 'Boston Massacre' in 1770, and did not by that defense alienate the good opinion of the people. In February, 1771, he was obliged to go to the south [due to] a pulmonary complaint. At Charleston he formed an acquaintance with Pinckney, Rutledge, and other patriots, and, returning by land, conferred with other leading Whigs in the several colonies. Continued ill health, and a desire to make himself acquainted with English statesmen, induced him [to go] to England in 1774, where he had personal interviews with most of the leading men. He asserts that . . . Colonel Barré, who had traveled in America, assured him that such was the ignorance of the English people, two thirds of them thought the Americans were all negroes! [Aware of] the feelings and intentions of the king and ministers, and hopeless of reconciliation, Mr. Quincy determined to return and arouse his countrymen to action. He embarked for Boston . . . and died when the vessel was in sight of land, April 26th, 1775, aged thirty-one years."

In short, he was of that weight that it seemed to depend upon his being present at the meeting whether or not there should be any measures in opposition . . ."[41]

They had dinner at Fairhill, Dickinson's country seat, "circulating the glass briskly," and agreed that when they got to the meeting at the City Tavern, Thomson and others would advocate radical measures, and Dickinson would then propose a more moderate course, which everyone would eventually fall in with. The plan worked; Dickinson became involved, and everything went according to schedule—except that Thomson dramatically fainted in the course of his radical harangue. There is no positive evidence as to whether or not McKean was there, but he had recently moved to Philadelphia and was living at an inn just two blocks north of the City Tavern: he might have attended the meeting, but would not have participated in the advance maneuvering by the leaders of the city committee.

At New Castle on June 29, 1774, McKean chaired a meeting which drew up a seven-point program that was immediately sent to the other counties over his signature, and that of his sister's brother-in-law, David Thompson, Clerk. These resolutions indicated that the freeholders and inhabitants of Newcastle County, or their leaders, knew exactly what they wanted, and could draft their plans with the skill and dexterity of "Philadelphia lawyers"—which is, indeed, what some of them were. The gist was as follows:

1. That the Act of Parliament, for shutting up the Port of Boston, is unconstitutional; oppressive to the Inhabitants of that Town; dangerous to the Liberties of the British Colonies . . .

2. That a Congress of Deputies, from the several Colonies in North-America, is the most probable and proper Mode of procuring Relief . . .

3. That a respectable Committee be immediately appointed for the County of New-Castle, to correspond with the Sister Colonies, and with the other Counties in this Government . . .

4. That the most eligible Mode of appointing Deputies would be by the Representatives of the People of this Government, met in their *Legislative Capacity,* but as the House of Assembly have adjourned themselves to the thirtieth Day of September next, and it is not expected his Honor our Governor [John Penn] will call them by Writs of Summons on this Occasion, having refused to do the like in his other Province of Pennsylvania, therefore that the Speaker of the Honorable House of Assembly [Caesar Rodney] be desired by the Committee now to be appointed, to write to the several Members of Assembly, requesting them to convene at New-Castle on any Day, not later than the First of August next . . .

5. That the Committee now to be chosen consist of thirteen Persons, to wit, THOMAS M'KEAN, JOHN EVANS, JOHN M'KINLY, JAMES LATIMER, GEORGE READ, ALEXANDER PORTER, SAMUEL PATTERSON, NICHOLAS VAN DIKE, THOMAS COOCH, JOB HARVEY, GEORGE MUNRO, SAMUEL PLATT and RICHARD CANTWELL, and that any seven of them may Act.

6. That the said Committee immediately set a Foot a Subscription for the Relief of such Poor Inhabitants of Boston, as may be deprived of the Means of Subsistence by the Act of Parliament, commonly stiled the Boston Port Bill . . .

7. That the Inhabitants of the County will adopt and carry into Execution all and singular such peaceable and constitutional Measures, as shall be agreed on by a Majority of the Colonies, by their Deputies, at the intended Congress . . .[42]

Kent and Sussex Counties, as it turned out, felt that Newcastle was a little too forward in its efforts to set the pace, and on July 21 the Kent County committee (including Caesar and Thomas Rodney, William Killen, Charles Ridgely, and others) tactfully informed Newcastle that although they had "some intelligence lately received from Sussex that the People of that County, greatly disapprove of New Castle as the Place of the Members of Assembly's meeting, and the Power of appointing deputies to Attend the proposed General Congress, being delegated to them," nevertheless, "we have the important purpose of this meeting so much at Heart, that we are willing to submit to some Things that might even look like imposition, rather than by refusing such a Submission, defeat or render it abortive." [43] Consequently, they were urging their leader, Speaker Rodney, to send out the letters that would call this very necessary meeting. Sussex County, they warned, was having a preliminary meeting at Lewes on July 23, and might not be equally cooperative.

To prevent discord, and to emphasize the common grievances against the British—rather than the rival claims of the three county seats: New Castle, Dover, and Lewes—McKean attended the meeting at Lewes and made one of the greatest oratorical efforts of his career. He spoke for two hours to a large audience consisting mostly of Sussex County farmers, many of them conservative and suspicious of politicians from New Castle. He listed the rights of the colonists under some twenty-seven heads, and then in the manner of Sam Adams pointed out the governmental measures by which they had all been violated.[44] He dwelt on facts that were known to his audience, and noted the limitations on the Lower Counties' iron industry, and curbs on the hat and wool trades. He made a particular point of the fact that farmers were prohibited from carrying their own wool across a ferry, "though the rivers, waters, havens, &c are given to us by our Charters."

McKean insisted that the Lower Counties "have been, and still are, the most loyal and dutiful of all his Majesty's subjects, and the most closely attached to the present Royal family" and said that "the present undeserved frowns of the parent state most probably arise from the base calumnies, wicked insinuations, and most false misrepresentations of the *Bernards, Hutchinsons, Olivers* . . ." He defended the conduct of Benjamin Franklin in London (who had recently made public some letters by Hutchinson and Oliver) and deplored the public humiliation and insult Franklin had been subjected to by Alexander Wedderburn, the British Solicitor General. Civilized countries, McKean said, respect emissaries from distant places and Franklin's "age, office, abilities, and character . . . might have exempted him from abuse, even among the rudest companies. His offense, strange to relate, was discovering to his country their false accusers."

In conclusion he urged the necessity for calling a Continental Congress to consider the grievances of the colonies, and appeal to the generosity of their *gracious Sovereign* before it was too late. The twenty-seven violations which he had mentioned were "a dreadful catalogue indeed." If only the King would "condescend to read the catalogue, and spend one hour apart from Lord North and the other authors of our calumnies, to meditate upon them." And, finally, he hoped—and this was a surprising note for McKean to strike—that "amidst [the Congress'] important affairs, they would fall on some honourable and safe expedient to put an end to our African slavery, so dishonourable to us, and so provoking to the most benevolent Parent of the Universe; that this, with our luxury and irreligion [were] probably the remote causes of our present alarming situation." This criticism of slavery was not one of the twenty-seven points and was McKean's only public statement on the subject. However, it expressed the idealism of 1774, and might have been an effective argument, even in Sussex County, at that time.

All in all it was a most successful presentation, producing the desired effect, for Sussex County quickly agreed to go along with the other counties. McKean later took full credit for this success, but the diplomatic urgings of the committee for Kent County must have been equally effective. They had written to their counterparts in Sussex, "We are sensible of the Unreasonableness and impropriety of the Conduct of the New Castle People on this Occasion, in undertaking to dictate to You and us a mode of Conduct and also fixing a Place for our meeting, without our Consent very convenient for themselves but very inconvenient for us; We think they might have been more Polite." [45] The Rodneys were the guiding spirits in Kent County, working with George Read and McKean, of Newcastle County, to bring the third county, Sussex, into line. They addressed this conciliatory note to Thomas Robinson, a member of the five-man committee of correspondence for the Lower Counties, who later justified Kent and Newcastle's apprehensions by turning Tory.

On August 1 the members of the Delaware Assembly, meeting as a special convention, came together at New Castle in response to Speaker Rodney's invitation. The credentials of the delegation from Newcastle County were signed by Thomas McKean as chairman of the county committee. As expected, the convention named Caesar Rodney, Thomas McKean, and George Read "or any two of them" as delegates to the Congress that was to be held at Philadelphia on the first Monday of September, 1774. The five-man committee of correspondence, that had been previously chosen, notified the other colonies of their action, and specifically informed Stephen Hopkins, Governor and Speaker of Rhode Island, who was coordinating the efforts of the numerous committees then groping their way toward a unified plan.[46]

In so doing, they joined the spontaneous response to the Intollerable Acts and the Quebec Act that was sweeping the colonies from one end to the other—a movement started by "Rhode Island and Providence Plantations" in May, but endorsed by cities, counties, and colonies nearly everywhere on the Atlantic seaboard. For example, Wethersfield in Connecticut as early as June 13 wrote to "the Committee of Correspondence for Philadelphia and Baltimore in Maryland," noting "we have wrote to the Committees at Newport, Boston & Portsmouth, Eastward, and to those at New York, Burlington, Philadelphia & Williamsburgh in Virginia, Westward, proposing the last week in July or first in August at New York or Philadelphia . . ." This letter was signed by Silas Deane, clerk of the local committee.[47]

The language of the resolutions appointing delegates to the Congress indicates that the Congress was looked upon as a meeting of the committees of correspondence, and the credentials show that a majority of the delegates were members of such committees.[48] They had not been chosen with any particular rule as to the number allotted to each state, and the manner of their selection likewise varied. The delegation from Delaware had been chosen by the members of the Assembly, informally (and illegally) called together by the Speaker, Caesar Rodney, because Governor Penn refused to convene the Assembly in the prescribed manner.

The delegation from Pennsylvania would have been chosen in a still more informal manner, because the Speaker, Joseph Galloway, would have supported the Governor; but Charles Thomson and the radicals, with the help of John Dickinson and some moderates, had applied pressure on the authorities with such skill that at the last minute the Governor decided to convene the Assembly, and have them appoint a delegation legally, with Galloway at its head. As a dignified retreat, and excuse for calling the Assembly, a step he had earlier refused to take, Governor Penn suddenly discovered an outbreak of Indian hostilities in the Ohio Valley.[49] New York's delegation indicated the confusion in that colony: five members were elected in the city and approved by various counties or districts within counties; Suffolk and Orange Counties chose their own; and in Kings County a self-appointed two-man committee, Simon Boerum and friend, unanimously elected Boerum as delegate.[50]

The instructions from Delaware were stronger than most, but the wording was still carefully guarded: after putting the best face possible on the legality of the selection, the instructions authorized the delegates "then and there, to consult and advise with the deputies from the other colonies, and to determine upon all such prudent and lawful measures, as may be judged most expedient for the Colonies immediately and unitedly to adopt, in order to obtain relief for an oppressed people, and the redress of our general grievances. Signed by order of the convention, Caesar Rodney, Chairman . . ."[51]

The election of delegates by colony and date was as follows:

June 3, Connecticut: *Eliphaet Dyer,** Roger Sherman, Silas Deane

June 17, Massachusetts: Thomas Cushing, Samuel Adams, John Adams, Robert Treat Paine

June 22–25, Maryland: Robert Goldsborough, Samuel Chase, Thomas Johnson, Matthew Tilghman, William Paca

July 21, New Hampshire: John Sullivan, Nathaniel Folsom

July 22, Pennsylvania: Joseph Galloway, *John Morton,* Charles Humphreys, Thomas Mifflin, Samuel Rhodes, Edward Biddle, George Ross, *John Dickinson*

July 23, New Jersey: James Kinsey, Stephen Crane, William Livingston, Richard Smith, John DeHart

* The delegates whose names are italicised had served previously in the Stamp Act Congress.

July 25, New York: James Duane, John Jay, Isaac Low, John Alsop, William Floyd, *Philip Livingston*, Henry Wisner, Simon Boerum, John Haring

August 1, Delaware: *Caesar Rodney, Thomas McKean*, George Read

August 1, Virginia: Peyton Randolph, Richard Henry Lee, George Washington, Patrick Henry, Richard Bland, Benjamin Harrison, Edmund Pendleton

July 6–8, ratified August 2, South Carolina: Henry Middleton, *John Rutledge, Thomas Lynch, Christopher Gadsden*, Edward Rutledge

August 10, Rhode Island & Providence Plantations: Stephen Hopkins, Samuel Ward

August 25, North Carolina: William Hooper, Joseph Hewes, Richard Caswell [52]

Altogether fifty-six delegates were sent from twelve colonies, some of whom were appointed too late to arrive for the convening of the Congress on Monday, September 5. North Carolina's delegates, leaving immediately after their election, arrived on September 14.[53] Many of the delegates had come to know each other through the intercolonial committees of correspondence; nine of them had met at the Stamp Act Congress nearly a decade before, being one-third of the total of that body. Several of the Southerners had had close associations with the North: Christopher Gadsden had lived in Philadelphia for a few years, and Silas Deane remarked that the South Carolinian "leaves all New England Sons of Liberty far behind, for he is for taking up his firelock and marching direct to Boston." [54] Two indeed had been transplanted from the North: William Hooper, a former Bostonian, had been a law student of James Otis's, and Joseph Hewes had left New Jersey in his late twenties for North Carolina, where he had become a member of the legislature. Quite a few had an older, unique bond as alumni of Dr. Francis Alison's; in fact the annual visitation of that school, scheduled for the second week in September, had to be postponed as too many of those expected were otherwise employed—they were so notified by the secretary of trustees, Charles Thomson, who by then was also Secretary of the First Continental Congress.[55]

When the Massachusetts delegation arrived in the vicinity of Philadelphia, on Monday, August 29, John Adams recorded in his *Diary*, "[After mid-day dinner] We stopped at Frankfor[d] about five Miles out of Town. A Number of Carriages and Gentlemen came out of Phyladaphia [*sic*] to meet us. Mr. Thomas Mifflin, Mr. McKean of the Lower Counties, one of their Delegates, Mr. Rutledge of Carolina, and a Number of Gentlemen from Philadelphia. Mr. Folsom and Mr. Sullivan, the N. Hampshire Delegates. We were introduced to all these Gentlemen and most cordially wellcomed to Philadelphia." [56] The most active member of the Pennsylvania delegation at this time was Thomas Mifflin, who entertained the Massachusetts and Virginia delegations with lavish hospitality, and served as a catalyst in bringing together delegates from the various colonies whose views, in many cases, were as yet not known to the others.

Rodney and Read had been the leaders in the preliminary moves in Delaware. McKean, like his old school-mate Charles Thomson in Pennsylvania, had been somewhat preoccupied by personal affairs and by his impending marriage. Nevertheless, the role he had played at the Stamp Act Congress and in the intervening years inevitably gave him a certain prominence, once the new Congress had assembled. Adams recorded in his *Diary* on his first night in Philadelphia, "By a Computation made this Evening by Mr. McKean, there will be at the Congress about 56 Members, twenty two of them Lawyers. Mr. McKean gave me an Account this Evening of the Behaviour of Ruggles at the former Congress in 1765. He was treated pretty cavalierly, his Behaviour was very dishonourable." [57]

The same Saturday night in Philadelphia Thomas Mifflin was host to a large assemblage, including Dr. John Witherspoon of the College of New Jersey, Richard Henry Lee and Benjamin Harrison of Virginia, Robert Treat Paine of Massachusetts, and Edward Rutledge of South Carolina.[58] Joseph Galloway, the conservative Speaker of the Pennsylvania Assembly, who had arranged to have himself named chairman of the Pennsylvania delegation in order to prevent radical action by the Congress, made the mistake of his life by not attending meetings of this sort during the weekend, retiring instead to his estate at Trevose in Bucks County, and writing a long description of the preliminary events in Philadelphia to William Franklin, the Royal Governor of New Jersey. Galloway would have been better prepared for the opening session on Monday if he had heard some of the toasts offered at Mifflin's party, and observed at first hand the meaningful looks exchanged across the table over such relatively harmless sentiments as this: "May the result of the Congress answer the expectations of the people." [59]

As for McKean, after spending a week welcoming the Massachusetts delegation and others, he hastened back to New Castle, there to be married on Saturday, September 3, to Sally Armitage. Thus he missed the roll call on Monday, when Caesar Rodney presented the credentials from the Lower Counties. He was present, however, on Tuesday, and thereafter attended for nearly nine years, with but one brief interruption, as a delegate from Delaware until the end of the war—despite having become, by 1774, a permanent resident of Pennsylvania. Only one other delegate to the Continental Congresses, Roger Sherman of Connecticut, surpassed this record.[60]

Galloway was in for a number of surprises, at least three of them on the first day. He was accustomed to dominating the Pennsylvania Assembly, and assumed that as chairman of the host delegation he would be able to steer the Congress in the same way. His chagrin can be imagined when his offer of the State House (later to be called Independence Hall) was refused in favor of the humbler and less imposing Carpenters' Hall, and also when a Virginian, Peyton Randolph, was elected as President of the Congress.[61] Another blow was in store for him: Charles Thomson, described as "the Sam Adams of Philadelphia" by the latter's cousin John, whom Galloway had pointedly excluded from the Pennsylvania delegation, was selected as permanent secretary of the Congress, though he was not a delegate. A few weeks later he received yet another shock; John Dickinson, whom he had excluded from the delegation, was chosen as an additional delegate on October 15. Galloway was no stranger to the arts of political manipulation, but he had been thoroughly outmaneuvered. He had expected intransigence from the New Englanders; the offensive of the Southerners caught him off guard.

Thomson's sudden appointment as secretary might have come as a surprise to him, and this was the public impression. However, Thomson was expert at shorthand and had frequently been called on to take minutes at conferences and congresses in the past, and his reputation for integrity had been proclaimed by the Indians, who, choosing him as interpreter-secretary, had christened him Wegh-wu-law-mo-end, "the man who tells the truth." [62] Married at Somerville, on Thursday, September 1, he was just returning to the city when he was informed of his appointment.[63] Watson's *Annals* describes the event as follows: "His appointment as Secretary to Congress was singular. He had lately married Miss Harrison, who inherited the estate of Harriton, where he afterwards lived and died. Coming with her to Philadelphia, he had scarcely alighted from his carriage when a message came to him from the President of Congress—then first in session . . . He went forthwith, not conceiving what could be purposed, and was told he was wished to take their minutes. He set to it as for a temporary affair . . ." [64]

A master stroke by the radicals at this point was to find an Anglican clergyman who agreed with the Presbyterians sufficiently to conduct a service for the Congress that would encourage resistance. This was the Rev. Jacob Duché of St. Peter's Church in Philadelphia, whose extemporaneous prayer on Wednesday, September 7 "filled every Bosom present," according to John Adams. The selection of Rev. Mr. Duché has usually been attributed to the genius of Sam Adams, but undoubtedly he was recommended by the local leaders; at the time of the Congress he had been married for nearly fifteen years to Elizabeth Hopkinson, sister of Francis Hopkinson. No member of the Congress could have known him better than Thomas McKean; Duché had been McKean's schoolmate at Dr. Alison's Academy, and Francis Hopkinson was McKean's brother-in-law. "The Collect for the day," Adams thought, "was most admirably adapted, tho this was accidental, or rather Providential." [65]

Philadelphia's residents, basking in their city's novel and favorable prominence, provided lavish, constant hospitality; pride and practicality for a while combined to submerge internal differences of opinion. On the same day an Anglican minister was chosen Chaplain of the Congress, a prominent Quaker entertained some of the delegates and local dignitaries in a friendly, but hardly plain, fashion. Impressed—but with the usual inaccuracies of spelling and titles, and providing Rhode Island with two governors—John Adams reported at length:

> Dined with Mr. Miers Fisher, a young Quaker and a Lawyer. We saw his library, which is clever. But this plain Friend, and his plain, tho pretty Wife, with her Thee's and Thou's, had provided us the most Costly Entertainment—Ducks, Hams, Chickens, Beef, Pigg, Tarts, Creams, Custards, Gellies, fools, Trifles, floating Island, Beer, Porter, Punch, Wine and a long &c.
>
> We had a large Collection of Lawyers, at Table. Mr. Andrew Allen, the Attorney General, a Mr. Morris, the Prothonotary, Mr. Fisher, Mr. McKean, Mr. Rodney— besides these we had Mr. Reed, Gov'r Hopkins and Governor Ward.
>
> We had much Conversation upon the Practice of Law, in our different Provinces,

but at last We got swallowed up, in Politicks, and the great Question of Parliamentary Jurisdiction . . .*

In the midst of such festivities the serious business of the Congress was going forward, and Joseph Galloway, the conservative leader, saw with dismay the formation of two factions: his own group which hoped "to form a more solid and constitutional union between the two countries, and to avoid every measure which tended to sedition, or act of violent opposition"; and another which "meant by every fiction, falsehood and fraud, to delude the people from their due allegiance, to throw the subsisting Governments into anarchy, to incite the ignorant and vulgar to arms, and with those arms to establish American Independence." [66]

Galloway's analysis as usual was prejudiced, but not without a factual basis, and if he had seen a paper which John Adams showed Patrick Henry, sometime in the course of the proceedings, his worst fears might have been confirmed. This was a memo, entitled "broken hints to be communicated to the committee of congress for the Massachusetts," written by Joseph Hawley of Northampton, and it produced a burst of approbation from Henry, "I am of that man's mind." [67] John Adams, after all, was a newcomer to the patriotic movement; comparative unknowns, such as Joseph Hawley, had done some profound thinking on the subject of independence, and the groundwork was already being developed:

> We must *fight,* if we can't otherwise rid ourselves of British taxation . . . It is *now* or never, that we must assert our liberty. Twenty years will make the number of tories on this continent equal to the number of whigs. They who shall be born will not have any idea of a free government . . .
>
> There is not heat enough for battle. Constant, and a sort of negative resistance of government, will increase heat and blow the fire. There is not military skill enough. That is improving, and must be encouraged and improved, but will daily increase . . .
>
> A certain clear plan, for a constant, adequate and lasting supply of arms and military stores, must be devised and fully contemplated. This is the main thing. This, I think, ought to be a capital branch of the business of congress.
>
> Quer[y], therefore—whether it is not absolutely necessary that some plan be settled for a continuation of congresses?—But here we must be aware that congresses will soon be declared and enacted by parliament to be high treason . . . [68]

McKean was of this militant school of thought, and probably had been for some time. The New Englanders who had come to Philadelphia with high hopes for leadership from John Dickinson, because of the reputation of the *Farmer's*

---

* John Adams' *Diary.* According to Konkle's *Benjamin Chew,* 137, a light-hearted verse was bandied about in this conversation:

> You ask me why lawyers so much are increased,
> Tho' most of the country already are fleeced;
> The reason, I'm sure, is most strikingly plain:—
> Tho' sheep are oft sheared, yet the wool grows again;
> And tho' you may think e'er so odd of the matter,
> The oftener they're fleeced, the wool grows the better.
> Thus downy chined boys, as oft I have heard,
> By frequent shaving, obtain a large beard.

Letters, soon found that they could rely with more confidence on such men as McKean, Rodney, and Charles Thomson. Dickinson excelled at drafting conciliatory petitions, and such petitions were necessary to convince peaceable people that every effort was being made to bring about a reconciliation. But when the time came for action, Dickinson seemed to be indecisive and vacillating, and the men who had already made up their minds found his behavior exasperating. By the middle of 1775 John Adams had lost patience with him completely and incautiously wrote to James Warren that "a certain great Fortune and piddling Genius . . . has given a silly Cast to our Whole Doings. We are between Hawk and Buzzard . . ." [69] With McKean and the Virginians, on the other hand, the feeling of mutual trust would grow.

Numerous committees and sub-committees were formed, as the sparring continued during the month of September. Sam Adams received a steady stream of messages from Boston: usually bad news and not infrequently false. Galloway took accurate measure of his great adversary: "He eats little, drinks little, thinks much, and is most decisive and indefatigable in the persuit [sic] of his objects." [70] The Rev. Dr. Duché's prayer had made a greater impression than it otherwise would have, perhaps, because it followed a rumor, as yet uncorrected, that the city of Boston had been bombarded. The fact was less dramatic; General Gage had merely removed a supply of powder from Cambridge.

More effective still were the Suffolk Resolves, a set of revolutionary propositions concocted by a county convention in Massachusetts (the county of Boston) condemning British policies in ringing language, which were rushed into Congress on September 17, and led to a unanimous resolution of support. The members hoped "that the effects of the united efforts of North America in [Boston's] behalf, [would] carry such conviction to the British nation of the unwise, unjust, and ruinous policy of the present administration, as quickly to introduce better men and wiser measures." [71] In the realm of propaganda loyalists like Galloway were hopelessly outmatched.

Again, as in the Stamp Act Congress, the policy of giving each state one vote, regardless of the number of delegates, was adopted. Patrick Henry's suggestion that representation should be based on population failed because of the lack of adequate statistics as to population, and the difficulty of determining the weight that should be given to slaves, also because of vociferous opposition from small-state men, particularly Thomas McKean. The chief advantage of having several delegates was that the workload in "greater committees," "lesser committees," *ad hoc* committees, and sub-committees could be shared by the various members; more time could be devoted to important matters by the key people, if they did not have to spread themselves too thin. Several committees required the attendance of at least one member from each colony, a policy which was necessary to obtain the views of each, but time-consuming for individual members.

The committee on the colonies' rights, sometimes known as "the Greater Committee," consisted of two members from each colony: McKean and Rodney from Delaware. At one point, in this committee, McKean argued that the Quebec Act should be considered a grievance because "the magnitude of the Law compels us to make a stand," and Protestants everywhere, including Quebec, would join in the opposition. The extreme radicals, he noted, tended always to emphasize "natural law" arguments in support of their positions, instead of the more legalistic arguments, based on the British constitution and the colonial charters, which offered known precedents, and thus, from McKean's view-point, would carry more weight with the dubious, on either side of the Atlantic.

While a "loyal address" to His Majesty, and comparable statements to the people of Great Britain, and to colonies *not* in the Congress were being prepared in committee, the two most fundamental questions of the day were being brought to the point of decision. These were the disposition of Joseph Galloway's plan of union, and the adoption of the non-importation, non-consumption, non-exportation agreement known as the Association. Galloway's plan was a brilliant effort to head off the Association, and it almost succeeded. His strategy was to adopt the radicals' premise—that an attack on one province was an attack on all—and create a constitutional union within the framework of the British Empire, which would safeguard American rights without breaking the ties with the mother country. His plan was anathema to the radicals, but it was warmly supported by several prominent delegates, including James Duane and John Jay of New York, and Edward Rutledge of South Carolina, who surprised everyone by announcing that he regarded it as "almost a perfect plan." It was debated off and on from September 28, when first presented, until October 20, when it was rejected by one vote (i.e. six colonies to five) and was "ordered to be kept out of the minutes." [72]

Galloway himself, ironically enough, was a member of the committee appointed the previous day "to revise the minutes of the Congress." [73] He was thus implicated in the decision to expunge all record of his plan from the minutes—a deed he would later complain about bitterly in many letters and pamphlets.* The other members of the committee, Thomas McKean, John Adams, and William Hooper, took care that the decision was implemented. The vote on Galloway's plan was to be the high-water mark of the conservative reaction.

---

* Galloway wrote to Gov. William Franklin of New Jersey (*New Jersey Archives*, 1st Ser., X, 579 f.) during the Congress, and immediately afterwards went to New York to see Gov. Cadwallader Colden. (*Loyalist Transcripts*, XLIX, 25 f., NYPL) In his post-war testimony before the Loyalist Commission, arguing that he was entitled to compensation by the British government, he produced a letter from Gov. Colden to Lord Dartmouth, dated Dec. 7, 1774, with this interesting passage: "Mr. Galloway and Mr. Duane tell me that at the close of the Congress they dissented from the proceedings and insisted to have their dissent entered upon the Minutes, but cod not by any means get it allowed." (*Ibid.*, 70) Still later, in 1793, he wrote to Thomas McKean, who was then Chief Justice of Pennsylvania in an effort to obtain permission to return to America, saying that he did not "act against America" until he actually joined General Howe's army in December, 1776. (McKean Papers, HSP, II, 108)

His statements on the subject were not consistent; in any case, his efforts were all in vain. The conflicting evidence is summarized in my article, "Joseph Galloway and the British Occupation of Philadelphia" (PMHB, XXX, 282 n.), as follows: "My opinion is that at the time of the Congress William Franklin, and others, were covering up for him; when he testified before the Loyalist Commission, he told the truth, but made it stronger than it needed to be; when he wrote to McKean he glossed over hostile acts, hoping that they had been forgiven or forgotten."

Never again would the moderates and Tories come so close to defeating or frustrating the plans of the radicals. The "clash of resounding arms" the following spring would convert a sufficient number of waverers so that a constitutional reconciliation was no longer feasible—the possibilities were then bluntly summed up by Patrick Henry as "Liberty or Death." [74] Military defeat was to stare the patriots in the face more than once, but from the political standpoint their cause had already passed the point of greatest danger.

The Association was the device by which the committees of correspondence strengthened their grip on revolutionary activities throughout the colonies. Having roundly condemned the policies of the "wicked ministry," and having provided for non-importation after December 1, 1774, and non-exportation "except rice to Europe" after September 10, 1775, the Congress provided "that a committee be chosen in every county, city, and town, by those who are qualified to vote for representatives in the legislature, whose business it shall be attentively to observe the conduct of all persons touching this association . . . ," and if anyone should be so rash as to violate its terms, the committee was to "cause the truth of the case to be published in the gazette; to the end, that all such foes to the rights of British-America may be publicly known, and universally contemned as the enemies of American liberty . . ." [75]

There had been considerable dissent and resentment over the exception of "rice to Europe," but many Southerners were convinced that non-exportation hurt the producers of staple crops more than anyone else, and the delegates were beginning to realize that public unity could only be reached through private concessions. The Association was passed on October 20, two days before Galloway's plan was finally disposed of, and it was the first step towards the practical union that would be necessary, if the Americans were ever to win their independence.

The Congress renounced the slave trade after December 1, provided for non-consumption of certain goods as an aid to the enforcement of non-importation, promised their "utmost endeavors to improve the breed of sheep," and went on to an explicit statement of the puritanical mood that so frequently accompanies revolutions:

> [We] will discountenance and discourage every species of extravagance and dissipation, especially all horse-racing, and all kinds of gaming, cock fighting, exhibitions of shews, plays, and other expensive diversions and entertainments; and on the death of any relation or friend, none of us, or any of our families will go into any further mourning-dress than a crepe of ribbon on the arm or hat, for gentlemen, and a black ribbon and necklace for ladies, and we will discontinue the giving of gloves and scarves at funerals.[76]

A moralistic and self-sacrificing attitude of this sort could hardly be permanent, but the revolutionary apparatus that was set up under the Association was to be a long-lasting thing indeed. The committees of correspondence, at the top, would gradually cease to exist, as the Second Continental Congress took over the function of coordinating the activities of the states; at the same time the growing network of committees that bound together the counties, the cities, and the towns would become self-perpetuating, and eventually merge with the legislative bodies that were set up under the new state constitutions. These committees tended to dominate all other institutions, especially during the early years of the war, so that eventually executive and judicial independence had to be wrested from them almost by force. The tri-partite system of government that was later to be regarded as typically American was *not* a characteristic of the early phases of the revolution.

On October 26, the Congress signed the Address to the King, approved an address to the people of Quebec, voted a resolution of thanks to the Pennsylvania Assembly for a grand celebration at the City Tavern on October 20, and other courtesies during the course of their sitting, and adjourned—having first agreed to return to Philadelphia on May 10, 1775, if their grievances had not by that time been redressed. As a reward for their labors they would receive little enough from the British government; they had to be satisfied with praise from their erstwhile hero, William Pitt, the Earl of Chatham: "I have read Thucydides and have studied and admired the master states of the world, it has been my favourite study, but I must declare and avow that for solidity of reasoning, force of sagacity, and wisdom of conclusion, under such a complication of difficult circumstances, no nation or body of men can stand in preference to the general Congress of Philadelphia." [77]

Chapter 10

The War Begins, 1775

Shortly after the adjournment of the First Continental Congress, the Chief Justice of the province of New Jersey, The Hon. Frederick Smyth (the judge who had sponsored McKean's promotion to Sollicitor and Counsellor at Law) took the unusual step of instructing a Grand Jury as to "the regulation of [their] personal conduct amidst the present commotions of the continent," and the Grand Jury "had the misfortune to differ from [him] in sentiment, both as to the origin and tendency of the present uneasiness." [78] They issued a public statement in the firmest possible language in which they set forth what might be called the radical Whig position, and the judge, to the satisfaction of everyone except the more extreme Tories, made "a very complaisant and conciliating reply." The Grand Jury's statement was quoted in a New York newspaper, dated November 17, 1774, in an article which expressed regret at omitting the judge's charge which had occasioned the exchange of views, and it was obviously a most effective bit of propaganda:

> If we rightly understood a particular part of your Honour's charge, you were pleased to tell us, that while we were employed in guarding against "imaginary tyranny, three thousand miles distant"; we ought not to expose ourselves to a "real tyranny at our own doors." As we neither know, Sir, nor are under the least apprehension of any tyranny at our own doors, unless it should make its way hither from the distance you mention . . . we are utterly at a loss for the idea thereby intended to be communicated. . . . But respecting the tyranny at the distance of three thousand miles . . . the effect, Sir, of that tyranny is too severely felt to have it thought altogether visionary . . . We cannot think, Sir, that taxes imposed upon us by our fellow subjects, in a legislature in which we are not represented, is an imaginary, but . . . real and actual tyranny . . . We cannot think, Sir, that depriving us of the inestimable right of trial by jury . . . is a tyranny merely imaginary . . . that an act

124

passed to indemnify, protect and screen from punishment such as may be guilty even of murder is a bare idea. That the establishment of French laws and popish religion in Canada, the better to facilitate the arbitrary schemes of the British ministry . . . has no other than a mental existence.

In a word, Sir, we cannot persuade ourselves that the fleet now blocking up the Port of Boston, consisting of ships, built of real English oak and solid iron, and armed with cannon and ponderous metal, with actual powder and ball; nor the army lodged in the town of Boston, and the fortifications thrown about it (substantial and formidable realities) are all creatures of the imagination . . .[79]

It must be remembered that in November, 1774, a British army of 3,000 men was occupying the city of Boston, which normally had a population of only 15,000.[80] General Thomas Gage, who had been in England when the news of the Boston Tea Party had arrived, and had helped to frame the new Quartering Act (one of the Intollerable Acts), had returned to Boston on May 13, 1774, with a dual assignment as Commander in Chief of the British army and Governor of Massachusetts Bay, replacing Governor Thomas Hutchinson who sailed for England, never to return.

A proper Bostonian and passionate Tory, Peter Oliver, had looked forward to Gage's arrival and the suitable chastisement of rebellious hot-heads, for "it was generally expected & hoped, that he had Orders to send to *England* several Persons, who had been declared by his Majesty's Law Servants to have been guilty of high Treason . . . but unhappily for the Publick the People were disappointed & the Traitors felt theirselves [*sic*] out of Danger." Upon reflection, Oliver tried to emulate the General, and noted that Gage "had both civil & military Government to conduct. The Task was arduous at this Juncture, & no Person could be more anxious than he was to support the former, tho' it was out of his Walk of Life . . ." [81] During the summer, however, Gage became convinced that the Americans would rather fight than yield, no matter how much force was used against them, and he so notified his government. His increasingly pessimistic dispatches merely caused him to lose favor with his superiors without gaining him any significant popularity on this side of the water.

Gage's policy was "to avoid any bloody Crisis as long as possible" [82]—a sensible course in the desperate situation he was at last beginning to understand—but, meanwhile, the friction between his troops and the local population increased from day to day. It was not that the troops were harassing the local people; on the contrary, they were kept away from them as much as possible. Rather, the Bostonians resented the presence of the army as such, while feeling a certain sympathy for individual British soldiers, many of whom were actually American volunteers. They kept teasing them, and encouraging them to desert to the American side, which many of them did. Then they were horrified by the strictness of the disciplinary measures that were taken to cut down on the desertion. They were especially appalled by the public floggings on the Boston common.[83]

Towards officers the attitude of the Bostonians was more ambivalent. The typical British officer was regarded as dashing, wealthy, and aristocratic; but at the same time violent, corrupt, and dissolute. The Boston girls, or at least some of them, found the British officers, especially the younger ones, irresistible, but the charm of these wicked foreigners was lost on their native, male rivals. General Gage's efforts to avoid a repetition of the Boston Massacre, either over a social conflict entered into by one of his officers, or over an attempted interception of an enlisted deserter, discredited him in the eyes of his army, and made his position almost impossible. When he ordered his men to apologize to the Americans, or recompense them for damages, they were naturally outraged. However, by avoiding an accidental flare-up during the winter of 1774–5, Gage had at least assured that the final decision for war would be made by the home government or, more specifically, by the King.[84]

William Pitt, the Earl of Chatham, helped to bring about the conflict unintentionally by proposing the right solution in the worst possible manner. On January 20, 1775, he rose in the House of Lords to demand the immediate withdrawal from Boston of the entire army, lock, stock, and barrel—doing so arrogantly, as his own proposal, without any effort to obtain the support of Lord North, Lord Dartmouth, or any of the Rockinghamites. Horace Walpole observed in his *Journal,* "Even the Opposition could scarce bring themselves to swallow either Lord Chatham's haughtiness or absurdity." [85] The King was now determined to send over General Sir William Howe, who would replace General Gage and adopt firmer measures, aimed directly at the ringleaders. As it happened, the troubles at Lexington and Concord occurred while Gage was still in command, but the determination of the British government had stiffened remarkably in January, 1775.

During the same time the Royal Governor of New Jersey, William Franklin, who was the natural son of the most famous Patriot and one of his most able enemies, had been keeping Lord Dartmouth, the Secretary of State for the American Colonies, informed as to the activities of the First Continental Congress. Governor Franklin relayed letters which he had received from "a Gentleman who is one of the Delegates"—Joseph Galloway—who was thus informing the British government of everything that went on at the revolutionary headquarters, while remaining free to deny knowledge of the use to which his letters were being put. Young Franklin handled Galloway skillfully and eventually won him irrevocably to the British cause. On December 6, 1774, for example, Franklin sent Dartmouth a copy of his friend's "Plan of a Proposed Union," and an "Idea of the Disposition of some of the principal Members of [the Congress]." So far as the public was concerned, Franklin said that the proceedings of the Congress, after its adjournment, were "not altogether satisfactory to many of the Inhabitants, yet at present [there is] little Reason to doubt but that . . . the Association . . . will be generally carried into Execution . . . [As to objectors] it is not in the Power of Government here to protect them. Indeed the Officers of Government [except in Boston] have but little or no Protection for themselves . . ." [86]

William Legge, Lord Dartmouth, had acquired a colonial reputation unique among his colleagues and peers and a list of correspondents to match; his pious interest in the new sect of Methodism, guided by Selina, Countess of Huntington, had given him a trans-Atlantic halo. His friendship with Benjamin Franklin began in 1765, at which time, and for an unduly long time, the latter had high hopes and illusions about his Lordship; this friendship had been inherited by William Franklin. Sharing the Franklins' optimistic delusions, Joseph Reed was also numbered, until 1775, among Dartmouth's correspondents—as, indirectly, were others in the colonies. These factors undoubtedly bore upon his appointment as Secretary for the Colonies. But by 1775, even his step-brother, Lord North, had recognised, as Walpole remarked, that he had "stayed long enough to prostitute his character and authenticate his hypocrisy." [87] In 1775 he was placed on a high but less accessible shelf, as Lord Privy Seal.[88]

During November and December, as Governor Franklin surmised, committees of observation and/or inspection were being set up in counties and cities everywhere, in compliance with the 11th Article of the Association. Penn's Lower Counties, like some in Virginia, had been divided into "hundreds," not, as in medieval times, to represent or produce a hundred warriors from each division, but for the peaceable purpose of supporting a hundred family-farms each. Varying in size, according to the supposed fertility of their soil, they were soon populated by many more than the earlier estimates. Now the original purpose seemed appropriate again, and revolutionary committees were set up in and for the respective Hundreds. Usually large groups, packed with people from the "lower orders" of society, they were subordinate to the committees of correspondence, which were smaller, more elite groups that included the foremost leaders of the resistance. The titles of these groups varied from place to place, sometimes changing from week to week; there was as yet no uniformity in such matters, and their terminology was confusing even to contemporaries. The principal result of the First Continental Congress was the establishment of this revolutionary network, which extended down to the smallest communities, and was not duplicated by their opponents on the other side. The forces loyal to the government had excellent intelligence, but lacked a grass-roots organization. The existing colonial governments gradually disintegrated as the real power shifted to these informal committees.

The establishment of local organizations led immediately to an intensification of political activity, and a multiplication of factions. It would be misleading to say that public opinion was "polarized"—there were too many contending groups. This was particularly true of the Philadelphia area, where the struggle would never be a simple contest between two groups. Historically, Philadelphia was the center of pacific beliefs and sects of all sizes and descriptions, both English and German, but it was simultaneously the nerve-center of the resistance. The less consensus there was, the more necessity for strenuous political activity. No single group, or pair of alternating factions, could claim control of this area at any time before the war broke out, or indeed for the next generation.

Thus, Pennsylvania politics was more bitter, and complicated, than the politics of most colonies for the entire lifetime of the revolutionary leaders. The Declaration of Independence did not settle matters, nor did the British occupation of Philadelphia in 1777, nor even the British evacuation in 1778. Factions which were thought to be utterly dead had a way of reviving ten or fifteen years later. A notable example was the old Proprietary Party, which included conservative Whigs such as Benjamin Chew, James and Andrew Allen, Edward Shippen, Jr., Edward and William Tilghman. Although still highly visible in 1774–75, dining with members of the First Continental Congress, practising military maneuvers with other gentlemen of the Associators, by 1776 this faction was eclipsed, and some, such as the Allens, became out-and-out Tories. Others, whose Loyalist temperatures were less feverish or fervent, who professed a cool neutrality, re-emerged in the 1780's and 1790's and came back into prominence again. The careers of individuals, therefore, must be judged by the rules of the arena in which they performed, and the meaning of the words they used in the various debates, such as Whig, republican, or constitutionalist, should be understood as forever changing.

In January, 1775, according to the *Diary of Christopher Marshall,* there were "meetings daily amongst the Quakers [and] members were enjoined not to concern themselves in the public disputes . . . to pay all humble and dutiful obedience unto the king or his ministers' mandates . . . not to join, nor to be in any of the city, county, provincial, or general committees . . ." [89] The radical committees by this time were in full operation. As early as the middle of 1774, they had been strong enough to force Governor Penn to call the Assembly together to select a delegation to the First Continental Congress, and with the formation of the Association in October they developed an impetus that could not be checked.

On January 23, 1775, there was a meeting of the county committees, which was referred to as a provincial convention, with Joseph Reed as chairman. Approximately a hundred delegates attended, from all counties "except from Bucks"—a county which then and later tended to take its name literally. This convention authorized the Philadelphia committee to serve as a committee of correspondence for the entire province, with power to call a future convention. They also decided that if any of the county committees had difficulty in enforcing the Association, the other committees should provide reinforcements. They "broke up the twenty-eighth, having finished all their business amicably." [90] The working alliance which was broached at this meeting, between the frontiersmen from the back country, who complained of being inadequately represented in the Assembly, and the equally vocal city radicals, would have a lasting significance.

Three military organizations were already in existence in Philadelphia, prior to the escalation of hostilities resulting from the bloodshed at Lexington and Concord: the City Troop, which had been organized in November, 1774, and was commanded by Captain Markoe, later by Captain Samuel Morris; the Infantry Greens, or "silk-stocking company," which was drilled twice a day by Captain John Cadwalader, who "had the kindness to set out his Madeira for the men to refresh themselves after drill;" and the Quaker Blues, a light infantry company of non-pacifist Quakers commanded by the Sheriff, Joseph Cowperthwait.[91] These were all independent outfits, private armies, subject theoretically to the Assembly, but more likely to heed the committees of correspondence if a disagreement should arise between the Assembly and the Philadelphia committee. The two

bodies worked together to defend American rights during the winter that inter-
vened between the Congresses, but the Assembly was much the more cautious
and conservative.

Although living in Philadelphia and engaged in private practice at the same
time—his work inevitably suffering from neglect [92]—McKean was still closely
identified with the Lower Counties, and would continue to be for several more
years. Nonetheless, by mid-summer, 1775, he joined the Philadelphia committee,
and became one of its chairmen. In March, 1775, he rode down to New Castle
for a meeting of the Assembly of the Lower Counties, and wrote to Sally in Philadelphia, after his arrival, disposing of all domestic news in one sentence, and
continuing in detail: "On Tuesday I made the report of the Proceedings of the
Convention [called by Caesar Rodney] here, on the second day of August last
[1774], and of the Delegates then appointed to attend the General Congress at
Philadelphia, also the Proceedings of the said Congress; which the House took
immediately into consideration, and approved of yesterday without a dissenting
vote." [93]

He added that the Delaware Assembly had appointed "the Same Government
[Rodney, Read, and himself] to attend the next Congress," and that they had
been instructed to avoid measures that might be disrespectful to their *gracious
Sovereign,* and to insist that each colony should have an equal voice in the deliberations of the Congress. In the Stamp Act Congress McKean had made the
point successfully, that "a vote by States was . . . a *sine qua non,*" [94] and a
decade later the point was even more crucial; McKean must have proposed and
insisted on the equal-voice instruction now, to strengthen his hand in Philadelphia. This time, incidentally, the delegates were legally appointed, by a duly
elected Assembly, and their instructions were signed by Caesar Rodney, as
Speaker.[95]

In Boston Sam Adams was as busy as ever, writing letters to various correspondents in the other colonies, and spreading tales of the British atrocities he had
seen, in order to counteract criticism of his fellow townsmen. The practice of
tarring and feathering, he wrote to Richard Henry Lee in Virginia, was indulged
in by the British and the Tories as much as it was by the Patriots. There had
recently been an incident, he wrote on March 21, 1775, in which some of the
"polite Gentlemen of the British Army" had paraded a poor victim right past
General Gage's house, but the General pretended not to know it. He had indeed
heard the tumult, "but thought that they were drumming a bad woman through
the streets! This to be sure would not have been a riot . . ." * Adams also reported some correspondence with mutual friends in London, dated from Decem-

---

* Cushing, ed., *Letters of Samuel Adams,* III, 207-9. Catherine Drinker Bowen in *John Adams
and the American Revolution,* 512, made a comment worth repeating: "The truth was the
American Revolution was engineered from first to last by a handful of men, by the sheer
contagion of private correspondence: Washington, Jefferson, Lee, Henry in Virginia;
Gadsden, Lynch, Judge Drayton in the Carolinas; John Jay in New York; Dickinson, Mc-
Kean, Rodney in the middle colonies; Chase in Maryland, Witherspoon in Princeton;
Roger Sherman in Connecticut. In Massachusetts the Adamses, Hawley, Hancock and the
rest talked eternally. No one within the reach of their voice or pen was allowed to forget
or to rest indifferent."

ber and January, "some Extracts from which I have thought it necessary to have inserted in our News Papers," and ended with a particularly alarming note which he had *not disclosed to anyone,* that revealed the thinking he apparently assumed his friend Lee shared. One of the letters from London had contained this passage:

> "I have been in the Country with Lord Chatham to shew him the petition of the Congress of which he highly approved. He is of Opinion that a solemn Renunciation of the Right to *tax* on the one side, and *an Acknowledgment of the Supremacy on the other* should accompany the repeal of all the obnoxious Acts. Without that, he says, the Hearts of the two Countries will not openly embrace each other with unfeigned Affection & Reconcilement." In this short Sentence I [Sam Adams] think it is easy to see that his Lordships plan of reconciliation is the same now with that which he held forth in his Speech at the time of the repeal of the Stamp Act. However highly I think of his Lordships *Integrity* I confess I am chagrind to think that he expects an Acknowledgment of the Supremacy in terms on our part. I imagine that after such an Acknowledgment, there may be a variety of Ways by which Great Britain may enslave us besides taxing us without our Consent.[96]

Unsatisfactory as Lord Chatham's reaction may have been, it was vastly more favorable than that of the British Government. Even before Lexington and Concord, the Lords and Commons had declared that the province of Massachusetts Bay was in a state of rebellion "countenanced and encouraged by unlawful combinations in several of the other colonies;" the news arrived in Philadelphia on April 13, and spread like wildfire throughout America.[97] Then, within a week, came the still more decisive news from New England which brought about the American union. Committees of correspondence everywhere forwarded the dispatches from Boston, and held mass meetings to consider the measures that should be taken—and the response was military from this point on. In the opinion of most people the time for resolutions had passed.

In Philadelphia, at five in the afternoon of April 24, a messenger galloped in from Trenton, "with the greatest haste, excitement in his looks, on his lips, and in his train. He rode up to the City Tavern . . . the members of the committee [of Correspondence] hurrying to meet him," and delivered his brief but alarming account of the battle at Lexington. Though incomplete in figures and confirmations and delivered too late in the day for public announcement, by the following morning the news was known to all, and thousands of people, "as if by common consent," gathered in the State House yard to hear what the city committee would propose. Before the day was over it was agreed by those assembled "to associate together, to defend with arms their property, liberty, and lives against all attempts to deprive them of it." Citizens were requested to inform the committee of whatever firearms they owned, so that these might be bought for the use of the new military organizations. The three existing organizations served as a nucleus, which was quickly augmented. This was the origin of the Philadelphia Association of Volunteers, which by June mustered nearly two thousand men, and was organized into three battalions under the respective commands of John

Dickinson, Daniel Roberdeau, and John Cadwalader, who were given the rank of Colonel.[98]

This prompt response, however, was unanimous in a typically Philadelphian manner; commanders and men were united in purpose but hardly in motives or viewpoints. Col. John Cadwalader was soon transferred from command of the Quaker "Greens," or "silk-stocking company." Col. John Dickinson of the First Battalion, despite his military eminence, would be instrumental in the drafting of at least one more humble petition to the British government, the famous "Olive Branch Petition" of July, 1775—which the king rejected. Others shared the cautious sentiments of James Allen, who explained in his Diary that "My inducement principally to join them is: that a man is suspected who does not: & I chuse to have a Musket on my shoulders, to be on a par with them; & I believe discreet people mixing with them may keep them in Order." [99] Nevertheless, this voluntary Association was inevitably to be expanded and made compulsory.

Thus, the war came before the Second Continental Congress convened on the tenth of May. The initial reaction to the clashes in New England proceeded from the colonial governments, and the committees. The Congress, meeting later, had to assume control over countless activities that were already in feverish progress. They advised and coordinated, and in an astonishingly short time, by common consent, they directed. But the initiative in most cases came from the hundreds of volunteers who formed armies, mounted expeditionary forces, and manned privateers on the high seas, even before they were requestd to do so. The physical effort required of the leaders in this unsettled time was almost incredible. The fact that commanding figures emerged who were able to assume control, and never once relax their grip, can be explained only by the supposition that many of them had foreseen the crisis, and prepared themselves for it, perhaps for years.

A welcome event for the revolutionary cause at this juncture was the return of Benjamin Franklin, who had been in England for a decade and now arrived in Philadelphia on May 5, 1775. His wife Deborah had died during his absence, the previous winter, and his daughter and son-in-law were living in the house which he had owned for years but had never seen.[100] On the day after his arrival, the Pennsylvania Assembly made him a delegate to the Congress that was about to meet, and after a short pause he moved swiftly on several levels to simplify and strengthen the revolutionary organization. In so doing, he was joining forces with Thomson, Reed, Mifflin, Clymer, and the reluctant Dickinson—as well as McKean and Rodney from the Lower Counties—in support of a faction which included many of his former opponents. Franklin was no longer a Quaker in his politics but a Presbyterian, and he helped move Pennsylvania from the Toryism of a Galloway, past the conservatism of a Dickinson, to the radicalism of the Philadelphia committee. In another year he moved even farther, to lend his prestige to an obscure group of revolutionaries who at this point were still unknown.

One of his first steps in the spring of 1775 was to persuade the Assembly to establish a Committee of Safety, which would supersede, or control, the provincial committee of correspondence, a large and amorphous group, and would have legal sanction for the exercise of its powers.[101] Despite the fact that more than half its members were Quakers, the Assembly, with only three dissenting, voted for the Committee of Safety, which was duly established on June 30. The Committee first met on July 3, and immediately announced approval of "the Association entered into by the good people of this colony for the Defence of their Lives, Liberties, and Property." For all practical purposes the Committee of Safety became the executive branch of the province for the period from June 30, 1775, to July 22, 1776, when it was replaced by a Council of Safety that lasted until the more formal revolutionary government of the state was organized.[102]

The Committee of Safety consisted of twenty-five members, more or less, with authority over the committees of observation and inspection which had been set up under the *old* Association of October, 1774. Sub-committees of the Committee of Safety sometimes included men who were members of other committees, but not members of the Committee of Safety—with representatives of the Lower Counties occasionally appearing among their numbers. For those who were trusted the formalities of residence were customarily ignored. A convenient device was to form six sub-committees of observation and inspection (one for each weekday) to meet at the Coffee House, down by the water front, and watch the arrival of vessels and inspect their cargoes.[103]

The Associators quickly began drilling. More than two thousand men were ready to parade on May 10, in ceremonies arranged to greet the incoming members of the Second Continental Congress. For this session, and hereafter when in Philadelphia, the Congress convened at the State House, having by this time accepted the formal invitation of the Pennsylvania Assembly. Peyton Randolph was elected President, and Charles Thomson, Secretary, a position he held until the Continental Congress was replaced by that of the Federal Constitution. Galloway remained in seclusion at his estate, Trevose, and refused to serve as a delegate, though officially urged to do so. The session of May 11th, at which the delegates presented their credentials, was opened with a prayer by the fiery Rev. Jacob Duché.[104]

McKean, Rodney, and Read represented Delaware as before, and were active in the affairs of the Congress out of all proportion to the size of their constituency. McKean was increasingly active in Philadelphia politics, but his movements here were more difficult to follow than those of his confreres, because he was living in the city and writing letters to his family only when he travelled elsewhere. Rodney and Read, on the other hand, were constantly writing to New Castle, and many of their letters have survived. Also, McKean's involvement with the city committee (which did not keep records) filled almost every hour not consumed by his responsibilities in Congress, which soon came to involve him in more than two dozen committees.

McKean was a member of the city's committee of observation and inspection by August, 1775, and Christopher Marshall noted that he became one of the chairmen of that body on August 18th. The hastily written entry was as follows: "Past seven, to meet [the] Committee in Philosophical Society's Room, where this evening were met forty-nine members, who proceeded to [the] choice of chairmen, when Joseph Reed, George Clymer, Thomas McKean, and Samuel Meredith were appointed to that service . . ." Members were fined sixpence for tardiness, one shilling for absence, and for unexcused departure from the meeting, five shillings. It is odd that the "Philosophical Hall" should have been the revolutionary hub; the Society had rented the Church School House on Second Street in 1770, and from this rather innocuous headquarters the central committee usually operated.[105]

This committee was in communication with the Committee of Safety, and was therefore a different, and no doubt more radical body, but the membership overlapped.[106] The functions of the group, which came to be known as simply "the committee," were to ferret out and expose people who were unfriendly to the Congress and the patriots' cause, to prevent profiteering by the merchants, and to encourage and sponsor defense measures.[107] McKean had joined one or more of the local committees informally in the spring, and was in an excellent position to make himself useful at the time the Congress was gathering. As a designated delegate for the Lower Counties, and a resident of Philadelphia, he had double claim to active membership. Representing the Lower Counties, which would in a few months attain individual status as the Delaware State, he was anxious to keep that province separate and equal in its relationship with the other colonies, and particularly with Pennsylvania; to that end he saw no inconsistency but, indeed, possible advantage in simultaneously serving as a member of the Philadelphia committee.* This kind of plural, and often complementary, office-holding would be characteristic of his entire career. The committee sometimes appointed appropriate persons "to assist the Committee of Safety" in trials or investigations and in various other functions, and by early fall these revolutionary groups had courts, prisons, guards, drum and fife corps, and a complete military apparatus—being virtually in control of the reorganized Associators.

In October, 1775, the committee appointed a sub-committee of seven members to prepare an answer to a "Memorial Presented by the People called Quakers" to the Assembly, against a proposed conscription measure, on the ground that "These gentlemen want to withdraw their persons and their fortunes from the service of the country at the time when their country stands most in need of them." [108] Historians have presented conflicting versions of what happened; the account of one eyewitness, committee member Christopher Marshall, follows:

> Oct. 29 . . . a committee of seven members, to wit, McKean, Clymer, Smith, Jones, Delany, Wilcox and Matlack, were appointed to prepare a draught . . .

---

* When Thayer, Lincoln, and Scharf & Westcott contradict each other frequently, when, in fact, the committee members themselves were imprecise, I had better avoid dogmatism about the relationship of these several committees. But, in agreement with Thayer, and from eyewitness accounts such as C. Marshall's, the detailed account of Scharf & Westcott, the documents found in *Pa. Archives,* Vol. III, 4th ser., the following hypothesis seems workable and tenable: the Philadelphia committee evolved from separate city and county committees, and persons from the Lower Counties (which were still part of the Penn provinces) were allowed to join, especially if of unquestioned patriotism, resident in Philadelphia, and owning property in Pennsylvania proper—all of which qualifications McKean filled. Further, in January, 1775, the conference of county committees had designated the Philadelphia committee as the committee of correspondence for the entire province.

Oct. 30. At six, went to meet [the] Committee at [the] Philosophical Hall, by ticket, where the Remonstrance to the Assembly in opposition to the one presented by the Friends, was read and approved of by the whole body that was there met, being seventy-four members, and we were ordered to meet in a body at this house, and so proceed to present it to the Assembly to-morrow morning at nine o'clock.

Oct. 31. Just before nine, went to meet the Committee at the Philosophical Hall. At ten, went, two by two, being sixty-six in number, to the State House. Our chairman, George Clymer, and Mr. McKean presented our Petition to the Speaker of the House, who ordered it to be read while we were all present, which was done accordingly.[109]

That very day—such was the speed of events—the city of Philadelphia received news of the King's proclamation that *all* the colonies were in open rebellion, and as Marshall noted, he "therein includes all his subjects within his realm that hold or maintain any correspondence with us . . ." With this news came the realization that the colonies' last hope for reconciliation, the "Olive Branch Petition," had been rejected. A few days before, on October 24, the first American state funeral had taken place, that of Peyton Randolph of Virginia. The services were held at Christ Church, the sermon delivered by Rev. Jacob Duché, chaplain to the Congress. Congress attended as a body, and so did the Philadelphia committee; a demonstration of unity, as well as of respect, which must have gratified McKean.[110]

A few days later, on November 9, 1775, the energetic Benedict Arnold, who had attacked Ticonderoga in May, reached the walls of Quebec, after a spectacular march across the wilderness of northern Maine. On November 13, 1775, the city of Montreal surrendered to a large, well organized American army under the command of General Richard Montgomery. In any consideration of the dilly-dallying in Philadelphia, the Americans' aggressive thrusts at Canada during 1775 must not be forgotten, efforts which almost succeeded in adding that vast province to the revolution, thereby making Congress the *Continental* Congress which it aspired to be.[111] Curiously enough, some conservatives like Robert Morris, who voted against independence in 1776, nevertheless heartily supported the invasion of Canada in 1775. The rhetoric of the public debates in the Quaker City was deceptive; the revolutionary leaders were committing treason in a big way, and were engaged in a military gamble of gigantic proportions. It is futile to speculate as to whether these leaders were indeed working for independence in January, 1776—as if men like McKean needed to be convinced of what they should do by reading Tom Paine's *Common Sense*.

Along with the activity of the committees, the work of the Congress proceeded apace. Those participants with a sense of history were amazed at the scope and intricacy of their task. As early as July, 1775, John Adams wrote to his wife, "When 50 or 60 men have a Constitution to form for a great empire, at the same time that they have a country of 1500 miles extent to fortify, millions to arm and train, a naval power to begin, an extensive commerce to regulate, numerous tribes of Indians to negotiate with, a standing army of 27,000 men to raise, pay,

victual and officer, I really pity these 50 or 60 men." [112] Adams was not borrowing trouble; he and his fellow delegates to the Congress *did* have these heavy
responsibilities, and they well knew it, even if they still had a year of hard work
ahead, to get the middle colonies to accept a declaration of independence. Mc-
Kean was one of those who understood the monumental challenge that confronted the rebels; a fact which John Adams emphasized at the time of his death,
writing, "In 1774 [at the first Congress] I became acquainted with McKean, Rodney, and Henry. Those three appeared to me to see more clearly to the end of
the business than any others of the whole body." [113]

The letters of Caesar Rodney to his younger brother Thomas provide a first-
hand knowledge of the reactions of the Delaware delegates at the time the Congress was convening. On May 8 he wrote from New Castle to his brother, at the
family estate near Dover, listing delegates from the south who were sailing up
the Delaware River, or travelling overland, on their way to Philadelphia. He
and George Read, he said, were to be accompanied part way from New Castle by
some of the local militia.[114] The next day the Assembly resolved that the sum
of five hundred pounds was to be drawn by the Trustees of the several Loan
Offices for the expenses of the three delegates.[115] On May 11 Rodney wrote from
Philadelphia describing the public welcome staged for the Boston delegation the
previous day, which was "Intended to Shew their approbation of the Conduct of
the good people of that Government, in the distressing Scituation of affairs
there." He learned that General Gage had acted somewhat against his better
judgment in ordering the troops to Lexington, but had been trying to destroy
arms, provisions, and bridges, and if possible to capture John Hancock and other
delegates to the Congress. He reported a conversation in which Hancock told
him "he had been to see that Small Company at Lexington Exercise, and had
not left them more than ten minutes when the Troops Came up, and that they
had no Suspision of any . . . ." [116]

Rodney's letter of June 20, 1775, contained more serious business: "I Can now
let you into a part of our proceedings in Congress—We have ordered Two Millions of Dollars to be Struck here as a Continental paper Currency, for the de-
fraying the Expences of Defending our Constitutional Rights and priviledges . . .
We have appointed Coll. George Whasington [sic] General & Commander in
Chief of all the Colony forces. General Ward (now with the army before Boston)
to be Major General & Second in Command . . ." [117] On June 29 Rodney and
McKean jointly wrote to the newly appointed General Washington, at his camp
outside of Boston, a letter which contained information, otherwise not recorded,
concerning one of McKean's pre-war activities: "The Bearer hereof Mr. John
Parke has taken his degrees of Bachelor and Master of Arts in the College of this
City and studied the law under one of us (Mr. McKean) for almost four years.
He is an Ensign in the 2d Battalion of the Militia here, and is desirous of serving
his country as a Volunteer under you." [118] Washington dutifully replied on
August 30 that he had made Mr. Parke an assistant Quartermaster-General, "an
office indispensably necessary in discharge of that important and troublesome

business." Moreover, he tactfully expressed the hope that Congressmen would appoint a few more officers from the colonies to the south of New England in the future, if possible.[119] Washington was never keen on New Englanders.

A tempest in the banished teapot occurred in Philadelphia in November, 1775, as Lady Washington was passing through the city on her way to join her husband. A ball was planned in her honor at the New Tavern, but certain leading Whigs objected that social affairs of this sort "appeared to be contrary to the Eighth Resolve of Congress" and asked her not to attend. The inevitable committee, "which was large and respectable," according to Christopher Marshall, met at the Philosophical Hall to consider the matter and concluded that no such festive welcome should be given either that evening or in the future. Not everyone was in agreement: a number of Southerners felt that the Philadelphians and New Englanders were being narrow-minded and puritanical. Christopher Marshall, who apparently was the one who had stirred up the tempest, matter-of-factly reported, "Col. Harrison came to rebuke Samuel Adams for using his influence for the stopping of this entertainment, which he declared was legal, just and laudable . . . all to no effect; so, as he came out of humor, he so returned, to appearance." [120]

The McKeans were among those who were *not* in a mood for having a ball, to honor visiting celebrities, that evening. Their first child, a boy, born on November 1, 1775, had died the same day.[121] The strain of these hectic months had been too much for Sally; the transition in her life from carefree independence to being the wife of an activist, responsible for his six children by a previous marriage, had been altogether too sudden. The war was reaching a critical stage at that point, too, with the surrender of Montreal to an American expeditionary force in November, and the imminent possibility of capturing Quebec. Others might not realize how high were the stakes for which the revolutionary leaders were gambling, but the McKeans were caught up in the effort too completely to be unaware or emotionally uninvolved. One of Benedict Arnold's right-hand men at Quebec (the man to whom he entrusted his dispatches for aid to General Wooster at Montreal, General Schuyler at Albany, and the Continental Congress) was Edward Antill of New Jersey, the brother-in-law of McKean's deceased brother Robert.[122] Sally McKean had to recover from her personal loss as best she could; her husband was too busy to help.

Meanwhile, for several years trouble had flared up intermittently over a fertile border area claimed by both Pennsylvania and Connecticut, and now the dispute threatened bloodshed and division which colonial unity could ill afford. In September McKean and Thomas Willing had moved that Congress should take an official position on the matter. Unsure of authority to arbitrate between individual colonies, even less sure of their ability to enforce such arbitration, Congress nevertheless attempted the task of reconciling this territorial conflict. On Saturday, November 4, Congress appointed McKean and Silas Deane of Connecticut "to wait upon the Honorable House of Assembly of Pennsylvania, now setting" with a copy of a resolution hastily prepared upon the subject.[123] The choice of a delegate who represented the Lower Counties, not Pennsylvania proper, in conjunction with Connecticut's representative, indicated Congressional recogntion of McKean's dual roles. And, thus, McKean became involved from the start in a dispute which amounted to an undeclared war between two states— a dispute that was not settled until he became Governor of Pennsylvania.[124] He also developed negative feelings about Silas Deane.

At about the same time, McKean was active in forwarding money to "the distressed citizens of Boston"—a project that had been begun as a propaganda stunt after the Boston Port Bill, but had turned into a serious relief project. George Read and Nicholas Van Dyke had conducted a subscription in Newcastle County in February, 1775, collecting some nine hundred dollars for the Boston committee, and "negotiat[ed] this matter with a friend in Philadelphia" for the transmittal of funds to the committee "for the distressed poor." [125]

Throughout the summer McKean had been raising money, and supplying arms and ammunition for the burgeoning military efforts over which Congress was attempting to assume control. As early as June 10, 1775, Congress had decided that each colony must provide the general public with processed goods, raw materials, or manufacturing sites, for which the colony would be credited. The Lower Counties were to collect saltpeter and sulphur to be made into gun powder in the city of Philadelphia.[126] McKean's first committee assignment in the Second Continental Congress was to work with James Wilson in setting up a Treasury, starting on July 29 when Michael Hillegas and George Clymer were appointed joint treasurers of the United Colonies, required to give a bond of $100,000 each.[127] McKean and Wilson also served on a committee with Eliphalet Dyer and Benjamin Harrison, which prepared instructions for recruiting officers.[128]

The most important of McKean's committees, however, was the Secret Committee, formed on September 19, 1775, for the purpose of obtaining gun powder and ordnance. Nine members were elected to this committee: Thomas McKean, Benjamin Franklin, Philip Livingston, John Dickinson, Silas Deane, Thomas Willing, John Alsop, John Langdon, and Samuel Ward. Five were to be a quorum, and "business [was to be] conducted with as much secrecy as the nature of the service will possibly admit." [129] McKean was appointed clerk of this Secret Committee.[130] On November 8 the committee was endeavoring to procure brass field pieces, and thousands of small arms, by arranging exports to "the foreign West Indies . . . as they [might] deem necessary." [131] Transactions of this sort immediately involved them with the French, the Spanish, and the Dutch, from whom they hoped to receive, and did receive, aid against the British. The Secret Committee, in many respects, was the forerunner of the Treasury Department, and must be distinguished from the Committee of Secret Correspondence, created two months later, which evolved into the Committee of Foreign Affairs in 1777, and eventually the State Department. In this period both committees operated on an *ad hoc* basis, and their functions and membership overlapped.[132]

British legislation on the subject of trade had by this time placed an intense strain on inter-colonial unity. The so-called Restraining Acts of March-April, 1775, had closed the ports of all the colonies except New York, the Lower Counties, North Carolina, and Georgia.[133] The Congress, consequently, began a protracted debate on whether British customs houses should be closed in all the colonies, to put the favored colonies on an equal basis with the others. The necessities of trade, international credit, a navy, and of closer political union, were all made starkly clear in the course of a lengthy discussion in committee-of-the whole, in which members from every section of the country participated.[134]

If any of the colonies had had any inclination to "go it alone," this was the moment when the final decision had to be made. The favored colonies, of course, were not likely to follow a separate course; if they had been, they would not have been favored. Nevertheless, it is significant that McKean spoke out emphatically against separating the interests of one colony from the others, in spite of the fact that the Lower Counties had been exempted from the British restrictions. Adams reported his friend's remarks as follows:

> *McKean*. I have 4 Reasons for putting the favoured Colonies upon a footing with the rest. 1st. is to disappoint the Ministry. Their design was insidious. 2. I would not have it believed by Ministry or other Colonies that those Colonies had less Virtue than others. 3. I have a Reconciliation in View, it would be in the Power of those Colonies, it might become their Interest to prolong the War. 4. I believe Parliament has done or will do it for us, i.e. put us on the same footing. I would choose that the exempted Colonies should have the Honour of it. Not clear that this is the best Way of putting them upon a Footing. If we should be successful in Canada, I would be for opening our Trade to some Places in G. B., Jamaica, &c.[135]

The debate lasted for weeks; the date of McKean's speech, outlined above, was October 12, 1775. On superficial reading, his third and his fourth points appear contradictory, but the latter was obviously closer to the general tenor of his argument. In mentioning a "reconciliation" he may well have been indulging in the ambiguous patois of the politician, but Adams would hardly have made these notes, disjoined though they are, had he not thought each point significant. His third and crucial point was that the exempted colonies might find it in their interest to prolong the war *even if a reconciliation were to come into view*. The fourth point made clear his expectation that the British government would soon penalize all the colonies, no matter what they did. This is in fact what happened under the Prohibitory Act of December, 1775.[136]

McKean was adaptable in his thinking on practical details; although he had a distinct animus against the British, he was not taking a doctrinaire line. If circumstances changed, the policy of the Congress on trade should be adjusted accordingly, but always for the purpose of strengthening the union. He was not thinking of one colony alone, and his eyes were fixed on the armies in Canada, where the fate of the continent might be determined. The final decision strengthened the Association, and the Congress thanked the four colonies for not taking advantage of the Restraining Acts. Some exportation was to be permitted to pay for the importation of arms and ammunition.

McKean's attitude towards independence was emphatically clear by the fall of 1775. Several weeks before the debate on the exempted colonies, John Adams recorded in his *Diary*, for September 23, "I walked a long Time this Morning, backward and forward, in the Statehouse Yard with Paca, McKean, and Johnson.

McKean has no idea of any Right of Authority in Parliament. Paca contends for an Authority and Right to regulate Trade, &c." [137] Thus, despite his legal loyalties, McKean was casting his lot with the American assemblies, or rather, with the Congress and its network of revolutionary committees, as against the British Parliament—while fully aware that his instructions from the Lower Counties were still "to concert and agree upon, such further Measures, as shall appear . . . best calculated for the Accomodation of the unhappy differences between Great-Britain and the Colonies, on a Constitutional Foundation, which the House most ardently wishes for . . ." [138] Those who complained, as did Joseph Reed, that it was all "a terrible wordy war," or who maintained that the struggle was "for the preservation of privileges, not for independence" were merely confused, he thought.[139] Plenary power, of all sorts, would have to be transferred to America. This much was clear. But how far such power should be transferred to new social classes in this country—that was a question of tactics. McKean would transfer power only so far as was needed to obtain independence.

He would grant greater representation to the western counties of Pennsylvania, and even to the working classes in the city and county of Philadelphia, in order to offset the conservatism of the metropolis, but he was certainly not in favor of a general social revolution, or of upsetting the existing pattern of property-holding.[140] Throughout his career he was consistent on these matters though at times he may have confused or misled observers. This was not one of the issues, however, on which he could be accused of dissimulation—at least, not at this time. The address of the city committee, signed by McKean as chairman, and published in the *Evening Post*, May 25, 1775, specifically stated: "[We] have no design or wish to alter those parts of the charter of laws of the province which secure to every man the enjoyment of his property, liberty, and the sacred rights of conscience. [We] wish only to see alterations made in such of them as *relate to representation in the province* and such as render the consent of the king and his governor necessary to give efficacy to our laws." [141] The city committee in this document was explaining its longstanding criticisms of the Assembly, and justifying its demand for a conference of county committees. As revolutionary rhetoric goes, the language was far from inflammatory.

People were baffled, however, by the variety of opinions expressed on all sides with ever-increasing stridency. Some of the most prominent leaders were radical on one issue, conservative on another. Families were divided, friendships were strained. Social discourse became difficult, even for those who had known each other for years, especially if there was the slightest suspicion that privately stated views were being quoted in hostile circles. The complaint of "A Reasonable Whigess," in a letter-to-the-editor in the *Evening Post* of November 16, 1775, was a clever, tongue-in-cheek gibe at the humorless dogmatism of the times, when old-fashioned values were constantly held up for reconsideration. There was more than a hint of conservative scorn for the manifold demands of the radicals:

> I am a young lady, who delights much in politics; and, if I know my own heart, am a warm friend to America. But my misfortune is, that some times, whilst I am contending for what I think is true liberty, I am told that I am a Tory; and perhaps

> the next day, expressing the same sentiments, that I am an outrageous Whig. As
> there are many of my acquaintance labouring under the same inconvenience I should
> be glad if any of your correspondents would favour me with a clear definition of the
> above characters, that I may conduct my conversation in future as becomes . . .
>
> A Reasonable Whigess [142]

The less amusing side of the prevailing confusion, and disagreement, arose
from the tendency of many over-vigilant committees to turn themselves into spies,
or political police. McKean was eventually to be known as the Grand Inquisitor
of the middle states, if not of the revolution itself; indeed, he was later to be
called the Fouquier-Tinville of the American Revolution. At this moment, however, he was still busy organizing resistance groups, setting up the revolutionary
apparatus, and gathering the threads of control into the hands of the Continental
Congress, which was to coordinate the local committees.[143]

McKean was not obsessed with details, but he never underestimated their
cumulative value; he was well aware that minor matters could define a much
greater principle. For example, when on December 14, 1775, he informed the
Congress that people in the middle colonies were still selling and drinking tea,
he was reminded that Congress had given them permission to do so. The actual
question then posed was whether the local committees should interfere with prac-
tices that the Congress had permitted. On February 13, 1776, Congress directed
"that McKean should request the City Comee to delay publishing the Sellers of
Tea in the Papers till further Order," thereby assuming control. In April Congress decided to allow the use of tea already in the country, but to forbid further
importation of it, a policy which McKean had strongly advocated on January
12, 1776.[144] The notorious beverage was obviously incidental to the question of
Congressional control. McKean was not hounding the dissidents personally, but
he was deeply involved and concerned over the necessity of unified action, and
clearly understood the importance of directing committee efforts into politically
useful channels. His opponents never forgave his efforts in these matters—a Tory
named John Smythe described him as "the violent raging rebel McKean." [145]

Yet if Tories could be found who were corresponding with Lord Dartmouth
and the British ministry, and if these Tories could be implicated in requests
for the dispatching of British troops, or the hiring of mercenaries, or fomenting
servile insurrection, or countenancing depredations by the savages on the frontier
—much ground could be gained. None of these possibilities was too far-fetched
to be believed in 1775.[146] In fact, the committees were already busy, as witness
a detailed letter from Caesar Rodney in Philadelphia to his brother Thomas as
early as October 9, 1775, which contained an un-selfconscious narrative of the
vigilante tactics of one group of radicals:

> On Friday about eleven Oclock at night Doct. Bearsly [or Kearsley] of this City
> was seized by Order of the Committee of Observation, for having wrote Letters to
> England injurious & destructive to us in the American Contnt, and wicked with
> respect to this City, and is now confined in Goal I gather with one Brooks who came
> here with Governor Sheen. Mr. Carter, an apothecary, who was in partnership with
> Speakman, and one Mr. Snowden, all of whom were aiding the Doct. in his plan—

You must know Bearsly has been a Considerable time since marked out as a thorough-power Torry, for which, together with his having insulted the people he was (since I came to Town last) carted through the streets.—But the offense for which he is now confined is this circumstance; On Wednesday last a ship sailed out of this Port for London, in which Mr. Carter was going passenger. A few days before she sailed Young Dewees, son of the Sheriff, went to pay Doct. Bearsly some money and coming suddenly in his Room found him and Carter together, with a bundle of Papers before them, which they gathered up in seeming confusion. This, with Bearsly's Torry Carrictor gave Dewees suspition, and he accordingly informed a few of the Committee who kept the matter secret, let the ship sail, and the passengers go down to Chester by Land to go on Board. On Thursday evening which was the day the passengers went, a small party was sent down to Chester. They stayed there that night in Cogg [incognito] and saw the passengers go on Board next morning. Then they immediately pushed on board, seized and examined Mr. Carter who in a little time told them that there were several Letters from Doct. Bearsly & Mr. Brooks and one Mr. Snowden, that he had the charge of them [the letters] and was concerned with them in the plan they had concocted, But that the Letters were then in the Custody of a woman down in the Cabin and that she had them concealed in a pocket sewed to the inside of her Shifty-Tails . . . The Letters were to Lord Dartmouth and other Ministers of State . . . The purpose and design was proposing their sending to Philadelphia five thousand Regulars, on which condition they would engage five thousand more here to join them . . . for that Great numbers of those who now wear Cockades and Uniforms were hearty in the Ministerial Cause . . .[147]

The Dr. Kearsley who was roughed up in this incident was a prominent citizen who had been elected to the American Philosophical Society on March 8, 1768, the same day that McKean was elected. He was well known to the revolutionary leaders and to everyone else in the city, but his prominence did not save him. Soon afterwards he "went out of his mind," and before the war was over he died "in confinement." Another Tory manhandled by the same mob was Isaac Hunt, a lawyer and graduate of the College of Philadelphia in the class of 1763. Hunt was the father of Leigh Hunt, the eminent English writer, who "but for these few hectic and brutal days in Philadelphia . . . might have been the first great American critic." Although Hunt was not treated as badly as Kearsley, he was hit in the eye by a stone before he was rescued, and this "dimmed his sight for life," according to his distinguished son.[148]

Thus, the Philadelphia committee, with McKean as one of its chairmen, was vigorously enforcing revolutionary law, even before the Assembly had been replaced, while the Continental Congress was attempting to assume over-all control. A reign of terror was being introduced, with selected victims as its targets. Bloodshed was kept to a minimum, systematic torture had not yet been thought of, but force and public humiliation were freely applied. Moderates like Dickinson were hardly aware of what was happening, and no one bothered to tell them.[149] But Tories like Galloway, who sometimes woke in the morning to receive pointed and ominous tokens of hostility, such as a parcel containing a carefully rigged noose, recognized the threat and fled the city, or conspired with British authorities to secure military aid.[150]

The leaders of the revolution were fully cognizant of what they were doing, but even they had no way of telling how far the violence would go. In the coming year McKean would find that many of his associates had become more radical than he, in his own mind, had ever intended to be. Perhaps Judge Smyth of New Jersey had had a point when he warned the Grand Jury against "the tyranny at [their] own doors." A certain blindness to the arbitrary and sometimes capricious conduct of the revolutionary committees was a necessary failing in the establishment of a separate American nationality.

Chapter 11

Independence, 1776

McKean's long-continued services to the cause of independence have never been fully recognized, because his instructions from the government of Delaware were to work for "the restoration of that harmony with the parent state which is so essential to the security and happiness of the whole British empire," [151] and these instructions prevented him from speaking his mind openly until the last critical days before the Declaration of Independence. He was as vigorous in promoting the national cause as any Adams or Lee, yet for months he had to work behind the scenes. His positions of influence in both Pennsylvania and Delaware gave him a strategic importance that no other member of the radical faction could duplicate, but his fate was that he had "to do the work of the Lord deceitfully," as John Adams put it.[152]

The radicals of New England and the South, confronted by the stubborn opposition of the middle colonies, sought instructions from their governments *ordering* them to vote for independence. In this way they hoped to sway the undecided, and bring the reluctant governments into line. The middle colonies, whether governed by their old colonial legislatures (as were Pennsylvania and Delaware) or by emerging revolutionary governments (as were New York, New Jersey, and Maryland), had issued strict instructions to their delegates in the Continental Congress to oppose independence. As a last resort, if persuasion failed, the radicals were prepared to overthrow any government that held out too long—and in the event they had to do this in Pennsylvania. The others were brought into the fold, in the nick of time, by a combination of propaganda, patience, and pressure skillfully applied.

McKean was working hand-in-glove with the radicals, but could not say so, then or later, without exposing himself to political attack. Instead, he adopted a policy for which a subsequent generation might have coined the slogan, "All power to the Congress!" * The only revolutionary group which he fully trusted was the Congress; he had been a member of the Stamp Act Congress and the First Continental Congress, and he knew the delegates from the other colonies. Here he had a comfortable majority, growing from day to day, and his policy was to refer all controversial matters to this body. By so doing, he could accomplish his purpose without violating his official instructions. In questions of regulating trade, distributing tea, supervising prisoner-of-war arrangements, inspecting jails, adjudicating inter-colonial disputes—always his vote was to transfer the decisions to Congress. The result of this policy might be strict, or it might be lenient, so far as his opponents were concerned, but the point in each case was to expand the jurisdiction of Congress.

As an indication of the Congressional factions with whom he was dealing, a list (See Table 1) of the ninety-two delegates who attended Congress from May, 1775, through the crucial first week of July, 1776, shows twenty-one conservatives, sixteen moderates, and fifty-one radicals—a clear majority for the radical faction. Four delegates remained uncommitted or uncertain, two conservatives finally chose another extreme, becoming Tory, but the eventual shift was toward the radical block, joining the men who were sure of their attitude toward independence, and clear as to the measures they would take to achieve it. The latter were of course aware of the growing discontent, the rising but aimless anger of the common people. Almost instinctively they kept probing in piecemeal actions which they hoped would not alienate the moderates, in order to provoke overreactions by the British, which would increase the local resentment. They also engaged in daring military gambles. In the process of deciding how far to go, they divided into factions which eventually solidified into the forerunners of political parties. These blocs were to be partly sectional and partly economic, but more than anything else they were the effect of personal temperament. The circumstances which influenced their development were as follows:

> Whereas the First Congress set out to do some fairly specific things (frame a set of grievances and determine a means of redress) and was in this sense an expanded Stamp Act Congress, the Second Continental Congress, had, from the very beginning, a war to administer in all its military and economic aspects. The effect of these new circumstances upon party development should be fairly obvious: while a political party could hardly develop in the space of two months, the growth of parties in a body meeting upon a permanent basis would be almost inevitable; and while the framing of a petition and a non-intercourse association might draw like-minded individuals together, the formation of political parties would be much more stimulated by the appointment of military officers, supply commissioners and emissaries abroad; the creation of a scheme of national finance, and the formulation of a federal system of government. Such were the fruits of Lexington and Concord.[153]

McKean was in the peculiar position of representing the Lower Counties in Congress, and informally representing Congress in Pennsylvania. He used the

* Lenin's slogan "All power to the Soviets" accomplished the same purpose. "Power to the People" is equally revolutionary, but it has a less specific strategic function.

authority derived from his Delaware constituents to perform his functions in Congress, and his prestige as a Congressman to influence the city committee in Philadelphia, to call meetings of the county committees to support the Congress, and so forth. No one could pin him down; he never violated the instructions of his constituents when he was acting in his capacity as their agent, but acting in other capacities he might be taking an entirely different line. By positioning himself to act in a dozen different areas simultaneously he freed himself to do what he wanted, though he could not talk freely in the Lower Counties until after Congress had made its decisive moves in May, 1776, urging the colonies to set up new governments, where "no government sufficient to the exigencies of their affairs" had previously been established.[154] Then, and only then, could he go back to New Castle, and boldly urge the Delaware government to make an open break with the past.

For months he had been working to strengthen Congress, and to build up the radical faction within it; now, at last, he could throw off the mask of compromise and openly advocate independence. The Delaware Assembly finally gave him the instructions he asked for on June 15, 1776, but even then they could not bring themselves to use the scare-word "independence." [155] McKean was wearing so many hats in the months that were climaxed by the Declaration of Independence, and rushing from one meeting to another with such split-second timing, that his role was blurred, and almost no one could define it. The following list of the positions he held omits his various trusteeships and temporary appointments, but it may help the reader to grasp the more important of his revolutionary functions:

Lower Counties
> Judge in New Castle: Court of Common Pleas, Quarter Sessions, and Orphans' Court, starting 1765

> Member of the Assembly, 1762–1779
> Member, Committee of Correspondence, starting 1766
> Speaker, at time of his wife's death, 1773 [156]
> Speaker, again, at time of British invasion, 1777
> (Acting President of Delaware, briefly, fall of 1777)
> Member, Constitutional Convention, Aug-Sept 1776

Pennsylvania
> Member of the city committee in Philadelphia. By virtue of a public meeting this committee became the committee of correspondence for the province.
> Chairman, starting August, 1775
> Colonel, 4th Battalion Pennsylvania Associators, May-Sept, 1776
> Chairman, or principal orator, at several mass meetings
> President, Provincial Conference, June 18–25, 1776
> Chief Justice under the new government, 1777–1799

Continental Congress
> (representing the Lower Counties—Delaware—*not* Pennsylvania)
> Member, Stamp Act Congress, 1765

Member, First Continental Congress, 1774
Member, Second Continental Congress, 1775-6, 1778-83
    President of the Congress, July-November, 1781
Member, Committees too numerous to mention

At the beginning of the year 1776 all eyes were focused on Quebec, which seemed to be the key to the continent. In the spring of 1775 Benedict Arnold and Ethan Allen had advocated invading Canada at once, before the British reinforced it. Congress hesitated, but was impressed by the danger of attack from the north along the traditional invasion routes used by the French in the previous war. On June 27, 1775, Congress sanctioned the invasion of Canada as a preventative operation, and also because its hand had been tipped by the motley groups which had attacked Ticonderoga and Crown Point even as the delegates were assembling.[157]

With Congressional approval Philip Schuyler, and later Richard Montgomery, marched through upper New York and forced the British General Carleton to abandon Montreal on November 13th. At the same time Benedict Arnold, a New Haven merchant-turned-general, who had received the surrender of Ticonderoga, led a hardy band northward through the Maine territory; they arrived at the St. Lawrence River, opposite Quebec, on November 8th, in bad shape from the hardships of the expedition, but determined to risk all in an assault on the city.* A few weeks later a small force under Henry Knox hauled mortars and cannon across the snow from Ticonderoga to Cambridge, Massachusetts, thereby rendering Boston untenable to the British, and forcing the evacuation of that city in the middle of March.

McKean had been in official correspondence with the armies of the north for several months, and on January 8, 1776—about the time that rumors of disaster at Quebec began to circulate in Philadelphia—he was one of three men appointed to "devise ways and means for furnishing the battalions destined for Canada with necessaries, and for expediting their march thither." [158] Not until January 19th, however, did Congress receive the full story from Edward Antill (brother-in-law of McKean's late brother Robert), who had left Quebec to obtain help on January 2nd, and arrived in Philadelphia via Montreal and Albany.[159]

A desperate attempt had been made on New Year's Eve, in a blinding blizzard, to storm the city of Quebec. Montgomery had been killed, Arnold badly wounded, some three hundred of their men taken prisoner, and a hundred more were killed, wounded, or missing. McKean was deeply involved in the ensuing effort to pump more men and supplies into the Canadian venture. He also proposed the establishment of a Canadian regiment, through the cooperation of some Anglo-American merchants in Montreal, with Moses Hazen as Colonel and

---

* The best recent account is in Gustave Lanctot, *Canada & the American Revolution, 1774–1783* (Toronto, 1967), translated from the French. Lanctot explains the ambivalent reaction of the French Canadians to the American, and later the French, bids for their support. The Americans were thought of as "les Bostonais," and unfortunately, Bostonians were considered violently anti-Catholic.

Antill as Lt. Colonel, and voted for the printing of some paper money to be sent to Canada to assist in the recruiting.*

On January 19th, the day of Antill's discouraging report, McKean wrote to George Read in New Castle, "I embraced the first opportunity of moving the Congress, after your favor of the 17th came to hand, to appoint the Field Officers in the Delaware Battalion and they have accordingly been just now elected by ballot, to wit, John Haslet, Esquire, Colonel and Gunning Bedford, Esquire, as Lieutenant Colonel . . . My dear Sir, you must come up here as soon as you possibly can, for I am almost wore down, being upon Four standing Committees, besides occasional ones, and owing to the multiplicity of business." [160] The pressure must indeed have been intense; McKean was not in the habit of complaining.

The multiplicity of business was compounded by citizens reluctant to cooperate, whose contracts with Congress were written for profit, not patriotism. The Secret Committee was constantly harried by the lack of gunpowder and was attempting to expedite its manufacture; at that time most of the colonies' powder mills were in the Philadelphia area. Here "the manufacturing of powder is carried on with Considerable dispatch and advantage," explained Paul Revere's instructions from Massachusetts, and he was "desired to . . . possess yourself as far as you Can of the Knowledge of making powder. VIZ Obtain an Exact plan of making powder [and] powder mill . . ." Armed with a note from Robert Morris to Oswald Eve, which remarked, pointedly, "A Powder Mill in New England cannot in the least degree affect your manufacture nor be of any disadvantage to you," Revere called upon Eve, owner of the mill near Frankford and under contract to Congress. Eve complied by briskly walking Revere through the mill, non-stop, without pause for observation or question, and with no advice offered. Revere later turned to a fellow New Englander, a canny man with the right friends on the right committees, and a month after his return he received the vitally needed plan from Sam Adams. In 1778 Chief Justice McKean neither commented nor questioned when Oswald Eve was attainted as a traitor.[161]

There was also "the Matter of inlisting Apprentices and small Debtors," which was referred to a three-man committee on January 27th. McKean was chairman of the committee, and for a short time looked with favor on this method of raising troops, but finally agreed with John Adams, who "has convinced me that you will get no army upon such terms. Even in Pennsylvania, the most desperate of imported laborers cannot be obtained in any numbers upon such terms. Farmers and traders give much more encouragement than laborers and journeyman." Such enlistments were soon rejected as bad policy.[162]

---

* JCC, IV, 78. Also Burnett, *Letters*, I, 332. On Jan. 27, 1776 "McKean moved on Behalf of Col. Hazen that he may have the Rank of First Colonel in Canada otherwise he declines the Service . . ." Two years later, on Sept. 29, 1778, Hazen wrote to McKean: "You, Sir, had a share in forming the original Establishment of this Regiment, which has been continued under your Patronage and Protection—I am particularly happy, that it has not Disappointed your Expectations . . . in Justice to the worthy officers I have the Honr. to Command, several of whom were appointed by your Recommendation, I must request your Interposition and friendly offices with Congress in their favour." (McKean Papers, I, HSP.)

Another of McKean's regular responsibilities in the Congress was his membership on the Committee of Prisoners. This committee was a veritable supreme court in its own right, and the *Journals of the Continental Congress* are filled with indications of its power. McKean's career as a Chief Justice can almost be said to have started here. A few illustrations will suffice to indicate not only his judicial role, but also the way in which the functions of this committee spilled over into military intelligence, and even into the directing of the war. A conservative delegate from New Jersey, Richard Smith, was carefully keeping track of McKean in his *Diary:*

Jan 30, 1776
      McKean informed Congress that 200 and odd Men in Tryon County are inlisted in the King's Regiment of Royal Emigrants. Mr. McKean [to whom the report below had been brought] was desired to acquaint Gen. Schuyler of it by Letter . . .

                                              Philadelphia, Jan 30, 1776
      Sir,
      A certain Duncan Campbell, Captain in the Royal Scotch Emigrants and now a Prisoner here, in a conversation yesterday with Capt. Wade of the Militia of this City, who is a relation to Sir John [Johnson] so far forgot himself as to mention to him that there were two hundred of that regiment in the neighborhood of Sir John.
      These Soldiers are supposed to be the McDonalds and Highlanders settled on the lands of Sir John.
      I am desired by the Congress to communicate this information to you, that these Soldiers and their Officers may be apprehended and detained as prisoners of war and not considered merely as Tories. If they are Soldiers and can be secured, they may possibly be exchanged for the like numbers of our friends in Quebec. [Thus, there would be practical advantages in giving jurisdiction to the Congress.]

Feb. 6, 1776
      Col. Heard attending with 18 Tories from Queens County, Crane, McKean, and E. Rutledge were named to take his account of the Expedition, which being reported, the Prisoners are ordered under Guard to N. York to be examined and secured by the Convention there, who are to report thereon to Us.[163]

Mar. 28, 1776
      McKean informed Congress that the Tory Prisoners in Philadelphia Goal have attempted an Escape and have provided Implements and a Ladder to escape this Night, whereupon Mr. McKean is to direct the Sheriff to confine Conolly, Smith, and Kirkland separately and get a sufficient Guard from the Barracks. [Kirkland actually made his escape May 7. He was a Colonel from South Carolina.][164]

And one of many such entries in *The Journals of the Continental Congress:*

April 5, 1776
      The Committee for Prisoners brought in a report, which was read: [Report in the handwriting of Thomas McKean.]
      . . . maturely considered the Letters from [a Brigadier General, a Lieutenant Colonel, two Captains, and Lieutenant, a Surgeon, and a civilian.]

. . . [Captain Duncan] Campbell be permitted to live with his wife in Burlington in Western Division of New Jersey . . .

That a list of the Prisoners of war in each Colony be made out and transmitted to the House of Assembly, Council, or Committee of Safety of such Colonies respectively, and that they be authorized and requested to cause a strict observance of the terms on which such prisoners have been enlarged [allowed to be at large], and also to take especial care that none of those confined by order of the Congress be suffered to escape; and also that the allowance to each prisoner be punctually paid by the Presidents of the Convention or of the Council or Committee of Safety of the Colony in which he resides; and where there are no Conventions by the Speakers of Assembly; which said Presidents or Speakers are hereby authorized from time to time to draw for the sums advanced in pursuance of this resolution upon the President of the Congress. [This would be through the Claims Committee, of which McKean was a member.] [165]

Finally the Committee and Congress reached a decision, and McKean wrote to General Philip Schuyler, on April 13, 1776:

. . . upon the whole the Congress have directed the Committee on Prisoners, of which I am one, to take your opinion, "Whether . . . the hostages taken in Tryon county [should be permitted to go home.]"

I congratulate you upon the evacuation of Boston . . . We have heard nothing lately about the much talked of Commissioners, but are determined to be prepared at all points.[166]

Thus McKean was working for independence with might and main in the Congress, no matter what his stance in the Lower Counties during these months. According to a Tory Captain, John Smythe, McKean's behavior toward the committee's detainees was sometimes harsh and threatening. On a visit of inspection early in 1776, "the violent raging rebel McKean introduced himself by abusing in the grossest terms, the King, Parliament and Ministry; the whole army and navy; and particularly Lord Dunmore and General Prescott. He told us for our comfort, that we should be retained for retaliation; that if Allen, or Proctor, or any of their leaders were executed, we should share the same fate; said we ought to think ourselves happy, not to be in irons, as their prisoners were always kept in irons by the British." [167]

McKean's severity in this instance was more a matter of policy than of temper, for he had already had occasion to write directly to General Prescott with his complaint that the American officers and soldiers "who were so unfortunate as to fall into the hands of the British forces both by land and sea, were treated with unprecedentd severities, which would probably compell [sic] the Colonists to retaliate . . ." [168] Furthermore, Smythe's case was a difficult one. He had escaped once, which aggravated matters, and on recapture had complained so bitterly of prison conditions that a Congressional committee was sent to investigate.[169] McKean may have suspected that Smythe would spread whatever he told him, as indeed he did, and that he would be a convenient channel of communication to the more important British leaders. In other cases he dealt with prisoners leniently, exchanging them or permitting them to live with their families, and he was always alert to prevent anyone's defrauding prisoners of their property.[170]

Committee assignments in the Congress were haphazard and, at this distance, difficult to follow. For every permanent committee there were usually several *ad hoc* committees for related functions, which could just as well have been given to the main committee. As an example of the Congressional method, on December 9, 18, and 26, 1775, and on February 2, 1776, four different committees were appointed to consider letters from General Philip Schuyler. McKean was on all four of them, but the other members varied widely.[171] His most important committees, however, were the Secret Committee, concerned with procuring supplies and material, and the Claims Committees and the Treasury, which arranged payment; also he attended the committee on Qualifications (for officers) and the committee for Prisoners (of war). In large part, civilian control over the miliary was maintained through the last two committees. Weak as it was, the Congress exercised a surprising degree of control over its widespread military forces all during the war.[172]

It should be emphasized that these were executive, not legislative, committees, and they carried with them the power to act. The Continental Congress still was an executive body, a plural executive, which turned to the state governments for the performance of specifically legislative or judicial functions. Not until the adoption of the Articles of Confederation in 1781 did the Congress become a legislature. In the early part of the war it was simply a revolutionary convention, assuming as much control over events as it could grasp, without written or constitutional limits.

McKean served on an especially large number of committees, though the committee-count is difficult to interpret. Before the turning point of July 4, 1776, McKean was a member of five standing committees and some thirty-three others, temporary or less important.[173] What is significant is that he was the only delegate from Delaware for months at a time, and was therefore entitled to membership on any committee which provided that each state should have a member. He was also appointed to numerous committees because of his residence in, and special knowledge of, Pennsylvania, or the city Philadelphia. Once again, his plural office-holding increased his power and influence, though burdening him with staggering responsibilities. When obligations in Pennsylvania and Delaware were added to his Congressional duties, and circumstances required a sudden burst of effort to coordinate all three, his total workload became almost incredible.

His military service was brief and undistinguished, consisting only of a tour of several weeks with the Pennsylvania Associators who were sent across New Jersey immediately after the passage of the Declaration of Independence. He was relieved from this duty, in time to attend the Delaware Constitutional Convention, and never re-enlisted in the armed forces, or entertained military ambitions of any kind. This was one form of vanity from which he was wholly free. As early as May 1, 1775, his name had appeared on a list of those "able and willing to bear arms" in the middle ward of Philadelphia (west of Fourth street, between Market and Chestnut streets) as a private in Captain John Little's company of the 2nd battalion.[174] Needless to say, he was too busy in Congress, and elsewhere, to be of much assistance to Captain Little.

The Pennsylvania militia early in the war was a vast, floundering paper organization, which included the names of every property-owner, or resident, in a given district that the local committee was able to dig up. These lists included Tories, who subsequently fled to join the British army, soldiers enlisted in other outfits, and people who never saw any military service. McKean's name appeared on several such lists, both in Pennsylvania and Delaware, but the presence of his name indicated little more than that he held property in the area, or wished to sponsor and encourage a local military unit.[175]

In November, 1775, when the organizations of which Captain Little's company was a part, the so-called Associators, were expanded and made compulsory for all males from sixteen to fifty, the situation was changed. In May, 1776, two more battalions were added to the original three: the 4th with Thomas McKean as Colonel, and the 5th with Timothy Matlack as Colonel.[176] McKean and Matlack had both been prominent on the seven-man committee which had prepared a remonstrance against the Quakers, while these measures were pending, and had led the procession to the doorway of the State House to present it to the legislature.

Accustomed as he was to top-level management, and finding the prospects of being a private in Capt. Little's company highly distasteful, McKean had found the proper solution. At the time, and for some time to come, military companies organized at the state level and volunteer groups from the back country elected— and demoted—their commanding officers, a democratic process which Washington approved in theory but sometimes found detrimental to military authority and discipline. Instant officers were also created by another process: the individual who, either entirely on his own or upon acceptance of an offer by the civil authorities, undertook to raise, and sometimes to equip a military unit, automatically took commanding rank. This latter approach would have been more to McKean's liking, and was entirely feasible for him. Blessing from the civil authorities—in this case, probably, the Committee of Safety—of his proposal to raise a military unit could be taken for granted. His talents of leadership and organization were publicly acknowledged, acclaimed at many mass meetings; recruiting or organizing the recruitment of a battalion would take time, but it could be done.

In February William Tilghman wrote to the commanding officer of the First Battalion, Col. John Dickinson, using terms with which Dickinson agreed as a politician but hardly as an old friend of McKean's, "Colonel McKean is a true Presbyterian and joins the violents . . . He is suspected of independency." [177] Before marching off to meet the British in July, these battalions were to participate several times in pressure-group activities in Philadelphia. McKean, who was certainly more at home on a public platform than in a bivouac area, realized that

the new units were, at the moment, more effective politically than they were militarily. The moderates were living in a never-never land; McKean had indeed
joined the violents—and yet he was still only suspected of independency!

In Pennsylvania the radical faction had got control of the committee network
in the elections of February 16, 1776.[178] Previously this network had been of a
mixed complexion, which had made it possible for moderates like John Dickinson
to take a leading part. Having obtained control, the radicals decided to call a
provincial convention on April 2nd,[179] but on March 4th the Philadelphia committee reconsidered, and on behalf of the entire apparatus decided to postpone
the convention "in order to see the event of sundry petitions now before the
House of Assembly." [180]

Meanwhile, disturbances were occurring in the Lower Counties, and Thomas
Robinson and Boaz Manlove of Sussex County were arrested by a light infantry
company in Dover, in spite of the fact that they were members of the Assembly
which was about to meet at New Castle.[181] Robinson had been one of the members of the committee of correspondence for the Lower Counties, but had always
been conservative, and he and Manlove were now considered Tories. They were
released after much talk on the part of George Read about "the breach of legislative privilege," but there was grumbling among the radicals over the danger
of permitting such obnoxious characters to go free. It was McKean who proposed "the best way of getting over the business," which was for Robinson to
make a solemn declaration of his innocence, and give security for his good behavior in the future.[182] The Lower Counties and the Eastern Shore of Maryland
were constantly exposed to attacks from British vessels, and the midnight raids
beginning to occur in Kent and Sussex Counties were demoralizing to the patriot
forces in Delaware, who were McKean's political constituents.[183]

The event which did more to change the climate of opinion than any other in
this period was the passage of the American Prohibitory Act by the British Parliament. Robert Morris laid a copy of this act before the Congress in Philadelphia
on February 26th, together with letters from England reporting that an army
of 25,000 would be sent to America, partly to the southern colonies.[184] The Prohibitory Act outlawed "all manner of trade and commerce" with the continental
colonies, and declared that all ships "with their cargoes, apparel, and furniture
. . . trading in any port or place of the said colonies, or going to trade, or coming from trading . . . shall become forfeited to his Majesty as if the same were
the ships and effects of open enemies . . ." [185] This was the most drastic act ever
passed by the British legislature with reference to America, and it struck the
advocates of reconciliation dumb. Charles James Fox, in the British Parliament,
prophesied truly when he said, "It is a bill which should be entitled, a Bill for
carrying more effectively into execution the resolves of Congress." [186] Accompanied, as it was, by the prospective hiring of foreign troops, it caused many a
moderate to think that independence had already been declared by the other
side. The more trusting souls seized on the fact that peace commissioners were
to be sent to negotiate with the colonies, but they grasped at straws.

The news of the Prohibitory Act caused "a large number of Philadelphians"
to apply to Congress for letters of marque and reprisal, authorizing them to serve

as privateers.[187] Congress debated at length, and on March 18 decided that only the ships of Great Britain would be subject to seizure, while Irish ships and those from the other British dominions would be exempt—with Pennsylvania and Maryland opposed to taking a public stand. The Lower Counties, on March 22, reaffirmed their instructions to their delegates in Congress to "embrace every favourable Opportunity to effect a Reconciliation," and to uphold the right of their colony to an equal voice in Congress, but they added a curious provision that: "Nothwithstanding our earnest Desire of Peace with Great-Britain . . . You are nevertheless to join with the other Colonies in all such Military Operations as may be judged proper and necessary for the Common Defence, until such a Peace can be happily obtained." [188] South Carolina, which had just received the news of the Prohibitory Act, voted on March 23 to send similar instructions, except that on the most critical question of all they were sufficiently vague not to preclude a vote for independence.[189] This was to be the formula for several of the colonies; they permitted such a vote without actually sanctioning it.

One of the reasons for postponing the provincial convention in Pennsylvania was to await the results of the elections of May 1, 1776, in the hope that these would provide a mandate for independence. In March the Assembly had finally yielded to appeals for greater representation for the western counties, and for the city of Philadelphia, by authorizing the addition of seventeen seats, setting the first of May as the date to fill them.[190] As the election approached, the radicals in Pennsylvania coordinated their strategy with the leaders of the Continental Congress, confident that their slates of candidates would be elected. But the moderates opposed to independence also drew up slates. To the surprise of almost everybody, the moderates won a stunning victory, electing three of their four candidates in the city: Andrew Allen, Samuel Howell, and Alexander Wilcox; the Whigs succeeded only in electing George Clymer. Several more moderates were elected from the backcountry, including James Allen, Andrew's brother, for Northampton County.[191] Recovering from the shock, the radicals quickly decided that a revolution would have to be engineered in Pennsylvania. "We cannot make Events," Sam Adams had written the day before the election—as if sensing defeat—"Our business is wisely to improve them." [192] This was to be the program for the future.

The radical "steering committee" was an informal group, of uncommon ability, consisting of such men as Christopher Marshall, Timothy Matlack, Dr. Benjamin Rush, James Cannon, Thomas Paine, and Dr. Thomas Young, formerly of Massachusetts and Rhode Island. Several members of this inner circle had not been elected to the city committee, nor were the last three in politics officially, but as a group they had learned to circumvent the committee, or to use it as a front. There was a wide range in their vocations as well as their ages: Rush was thirty-one, Marshall, a retired Quaker druggist, sixty-five. Mathematics professor James Cannon was thirty-six, Matlack, an unsuccessful brewer, was forty-six, journalist Tom Paine thirty-nine, and Dr. Young forty-four. They were in constant touch with the "brace of Adamses" and certain other members of Congress, most notably Thomas McKean. Dr. Young had been a lieutenant of Sam Adams' in Boston, and was now helping his former leader to pull the strings

POLITICAL BLOCS, SECOND CONTINENTAL CONGRESS, MAY 10, 1775 to JULY 8, 1776

Radical	Moderate	Conservative	Uncertain
New England			
J. Langdon (N.H.)			
J. Bartlett (N.H.)			
J. Sullivan (N.H.)			
W. Whipple (N.H.)			
J. Adams (Mass.)			
S. Adams (Mass.)			
E. Gerry (Mass.)	T. Cushing (Mass.)		
J. Hancock (Mass.)			
R. T. Paine (Mass.)			
S. Ward (R.I.)			
W. Ellery (R.I.)			
S. Hopkins (R.I.)			
R. Sherman (Conn.)			
O. Wolcott (Conn.)			
E. Dyer (Conn.)			
S. Deane (Conn.)			
S. Huntington (Conn.)			
W. Williams (Conn.)			
The Middle Colonies			
[*H. Wisner*] (N.Y.)	[*F. Lewis*] (N.Y.)	P. Livingston (N.Y.)	S. Boerum (N.Y.)
L. Morris (N.Y.)	P. Schuyler (N.Y.)	[*R. R. Livingston**] (N.Y.)	
[*W. Floyd*] (N.Y.)	*J. Hart* (N.J.)	J. Duane (N.Y.)	
A. Clark (N.J.)	W. Livingston (N.J.)	J. Alsop (N.Y.)	
J. Witherspoon (N.J.)	J. DeHart (N.J.)	G. Clinton (N.Y.)	
R. Stockton (N.J.)	*T. Stone* (Md.)	J. Jay (N.Y.)	
F. Hopkinson (N.J.)		R. Smith (N.J.)	
B. Franklin (Pa.)		S. Crane (N.J.)	
J. Morton (Pa.)		J. Kinsey (N.J.)	
G. Ross (Pa.)		*J. Wilson* (Pa.)	
T. Mifflin (Pa.)		*J. Dickinson*** (Pa.)	
T. McKean (Del.)		*R. Morris*** (Pa.)	
C. Rodney (Del.)		*T. Willing** (Pa.)	
S. Chase (Md.)		*C. Humphreys** (Pa.)	
C. Carroll (Md.)		A. Allen (Pa.)	J. Rogers (Md.)
W. Paca (Md.)		E. Biddle (Pa.)	R. Alexander (Md.)
T. Johnson (Md.)	R. Goldsborough (Md.)	*G. Read** (Del.)	J. Hall (Md.)
M. Tilghman (Md.)			
The South			
R. H. Lee (Va.)	B. Harrison (Va.)	*C. Braxton* [*?] (Va.)	
T. Jefferson (Va.)	E. Pendleton (Va.)	*J. Hewes* (N. Ca.)	
G. Wythe (Va.)	W. Hooper (N. Ca.)	*E. Rutledge* [*] (S. Ca.)	
F. L. Lee (Va.)	H. Middleton (S. Ca.)	J. Zubly (Ga.)	
T. Nelson, Jr. (Va.)	*T. Heyward, Jr.* [*] (S. Ca.)		
R. Bland (Va.)	T. Lynch (S. Ca.)		
G. Washington (Va.)	*T. Lynch, Jr.* (S. Ca.)		
P. Randolph (Va.)	J. Houston (Ga.)		
J. Penn (N. Ca.)			
R. Caswell (N. Ca.)			
C. Gadsden (S. Ca.)			
A. Bulloch (Ga.)			
L. Hall (Ga.)			
B. Gwinnett (Ga.)			
G. Walton (Ga.)			

NOTE: The Second Continental Congress convened May 10, 1775. The numbers of delegates to the Continental Congresses, dates of their election and thus attendance, varied widely from state to state for a number of years. e.g., the New Jersey delegation present July 2, 1776 had just been elected, on June 21, and some Signers were not elected till mid-July or later in 1776.

Italics represent those congressmen present for the vote on Lee's resolution for independence, July 2. Some of those opposed on July 1, approved the final vote for the sake of unanimity; those who altered votes are bracketed. * indicates opposed, and ** abstained. New York delegates had to abstain until further instructions, which were received, in favor, July 19. Therefore their names are bracketed with presumptive votes. As no individual's vote was recorded at the time, the tally is unofficial, representing opinions and recollections of members and their contemporaries.

Delegates not present for any part of this period are omitted here. Of the many sources used, including MSS, the principal ones are the *JCC*, Burnett's *Letters*, D. Malone's *The Story of the Declaration of Independence*, and *DAB*.

in Philadelphia. Hawke states that "Sam Adams' hidden hand . . . was . . . probably involved in every decision made by the city committee between February and July of 1776." [193]

The "steering committee" met constantly, as the election returns came in. On the evening of May 3, said Christopher Marshall, they consulted with Thomas McKean, then all trooped over to Samuel Adams' lodgings and "stay'd a good while in Conversation with him . . ." On May 10, the day of John Adams' motion that new governments should be established where there was "no government sufficient to the exigencies of their affairs," they again visited McKean and "thence to Saml. Adams Lodgins." [194]

On May 6 two British warships, the *Liverpool* and the *Roebuck*, left their stations at the mouth of the Delaware River and proceeded upstream, creating consternation in New Castle and Chester. This was the kind of event that Sam Adams knew how to improve on, and the rumor soon spread that New Castle had been burned to the ground. In fact, the *Roebuck* had become snagged on the 7th, and although she eventually floated free, she was subjected to heavy attack and considerable damage by armed row-galleys, whose spirited crews forced both ships to return to their stations, dispelling the myth of their invincibility. However, Philadelphia's complacency had been jarred by the sound of cannonading, and George Read wrote McKean, urgently requesting immediate supplies of powder and lead.[195]

John Adams' motion of May 10 was passed with surprisingly little difficulty because John Dickinson, who was still in favor of reconciliation and might have been expected to oppose the measure, did not feel that it applied to Pennsylvania.[196] This province, Dickinson thought, had a government that was entirely sufficient, and had already contributed more men and material in the present contest than any of the others. Surely Adams was not referring to Pennsylvania. Serene in his misconception, he left for a short vaction at his estate near Dover, Delaware [197]—as Galloway had retired to his country estate at a critical moment some two years earlier.

After Dickinson had departed, however, Adams, by adding an unusually strong preamble to the resolution, made clear that Pennsylvania was indeed included in the original motion, and that his maneuver was not to be ignored. He spelled this out in unmistakable language, and the resolution, once passed, was to be the lever releasing McKean from the instructions which had bound him thus far: "it appears absolutely irreconcileable to reason and good Conscience, for the people of the colonies now to take the oaths and affirmations necessary for the support of any government under the crown of Great Britain, and it is necessary that the exercise of every kind of authority under the said crown should be totally suppressed." *

From May 13 to 15 a bitter debate was waged, with both sides alert this time

---

* JCC, IV, 357-8. Jensen, *The Founding of a Nation*, 684, says: "The resolution of 10 May needed a preamble and Congress appointed John Adams, Richard Henry Lee, and Edward Rutledge to prepare one. The preamble John Adams wrote provided the theoretical foundation for revolution which Jefferson was to elaborate in the Declaration of Independence a few weeks later, but its immediate purpose was to justify a revolution in Pennsylvania."

to the revolutionary nature of the preamble. James Duane of New York cried out passionately, "You have no Right to pass the Resolution—any more than Parliament has." This was interfering in the internal affairs of the colonies with a vengeance. "Why all this Haste? Why this Urging? Why this driving? . . . I do protest vs. this Piece of Mechanism, this Preamble." [198] Thomas McKean suavely replied, still wearing the mask with which he had puzzled people for so long, that he thought "this Measure the best to produce Harmony with Gt. Britain." Harmony, apparently, on American terms! [199] Lest any confusion remain, he didn't "doubt that foreign Mercenaries are coming to destroy Us. I do think We shall loose our Liberties, Properties and Lives too, if We do not take this Step." Immediately afterwards Sam Adams signaled the importance of the occasion by making a short speech in Congress, which he rarely did, emphasizing that "We cant go upon stronger Reasons, than that the King has thrown us out of his Protection. Why should we support Governments under his Authority?" [200]

The implications of the preamble for Pennsylvania, at least, were brought out by young James Wilson, of Carlisle, who with skill and courage filled in for the absent Dickinson. He warned without equivocation that "In this Province if that Preamble passes there will be an immediate Dissolution of every Kind of Authority. The People will be instantly in a State of Nature." He urged delay and pointed out that many delegates had been placed under restrictions by their constituents, and could not exceed their instructions. Denying the authority of the King would be, in effect, to break the last link with the mother country, for the Congress had already challenged the jurisdiction of Parliament. Providing for government where there was no government was perfectly acceptable, but the preamble raised a whole set of new questions. Why not print the resolution without the preamble? "Will the cause suffer much, if this preamble is not published at this time?" [201] Wilson had a genius for defending unpopular causes; the radicals could vote him down more easily than they could answer his questions.[202] Even so, the vote was close: six colonies to four. North Carolina, New York, New Jersey, and Delaware were against it; Georgia was absent, and Pennsylvania and Maryland abstained—with Maryland walking out until its delegates had received further instructions.[203]

If Maryland's defection were to spread to Pennsylvania, the radicals would be dangerously divided. Extraordinary efforts, beyond everything done in the past, would now have to be made to hold Pennsylvania in line, and to win over Delaware and the other middle colonies. McKean at long last discarded the mask. That same evening "at seven [Christopher Marshall] went and met a large number of persons at the Philosophical, by appointment (Col. McKean in the chair), where was debated the resolve of Congress . . . respecting the taking up and forming new governments in the different colonies." [204] The meeting did not break up until after ten o'clock, and then adjourned until the following afternoon, with a meeting in the morning on another subject, their conduct toward Quakers on the 17th, which Congress had declared to be a fast day. Marshall made no mention of a new chairman at the adjourned meetings, so presumably

McKean still presided. On the afternoon of the 16th they "concluded to call a convention with speed; to protest against the present Assembly's doing any business in their House until the sense of the Province was taken in that Convention . . ." [205] This was the critical decision, so far as Pennsylvania was concerned. They would prevent the Assembly from acting.

Friday, May 17, was the fast day, or Congress Sunday, as it was called, and the radicals exerted themselves tirelessly in gathering names on a petition from the City and Liberties of Philadelphia, urging a mass meeting on Monday morning "to take the sense of the people respecting the resolve of Congress . . ." [206] On the evening of the 18th the city committee voted, with only five members dissenting, to hold such a meeting on Monday morning, the day the Assembly was supposed to convene. Sunday, the 19th, was likewise filled with politicking, contrary to the custom of the Quaker City. Propaganda in both English and German, some of it written with the master-touch of Tom Paine, was widely circulated, though it had been printed before the decision to hold a mass meeting: "CONVENTIONS, my Fellow-Countrymen, are the only proper bodies to *form* a Constitution." The Assembly, it was argued, could not suppress the royal authority because that was something that could only "be done *to them,* but cannot be done *by them.*" [207]

The mass meeting on Monday morning, May 20, in the State House yard was dominated by four of the five colonels * of the Philadelphia battalions now officially formed.[208] Col. Roberdeau was the moderator, and the principal orators were Col. McKean, Col. Cadwalader, and Col. Matlack. The fifth, John Dickinson, was not there and would not have had anything to do with such a meeting in any case. Despite rainy weather, some four thousand people managed to crowd into the brickwalled enclosure, and in subsequent reports to the backcountry this number was magnified to six or seven thousand. John Adams thought the proceedings were conducted "with great order, decency, and propriety," [209] but Dr. James Clitherall, a visitor from South Carolina, noted that even "Col. Cadwalader, one of their favorites, was grossly insulted . . ." for proposing modifications in one of the resolves that was adopted at the end of the meeting.[210]

McKean, on the other hand, rode the crest of the wave of public opinion with perfect aplomb, as three dignitaries in one: colonel, chairman of the city committee, and delegate from Delaware to the Continental Congress. Peter Force's *American Archives* contain an account of his masterful leadership, taken from a contemporary newspaper, as follows: [211]

> Colonel Thomas McKean informed the meeting that the committee of the City and Liberties, apprehending the dangerous tendency of the said instructions [against independence], had presented a memorial to the Honorable House of Assembly praying that they might be recinded: and the House, taking the said memorial into their consideration, did, as the last act of that Body, in their late session, determine *not to alter the said instructions.*

* How many Colonels' Revolutions there have been in the world since that time! The principle that seems to work in such situations is this: when a military organization becomes involved in a revolution, its leaders—for their own safety and the safety of the public—must play a leading role in the revolution.

Upon motion: Resolved unanimously: That it is the opinion of this meeting that the said instructions have a dangerous tendency to draw this Province from that Happy union with the other Colonies which we considerd both our glory and protection.

On motion, Resolved (with only one dissenting vote) That the present House of Assembly, not having the authority of the People of this City and Liberties, against the power of said House to carry the said resolve of Congress into execution.

Resolved unanimously: That a protest be immediately entered by the People of this City and Liberties, against the powers of said House to carry the said resolve of Congress into execution.

It being moved, and the question thereupon put, whether the present Government is competent to the exigencies of our affairs, *the same was carried in the negative unanimously.*

Resolved unanimously: That a Provincial Convention ought to be chosen, by the People, for the express purpose of carrying the said Resolution of Congress into Execution.

As some difficulties may arise respecting the mode of electing members for the Convention: therefore:

Resolved unanimously: That the Committee of the City and Liberties of Philadelphia be directed to send the aforesaid throughout the Province and to call together a number from "The Committee" of each County, to hold a Provincial Conference, in order to determine upon the number of which the convention for framing a new Government shall be composed and the manner in which they shall be elected.

The "Liberties" referred to were municipal divisions bracketing the city proper. The north end of town, from Cohockson Creek to Kensington, was known as the Northern Liberties, and the other limit, including the Society Hill section and Southwark, was called the Southern Liberties, "with a surplus population of a baser sort," in Watson's estimation. However, even the baser sort were patriotically uplifted by McKean's persuasive oratory, and the City and Liberties presented their unanimous thanks to the Committee "for their zeal, fidelity, and steady attention to the duties of their important station," which the Committee's chairman, Col. McKean, "accepted and politely acknowledged." Acting promptly upon the meeting's final resolution, the chairman and committee wrote to the backcountry, modestly explaining that "Our situation makes us a kind of centinels for the safety of the Province; and to prevent our friends from being deceived by specious impositions we give this open notice as an instance of our good will to them." After which amiable notice, Col. McKean came to the point, informing the county committees that there would be a conference in Philadelphia on June 18, to which they were requested to send delegates. Further, the city committee considered the present occasion of such importance that they were dispatching "some of [their] Committee and fellow-citizens into each County" to explain everything that had happened and to solicit their support.[212]

In accordance with the procedures thus publicly adopted, Col. Roberdeau addressed a forthright communication to the Assembly "by the Direction of the Inhabitants of the City and Liberties."[213] The city committee also prepared material for posters and broadsides to be distributed throughout the province, in which they summed up their argument in terms everyone could understand: "to prevent your being deceived we tell you concisely, until we can prepare the matter fully for you, that you either are or will be called upon to declare whether you will support the Union of the Colonies, in opposition to the Instructions of the House of Assembly or whether you will support the Assembly against the Union of the Colonies . . ." [214] Here, again, it was All Power to the Congress, which had sanctioned the overthrow of the government of Pennsylvania, or of any other government that was not *sufficient*. Elated by such activity, and his participation therein, a young Committee-member, Dr. Benjamin Rush, wrote to his bride of four months, "General Mifflin and all the delegates from the independent colonies rely chiefly upon me," then, honesty overcoming enthusiasm, he crossed out "me" and continued more objectively, "Colonel McKean and a few more of us for the salvation of this province." [215]

The conservatives naturally drew up a protest against the radical actions of the town meeting and circulated it widely in the city and its environs. It was carried by its supporters, two by two, up and down the streets "to be signed by all (tag, long tail, and bob) . . . and much promoted by the Quakers." [216] One or two of the counties sent petitions to the Assembly requesting specific changes that would be more moderate in their effect than the radicals' program. At the same time there were others who were criticising the actions of May 20 from an unexpected viewpoint. Caesar Rodney, McKean's closest confederate in Delaware, wrote to his brother on May 22, "The people in this City I think have Acted rather unwisely . . . If the present assembly Should take order in the matter [of changing instructions, etc.] the work would be done in one Quarter of the time— However [this was his concession to McKean's judgment] many of the Citizens seem to have little or no Confidence in the Assembly." [217]

The immediate problem for Rodney was to decide whether or not Delaware must risk the turmoil then beginning in Pennsylvania, in order to change the instructions of its delegates, and at first he was not sure how to proceed. "With us below [in the Lower Counties] I hardly know what Step will be best—in our County [Kent] a new Choice Could not mend the Ticket, but might make it worse—in the other Counties there is verry little probability of an Alteration for the better." By May 29, however, he was in a more optimistic mood, and had adopted a sensible plan of action, which proved effective. "I don't doubt the Assembly will Act prudently," he wrote, "if otherwise, it will then be time enough for the people to take the matter up in another way." [218]

Two days earlier, on the Philadelphia Common, between Chestnut and Walnut Streets, west of the State House, there had been an impressive military review, with Associators, militia, and Continental troops lined up before "the Congress, General Washington, Gates and Mifflin, accompanied by a great number of other officers, most of the Assembly, the Presbyterian Clergy, who were here at the Sinod—and 21 Indians of the Six Nations who gave the Congress a Wardance Yesterday." Evidently, this was enough to restore Rodney's confidence, despite qualms shared by several other members of Congress over the reliability of the Iroquois. That tribe had traditions of friendship with their Brother Onas, the Proprietor of Pennsylvania, and with the Quakers, which might lead them to oppose the revolution. As events proved, these fears were justified. Rodney's confidence, so far as the Iroquois were concerned, was short-lived.

McKean was notably fond of ceremony, and with such an opportunity for pompous display, he probably wished to remain in Philadelphia long enough to participate in the military review. But by the 29th he was in Reading, as a spokesman for the city committee in their effort to arouse enthusiasm among the county committees.[219] Meanwhile, he had written to them in his capacity as president of the committee, as follows:

> We need not remind you that you are now furnished with new motives to animate and support your courage. You are not about to contend against the power of Great Britain, in order to displace one set of villains to make room for another. Your arms will not be enervated in the day of battle with the reflection that you are to risk your lives or shed your blood for a British tyrant; or that your posterity will have your work to do over again. You are about to contend for permanent freedom, to be supported by a government which will be derived from yourselves and which will have for its object, not the emolument of one man or class of men only, but the safety, liberty and happiness of every individual in the community. We call upon you, therefore, by the respect and obedience which are due to the authority of the United Colonies, to concur in this important measure. The present campaign will probably decide the fate of America. It is now in your power to immortalize your names by mingling your achievements with the events of the year 1776—a year which, we hope, will be famed in the annals of history to the end of time, for establishing upon a lasting foundation the liberties of one-quarter of the globe.[220]

Reading was the county-seat of Berks County, which had a large German population and was considered one of the keys to the backcountry. The response from this area was to be more than satisfactory; by June 1 an able delegation, including Joseph Heister (who would be Governor of Pennsylvania in 1820) had been selected for the Philadelphia conference.[221] At the same time James Cannon, Timothy Matlack, and Dr. Thomas Young also visited towns in the west. Some members of the "steering committee" visited several counties, and everywhere they were cordially received.

Conservatives tried to create an unfavorable climate of opinion, but without success. From Philadelphia, Edward Shippen sent a warning to Jasper Yeates, at Lancaster: "I am desired by some friends of mine to write you a line by this opportunity, to appraise you that a certain bawling New England man called Doctor Young, of noisy fame together with Joseph Barge is going up to Lancaster to endeavor to persuade the people there to join in the late attempt to dissolve our Assembly, and put everything into the hands of a Convention . . ."[222]

A little-known teacher of mathematics, James Cannon, was one of the most effective of the radical propagandists at this time, perhaps because his radical views were so thorough that they encompassed even his own profession; in two months he was to state, answering critics of the Constitutional Convention's members, "All learning is an artificial restraint on human understanding." [223] As

Secretary of the Committee of Privates of the Pennsylvania Associators, he was able to exploit the grievances of the Associators throughout the counties, especially those disenfranchised under the old regime. He developed a committee of correspondence within the Committee of Privates, reaching numerous battalions in the back country through his own channels. For a military machine, this committee was far too democratic; as a vehicle for agitation it was a smashing success.

For the revolutionaries in the middle colonies, the month of May was thus a busy one, but not the climax; the pace was to quicken in June to the limits of human capacity, as the embattled conspirators realized that time was running out. Nothing could be omitted now that would contribute to the cause, for the more radical colonies were losing patience, reaching the point beyond which they could no longer be restrained. If the middle colonies could not be maneuvered into joining the rest before that point was reached, the union of the colonies, on which everything else depended, would be irretrievably lost.

Several of the delegates had received clear warnings of the danger. Sam Adams heard from Joseph Hawley that "The people are now ahead of you and the only way to prevent discord and indiscretion is to strike while the iron is hot. The people's blood is so hot as not to admit of delays . . ." [224] It was possible, Hawley wrote, that Congress itself would be dispersed by an angry mob which would then "dictate for the whole continent." Even the conservative Robert Morris was urged on by Charles Lee, chafing in Virginia—"For God's sake why does your Congress continue in this horrible, nonsensical manner? Why not at once take the step you must take soon? . . . you will force at last the people to attempt it without you—which must produce a noble anarchy." [225]

Still, that final step would not be easy. The middle colonies were not yet "matured for falling from the parent stem," no matter what the pressure; [226] the elections of May 1 in Pennsylvania had proved that. The moderate leaders who reflected public opinion in this area were not fearful of the British so much as they were of anarchy in their own governments. The "massive, articulate urban public opinion" of Philadelphia (not to mention New York and Baltimore) had to be taken into account, and required political skill of the highest order—or brutality—to change it. [227] Since the moderate leaders in many cases were the radicals' best friends, and had hitherto been their political allies, as Dickinson, for example, had long been close to McKean, the course of wisdom had a strong appeal. But Dickinson would have to be neutralized politically, even destroyed, if he could not be converted, regardless of friendship. The inexorable logic of revolution could not be denied. The Pennsylvania Assembly would have to be swept aside, as well as the rest of that government; the Governor of New Jersey, William Franklin, and of Maryland, Robert Eden, must be rendered harmless. The legislature of the Lower Counties likewise had to be put to the test, and might have to be displaced as abruptly as that of Pennsylvania, if it faltered. Indeed, many painful actions would have to be taken—and McKean would take part, directly or indirectly, in all of them. (See Table 2) No one else had as many divergent responsibilities and roles. [228]

At the precise moment that McKean was engaged in closing down the colonial courts in Pennsylvania, as chairman of the Philadelphia committee, he was also establishing clandestine contact with French merchants in Martinique, as a member of the Secret Committee of Congress. In the winter of 1775–76, the Quaker City received three mysterious visitors, the first of whom, Achard de Bonvouloir, purportedly a Flemish merchant, was actually an agent from the French Foreign Minister, Count Vergennes. He had been instructed to report on the situation and to intimate to the proper persons that the French government might soon be willing to aid the revolutionary leaders, in an entirely unofficial but practical way. Devious though the visitor's approach was, the members of the two Secret Committees were equally experienced in intrigue, and apparently superior in propaganda—of which Bonvouloir's report to Vergennes is somewhat amazing proof. "Everybody here is a soldier; the troops are well dressed, well paid, and well commanded. They have 50,000 men under pay and a large number of volunteers who desire none." And Bonvouloir concluded, "Nothing frightens them. Take your measures accordingly." The Committee of Secret Correspondence and the Secret Committee worked together in negotiating the details of this entente cordiale. They dispatched Silas Deane to Paris and William Bingham, a young Philadelphia merchant, to the West Indies to arrange for transfers of cargoes.[229]

On June 3, 1776, two letters were sent from Philadelphia to Martinique, in connection with William Bingham's mission; the first was signed by Thomas McKean, Richard Henry Lee, Benjamin Franklin and Robert Morris, and the second by Benjamin Franklin, Benjamin Harrison, Robert Morris, and John Dickinson—who was still in the inner circle, for some purposes.[230] The two other visitors to Philadelphia were also French, with a like purpose, but in truth unofficial. Emanuel de Pliarne and Pierre Penet had become partners, in France, with the explicit but private intention of trading munitions for American goods. Forwarded by General Washington to the Congress, they reached an agreement with the Secret Committees, and returned to France in May. This contract proved too unofficial; unsanctioned by France, it could only be protested or corrected there, and provided little but faulty matériel and headaches for the Committees.[231]

Not by coincidence, the Philadelphia committee on June 3 approved an official communication "To the Worshipful Justices of His Majesty GEORGE, the Third, of his Courts of Quarter Sessions and Common Pleas for the County of Philadelphia" (signed by Thomas McKean, as chairman), in which they respectfully but somewhat testily urged: "It is with concern that the Committee have beheld some persons in office in this Province so influenced by their salaries as to prefer their own immediate power and interest to that of their country and their posterity . . . Upon the whole, the Committee think it their duty to themselves, their constituents, and to the Congress to request your Worships to postpone the business of the above-mentioned Courts until a new Government shall be formed." [232] McKean (as Colonel) was requested to present this memorial, and steps were taken forthwith to mobilize the Philadelphia battalions, and other groups, to support the radicals' entire program.

In addition, the Congress itself moved to back them up, by prearrangement with the delegates from Massachusetts and Virginia, as indicated by Sam Adams' letter to James Warren on June 6 that "tomorrow a motion will be made, and a Question I hope decided . . . This being done, Things will go on in the right Channel and our Country will be saved." [233] He was referring, of course, to the motion by Richard Henry Lee, seconded by John Adams, on June 7 that "That these United Colonies are, and of right ought to be, free and independent States . . ."

The pressure was more than the Pennsylvania Assembly could bear. In a last-ditch effort to save its skin the Assembly voted, on June 8, to permit its delegates to Congress to concur with the other delegates in all measures except those regulating their "internal government and police." [234] Thus, Pennsylvania acted in what appeared to be a decisive manner, before the Lower Counties or the other middle colonies, despite the foreboding by Caesar Rodney and others that the calling of a conference to replace the Assembly there would slow matters down. The new instructions were not written formally until June 14, but the delegates from all the colonies were aware that Pennsylvania had changed its instructions. The New York and Maryland delegations immediately wrote to their governments, asking—as the letter to Maryland put it—for the "fair and uninfluenced sense of the people" back home.[235] McKean's schedule at this point called for a flexing of the political muscles of the five battalions of Associators in Philadelphia on the 10th—to influence the leaders from the other colonies primarily, since Pennsylvania had already changed its instructions—and then a quick trip to New Castle for a meeting of the Assembly of the Lower Counties on the 14th, hopefully to persuade that body to fall in line.

The polling of the battalions on the 10th was marred by an incident involving a part of McKean's command, which "seized a Jew, for mal-practice, cursing the Congress, declaring his willingness to fight against them, &c." This unfortunate man was treated roughly, but excused himself by giving information against one Arthur Thomas, a skinner, who "had been frequently complained of ever since Dr. [Kearsley's] affair." [236] A mob, which included some of McKean's soldiers, then flew to Thomas' house and pillaged it. Christopher Marshall reported that the First Battalion voted to support the resolves of Congress, of May 15, "except two officers in the Foot, two officers in the [light] infantry, and about twenty-three privates . . ." In the Second Battalion the vote was unanimous "except two privates." [237] In the third Battalion a lieutenant refused to put the question, which "gave great umbrage to the men, one of whom replied to him in a genteel spirited manner," according to the *Evening Post*.[238] Marshall was not present when the Fourth and Fifth Battalions (McKean's and Matlack's) voted, but was under the impression that they supported the Congress "to a man."

Altogether some fourteen hundred Associators voted to uphold the Congressional resolves "at all hazards"—a satisfying demonstration of McKean's premise that this infant army was politically adult enough, for the moment, to allow democratic disciplines to take precedence over military. If his point was not clear, his procedure was; another officer of the Pennsylvania Associators, Richard Peters, when asked how many men he commanded, replied a bit ruefully, "Not one, but

I am commanded by ninety." [239] Accordingly, Colonel McKean signed his report with a phrase that would cause most military men to shudder, "By order of the Battalion," writing as follows:

> At a meeting of the Associators of the Fourth Battalion of the City and Liberties of Philadelphia, on the usual place of parade, in consequence of notice given to them on the 6th instant . . .
> Present: The Officers and Privates of nine Companies.
> The Colonel, Thomas McKean, informed them that since he had proposed this meeting for the above, among other purposes, he had been waited on with the following Resolution of the Committee of Privates of the five Battalions [supporting the Congressional Resolve of May 15, signed by James Cannon, Clerk] . . .
> He said he was happy to find that his own idea of the propriety of this measure was supported by so respectable a body as the Committee of Privates . . .
> No arguments or persuasions were urged for or against the above propositions, and all present, amounting to upwards of four hundred, showed their hearty approbation of the whole transaction by three huzzas.[240]

Meanwhile Richard Henry Lee's motion for independence was being given the thoughtful treatment it deserved. Even the most ardent spirits realized that careful timing was of the essence, if the Congress were to achieve the necessary unanimity on this all-important qustion. The original motion had been made on June 7; the next day it was referred to a committee of the whole, and John Hancock yielded the chair to Benjamin Harrison of Virginia. On Monday, the 10th, *before* the battalions were polled on the Commons, the adoption of the resolution was urged from the floor of Congress by Richard Henry Lee, John Adams, George Wythe, Elbridge Gerry, Thomas McKean, Thomas Jefferson, and Samuel Adams.[241] The conservatives managed, however, to postpone the question until July 1st, and the radicals agreed, since the middle colonies were not quite ready. Edward Rutledge of South Carolina expressed the views of some when he declared there was no point in pressing the measure "except the reason of every Madman, a shew of our spirit." [242] It was decided nonetheless "that no time be lost, in case the Congress agree thereto, that a committee be appointed to prepare a declaration . . ." On the 11th a five-man committee was appointed: Thomas Jefferson, John Adams, Benjamin Franklin, Roger Sherman, and Robert R. Livingstone. It was further resolved that a committee be appoined to prepare a plan of confederation, and another to consider the mode of forming alliances with foreign powers.[243]

Tuesday, June 11, was also the day the Delaware Assembly was due to meet, and McKean had to hurry down to New Castle to present the Congressional resolves of May 10th and 15th. Meanwhile, in Philadelphia, the political machines which he had helped to put in motion continued to grind away in his absence. On the 12th he was chosen by Congress as the member from Delaware on the committee to draft articles of confederation; [244] on the 13th the Secret Committee managed to send a supply of lead and power southward to suppress an insurrection of Tories in Sussex County; [245] and on the 14th (the day of McKean's presentation at New Castle) Franklin, McKean, and twenty-three others were chosen by the city committee as Philadelphia's delegation to the Conference of Committees that was scheduled to meet in Carpenters' Hall on June 18th.[246]

The 14th was also the day when the Provincial Congress of New Jersey declared Governor William Franklin in contempt for summoning the Assembly of that province, and attempting to by-pass the radicals.[247] With Congressional blessing the Provincial Congress ordered their Royal Governor, son of Pennsylvania's most prominent patriot, arrested and stopped his salary; after a few days of negotiation he found himself under the jurisdiction of the Committee on Prisoners, which McKean headed.[248] Then, at this late date, June 22, New Jersey sent a new delegation to Congress, with McKean's brother-in-law, Francis Hopkinson, as a member, and such other "independent souls" as Dr. John Witherspoon of Princeton, and Richard Stockton, father-in-law of Dr. Benjamin Rush.*

In Maryland, Governor Robert Eden was disposed of more easily; a convention simply requested him to leave, and he went aboard a British man-of-war. When the Delaware Assembly met, on Friday morning, June 14, "Mr. McKean delivered in at the Chair a certified copy of a Resolution of Congress, of the fifteenth of May last, which was by order read . . . [and by special order read a second time]." [249] The Speaker was Caesar Rodney who had not been idle in preparing the ground—Delaware had fallen behind Pennsylvania, and the debates this day would test his decision to leave the matter of independence to the discretion of the legislature. He was not disappointed; the Assembly voted unanimously to approve the above resolution, and on Saturday afternoon they framed new instructions for their delegates in Congress, and established a temporary new government.

The new instructions, which did not mention independence, simply permitted the delegates to concur with the delegates from the other colonies in forming compacts and concluding treaties and "such other measures as shall be judged necessary . . ." with the usual reservation "to the people of this Colony, the sole and exclusive right of regulating the internal government and police of the same." [250] It should be emphasized, however, that the delegates were equally free not to concur with the others, and this was what George Read decided to do on July 1. The question had not been finally disposed of, after all; John Adams was leaping to conclusions when he wrote that "McKean has returned from the Lower Counties with Full Powers." [251] McKean was released from the ironclad instructions which had limited him up to this point, but Delaware was not yet bound and delivered.

The temporary government then made Caesar Rodney the chief executive of the state, replacing Provincial Governor John Penn, but otherwise all persons

* George E. Ross, *Know Your Declaration of Independence and the 56 Signers* (New York, 1963), 38–42. ". . . when New Jersey ousted its royal governor in June of 1776 and elected five new members for the Continental Congress . . . Witherspoon was the leader of the movement to oust the royal governor . . . he and four companions—called the 'five independent souls' by John Adams—were sent as delegates." Ross does not locate the quotation, and neither does Burnett, who also uses it.

The newly appointed delegates signed the Congressional declaration of secrecy, of Nov. 9, 1775, as they were required to do. Hopkinson inserted his name at the foot of a column, *before* McKean's, but "28 June" appears in Charles Thomson's handwriting after his name.

holding office, civil or military, in the name of the King were to continue as before, "until a new government shall be formed, agreeable to the Resolution of Congress of the fifteenth of May last." [252] McKean, therefore, did not lose his position as a judge in Newcastle County by this resolution. As for Rodney, immediately after the adjournment of the Assembly he hurried south to investigate the report of a Tory uprising in Sussex County. He was thus in Lewes on the 26th when he heard from George Read and others that the Assembly had more business to perform, in order to raise its quota of militiamen, to consider articles of confederation, and to take care of several other matters referred to them by the Congress. Apparently, he was back at his home in Dover when he received the still more urgent "express" from McKean that he was needed in Philadelphia to support the Declaration of Independence.[253] McKean had returned to Philadelphia—probably on Sunday, the 16th—to participate in the meetings of the city committee, which was preparing on Monday for the Conference of Committees that was to meet at Carpenters' Hall on Tuesday. He had a vital interest in the preparations, for he was slated to be the President.

The city committee had its plans for the Conference of Committees well in hand. Merely to survive in the uncongenial atmosphere of Philadelphia, a radical revolutionary committee of this sort had to organize its activities with supreme efficiency. Such a group could not hope for a generally favorable public response to excuse or conceal blunders, but rather, could count on an intelligent, dedicated, and experienced opposition to its every move. Very early on the morning of the 18th, the committee made last-minute arrangements "upon the mode to open the Conference," and then adjourned till nine at which time they met again "to introduce some of the country members, who are strangers." [254]

At ten o'clock or a little later "Colonel McKean, as Chairman of the City Committee, declared the motives which had induced that Committee to propose the holding of the present Conference, and then laid on the table a certification of Deputies appointed to attend." [255] There were ninety-seven members present, with a few more still expected. McKean and Benjamin Franklin headed the list for the City of Philadelphia, but Franklin was unable to attend, so McKean—as planned—was made President. Joseph Hart of Bucks County was made Vice President, Jonathan Bayard Smith and Samuel Cadwalader Morris, Secretaries. By and large it was an inexperienced, undistinguished group, more remarkable for organizational dexterity than wisdom. The leaders of the counties were listed as follows:

> Philadelphia County—Col. Henry Hill
> Bucks County—John Kidd, Esq.
> Chester County—Col. Richard Thomas
> Lancaster County—William Augustus Atlee, Esq.
> Berks County—Col. Jacob Morgan
> Northampton County—Robert Levers, Esq.
> York County—Col. James Smith
> Cumberland County—Mr. James McLane
> Bedford County—Col. David Espy
> Westmoreland County—Mr. Edward Cook [256]

William A. Atlee of Lancaster was the only one of these men to become important in McKean's life, or in the history of the province. In another year he was to join McKean on the Supreme Court of Pennsylvania, and to serve simultaneously as a Commissary of Prisoners and committee leader in his county. That same evening, another future member of the Supreme Court was publicly recognized as a man to be reckoned with, when the city committee in a late session decided that George Bryan, a merchant and judge, was "to take upon him the collectorship" of the port of Philadelphia.[257] On Wednesday, the 19th, the Conference decided in rapid succession that the city and the various counties were to have one vote each (thereby winning the allegiance of the backcountry); that the Congressional resolution of May 15th was approved; that the present government of the province was *not* competent to the exigencies of their affairs; and that a Constitutional Convention should be called in a few weeks to consider and establish a new government.

During the next two days, the delegates reviewed details of voting, clearly intending to enfranchise many new voters, while at the same time selectively disenfranchising others. Every Associator, they said, should be entitled to vote—a revolutionary proposition. Voters should be twenty-one years of age, they should have one year's residence, and should have paid taxes or been assessed toward the same. The places for holding elections were specifically designated—McKean's old property at Chatham "commonly called the Half-Way House" was to accommodate the residents of London Grove, New London, Londonderry, and East and West Fallowfield.[258] All voters should take an oath of affirmation that they would no longer bear allegiance to George III, and "no person who has been published by any Committee of Inspection or Committee of Safety in this Province . . . and has not been restored to the favour of his country [shall vote]." Such a provision, of course, would give the committees the whip-hand over the Constitutional Convention.

On Friday, the 21st, the delegates in their zeal to exclude the unworthy blundered into another decision, which probably lost them a great deal of popular support. Not only were the prospective members of the forthcoming Convention to be required to take an oath against George III, but another oath:

> [that they] do profess faith in God the Father, and in Jesus Christ, his Eternal son, the true God, and in the Holy Spirit, one God, blessed forevermore; and do acknowledge the Holy Scriptures of the Old and New Testaments to be given by Divine Inspiration.

The spirit behind such a requirement was contrary to the libertarian traditions of William Penn's "holy experiment" and was dictated by a blindly partisan view of the political advantages that could be obtained. Many potential supporters were offended: Quakers, Anglicans, Jews, Catholics, Deists, and certainly the uncommitted. Christopher Marshall, who had strenuously advocated this measure as a delegate from the city, complained a few days later about the adverse reactions, revealing the mood in which it was adopted: "Sundry of my friends," he wrote, "who, I believed, were really religious persons . . . now declare that no such Belief or Confession is necessary, in forming the new government. But their behavior don't affect me, so as to alter my judgment in looking upon such a Confession to be essentially necessary and convenient." [259]

The most significant maneuver of the Conference, however, was the carefully orchestrated effort to discredit the Pennsylvania Assembly, and the Committee of Safety. The technique was to accuse the existing legal bodies of failing to provide ammunition and supplies for the armed forces, especially the thirteen row-galleys that had attacked the *Roebuck* and the *Liverpool,* and for the five battalions of Associators. Testimony was brought in from the commanders of the row-galleys, the Patriotic Society of the City of Philadelphia, the Committee of Privates (James Cannon), and even the Committee of Safety (in the form of a minute written by Robert Morris).[260] Morris, who represented the conservative element of Pennsylvania in the Congress, had tried to get Congress to stand behind the Committee of Safety—of which he was also a member—but had failed, and his attempt was quickly turned against him. He had urged the Congress to ask the Committee of Safety explicitly for military aid, because "he much doubted if they would be obeyed unless so authorized," and when the Congress refused after long debate, he had violated the rule of secrecy by writing a memorandum on the spot and getting three of his fellow-members in Congress to witness it.

The essence of this curious document was the confession "that the Assembly of said Province had adjourned on the 14th instant without having been able to carry into execution the Resolves of the Congress of the 3rd instant for raising six thousand Militia for establishing a flying camp." Since the Committee of Safety was "in the recess of the Assembly the Executive Body of the Province," yet was unable to act without bolstering from the Congress, the implication was clear that the Conference in Carpenters' Hall would have to assume governmental powers which normally belonged to the Assembly. Congress had understood that the radicals in Pennsylvania were determined to effect a revolution, and a majority in Congress was actively supporting the radicals. For this reason they had refused Morris' plea to support the Committee of Safety. McKean, as President of the Conference, had not hesitated to make public Morris' confidential memorandum, which clinched the Congressional alliance with the radicals, and sealed the doom of the Pennsylvania Assembly. No wonder McKean and Morris never liked each other afterwards.

The "flying camp" was to be a force of 10,000 men, to defend the middle colonies from invasion: 6,000 from Pennsylvania, 3,400 from Maryland, and 600 from Delaware. This force was to be sent to Perth Amboy, New Jersey, to stand off the British threat to this area until the end of the year, or until the regular troops could be mobilized for this purpose.[261] The situation of the rebels was desperate: the Canadian venture had failed, a confederation of the colonies was still being debated in committee, and the British were arriving in the New York harbor with a peace commission on the one hand, and an overwhelming military and naval force, on the other. The Conference decided on its own authority, with Congressional backing assured, to raise 4,500 men "to be added to the 1,500 now in service" for the state's quota, and to keep them under arms until December, 1776, "unless sooner discharged by Congress," paying them a penny-a-mile for their travels. Pennsylvania was to provide two major generals for the flying camp, and Maryland one, in keeping with the recommendation of Congress. That body, in fact, directed and controlled events in this period to an astonishing degree, and in detail, from the specific choice of Major Generals down to some of the military reviews held on the Philadelphia common.[262] Under the auspices of the flying camp McKean was to march across New Jersey, at the head of the 4th Battalion, shortly after the Declaration of Independence was passed.

The Conference was not finished, however. The Declaration of Independence was still a week in the future, and by no means assured. Under McKean's leadership, the Conference proceeded to return the favor of the radicals in Congress by formulating their own declaration of independence, to precipitate similar action by the national body. A committee consisting of Benjamin Rush, James Smith, and Thomas McKean was appointed on a Sunday afternoon to prepare a draft for submission the following morning, Monday, June 24. Benjamin Franklin had apparently also been slated for this committee, but because of illness (gout, or the after-effects of his precipitous return from Canada), he had been unable to attend the Conference as an official member. Nevertheless, the political machinery was now working at such speed that his name was given out in advance as a member of the committee, and historians have so stated ever since.[263]

How the committee managed in a single night to prepare, and agree on the resounding declaration of June 24, which McKean delivered to the Congress the following afternoon, is a mystery, unless, perhaps they had earlier consulted the Congressional committee of five, appointed for a like purpose. Franklin was to have been on both committees, and his diplomatic gout would have given him time to devote to these important labors without the effort of meetings with the general public.[264] Jefferson is known to have written a letter to him (though in the same city) on the 21st, asking him to read and criticize an unnamed document—which may have been the Declaration of Independence in draft.[265] It is entirely possible that the Pennsylvania committee consulted both Jefferson and Franklin, and that they did so a day or two before their actual appointment on Sunday afternoon; there were several examples in this period of official announcements as well as propaganda releases prepared ahead of time, to allow for coordination, printing, and distribution.[266] The language of the Declaration of the Deputies of Pennsylvania bore a remarkable resemblance to the early drafts of Jefferson's Declaration, including some of the ideas and expressions eliminated in the final and more famous form.[267] The preamble of the Pennsylvania document went as follows:

> WHEREAS George the third, King of Great Britain, etc., in violation of the principles of the British constitution, and of the laws of justice and humanity, hath by an accumulation of oppressions, unparalled in history, excluded the inhabitants of this, with the other American colonies, from his protection; and whereas he hath paid no regard to any of our numerous and dutiful petitions for redress of our complicated grievances, but hath lately purchased foreign troops to assist in enslaving us, and hath excited the savages of this country [to make war against us] also the negroes, to embrue their hands in the blood of their masters, in a manner unpracticed by

civilized nations . . . and whereas, the obligations of allegiance (being reciprocal between a king and his subjects) are now dissolved . . .[268]

This, no doubt, is what the Declaration of Independence would have sounded like, if Thomas McKean had been its author. There is no evidence that McKean personally composed the document, more than any of the other members of the committee, but he was frequently the penman and spokesman for committees, and the language echoes other statements of his and the philosophy of the Rev. Francis Alison. The reference to the blacks, however, was too divisive in a statement of this kind.[269] The Congress was later to decide that this issue was best omitted, no matter which side one argued—whether blaming the king for the institution of slavery, or conversely for inciting a slave rebellion—or straddling, as Jefferson managed to do. Accordingly, in the finished work Congress confined itself to the more discreetly vague language now so familiar: "He has excited domestic insurrections amongst us, and has endeavoured to bring on the inhabitants of our frontiers, the merciless Indian Savages, whose known rule of warfare, is an undistinguished destruction of all ages, sexes, and conditions." The Indians apparently were beyond the pale, but where the blacks stood no one was bold enough to declare.

Then, having set forth the basis for their actions, the Conference resolved—in legal language, but with utter illegality: "*We,* the *deputies* of the people of Pennsylvania, assembled in *full* provincial conference, for forming a plan for executing the resolve of congress of the 15th of May last, for suppressing all authority in this province, derived from the crown of Great Britain, and for establishing a government upon the authority of the people only *do,* in this public manner, in behalf of ourselves, and with the approbation, consent, and authority of our constituents, *unanimously* declare our willingness to concur in a vote of the congress, declaring the United Colonies *free* and independent states . . ." The statement, as published, was signed by Thomas McKean, President, but the minutes of the Conference indicate that it was also "signed at the table" by all members present. The formal signing of this paper was to constitute an important precedent for the signing of the Declaration of Independence the following week, and for the same reason, according to McKean: "to prevent traitors or spies from worming themselves amongst us." [270]

Finally, the conference put teeth in their pronouncements by limiting the freedom of travel in Pennsylvania, and specifically by strengthening the local committees which were already strong. They provided for the "examination of all strangers or persons travelling" and required that the committees give passes to the people in their jurisdiction who had to move to and fro. Suspicious characters could be detained "unless they produce a pass or certificate from the City, County, or District Committee from whence they last came." The rationalization for this abrogation of freedom was that it was only a temporary necessity, and would happily pave the way for a Constitutional Convention which would confer compensatory benefits.

An Address to the People of Pennsylvania, which had been sent out over McKean's signature on the 22nd, noted that the people's representatives had experienced an unexpected unanimity in their councils and were aware of growing popular support. With pious complacency they announced: "Divine Providence is about to grant you a favour which few people ever enjoyed before, the privilege of choosing Deputies to form a government under which you are to live . . . You will not, therefore, be surprised at our fixing the day for the election of Deputies so early as the 8th of next July." The Constitutional Convention itself was to meet on the 15th.

The denouement of this unruly Conference, which had deliberately destroyed public confidence in the Assembly and the Committee of Safety, was the recommendation to the forthcoming Convention that they should choose delegates to the Congress and an entirely new body, a Council of Safety, which would exercise military and executive powers for six months, unless a new government had been formed in that time.* The superseded Committee of Safety was specifically denied control over the obstreperous crews of the row-galleys, and their appointment of a certain Samuel Davison as Commodore of the fleet was not upheld. The thirteen captains had informed the Conference that they would not under any circumstances accept Davison, nor would they resign their commissions. They got away with this defiant gesture, presumably, because such action was exactly what the leadership of the Conference wanted. The Committee of Safety, a strange medley containing a few moderates but also many strong patriots,[271] was left howling with pain as well as fury. On July 2, while Congress was voting for the Declaration of Independence, the Committee of Safety issued the following testament to their hurt feelings:

> The Committee doubt not the purity of the intention which produced this Resolution [limiting Davison's command], and by which their power in so important a Branch is so greatly mutilated, if not altogether destroyed; They well know the regard due to the Representatives of the People, & are disposed to submit to the recommendation, tho' wounded and dishonoured by it. But they would have it understood that the Continuance of many of their Board under such circumstances is of necessity, as no Body of Men can at present be appointed to supply their places, and as they perhaps may, fettered in their authority as they are, still render some small services to their Country; They however think it incumbent on them to declare that many bad Consequences may probably proceed from a divided Command. Military authority is not of a nature to be participated, and when attempted the greatest mischiefs commonly flow from it.[272]

---

* John H. Powell, *General Washington and the Jack Ass* (1969), 151, describes this as in "inept Conference." I do not agree. The Conference accomplished everything it set out to do. Powell states that it was "palpably inane" for them to restore power to the Committee of Safety, after destroying confidence in it, but what they did was call for the establishment of a new body, to be called a *Council of Safety*. Such a body was in fact created and acted as the provisional executive of the state from July 22, 1776, to March 13, 1777. Thus, there was an interregnum of only about one month, during which the Congress and the Philadelphia committee, with the prestige that the Conference had given them, retained control of the armed forces. In this interval the network of committees throughout the state worked well. Dissidents quickly fell into line, as indicated by the statement of the Committee of Safety, quoted in the text. It should be noted further that Christopher Marshall and other members of the Philadelphia committee consulted with Sam Adams (the master wire-puller) on Sunday, the 23rd, and then went directly to see the delegates at Carpenters' Hall. (*Diary of Christopher Marshall,* June 23.) They also consulted Sam Adams on June 30.

McKean went his way unscathed. The enemies he had made in the last few days were powerless, and as long as he rode the whirlwind their hatred was tinged with awe. The meeting at Carpenters' Hall adjourned with resolutions of thanks to him as President "for his impartiality and close attention to the business of this Conference," and to the Committee of the City and Liberties of Philadelphia (which he headed) for "their unwearied endeavours in the publick service." On Tuesday, the 25th, he presented to Congress the declaration of independence drawn up by the deputies of Pennsylvania, and that evening he attended a dinner at the Indian Queen Tavern on Fourth Street for the members of the Conference, where toasts were drunk to "The Congress," "A Wise and Patriotic Convention to Pennsylvania on the 15th of July," and "Lasting Dependence to the Enemies of Independence." [273]

There was a general feeling of satisfaction with a job well done in Pennsylvania, although clouded by a deep concern over the deteriorating situation of the colonies militarily. Perhaps more attention should have been paid to the Constitutional Convention scheduled to meet on the 15th, but the Declaration of Independence was soon to be brought up again in Congress on the 1st, and in the interim numerous details needed attention: arrangements by the Secret Committee, exchanges of prisoners of war, and questions as to what had gone wrong in the Canadian expedition. The last few days of June, on McKean's calendar, appeared to offer a well-earned breathing spell. On June 29, however, Congress resolved "to order a German Battalion to be raised, as soon as possible," and the Congressional President Hancock requested the Committee of Safety in Pennsylvania to attend to it. In this situation—an interregnum between the discredited Committee of Safety and the yet-to-be-created Council of Safety—this task in fact had to be, and was, assumed by the only competent body, McKean's Philadelphia committee.[274]

On Monday, July 1, Congress assembled to consider again the advisability of declaring independence. The news, or rumor, that the great question would be brought to a vote on that date had been widely publicized, and therefore Congress refused the request of the Maryland convention that they postpone consideration further, to give the doubtful colonies more time.[275] July 1 was the deadline, and the Maryland radicals (including several recent returnees from Franklin's Canadian trip) had been making the most of it.[276] "I have not been idle," Samuel Chase had written to John Adams, "I have appealed *in writing* to the people. County after county is instructing." [277] As a result of these efforts a unanimous resolution had been achieved, in time to be read on Monday morning to the delegates in the assembly room of the Philadelphia State House.

New York, on the other hand, had reached no decision and their delegates were forced to announce that they were not authorized to vote, one way or the other. On behalf of the New Yorkers, in a guileless and matter-of-fact manner, George Clinton "asked permission to abstain, which was granted." [278] Formal approval of this sort was not necessary. The delegates could simply have refrained from voting, or stepped behind the bar and been recorded as technically "absent," but by this device Clinton effectively removed himself and his colleagues from the debate, thereby gaining for New York some additional time for thought, denied to the others. It was one of the more adroit parliamentary ploys of the week.[279]

According to the order of the day Congress then resolved itself into a committee of the whole, with the corpulent Benjamin Harrison in the chair, to debate the subject discussed so many times before, and to test fate with a vote that would be reported to the Congress (the same men, in the same room) in a less-than-final form, permitting minor adjustments prior to an official announcement. Altogether the debate lasted nine hours, and was an occasion of the utmost gravity. John Dickinson set the tone with a long, and carefully prepared, address in opposition to a declaration at this time—on the ground that the states had no settled governments of their own, had received no foreign aid, and had not yet set up a working confederation—all of which he deemed necessary prerequisites for separation from the mother country.[280]

His arguments and his sincerity deeply impressed his listeners, but what he said exactly is not known. He later wrote a recapitulation of his address as he wished he had given it, a polished oration like one of Cicero's. Historians have expatiated at length on its eloquence, but the resemblance of this address to the original was unconvincing to those who were there. John Adams, who replied immediately, not once but twice, at the request of the New Jersey delegates who entered as he was finishing his first effort,[281] noted in a letter to McKean many years afterwards: "Mr. Dickinson printed a speech which he said he made in Congress against the declaration of Independence: but it appeared to me very different from that which you and I heard." [282]

When Adams had finished his rebuttal, James Wilson announced that although he had usually heretofore agreed with Dickinson, he felt that he should "obey the instructions" of the Conference of Committees in Pennsylvania and support the declaration. Paca, McKean, and Rutledge spoke, perhaps others, but no minutes were kept of debates in the committee of the whole.[283] The vote revealed, however, that the radical faction in Congress had run into unexpected opposition: with Pennsylvania and South Carolina in the negative, Delaware split, and New York with quiet detachment awaiting events. McKean commented later, "The Delegates of Pennsylvania, who voted in the negative, were John Dickinson, Robert Morris, Charles Humphries & Thomas Willing, Esquires; those in the affirmative were John Morton, Benjamin Franklin and James Wilson, Esquires. For Delaware, my vote was for Independence, my Colleague George Read, Esquire, voted against it." [284] Read's vote had evidently caught McKean by surprise, and was obviously unanticipated by Caesar Rodney, who was performing his duties as Speaker in Dover, under the impression that his two associates, with whom he had served for ten years as co-spokesman for the Lower Counties, were in agreement, at least on fundamentals.[285]

McKean's characteristic response, as described in a letter to Rodney's nephew in 1813, was to take instant action: "Whereupon, without delay I sent an Express (at my private expence) for your honored Uncle Caesar Rodney, Esquire, the remaining member for Delaware . . ." [286] He was not worried about Rodney. There would be no second surprise; the only question was whether Rodney could arrive in time. Dover was eighty miles distant, and the weather was bad. Christopher Marshall noted in his Diary for that date, "I went home near 4 came on a thunder gust with rain cleared up by Six," [287] and Rodney himself wrote, "I arrived in Congress (tho detained by Thunder and Rain) time Enough to give my Voice in the matter of Independence." *

The unnamed and unsung rider, who must have used relays of horses, arrived safely in Dover about midnight, and alerted the slumbering Speaker—and Rodney got to Philadelphia on July 2 in time for the afternoon vote. Again, the weather was poor: "before 10 came on a heavy rain Continued till past 2, cleared up by 5," in Marshall's tortured prose.[288] McKean's description of Rodney's arrival, continuing his letter above, was that he met him "at the State-house door in his boots & spurs, as the members were assembling; after a friendly salutation (without a word on the business) we went into the Hall of Congress together, and found we were among the latest. proceedings immediately commenced, and after a few minutes the great question was put: when the vote for Delaware was called, your uncle arose and said; 'As I believe the voice of my constituents and of all sensible & honest men is in favor of Independence, and my own judgment concurs with them, I vote for Independence,' or in words to the same effect."

The debate had been continued for a second day, on motion by Edward Rutledge of South Carolina, who had implied on the 1st that the delegates from his state might soon be willing to join the majority, despite their personal views, for the sake of unanimity.[289] Rodney had missed hours of debate, but had no doubt as to how he was going to vote; he was not one of those who thought that the declaration was premature. As for McKean, he must have had difficulty remaining quietly in his seat all day, while elsewhere the city committee was busily preparing for the Convention, struggling against time and lack of equipment to prepare the Associators' battalions for marching—and while thunder and rain competed with the voices within the hall.

When the vote was finally taken, Charles Thomson, Secretary of the Congress, turned over the paper on which Richard Henry Lee's original motion was scribbled, and jotted down the results, beginning with New Hampshire and proceeding south in the customary manner. For a reason unknown, Maryland voted last.[290] New York perforce remained mute. Pennsylvania's vote had been changed by the fact that Dickinson and Morris withdrew behind the bar, and abstained.†
South Carolina, as promised, had switched, and Delaware, thanks to the efforts of the exhausted and unwell Rodney, had exchanged impasse for the winning

---

* Caesar Rodney to Thomas Rodney, Philadelphia, July 4, 1776, in Ryden, *Letters to and from Caesar Rodney*, 94–5. Caesar Rodney did not mention his mode of travel: it has been generally assumed that he rode horseback. However, Thomas Rodney later said that his brother went by his carriage to Philadelphia, which, in view of his precarious health and the weather, would have been more logical and safer. This would account for his arrival later than might be expected; a carriage would have been "detained by Rain" in the crossing of swollen streams and fords more than a rider. McKean's description of Rodney in "boots and spurs" need not be construed too literally. The phrase was an idiom for *haste,* and even so, "boots and spurs" were the accepted costume for travel; sometimes a carriage horse had to be mounted as well.
† Had contemporary writers used the word "abstained," instead of "absent" or "present" (in the parliamentary sense), much confusion would have been avoided.

side. By the unit rule, it could now be said that the declaration had passed *without a single dissenting vote*.

It remained to consider the terms of the declaration, in a line-by-line scrutiny, and Congress immediately began what Jefferson called the "depredations" of the document.[291] Dr. Witherspoon of Princeton, in a Scottish burr, moved to strike out the word "Scotch" from the sentence accusing Great Britain of sending over "not only soldiers of our common blood, but Scotch and foreign mercenaries to invade and destroy us." The word was struck, and so was the sentence in which it stood.[292] Other changes were made, in the interests of brevity and political expediency, and on the whole the editorial work was well done, though the process was painful to the author, and lasted for the better part of the next two days. Jefferson particularly regretted that his condemnation of the slave trade was overruled; it "was struck out," he wrote, "in complaisance to South Carolina and Georgia, who had never attempted to restrain the importation of slaves, and who, on the contrary still wished to continue it." Then he added, "Our northern brethren also I believe felt a little tender under their censures; for tho' their people have very few slaves themselves yet they had been pretty considerable carriers of them to others." [293]

McKean was less interested in the words adopted for progaganda purposes than he was in the practical measures, political and military, that would be taken to enforce them. His duty as a delegate had been accomplished for the time being; he must become a Pennsylvania politician again, and a soldier, in rapid succession. On July 2 the Pennsylvania Committee of Safety, prodded by the real executive, the Philadelphia committee, and on July 3 by the Congress, moved for the activation of the flying camp in response to an urgent request from the New Jersey Convention, asking for as many troops as could be spared from the middle colonies. Until the flying camp was organized, "the Philadelphia Associators were asked to come forward," to face the British in New York and "to hold in check the troublesome Tories of Amboy." [294] At the same time delegates had to be nominated for the Pennsylvania Constitutional Convention, which had been called for July 15 (with elections on the 8th), and the Associators wanted to have their say before being required to march against the enemy.

On July 3, the Committee of Privates, and a number of like-minded citizens, met at Thorn's School where three speakers, James Cannon, Timothy Matlack, and Dr. Thomas Young "flourish[ed] away on the necessity of chusing 8 persons to be proposed to the publick for their Concurrence . . . for our Representatives in Convention." [295] The speakers, according to Christopher Marshall, "expatiated greatly upon the Qualifications they should be possessed of, viz. Great learning, Knowledge in our History, Law, Mathematicks, &c." [296] McKean hoped that such paragons could be found and would be willing to serve, but he had little time for political recruitment, and none for being a candidate himself; he was now deeply involved in preparing his own battalion, in liason work between the Congress and the military—in whatever time could be spared from the events in the assembly room of the State House.

July 4 dawned clear and bright.[297] At six o'clock in the morning Thomas Jef-

SUNDAY	MONDAY	TUESDAY	WEDNESDAY
	Note: McKean was the only Delaware delegate in Congress, from the first of June until the 25th or 26th, when Read joined him. Rodney did not arrive until July 2. Thus, McKean	attended Congress daily, if not always the whole day, in this period. McKean was a sub-chairman, often acting Chairman of the City Committee as well.	
2	**3** The City Committee approves memorial to the County Magistrates, requests that Col. McKean present it. Accompanied by Committee members, Col. McKean presents the memorial at the Courthouse.	**4** Congress resolves to raise a flying camp for the defense of the middle colonies.	**5** Congress in session.
9	**10** Vote on Lee's resolution tabled till July 1; Congress resolves to appoint committee to prepare articles of confederation, & appoints committee to compose a declaration of independence, in event Lee resolution approved. Col. McKean polls 4th Battalion on Congress' May 15th resolution, & on public resolution of May 20th; both approved unanimously.	**11** Congress in session.	**12** Committee on articles of confederation appointed, includes McKean as member for Delaware. The City Committee considers procedure, & election of delegates to Pennsylvania Conference of Deputies, to convene June 18.
16	**17** The City Committee decides on agenda for the Conference.	**18** The Conference convenes at 9 a.m. elects McKean chairman. The 104 members meet daily at Carpenters' Hall, through June 25.	**19** The Conference resolves to call a Constitutional Convention to form a new state government, to raise militia for the flying camp; decides upon qualifications for delegates elected to the Convention. Various minor disputes settled, the affairs of the state considered in general.
23 The Conference appoints McKean & two others, to prepare a declaration in support of Congress, to be reported next day.	**24** McKean presents declaration to the Conference; McKean ordered to present declaration, unanimously approved, to Congress.	**25** The Conference concluded, McKean presents their declaration to Congress. In celebration of success, Conference members given a banquet at Indian Queen Tavern.	**26** Congress in session. City members of Conference & City Committee decide upon instructions to be issued for the election, July 8, of delegates to the Constitutional Convention called by the Conference for July 15.
30	**1 JULY** Congress in committee of the whole debates Lee's resolution for independence for nine hours; final vote postponed till next day. McKean sends express for Rodney, to break Delaware's tie.	**2** Congress resumes debate; Rodney arrives. Final vote, twelve in favor, New York abstaining. Debate on formal Declaration begins in committee of the whole.	**3** Debate on Declaration continues. At New Jersey's request, Congress asks City Committee and Pennsylvania Committee of Safety for troops to be sent to New Jersey.
7	**8** The City Committee, as a body, & Congress attend public proclamation of Declaration of Independence, in State House Yard. The Declaration is also proclaimed to Associators' Battalions, in formation on the Commons. Delegates elected to Convention called for July 15.	**9** Congress advances $100,000 to Committee of Safety, for the City Committee, to expedite preparations for departure of the Associators' Battalions.	**10** Congress in session; joint committee meetings.
14	**15** The Associators' Battalions begin to march into New Jersey.	**16** Between July 15 and July 18, Col. McKean, in command of the 4th Battalion, leaves for Perth Amboy, New Jersey.	17

THURSDAY	FRIDAY	SATURDAY
		1 JUNE The City Committee decides to support Adams' May 15 resolution; to present a memorial to the County Courts, requesting that they adjourn until further notice.
6 Congress in session.	**7** R. H. Lee's resolution for independence, seconded by J. Adams, is presented to Congress.	**8** Lee's resolution considered by Congress in committee of the whole, tabled until June 10.
13 McKean leaves Philadelphia, to present Congress' May 15th resolution to the Delaware General Assembly, in session at New Castle.	**14** Delaware General Assembly approves May 15th resolution & McKean given certified copy of resolution of approval to present to Congress. City Committee elects 25 deputies to the Provincial Conference, including McKean.	**15**
20	**21**	**22** ⟶
27 Congress in session.	**28** Congress in session.	**29** Congress resolves to request that the Committee of Safety (and City Committee) raise a German battalion.
4 At Congress' request, City Committee sends express to the Military Convention meeting at Lancaster, urging them to expedite the flying camp. Congress asks delegates from New York, New Jersey, & Delaware, commanding officers of Associators' Battalion, & Committee of Safety to meet next day to consider & plan immediate defense measures. Congress approves the Declaration of Independence; orders copies printed immediately. 10 p.m., City Committee meets to consider above requests & approves.	**5** 7 A.M., at State House, members of Congress, committees & officers of Associators' Battalions meet to plan measures necesary to defend New Jersey. Col. McKean elected chairman of this joint committee.	**6** City Committee considers nominations of delegates to Constitutional Convention; plans for formal announcement of the Declaration of Independence, July 8. Through July 15, meetings under direction of the joint committee, McKean chairman, to arrange for supplies, prepare for departure of Associators.
	12 The Committee considering the articles of confederation, makes first report to Congress.	**13** Joint committee meetings.
11 Congress in session; joint committee meetings.		
18 ⟶		**22 (Monday)** Col. McKean and 4th Battalion arrive Perth Amboy, New Jersey Col. McKean remains in New Jersey till August 23; he returns to Philadelphia on August 25. GRC

ferson noted that the temperature was 68° Fahrenheit, and that the wind was blowing from the south-east. Even in the heat of the day the mercury rose no higher than 76°.[298] The New York post arrived at eleven o'clock with news that one of General Washington's guards had been executed near that city the previous Friday for a plot to assassinate some staff officers and blow up the magazines, on the arrival of the British fleet, and that "the number of transports from Halifax now arrived at Sandy-Hook amount[ed] to 113 Sail." [299] Soon there would be 25,000 British soldiers in the New York area, who could undoubtedly overwhelm the local defenses and advance in any direction they chose.

The Congress therefore dealt with immediate problems first, before resuming debate on the wording of the Declaration of Independence, and later a committee of the Congress worked long into the night on military plans, after the great consummation for which the 4th of July became famous. The city committee was asked to get in touch with the Lancaster Military Convention, of which George Ross was President, "to expedite the six thousand men [for] the Flying Camp . . . to march directly for Brunswick." [300] They were also asked to join a leadership meeting at seven o'clock the next morning, July 5, to concert measures for the security of New Jersey. The leadership committee was to consist of the delegates in Congress from New York, the Jerseys, Pennsylvania, and the Lower Counties, representatives of the city committee, the field officers of the five battalions already mobilized, and for the sake of public relations the Committee of Safety.

Thomas McKean, whether he was willing or not, was the logical choice for chairman of the leadership committee, and of necessity he spent much of the 4th, in and out of the assembly room, making arrangements for convening this emergency committee and planning the forthcoming campaign.[301] He was inexperienced in military matters, but if he had ever had military ambitions, this would have been his chance to shine. Many a revolution has been subverted, and many a dictatorship erected, on a power-base less secure than McKean's.*

Some thought that the Associators "were not well prepared for field service, only looking to be called on for operation near home," but the entire city rallied around to improvise the needed supplies.[302] "The good women of the town looked after lint and bandages; awnings, sails, and canvas were sought for tents; clock and window weights were collected to be cast into bullets; six cannon were procured . . . the arms of non-associators were seized for the public use," and skilled labor was "restrained from going into the field." [303] John Adams later explained, "Mr. McKean was not then present for he had so many avocations in Delaware, and as Attorney General in Pennsylvania [*chairman of the city committee* would have been more exact] that he could not constantly attend in Congress." [304]

As it happened, the military expedition then planned was not especially significant, but the intense activity in Congress and throughout the city on the 4th helps to explain the confusion which later arose over the signing of the Declara-

---

* For a comparison one needs only to recall the planning of the first Italian campaign in Paris by Napoleon Bonaparte.

tion of Independence. When the members got back to their interminable rewording, the main issues had already been decided. McKean's description of the occasion was, "I do not recollect any formal speeches . . . We had no time to hear such speeches, little for deliberation—action was the order of the day." [305]

At about two o'clock in the afternoon the entire document was finally approved unanimously by the twelve colonies voting. The New York delegates were sure they would ultimately be allowed to join, but the formal consent of their government was not forthcoming until July 9, and the news of their approval was reported to Congress on the 15th.[306] On that date they signed the copy of the Declaration that was then being carefully guarded by Charles Thomson, Secretary of the Congress.[307] Caesar Rodney, who was one of the few members of Congress to write a letter on the 4th, informed his brother in Dover that he had arrived in Philadelphia on time, and added, "We have now Got through with the Whole of the declaration and Ordered it to be printed, so that you will soon have the pleasure of seeing it—Hand-bills of it will be printed and sent to the Armies, Cities, County Towns &c To be published or rather proclaimed in form . . ." [308]

The official business of the 4th was concluded by the order that the Declaration be authenticated (which it was by Hancock, as President, and Thomson, as Secretary), and that the committee which had presented it should see to its printing.[309] Also, as John Adams noted in his *Autobiography*, Franklin, Jefferson, and he were instructed to prepare a device for a seal of the new United States of America.[310] Sometime after the crucial decision in the assembly room, William Hurrie, who had been waiting since early morning in the steeple (or belfry) for news of the event, and had begun to wonder if it would ever come, heard a shout from a boy down below, "Ring, Ring," and he began to toll the now famous bell with the Biblical inscription, "Proclaim liberty throughout the land"—and the excitement and confusion were increased.[311] What happened thereafter is a matter of dispute. Jefferson and Adams always maintained that the original copy of the Declaration (on a paper which has since disappeared) was signed by at least some members, besides the President and the Secretary, on the 4th.[312] McKean insisted that "no person signed it on that day nor for many days thereafter."*

This controversy did not begin immediately, however. For the moment it was sufficient to say that McKean did not sign on the 4th, and was not aware that anyone signed—if indeed they did. He had more than enough to do, preparing for the meeting the next morning, and for the military expedition in which he

* Burnett, ed., *Letters,* I 528 f. attaches more importance to this statement of McKean's than to the contrary statements of Adams, Jefferson, Franklin, and several others, combined. He discounts most of the Signers' statements on the ground that they were written late in life, and that they contain minor inaccuracies; for example, he notes Jefferson's reference to Mr. Dickinson. It is possible, however, that Dickinson was physically present on the 4th—though abstaining. John Trumbull, a painter of the Revolution who was known to have consulted both Adams and Jefferson, depicted Dickinson as present in his "Presentation of the Declaration of Independence to Congress." Trumbull worked under a Congressional commission, and also did the painting in the Rotunda of the Capitol, on the same subject, and it is probable that knowledgeable critics would have raised a howl if there had been glaring blunders, when his work first appeared. (See Scribner's *Concise Dictionary of American Biography*, New York, 1964, and Lossing, *op. cit.,* II, 204.)

would soon participate.* These preparations continued for many hours, interrupted only by efforts to coordinate the activities of the various groups to which he belonged: the Secret Committee of the Congress, the Delaware delegation, the city committee, and the 4th Battalion. Christopher Marshall's *Diary* notes that members of the tireless local committee were present at the Philosophical Hall until past 11 p.m., and that "an Express was sent off from this committee near 10 o'clock by request of the Committee of Congress with a letter to the meeting of officers at Lancaster in order to request them to expedite the 6,000 men appointed to Compose the flying Camp. and to march directly for Brunswick in the Jersies . . . [also] the sd. Committee of Congress requested this Committee to meet a Committee of the members of New York. Jersies. lower Counties. officers of ye 5 Batalion & Safety at 7 tomorrow morning at State house . . ." [313]

McKean had no time to write a memorandum that night for the benefit of history. He had no reason to suspect that his name would be omitted from the Declaration, when the first printed copies of the engrossed document were distributed the following year, and that he would be worried until his dying day about establishing the facts of what happened in Congress on the 4th of July, 1776. [314] So far as he was concerned, at the time, it was not a literary occasion but a military crisis. Granted the necessity of counteracting the peace commission which the Howe brothers would soon present, the great necessity was that of facing the 25,000 peace commissioners they were bringing with them. McKean was occupied with tangible facts rather than abstractions. The Declaration would be judged ultimately by the success of its defense.

His friend, Thomas Jefferson, was more sensitive to the fate of the document itself and "took notes in [his] place while these things were going on, and at their close wrote them out in form . . ." † According to Jefferson, "the Declaration thus signed on the 4th on paper was engrossed on parchment, & signed again on the 2nd of Aug. Some erroneous statements of the proceedings [have] got before the public . . ." It should be noted also that the final paragraph of the Declaration made signing almost obligatory: "We, therefore . . . mutually pledge to each other," etc.—as in the case of the Association of 1774, the agreement of

---

* As Boyd and Malone, and others who have looked into the matter carefully, have indicated, the question is by no means closed. My own view is that McKean was too busy on the 4th, with responsibilities outside of Congress, to be aware of the signing of the Declaration by most, if not all, of the others. It is not necessary to challenge anyone's memory. McKean was the only one who was out of step. As Boyd puts it, "No member of Congress ever stated in so many words that a Declaration was *not* signed on 4 July, except for the statement of Thomas McKean in 1812." Several others specifically stated that there was a signing on that date, and in my opinion there is much circumstantial evidence to support them.

† No one knows *when* Jefferson put these notes in form, and several writers have insisted that it was not until many years afterwards, but Boyd's conclusion was that he did so shortly after the debates. In *The Papers of Thomas Jefferson,* I, 301 f., Boyd writes: "Jefferson, as Adams said, was always 'prompt and explicit' in the Congress and throughout life conducted business, especially paper work, with dispatch and efficiency. It seems plausible to assume, therefore, that, especially during Aug. 1776, Jefferson had . . . an opportunity to put his rough notes in form . . . In the absence of evidence to the contrary . . . Jefferson's statement as to the Notes being put in form at the close of debate should be given much weight . . ."

Thus, although we cannot be certain, these notes of Jefferson's are probably the best single source of information concerning the signing of the Declaration of Independence.

secrecy of 1775, and Pennsylvania's declaration of independence only ten days earlier.[315]

Henry Melchior Muhlenberg, the great Lutheran leader who was never enthusiastic over political entanglements, wrote in his *Journal* for the 4th, "Today the Continental Congress openly declared the united provinces of North America to be free and independent states. This has caused some thoughtful and far-seeing *melancholici* to be down in the mouth; on the other hand, it has caused some sanguine *miopes* to exult and shout with joy." [316] Charles Biddle's Autobiography contained the significant notation: "On the memorable Fourth of July, 1776, I was in the old State-House yard when the Declaration of Independence was read. There were very few respectable people present. General *** spoke against it, and many of the citizens who were good Whigs were much opposed to it . . ." [317]

Scharf and Westcott believed that the General was John Dickinson, and that Biddle had confused the date with the 8th, when a formal ceremony was arranged for the reading of the Declaration by John Nixon. However, Dickinson had spoken at length in Congress, and it would hardly have been in keeping with his retiring nature to have immediately appealed to the crowd outside. Furthermore, he was not yet a General—more likely, it was his brother, Gen. Philemon Dickinson, giving a spontaneous response on the 4th. The affair on the 8th was more carefully managed, with enthusiastic throngs of patriots present, and official representatives of many influential groups. Mrs. Deborah Logan, who was present on the 4th, made the comment, "The first audience of the Declaration was neither very numerous or composed of the *most respectable* class of citizens." [318] Presumably these sporadic and unplanned events occurred on the afternoon of the 4th, before the committees got down to the serious business of the evening, to implement Jefferson's inspiring statement.

The 5th was "cloudy like for falling weather" when the leadership committee met at seven in the morning to take measures for the safety of New Jersey.[319] McKean was called to the chair. It was decided (and ordered) that all "available military force march without delay to Trenton . . . thence to such points as were threatened . . . except three battalions that were dispatched to New Brunswick." [320] These groups were to remain in the field until the flying camp of line troops was ready to replace them.[321] In Congress it was "*Resolved*, That Copies of the Declaration be sent to the several Assemblies, Conventions, and Councils of Safety, and to the Several Commanding officers of the Continental Troops, and it be proclaimed in each of the United States, and at the Head of the Army." [322]

The Philadelphia committee immediately made arrangements for the meeting of the 8th, going into such details as the selection of The Associators who were to take down the King's Arms, and "convey [them] to a pile of casks erected upon the Commons for the purpose of a bonfire . . ." [323] Christopher Marshall wanted the bonfire and the other celebrations postponed for one day, so that they would not detract from the elections on the 8th, but he was overruled. For the procurement of the urgently needed supplies and arrangements, which included providing for the support of families whose breadwinners were leaving, committees were organized for each battalion—for the Fourth, George Green, Frederick Dashun, and Peter Knight. The needed funds were disbursed by the titular executive, the Committee of Safety, to whom Congress had advanced one hundred thousand dollars for the purpose. And on behalf of the Fourth, its commanding officer, Col. McKean himself ordered powder, lead, and muskets.[324] The revolutionary machinery was now in high gear; the doubts and hesitations of the previous weeks had been resolved. The activities so commenced were to continue for the next several days and weeks; the enthusiastic response of the people was never to be higher. Mutterers lapsed into silence.

Letters were sent to the various county committees, the Sheriff of Philadelphia was given detailed instructions for the celebration at noon on the 8th, and all members of the city committee were ordered to attend. A slate of eight delegates to the Constitutional Convention was chosen, and nothing that would lead to their election was overlooked. The city committee and the Committee of Safety (occasionally called the Council of Safety, although the latter was not yet in existence) vied with each other in making preparations, but the city committee had an advantage in this competition, since the Associators were more directly under their control.

On the 8th the city committee met at the Philosophical Hall at 11 a.m. and marched in a body to the State House yard, where in the presence of a huge multitude the Declaration of Independence was read aloud by John Nixon. "The company declared their approbation by three repeated huzzas." [325] Afterwards—delayed somewhat by frequent stops at the local taverns—the crowd attended the proclaiming of the Declaration at the head of each of the five battalions, and in the evening there were bonfires. The Adamses and Thomas Jefferson were not featured, though they must have been present. Jefferson was later to take great pride in his authorship of the Declaration, as one of the three greatest achievements of his life, but at the moment he was still smarting from the omissions and the elisions made by the Congress. He regretted some of the missing passages, and did not feel that the end result was entirely his.[326]

Not until July 9 did the New York Provincial Convention ratify the decision for independence, and send word to the delegates in Congress that the Declaration was now in truth the *unanimous* decision of the thirteen United States. That evening at six o'clock General Washington assembled his troops in parade formation and had the document read at the head of each brigade, leading to a similar celebration in New York.[327] An equestrian statute of George III was toppled and "the lead wherewith the monument was made [was] run into bullets, to assimilate with the brains of our infatuated adversaries, who, to gain a peppercorn, have lost an empire," as The *Pennsylvania Journal* reported on July 17.[328] Ebenezer Hazard, writing of the incident, remarked, "His troops will probably have melted majesty fired at them"—an accurate guess, for the statue was taken to the home of Oliver Wolcott in Connecticut, and there in the backyard converted into an estimated 42,000 bullets, which must have compensated Wolcott for his absence from Philadelphia when the vote was taken, and his inability to sign the Declaration until October.[329] An alleged sequel, noted by Watson, was the beheading of a marble statue of William Pitt by some Tories; however, the

Annalist was forced by his historical conscience to admit that there was a plausible rumor that it was really an old statue of George II.[330] Either way the story fanned patriotic fervor.

Disturbed by its increasingly slipshod procedures during the days of crisis, Congress on July 10 appointed a three-man committee "to prepare rules for the conduct of Congress." Thomas Jefferson, Robert Treat Paine, and Edward Rutledge were the members, and the resulting manual, which was later referred to as "Jefferson's Rules," dealt with such matters as determining who was absent and who was present at the time of a vote, who was entitled to vote, and how the votes should be counted.[331] By July 11 the first companies of Associators left Philadelphia by water for Trenton. Such departures were to continue for a period of two weeks.[332] The tardy vote on the Declaration (and the signing) by the New York delegates on the 15th thus occurred after the tension had been eased and succeeded by a series of rapid actions at all levels of the community.

At about the time the 4th Battalion departed, the Congressional committee appointed on June 12 to draw up articles of confederation made its report to Congress, beginning a debate which was to continue sporadically all summer; McKean attended at least one session of this committee while it was drafting the proposed articles. Delaware's insistence that each state should have one vote was often referred to in the course of the debates, and was regarded by Chase of Maryland as "the most likely to divide us." [333] Others wanted to fix the proportionate strength of the states on the basis of money contributed, or population, but Delaware, as had been the case for more than a decade, was adamant. Franklin complained that "the Delaware counties [have] bound up their Delegates to disagree to this article . . . [it was] very extraordinary language to be held by any state, that they would not confederate with us unless we would let them dispose of our money . . ." [334]

The 4th Battalion * left Philadelphia by companies sometime in the middle of the month, and arrived at General Mercer's headquarters at Perth Amboy in full battalion strength on Tuesday, July 23.[335] McKean wrote a long letter to his wife on Friday, the 26th, describing his first contact with the enemy. This was to be his only combat experience while serving in a position of military command,

---

* Silas Deane had written a letter to his wife early in June, 1775, with a colorful description of the appearance of the Philadelphia Associators: "The uniform is worth describing to you. It is a dark-brown (like our homespun) coat, faced with red, white, yellow, or buff, according to their different battalions, white vest and breeches, white stockings, half boots and black knee-garters. The coat is made short, falling but little below the waistband of the breeches, which shows the size of a man to great advantage. Their hats are small . . . with a red, white, or black ribbon, according to their battalions, closing in a rose, out of which rises a tuft of fur of deer (made to resemble the buck's tail as much as possible) six or eight inches high. Their cartouch-boxes are large, with the word LIBERTY and the number of their battalion written on the outside in large white letters . . . their cartouch-boxes are hung with a broad white horse-leather strap or belt, and their bayonets, etc. on the other side, with the same, which two, crossing on the shoulders diamond-fashion, gives an agreeable appearance . . . The light infantry are in green . . . They exercise in the neighboring groves, firing at marks and throwing their tomahawks, forming on a sudden into line, and then, at the word, breaking their order and taking their parts to hit the mark. West of this city is a large open square of nearly two miles each way, with large groves on each side, in which, each afternoon, they collect, with a vast number of spectators." Scharf & Westcott, *History of Philadelphia,* I, 296.

though he was later to have numerous brushes with violence, while acting in other capacities. Vivid and accurate, his account was as follows:

My dear Sally,

Your favor of the 21st instant I received on Wednesday by George Armitage, who is in Captn Purviance's company. I am happy in your prayers and good wishes. The articles you mention in your Lrs to have sent me are all safe come to hand. Be pleased to send me my saddle and bridle by some safe conveyance to this place. I think the Bordentown stage will be the best way, if you write to Mr Borden to forward it.

On Tuesday morning I marched in here in full parade with 360 odd men in the Battalion, officers included; two of my companies are still in Philadia, but I expect one of them here soon, which will make my Battalion pretty respectable. Some of my men got sick at Trenton by drinking the water there & lying on the ground in Camp, but they all recovered excepting two or three, who remain unwell. I wish Doctr Harris would come up here immediately, his delay is inexcusable

I am at the time of writing this within about six hund yards of the Enemy, hundreds of whom I have seen every day since my arrival, and not an hour passes without seeing a great many of them. On Wednesday, a little after dark, as I stood near a little Battery of two four pounders close on the Sound within fifty feet of Courtlandt Skinner's house, I decryed a shallop sailing close along the Enemy's shore (the distance about the width of Christiana at the Ferry, or a little more) and ordered the Centinel to hail her to bring too; they made no answer; the same was done a second time without any ans. upon which I ordered the Centinel to fire, which he did, and then one of four pounders was discharged; but a very heavy rain falling at that instant and the wind being very high, and the night very dark insomuch that we could not see the shallop, except when it lightened, she went around the Island to the men of war, and the matter ended there. These were the first guns I ever ordered to be fired agt human Beings, if I may be allowed to call the Enemies of Mankind such.

Yesterday about four a clock in the afternoon, 5 more shallops sailed along in the same manner, when our two guns (being all we had in Town, Captn Moulder's of Philadia his two field-pieces being in our Camp, half a Mile off) were discharged—I was in the Camp, where I had received orders from the General to hold my Battalion in readiness to march into the Town at a minute's warning; we got under arms and I never saw more alacrity for any thing, than they shewed universally for an Engagement. I left them under Lt Colonel Dean to be marched to Town, whilst I mounted my horse and waited on the General in Town for orders; on the road which is a strait & wide lane (something like market street) all the way from the camp to the Sound, and in a line with the Enemies Batteries, about twenty Cannon Balls flew close to me sometimes on one side and sometimes on the other and some just over my head, and made such a noise thro' the Air that my horse was frightened & would scarcely go along; I confess I was not a little alarmed myself (being the first time I had ever heard a cannon ball) but clapped spurs on my horse and rode on amidst the balls to the General's, where I had just received orders to make the Battalion halt until further orders, and was going to execute them when on turning round I saw a horse shot thro' the neck with a four pounder within much less distance than the width of Market street from me—The fire was so incessant and so direct on the street I had to return, that some Gentlemen begged of me to wait a little, but as the troops under my care were in full march, and Colonel Miles's Battalion close behind them, I thought it my duty to stop them, as some of them otherwise would probably be killed without a chance of effecting any beneficial service. On my return I found the fire hotter than before (the Enemy then playing from three Batteries of 3 or 4 guns each) but thro' God's favor I escaped unhurt and marched the troops to the Camp. By the balls we picked up we found they had from 4 pounders to 18 pounders, some of which are in my camp—The Shallops got by, tho, Captn Moulder had got on the bank without any covering & fired several good shots at them. His Artillery comp^y were exceedingly exposed as they stood on the bank at the end of the street or lane I before described. Upon the shallops having got out of our reach our cannon ceased, as did that of the Enemy. The actions continued about half an hour, the Enemy fired about 60 shots, and our few cannon about 20, as they always gave us three for one. A private in Captn Weed's comp^y Col. Bayard's Battalion (an Apprentice of Captn Weed's) being in the Guard-house near the roof (the Court-house is the Guard-house) was killed, and another in the same Battalion was wounded but not dangerously—No other damages done except the killing the horse, and about a dozen shot thro' the houses—The Enemy fired well, and so did our Artillery, many shots on both sides hitting within a few feet of the spots they were intended for. I am pretty well, tho' as Field-Officer of the day, yesterday I was obliged to ride in the heat of the Sun and also in the night to assist [?] all our Guard & our Posts, which extend about four Miles. God Bless you.

                                                                Tho M:Kean [336]

Edward Burd of Lancaster and Reading (who was soon to be a prisoner of war, and after his exchange Prothonotary of the Supreme Court under McKean for many years) wrote a letter on the 28th, which tended to corroborate McKean's account: "There has been a Cannonade at Amboy brought on by our firing at the Vessel which was aground; We lost one man killed and one wounded—Tho' report has magnified it into a very important action. There are so many falsehoods spread abroad, that I never give credit to the first one, nor till I hear it confirmed several times." [337]

PART IV

CONSTRUCTIVE
POLITICS

Chapter 12

Revolutionary Governments, 1776–77

In May, 1777, a year before he died, the agonized and decrepit Earl of Chatham overcame his various ailments sufficiently to "crawl to the House of Lords" and deliver an address as remarkable for boldness of spirit as it was for feebleness of delivery. The great war minister, leaning on the arm of his son, William Pitt, the Younger, called on his country to admit that it had been mistaken, and to remove its armies from America forthwith:

> You may ravage—you cannot conquer; it is impossible; you cannot conquer the Americans. You talk . . . of your powerful forces, to disperse their army: I might as well talk of driving them before me with this crutch! . . . If you conquer them, what then? You cannot make them respect you, you cannot make them wear your cloth . . . coming from the stock they do they can never respect you . . . You have said, "Lay down your arms," and America has give you the Spartan answer: "Come take." . . . We are the aggressors. We have invaded them as much as the Spanish Armada invaded England.[1]

The following November, and again in December, he poured forth his soul in a series of addresses containing the accumulated experience of a lifetime spent in the service of his country, before a curiously indifferent House, urging and pleading—with unsurpassed eloquence—for a return to the virtues of a by-gone era:

> But yesterday and England might have stood against the world: now none so poor to do her reverence. I use the words of a poet, but, though it be poetry, it is no fiction . . . you may traffic and barter with every pitiful German prince that sells and sends his subjects to the shambles of a foreign prince; your efforts are for ever vain and impotent . . . your own army is infected with the contagion of these illiberal allies. The spirit of rapine and plunder is gone forth among them . . . it is not

189

the least of our national misfortunes, that the strength and character of our army are thus impaired: infected with the mercenary spirit of robbery and rapine—familiarized to the horrid scenes of savage cruelty, it can no longer boast of the noble and generous principles which dignify a soldier . . . Besides these murderers and plunderers, let me ask our ministers, what other allies they have acquired: . . . Have they entered into alliance with the king of the gipsies? Nothing, my Lords, is too low or too ludicrous to be consistent with their counsels . . . My Lords, if I were an American as I am an Englishman, while a foreign troop was landed in my country I never would lay down my arms—never—never—never! [2]

Chatham could no longer bend the government of England to his will, but the noble spirit of these magnificent addresses struck a spark with the Americans of that generation—whose conduct, indeed, had helped to inspire his eloquence—and many of them were encouraged to try to create new governments on this continent that would be worthy of respect. This spirit was so general in the early period, sweeping along so many of the Americans, that the insistent rhetoric of their speeches, their letters, and their prayers sounds artificial to a less idealistic generation. But there is no mistaking the sincerity of the tone, whether found in private communications or in public manifestoes.

Witness Thomas McKean, at headquarters in Perth Amboy, writing to "Dear Sally" on Aug. 7, 1776, that he did not expect to be included in the Constitutional Convention of the Lower Counties at New Castle, and really wished "to be rid of all public employments, tho' that I fear is impossible, but I must make a struggle for it, as I am injuring my fortune and my health rather too much—too much, did I say, no nothing is too great a sacrifice to preserve the liberties of my country. My life shall follow the loss of them." [3] At the time of this writing he was forty-two, older than most of the men around him; nevertheless, he would not know the luxury of retirement from strenuous and bitterly contested public employments until he was in his seventy-fifth year.

The military skill of the Americans, at the beginning of the war, was notoriously unequal to their valor. Their forces in the New York area were driven back from one defensive post to another, and many enthusiastic volunteers were captured by the enemy almost before they began to fight. Colonel Daniel Brodhead reported to his friends in Philadelphia, "Upon the whole, less Generalship never was shown in any Army since the Art of War was understood, except in the retreat from Long Island, which was well conducted . . ." [4] Before the campaign was over, some of the battered Pennsylvania battalions were consolidated by General Washington in a regiment under Col. Brodhead's command, and that harassed officer was enquiring anxiously whether his troops were considered as Continental volunteers or as Pennsylvania soldiers "subject to the order of [the] Convention." He wondered whether his units would be filled by drafts or by recruiting, and whether promotions would be "settled upon a more respectable footing than at present." At the moment, he complained, a Lieutenant Colonel commissioned by Congress "as of yesterday, takes rank of me to-day." He also pointed out that Continental prisoners of war would be exchanged before state troops, and that this was causing a morale problem in some units.[5]

One of the first prisoners from Pennsylvania was Edward Burd (who would soon be Prothonotary of McKean's Supreme Court). The truth of Col. Brodhead's observations as to the uncertain status of the Pennsylvania troops was amply demonstrated by Burd's description of General Washington's surprise at Burd's good fortune in getting himself released. Writing on December 12, 1776, to his father, James Burd, who had served as a Colonel in the French and Indian War, Burd described a typical military mix-up to an old soldier, who would fully appreciate how much difference a small slip of paper could make:

> I am at last so fortunate as to be exchanged, though it happened not by intention, but accident. General Washington sent about ten or twelve prisoners to New York, and intended to name the persons who were to be sent in exchange; but Gen. Howe took the first Major, Captains, Lieutenants, &c, who happened to be on his list of prisoners, and sent them in exchange. I happened to be the first Major, and was therefore so lucky as to be returned. General Washington was surprised to see me. However he was so polite as to tell me, that from the character I bore he was satisfied with my being the person, though he did not like the mode, especially as I was in a Standing Regiment . . .[6]

Matters of rank and precedence were of vast importance in the military world, as the recently enlisted civilians in the American army were learning every day. McKean wrote to General Washington from Perth Amboy on August 10, inquiring "whether, when a Brigade is drawn up, and the oldest Colonel takes the Right, his Battalion is to be on the right with him; that is, whether the Colonel gives rank to the Battalion," [7] and received in reply a four-page letter in Washington's own hand, attempting with some difficulty to straighten him out. Washington may have been uncertain as to the correct answer, or he may have been worried about making himself clear to a Philadelphia lawyer; on safety's side, he added a post-script almost as long as the original letter—all this is the face of the enemy—as follows: "Perhaps I may not have fully understood the tendency of the question propounded to me & consequently have given an indecisive answer—the Idea I meant to convey is this, that the Regiment takes Rank from the time it is raised, and cannot be deprived of that Rank by the change of its Colonel—if therefore three Regiments should be formed into a Brigade, the eldest of these Regiments will take the Right, although it is Commanded by the Youngest Colo., but if there shd be no Genl. Officer to comd these three Regiments the Senior Colonel of course does it—not the Colonel of the Senior Regiment—In short [and so on]." [8] The reasons for McKean's inquiries were not clear; perhaps he wanted special privileges for his battalion because of his own seniority. Washington's letter, whatever its military usefulness, was carefully saved and sent to Sally, who was beginning to organize McKean's papers.[9]

McKean's own letters in this period reveal an intense concern over the political situation in the Lower Counties, his power base, which he had neglected for so many weeks before the Declaration of Independence in his preoccupation with Pennsylvania affairs. "Please to let me know, whether Messrs. Read and Rodney are again returned to the Congress, and also all the News of the city," he had written to Sally on August 1st.[10] One of the disadvantages of service in the field was the absence of news, and for someone who had been at the center of affairs for so long this sudden exile was a difficult trial. Perhaps he had premonitions of political defeat; there was much dissaffection to the revolutionary cause in Sussex and Kent Counties, and Newcastle County was not altogether immune. McKean and Rodney were subject to increasing attacks in their home districts, because of their close connection with each other and their conspicuous leadership, while Read's vote against Lee's resolution of independence and thus against the Declaration (which, however, he signed) and Dickinson's opposition to these measures were a great deal more popular with Delaware's conservative farmers. Dickinson, like McKean, was a man who could hold office in either Pennsylvania or Delaware, and although temporarily eclipsed in the former state, his star was high in the latter.

The central and southern parts of Delaware were isolated and remote. Few travellers passed that way, and the local farmers were seldom exposed to new ideas. The radicals from the north were frequently irritated by the southerners' "changeless loyalty to the old order," [11] and the committees of inspection which had been duly appointed in that area had run into constant opposition, and even an armed "insurrection" in Sussex County in the spring of 1776.[12] McKean was aware of this attitude, and was apprehensive. As things turned out, Rodney was the victim, not McKean, in the elections of August 19 for the Delaware Constitutional Convention (because Kent was more conservative than Newcastle), but both were marked men. By late autumn they had both lost their positions in the Continental Congress, for the first time since the Congress had been formed.

Such speculations as to the coming months at New Castle were undoubtedly going through McKean's mind as he posted guards at Amboy, and fretted about the state of his health. His tour of duty in the military was the first time he had ever been concerned about his physical condition. "I am better in health within these two days," he wrote Sally on August 1st, "than since I left Philadelphia, owing in a good degree to my bathing in the Evening in the salt water here. There is a very neat little Bath-house erected some years ago, but still in good order, which I propose to frequent as often as I can." [13]

One suspects that McKean's relations with his men were only fair. He had been a judge and a top-level politician too long, and had lost the habit, forced at best, of associating with ordinary people on terms of equality. He got along with his fellow officers reasonably well, but the enlisted men were another matter. Later he wrote to Joseph Reed that he had under his command "some of the most rude, turbulent, impudent, lazy, dirty fellows . . . that I have ever beheld." [14] The men probably reciprocated the distaste. Indeed, McKean must have received more deference and respect from General Washington, and other high-ranking officers, than he did from his own troops. One of his soldiers publicly recalled (inconveniently, during McKean's first gubernatorial campaign) that "from his tyrannical, arbitary, imposing conduct upon the soldiery, not a single man in the battalion either loved, feared, or respected him . . . They even looked upon him as a base, tyrannical, over-bearing coward." [15] His vanity undoubtedly suffered as he discovered his lack of aptitude for the military calling.

All his life he was to have difficulty in give-and-take situations, except with people in positions of power, and even then his temper was short.

Some of the officers, he wrote Sally, had received visits from their wives at headquarters, "and I hear Mrs. Roberdeau intends to stay a fortnight longer;" but, he hastened to add, "I confess I have not a wish to see you or any of my female relations in a Camp, or in an Army, which may be drawn into action every day, nay every hour." [16] He relented a week later, however, and told her to put their servant, Alister, in new livery and come to the camp briefly, leaving the children with their grandparents at Bordentown.[17] He was bothered that he could not compete with his brother officers socially, as he had not made adequate preparations. "I have dined with the Generals, Colo. Miles, Bayard &c. since I arrived here, who keep so much better tables than I do, that I shall be at a loss to return the complimts, as I did not expect any delicacies when I left Philada." [18] He commented on the homesickness of some of his men, and evidently shared it. His letters always ended with great affection. "Give my love to Josey and Robert; kiss Nancy for me; Love me and pray for me . . ." [19] Sally McKean apparently had an unusually warm relationship with her new family at this time, for it must be remembered that these were her step-children. Her only child had died.

Thus, when McKean received word that Caesar Rodney had failed of election to Delaware's Constitutional Convention—defeated by a faction in Kent headed by Dr. Charles Ridgely, despite his many services as Speaker of the Assembly, and delegate to Congress—and when Rodney wrote him that *he* had been elected to the Convention, and that his presence was urgently required at New Castle, McKean did not hesitate. Each of the three counties had been allotted ten delegates, and in the elections, August 19, the conservatives swept Sussex and Kent Counties, even winning part of the Newcastle delegation.[20] Important as the meeting would be, it was now more so for the convention would not only determine the state's future form of government, but also perhaps the extent to which it would continue to support the revolution. Here he could be of greater service, and as the Associators were about to be mustered out anyhow, this was the call of duty.[21] Fortunately, he was able to resign his commission and comply with Rodney's request, arriving at New Castle by way of Philadelphia in time for the opening session on August 27.* Neither of the two men liked the make-up of the

---

* Caesar Rodney wrote to his brother on Aug. 28, "As soon as I Recd the accounts from Kent and Newcastle of the Elections I wrote to Mr. McKean at Amboy and desired he would give immediate attendance at the Convention. He got my Letter and in Consequence thereof Came to Philadelphia on Sunday Night last, and set out Yesterday morning [Tuesday, the 27th] very early to Newcastle." (Ryden, *op. cit.*, 105.) Thus, incidentally, McKean had only one day in Philadelphia during which he could have signed the engrossed Declaration of Independence, and presumably did not do so at that time. He and Rodney were greatly preoccupied with the forthcoming Delaware Convention.

Benjamin Franklin had written McKean at Perth Amboy on Aug. 24, not knowing that he was about to leave the army, saying: "I heard your letter read in Congress relating to the Disposition of the German Troops . . ." and suggesting a strategem by which propaganda leaflets could be smuggled into the Hessian camp, with a little tobacco in each package, so that "it would be divided among them as Plunder before the officers would know the Contents of the Papers & prevent it." (McKean Papers, HSP, I and Burnett, *Letters,* II, 90.)

Convention, and both feared that it would exceed its prerogatives by assuming control of the government—the usual first step of revolutionary bodies, as they well knew.

The justice of their fears as to the complexion of the group was confirmed when George Read, who had voted against independence only a month before, was made president of the Convention.[22] True, Read had signed the engrossed Declaration, when it was presented to the members on August 2, and was still a warm friend to American liberty as he understood it, but Rodney and McKean had not forgotten the jolt he had given them on the first of July. The rift in the triumvirate was widened by Read's suggestion that Rodney should be allowed to serve as the single delegate for Delaware in the Continental Congress, provided the Convention at New Castle approved of the change.[23] McKean had learned of this suggestion during his brief visit with Rodney in Philadelphia, on his way to the Convention, and had objected to the precedent of allowing the Convention to make this decision, for fear they would use the appointment as an entering wedge for other actions which "they would willingly be at," and Rodney had agreed with him.[24]

McKean viewed the move as a plot to get rid of both him and Rodney: Rodney would not be in the Convention, and now he himself was to be eased out of Congress. Obviously they would have to defend themselves as best they could; Read's suggestion was not to be regarded as merely a practical means of obtaining immediate representation for the state. No one understood more clearly than McKean what a run-away convention could do to humiliate established authorities—had he not recently presided over just such a meeting in Pennsylvania? If a radical Conference of Committees could destroy a conservative Assembly, a conservative Convention could certainly eliminate radical delegates to Congress in the same manner. Rodney reported to his brother on August 28 that McKean had instantly decided that "they" should not turn him or anyone else out. He had said that "for his part he is tired of attending the Congress . . . [but] if they are determined to do these things by the Strength of their Majority, he will try the Strength of the County with *them* even at the risk of the Court House." [25]

There has long been a tradition that McKean was such a dominant figure at this Convention that he *wrote* the state's revolutionary constitution, by himself in a single evening. This myth had its origin in a letter McKean wrote to Caesar A. Rodney (nephew of Caesar Rodney, the Signer) in 1813; it was elaborated on by Sanderson in the 1820's and embellished still more by Roberdeau Buchanan in 1890.[26] McKean's statement in that letter was, "I went to Newcastle, joined the Convention for forming a constitution for the future government of the State of Delaware (having been elected a member for Newcastle county) which I wrote in a tavern, without a book or any assistance." By the time the story reached Buchanan it had acquired a few more detailed adornments, as follows: "Immediately upon his arrival, after a fatiguing ride, he was waited upon by a committee of gentlemen, members of the convention, who requested that he would prepare the constitution for them. He retired to his room at the public inn, sat up all night, and wrote the constitution *without the aid of a book or the least assistance.*

At ten o'clock the next morning, it was presented to the convention, by whom it was unanimously adopted . . . This has been justly regarded as the greatest act of Mr. McKean's life . . ." [27]

Unfortunately, the facts were not so flattering. McKean was not a member of the dominant faction at the Convention; he had had no time for advance preparation with anyone except Caesar Rodney, who had not been elected; he was frequently frustrated by actions he disapproved, which had been decided "out of doors;" and he was obliged to request leave for a week because of the illness of his son and nephew, and the death of his sister, Dorothea Thompson. The journals of the Convention record that the first session was called to order on Tuesday, August 27, and while the Convention was being organized—from Friday, the 30th, until Friday, September 6—McKean was absent, at the Thompson's home at Red Lion Hundred, attending his sister's funeral.

During that week, George Read was elected president of the Convention, rules were adopted, and committees were appointed for the framing of a bill of rights and a constitution. The former was adopted on September 11, and the latter was agreed to in substance, with a few important exceptions, on the 18th. The language of the constitution was fully approved on the 20th, and the Convention adjourned on the 21st,[28] George Read having been chairman of the two most important committees as well as president of the Convention. No wonder Read's grandson and biographer took pains to refute Sanderson's account of McKean's writing this constitution.[29] And no wonder a modern historian, John A. Munroe, has concluded that "the final draft was more probably a cooperative work to which many minds contributed." [30] McKean's paper-work on the night of his arrival might have been an agenda for the Convention, or an outline of the constitution, to be coordinated with the other leaders. A third, and more plausible explanation was that McKean, who was familiar with the Pennsylvania bill of rights, which appeared in the *Pennsylvania Gazette* for August 21, might have drafted a similar one for Delaware, and years later confused this with the drafting of a constitution.[31] Any one of these projects would have been a major intellectual undertaking.

In view of McKean's caution, if not hostility, towards Read, it is noteworthy to find the latter writing in such friendly terms about him, as in the following letter to Rodney, on August 30: "Mr. McKean has been absent since yesterday Noon his Son being sick at Mr. Thompson's—Your Hble Servt. is in the Chair which he wants size as well as Capacity to fill." [32] Also (as quoted in a letter from Rodney to Haslet, on September 12): "Our business has been delayed in Convention by the death of Mrs. Thompson, the sister of Mr. McKean, who was burried this day, Mr. McKean's Eldest Son lies dangerously ill at Mr. Thompson's house, and I know not when he can attend." [33] Manifestly Read considered McKean a useful and necessary member of the Convention, not an enemy.

Mrs. Thompson died on the 2nd, and McKean wrote a characteristic letter to Sally on that date, explaining the arrangements that had been made, and then disguising the whole experience, which must have been an emotional one, in the conventional trappings of religion. The religion was no doubt sincere, but it smothered the emotion and allowed only a breath of feeling to come through, the pain he felt at the loss of so many of his family:

> At nine o'clock this morning precisely my sister Thompson took her departure for the region of spirits to join her parents, brother & daughter, and the whole righteous choir in Heaven, in singing Hallelujah to the most High—She will be buried at Newcastle along side her daughter on Wednesday about twelve o'clock.
>
> Josey M'Kean has had a severe time of it; ten days continual fever; everything has been done for him since I came that (I believe) could be done, and I now have hopes of his recovery. I shall be glad to see you at Newcastle on Wednesday, if you can come then.
>
> You may come down in the Chariot or Chaise, and make Sam drive you. If Josey recovers, he must return Home with you as soon as he can ride.[34]

McKean returned to the Convention on Friday, September 6, and his brother-in-law, John Thompson, a political ally as well, returned the following week.[35] On the 7th McKean was added to the committees for preparing a bill of rights and a constitution, and the work of these committees proceeded more rapidly because of his attendance.[36] Despite the earlier fears of the radicals, the Convention made no efforts to take over the functions of the government, except to expedite the military operations that were already under way. Caesar Rodney in Philadelphia kept in close touch with George Read, and was able to write on the 11th to his brother in Dover, "From what I can learn of the Convention at Newcastle—They will attempt nothing but Barely the framing a plan of Government Except what may be necessary for the dispatching the flying Camp Battalion. Mr. Read lets me know that matters go on Sloely, and that the members of Kent & Sussex grow uneasy to get home—This is (I know) as it used to be with them." [37] By restraining their activities in this way, the Delaware Convention kept radicals and conservatives working together in harness, and did not tear the state apart, as Pennsylvania had been torn.

On the 17th Read wrote to Rodney that because of the "daily amendmts" he had not been able to keep up his correspondence, but that things were now pretty well in hand. A Declaration of Rights and Privileges had been drawn up, based on the Pennsylvania and Maryland drafts, which he "did not think . . . an object of much curiosity"—presumably because the delegates had been content to borrow so much of their language from other states.[38] Also, the general heads of the new frame of government, he believed, were at that point almost complete. Events were to prove, however, that this happy state of affairs was actually the calm in the center of a hurricane, because several practical questions as to the way in which the new government would be established had been left until last. The lightning and thunder were about to begin and, as might be expected, McKean was the one who invoked the storm. Read was genuinely surprised at the great burst of passion that arose at the end of the Convention, when the issues which were theoretically the most difficult had already been settled.

For example, the Convention had dealt with the slavery question and, while reluctant to declare the equality of all men, had decided to prevent an increase in the existing slave population, by outlawing the slave trade. The article that was adopted was as follows: "No person hereafter imported into this State from Africa ought to be held in slavery under any pretence whatever; and no negro, Indian, or mulatto slave ought to be brought into this State, for sale, from any part of the world." The Convention had also considered ways in which to separate church and state, and had declared that "no clergyman or preacher of the gospel of any denomination shall be capable of holding any civil office in this state, or of being a member of either of the branches of the legislature while they continue in the exercise of the pastoral function." McKean had led the fight to expunge this clause; in one of the only cases in which the record indicated the yeas and nays he lost by a vote of 20 to 5.[39] Unwilling to exclude clerics like Dr. Alison and Dr. Witherspoon from the political process, McKean was not unaware of the potential Presbyterian predominance in the new revolutionary electorate, but the issue had been decided in a decent, parliamentary manner, and without anger.

The explosion on the evening of the 18th was described by McKean in a long letter to Rodney the next day "while the facts [were still] recent and fresh" in his memory. The thirty articles of the proposed constitution had all been agreed to, except for the last three, but "in reading one of [them] after nine o'clock last night we got into great heats." [40] The president of the new government, according to the draft which McKean said he had prepared, would have been "a discreet, modest & respectable Magistrate and useful member of Society," but instead he was likely to be "a very powerful & dangerous man." McKean, at this stage, was still trying to limit the state's authority, and was less far-sighted than some of his conservative colleagues. Apparently he did not imagine, as yet, the role he would soon be playing in strengthening the hand of the executive (and the judiciary) in the state governments that were presently being formed. Like most of the members of the convention he was groping his way from day to day, changing his mind occasionally or compromising, even on basic principles of government.

Another dispute arose on the heels of the first when Mr. Basset moved, and Dr. Ridgely seconded, the motion that the next elections should be held on October 21. This, McKean wrote, "displeased me, and some others who had no private selfish views, very much." [41] He argued vehemently that an election held so soon would penalize Colonels Haslet and Patterson, and their two battalions, and that these men who were away from home, risking their lives for their country, would probably be unable to win offices or distinction under the new government, but "I might as well have harangued the walls—the matter had been settled out of doors, and the new elections and the loaves and fishes, were to be secured at all events."

Then came the climax, and again it seemed to McKean to be part of a plot by the conservatives to control the new government. Mr. Basset moved, and Dr. Ridgely seconded, the motion that the General Assembly of the new government should meet at Dover—thereby perhaps removing the capital of Delaware from New Castle. McKean thought he recognized a deadly challenge, and did his best to stave it off:

I answered the Gentlemen, that the Seats of Justice in each county, and the seat of Government for the colony, were fixed by acts of Assembly, and that we might as well remove the one as the other, and indeed repeal any other laws or make any new one we thought proper—that we were not vested with the legislative power, being expressly chosen for the purpose of "ordaining and declaring the future form of government for this State," which being a special purpose excluded an Idea of any other being delegated, as no other was mentioned—that the Sovereign power of the state resided in the people collectively, and they had delegated a certain portion of it to us, which if we exceeded we were usurpers & tyrants—However the matter had been determined out of doors as usual, and no reply was made (for truly none could be made) . . .[42]

How much his attitude had changed since the Conference of Committees in Pennsylvania! Strangely, no one pointed out his inconsistency; an *argumentum ad hominem* might have been the best reply in these circumstances, but no one dared to attack him yet. He would have taken it as an attack on the sovereign people. Some members of the Convention, surely, were familiar with McKean's connection with the "tyrants & usurpers" in Pennsylvania; this may have been what deterred them. It was more convenient to vote him down. The upshot was that after much sparring over the lateness of the hour, the number of absentees, and whether or not the previous question should be put, McKean was defeated 14 to 11, primarily by the Kent and Sussex delegations.

"Upon this I told the President that I could not with honor, nor in conscience, sit any longer in such an Assembly, and took my hat and withdrew, being followed by VanDike, Jones, Robinson, &c. but before Mr. Thompson and Mr. Evans came away, the other Gentlemen moved to adjourn, which was done whilst there were twenty (including the Presid.) which was just a quorum . . ."[43] The next day the dispute was straightened out, and the disagreement blew over, but obviously there had not been anyone there *to ring the changes on conscience,* as McKean had done at the Stamp Act Congress. The chief difficulties had come over the control of the prospective government, rather than over the form it was to take.

The constitution that was drafted was a moderate document that was to serve the state of Delaware for the next sixteen years.[44] It was the first of the state constitutions to be approved by a convention specially elected for the purpose, the procedure that was later considered "correct," but it was not submitted to the people afterwards for ratification. The duly elected delegates did not care to risk any further expression of public opinion from an ulta-conservative agricultural community, isolated on a peninsula subject to interference by Tory raiders and British sea power. By the adoption of this constitution the Lower Counties officially became "The Delaware State."

The terms of the constitution bore a remarkable resemblance to those of the British government, and at the same time approached the American norm that was gradually being established, as state after state set up their revolutionary governments.[45] The Delaware government was far from radical, and had few of the eccentric features that characterized the Constitution of 1776 in Pennsylvania. As in most of the new governments, during the early part of the revolution, the executive and judicial branches were weak and were dominated by the legislature. The American leaders had had long experience in controlling legislative bodies, and tended to regard legislatures as the embodiment of the will of the people.

It would have been heresy at this early date to suggest that the executive or the courts might on occasion be more representative of public opinion than the branch then commonly referred to as the "popular" branch. There had been periods in English history, to be sure, when the King or the judges had defended the rights of the people, as against the entrenched interests of the parliamentary big-wigs, but these episodes were foreign to the experience of the Americans. Not until after they had absorbed a few sad lessons on the possibilities of legislative tyranny could they subject their favorite prejudices to a somewhat more critical analysis.

There was to be a bicameral legislature known as the General Assembly, with an upper house called the Legislative Council and a lower house called the House of Assembly.[46] The Council would have three members from each county, rotating so that each county would elect one member every year, who would serve for three years. The members of the Assembly were to be elected annually, seven from each county; it would be similar to the colonial Assembly. Only freeholders owning "fifty acres of land or more well settled, and twelve acres thereof cleared and improved, or . . . [freeholders] otherwise worth Forty Pounds" were to have the right to vote, as before the revolution. Money bills were to originate in the Assembly, but they could always be altered, amended, or rejected by the Council.

A president enjoying a three-year term would be elected by the General Assembly—with a privy council of four members, two chosen by the Council and two by the House, whose chief function was to limit the president's initiative. The president, in conjunction with the entire legislature, would name judges for the Supreme Court and the Admiralty Court, the judges to hold office during good behavior. In conjunction with the privy council the president could lay an embargo "not exceeding thirty days" during a recess of the General Assembly, and could call up the militia with the consent of the privy council, and thereafter act as its commander-in-chief. He could not, however, prorogue, adjourn, or dissolve the General Assembly. The highest court of the state was to be a Court of Appeals consisting of the president and six members-at-large appointed by the legislature. Justices of the peace were to be appointed by the president, with the approval of the privy council, but from a list made out by the General Assembly. In case of the death or absence of the president, the speaker of the Council would take his place, and after him the speaker of the Assembly. It was under this provision that McKean was to become Acting President at the time of the British invasion.

Elections to state and county offices were to be held every year on October 1st, and the General Assembly was to convene on the 20th. Delegates to Congress were to be chosen each year by a joint ballot of the two houses, which thus controlled the relationship of Delaware with the other twelve states. Amendments to the constitution could only be made by a vote of five-sevenths of the House and seven-ninths of the Council, but certain provisions were declared to be unamend- able, such as the prohibition of the slave trade. The English common law, and as much of the English statute law "as had been heretofore adopted in practice," were proclaimed to be in force, as if the revolutionaries were anxious to show that only they were faithful to the true spirit of English institutions—except, of course, in matters of religion. The framers had tried, in every way they knew, to introduce checks and balances separating the executive, legislative, and judicial functions, but the legislature was to exercise such powers of appointment and review, including the appointment of officers of the army and navy, that it would dominate the other two branches for a long time to come.

The actual use that the new legislature would make of its power remained to be seen; this was what had disturbed McKean for months, and it continued to do so. Presumably his days in Congress were numbered, for the conservatives would surely throw him out, once they came to power. Meanwhile, he had to hurry back to Philadelphia to attend Congress, and to find out what was going on in the Constitutional Convention of Pennsylvania, which had been meeting there since the middle of July. In this period, McKean's life was exclusively dedicated to public service; he was never to have time to think about or to take proper care of his private affairs. The Delaware Convention was dissolved on Saturday, Sep- tember 21, and McKean returned to Philadelphia immediately.

In Congress on Wednesday, the 25th, he was appointed to a committee of thir- teen, one from each state, to purchase blankets and clothing for the Continental Army, and on the 27th he was appointed to a committee of three, with Edward Rutledge and William Hooper, to deal with certain resolutions of the Conven- tion of New York relating to General Schuyler.[47] The less he could rely on the conservatives in Delaware, the more he had to place his confidence in the radical leaders in Congress. His position with his constituents at home had been pre- carious ever since he had thrown off the mask, and come out openly for inde- pendence, back in the month of May.

The Congress was still operating by consensus. The Articles of Confederation, drafted by a committee headed by John Dickinson and presented to Congress in July, 1776, had been debated for about a month and dropped in August.[48] They were taken up again in April, 1777, but were not agreed upon by Congress and sent to the states for ratification until November, 1777—and because the state of Maryland held out on the issue of Congressional control of western lands, they were not finally ratified until March, 1781, by which time the war was prac- tically over. In the meantime the states were held together, contrary to the pre- dictions of many experts, by the good sense and mutual respect of the revolu- tionary leaders, provided each man's "heartiness" in the cause was beyond dis- pute.

In this sense the arrival of the British army, and their occupation of certain seaboard cities, greatly aided the patriots, because the more overt loyalists fled to the protection of the British army, and the citizens who remained could be trusted, though they might have to be watched. The presence of a foreign army separated the sheep from the goats, and made the work of the revolutionary committees easier. The clearer the line between the British and American forces, the better for both sides. Neutral, or disputed, territory like the Delmarva Peninsula presented special problems.

One of the best examples of the willingness of the revolutionary leaders to tolerate divergent views—and the limitations of their tolerance—was that provided by the career of John Dickinson in the months after he had voted against independence.[49] Other members of Congress had voted against Lee's motion in July, but had signed the engrossed parchment on August 2nd. By that date, Dickinson was no longer qualified to sign, having been replaced as a delegate, but there was no indication that had he been, he would have changed his mind. He was not the indecisive person he has so often been called, but on the contrary was one of the most decisive and idealistic men in his generation. Furthermore, he and McKean were the only two members of Congress who took up arms in defense of their country in the year following the Declaration, and Dickinson did so promptly in spite of the fact that he had voted against the policy that was adopted.

Dickinson and McKean both commanded battalions of the Pennsylvania Associators, and Dickinson as the senior Colonel was originally the commanding officer of the whole force. However, some of the soldiers held an impromptu election and chose Daniel Roberdeau as their commander in his stead, and the Constitutional Convention in Pennsylvania later confirmed the choice made by the men, as part of their campaign to discredit the Assembly which had commissioned the leaders of the Associators in the first place. The Convention had already removed Dickinson from his position as one of Pennsylvania's delegates to the Congress.

Dickinson thereupon resigned his commission and retired to his estates—only to reenlist as a private soldier in the Delaware militia, in time to be wounded in the shoulder in a skirmish at the Head of Elk. With John Evans of Newark, he was chosen by the new government of Delaware as a delegate to Congress on November 8, when Read was re-elected but McKean and Rodney dropped. This petty revenge on the radical faction soon lost any sweetness; for many months the state was not represented in Congress because Read, as Speaker of Delaware's Legislative Council, was too busy to attend, and Dickinson and Evans refused to serve, pleading illness—which, in Dickinson's case, at least, was true for some time.[50]

Later Dickinson was to serve as President (Governor) of Delaware, then in Pennsylvania as President of the Supreme Executive Council, holding both positions before the war was formally terminated. In a speech before Congress in 1779, he explained the principles which had guided him:

> Two rules I have laid down for myself throughout this contest, to which I have constantly adhered, and still design to adhere; first, on all occasions where I am called upon, as a trustee for my countrymen, to deliberate on questions important to their happiness, disdaining all personal advantages to be derived from a suppression of my real sentiments, and defying all dangers to be risked by a declaration of

them, openly to avow them; and, secondly, after thus discharging this duty, whenever the public resolutions are taken, to regard them though opposite to my opinion, as sacred, because they lead to public measures in which the Commonwealth must be interested, and to join in supporting them as earnestly as if my voice had been given for them. If the present day is too warm for me to be calmly judged, I can credit my country for justice some years hence.[51]

Dickinson's confidence that his countrymen would eventually do him justice was based on a generous estimate of their good will and fair-mindedness. Unfortunately, his reputation was permanently branded by his vote against independence, and the strictures of John Adams and the radicals continually haunted his public life. It was particularly disheartening that he should be charged with timidity and indecisiveness, and an undue concern for the security of private property, by John Adams—who was at one point to be the leader of the High Federalists—when he himself remained a liberal humanitarian. McKean, to his credit, never joined in the criticisms of Dickinson and, though they had their differences in moments of political passion, they ended their days as Jeffersonian democrats, and friends to the last.

Charles Thomson was another strong patriot who retained a proper respect for John Dickinson's integrity and public spirit, writing him on August 16, 1776, when Dickinson was at his lowest point: "There are some expressions in your letter, which I am sorry for, because they seem to flow from a wounded spirit . . . [your countrymen] did not desert you. You left them. Possibly they were wrong in quickening their march and advancing to the goal with such rapid speed. They thought they were right, and the only 'fury' they showed against you was to choose other leaders to conduct them." [52]

On October 3, 1776, the Secret Committee of the Congress was empowered to take such measures as they deemed necessary for the purchasing and arming of a frigate and two cutters, with the expectation that the frigate would make "a cruize in the British channel against our enemies." [53] A few days before, without publicity, Congress had chosen Benjamin Franklin, Thomas Jefferson, and Silas Deane, who was already in Europe, to represent them at the court of Louis XVI in Paris, where naval expeditions of this sort could be financed and organized.* Jefferson's wife was ill at the time, so he declined the appointment, and his place was taken by Arthur Lee who was then in London.

McKean had been an active member of the Secret Committee before his departure for military service in New Jersey, and presumably was privy to these plans which were later implemented by a small fleet, under joint Franco-American sponsorship, commanded by John Paul Jones.[54] On a more mundane level, Councils of Safety and Committees of Inspection everywhere were instructed to

---

* Carl Van Doren, *Benjamin Franklin* (New York, 1938), 563–5. On his departure for France Franklin left his papers with Joseph Galloway, his lawyer, who was to have been one of the executors of his estate. Galloway was still in retirement at Trevose, fuming at the course of events, but giving no outward indication as to his future plans. Late in November, 1776—while the British were advancing across New Jersey, and before their set-backs at Trenton and Princeton—Galloway swam his horse across the Delaware River, and fled to the protection of the British army.

collect blankets, linen, and woolens, suitable for the army and forward them to designated points. In Delaware it was George Read who headed the operation, and by the middle of November, he and Rodney "sent to the care of Thomas McKean, Esqr. in Philadelphia by John Palmer, Shallopman, sixty Blankets and all the Cloths of any kind . . . suitable for the Delaware Battalion." [55] This battalion had gone to the defense of Philadelphia after the departure of the Pennsylvania Associators.

McKean was in Philadelphia in late September and early October; about the 10th of October, he returned to New Castle for a week or so of politicking, in preparation for the Delaware elections on the 21st. He was able to get himself included on a slate of nominees, and was one of the few radicals, or Whigs, elected to the new Assembly. But before the elections were held he had to return to Philadelphia to join a protest movement against the ultra-radical constitution that had been adopted by the Convention in Pennsylvania, under the leadership of James Cannon, and with the apparent sanction of Benjamin Franklin.

Immediately upon publication, the Pennsylvania constitution had been greeted by a storm of opposition, raised not only by conservatives like Dickinson, who felt that the Convention had been illegal and tyrannical from the beginning, but also by disgruntled radicals like Christopher Marshall and Benjamin Rush, who objected to one provision after another, and who now proposed to launch a full-scale campaign of opposition against it, comparable to the previous campaign against the Assembly, using many of the same techniques.[56] McKean, who had done so much to launch the Convention, was also disenchanted with the Pennsylvania constitution, and was prepared at this point to throw in with the opposition in the hope of obtaining a new convention, to draft a document more nearly similar to that of Delaware. He was in the odd position of being almost-too-radical in Delaware, and almost-too-conservative in Pennsylvania.

On October 17 there was a well-organized meeting at the Philosophical Hall, with printed tickets, "where met a large number of respectable citizens in order to consider of a mode to set aside sundry improper and unconstitutional rules laid down by the late Convention, in what they call their Plan or Frame of Government . . ." [57] The meeting passed numerous resolutions and made preparations for a "general town meeting" at the State House on Monday, the 21st, the proceedings of which were "to be printed and immediately transmitted to all the Counties of the State." [58] The radicals were temporarily abashed by the universal criticism of their work—in the city, if not in the outlying districts—and permitted the conservatives to organize against them with as much impunity as they had enjoyed in organizing against the distant British government.[59] McKean considered the forthcoming mass meeting of such great importance that he remained in Philadelphia to participate in it, rather than return to Delaware for the Assembly and Council elections, which were to be held on the same day.

The meeting in the State House Yard, the evening of October 21, was attended by about fifteen hundred people, and was conducted "with prudence and decency till dark." [60] Colonel John Bayard was chairman, and there were several speakers both for and against the new constitution. In favor were the chief architects of the radical persuasion: Cannon, Matlack, Young, and Smith; and against were Dickinson and McKean, the two members of Congress who, despite their political differences, had taken up arms together, and were now joining forces again in opposition to Pennsylvania's extreme radicalism. The discussions being inconclusive that evening, the meeting was adjourned until nine o'clock the next morning, at which time they were vigorously continued. The debate was carried on at a high intellectual level, but the opposition forces who had called the meeting had prepared their strategy, or their audience, more carefully, and the resolutions that were passed were highly critical of the proposed constitution.

The new government, it was said, "unnecessarily deviate[d] from all resemblance to the former government of this state." Also, and more notably, it differed from "every government that had lately been established in America on the authority of the people." [61] The resolutions expressed disapproval of the single-house legislature which had the power to remove judges from office at pleasure, and selected the executives and controlled them through the regulation of their salaries. The Supreme Court was attacked on the ground that it had original jurisdiction in some cases, but no Court of Appeals over it to correct its mistakes, or abuses of its power. The oaths prescribed by the new constitution were "unprecedented on this continent," and the odd method of amendment by a Council of Censors every seven years—a throwback to classical antiquity—might mean in practice that all amendments would be delayed until the need for them had passed.

McKean's position in the course of these debates is not clear from the records, but he had publicly opposed the constitution from the beginning, and only consented to serve under it when the leaders of Congress began to fear that the opposition forces in Pennsylvania were jeopardizing the entire revolution. His thinking on the subject had not yet matured, but he did feel an instinctive alarm at the new government's more democratic features.[62] Whatever the opposition had in mind, they accomplished relatively little.[63]

Within a week he had bounced back to New Castle to attend the General Assembly under the recently completed Delaware constitution, writing to Sally on October 31st, "I arrived here about dark the day I left you, and am well—Mr. Read is Speaker of the Council and Mr. McKinly of the Assembly—They were both chosen before I got down." [64] He was the only prominent Whig who had been elected to the Assembly, and knew that he would be given no voice in the selection of a Speaker. Indeed, it is possible that he owed his election in Delaware almost entirely to the fact that he had been helping John Dickinson and the conservative element in Pennsylvania, in their opposition to the radical constitution in the state. Dickinson still had enormous influence in Delaware, and McKean's participation in the public meetings in Philadelphia on October 21–22, far from being irrelevant to his political future in New Castle, may have been the direct cause of his success. The conservative leanings of the Delaware electorate were well known to everyone, and McKean had given serious consideration to the approach that he would make to his constituents in the days before his departure for the Philadelphia meetings. His electoral stance at home was certainly based on accurate information as to the state of public opinion there, for his participation in the Delaware Convention had kept him in close touch with all of the political leaders.

In Sussex the majority was not merely conservative, but downright "Tory" in the opinion of many observers. The situation was so bad that one Henry Fisher sent an "express" from Lewes to the Council of Safety in Pennsylvania, in care of Colonel McKean, and the latter endorsed it at New Castle on October 30th, forwarding it to Philadelphia. The election in the town of Lewes had "exhibited such a scene of disaffection to the common cause of America," according to this message, as had not been seen since the beginning of the struggle. "The few friends of America in this County [were] almost worn out with perpetual Contention . . . the streets resounded with huzzas for King George and General Howe . . ." [65] In short, the patriots needed protection. Mr. Fisher's letter was received by the Pennsylvania authorities, and transmitted on November 1st to Congress which immediately ordered "a part of a Virginia regiment now on the Eastern Shore of Maryland to march to Dover" and there to await further orders.[66] The new government in New Castle was meeting at a time of intermittent civil strife, complicated and intensified by the presence of enemy forces.

While these events were transpiring, the House of Assembly on the 30th appointed McKean, Cook, and Robinson a committee to confer with a like committee from the Council "on the forming a device and making a Great Seal for this State," [67] and on the next day McKean, Robinson, and Ridgely were appointed a committee for enlisting a Delaware battalion to join the service of the United States.[68] Both of these committeeships were established before McKean had had time to write his first letter to Sally, on the evening of the 31st. The ploy was to keep McKean busy with details of this sort, while on November 7 he and Rodney lost their all-important positions in the Congress, which they had held from the beginning. He was not to be kept down, however, for he continued to be an active member of the city committee in Philadelphia, and was soon chosen Speaker of the Assembly in Delaware, and suddenly became Acting President of that state by the fortunes of war, despite the fact that he was the only radical leader in the lower house of the legislature.

Having been removed from Congress, McKean concentrated all the more directly on Delaware and Pennsylvania politics. There was still much to be done, for the patriot forces were in disarray in both states. The General Assembly of Delaware remained in session for another few days, adjourning without having chosen a president of the council under the new constitution, but authorizing and empowering the conservative delegates to Congress, "or any one or more of them" to act on behalf of the state, supposedly under the direction of a Council of Safety, which was "to act during the recess of the legislature." [69] McKean then returned to Philadelphia, where he threw himself into the activities of the city committee, and kept himself busy rounding up, hearing, and meting out punishment to persons suspected of Tory sympathies.

On November 25, 1776, there was a meeting at the Indian Queen Tavern on Fourth Street, with McKean as chairman and John Chaloner as clerk, and some seventy-two committee-men or observers in attendance. The proceedings were formal, though of questionable legality, and the minutes contained such entries as the following:

> On motion, Resolved una. That Mr. Wm. Imlay, late of New York, be requested to attend . . .
>
> Mr. Wm. Imlay appeared and offered reasons to the Co. met, why he ought not to be accused as an Enemy to his Country, and then withdrew . . .
>
> Moved That Mr. Daniel Smith be requested to attend this meeting immediately & bring his day book of Saturday. Agreed to unanimously.
>
> Capt Barnes, Mr. Hennersly was appointed to request Mr. Smith to attend.
>
> Mr. Smith attended & Informe'd that he thinks Jos. Stanbury sung God Save the King, in his house, & a number of persons present bore him Chorus, on the 15th October, 1776 . . .
>
> Moved that Mr. Proctor & Mr. Blewer be desired to request the attendance of Robert Saunders, Mr. Smith's Barr Keeper [etc.] [70]

Joseph Stan[s]bury later wrote two letters to the Council of Safety from the New Jail, on December 6 and 10, in which he complained bitterly of the harshness of the treatment he had received. He had been examined and dismissed previously by the Council for his alleged offense of October 15, but was questioned again "whether I sung God Save the King or joined in the Chorus? both of which I answered in the negative." Nevertheless, he had been ordered to jail, without being given a reason or a mittimus, and had been held in "irksome confinement." He said he had no idea of the "stile and authority" of the persons who had assumed jurisdiction over him, and insisted that if the people at the Philosophical Society's Hall had had any new charge against him, they might have had a pretext for their action, but they had made no such claim.[71]

In spite of these activities, or perhaps because of them, the radicals in Pennsylvania were having difficulty in setting up their new government.[72] The conservatives under the leadership of John Dickinson refused to hold office, until a more moderate convention had been called to repair the damage done by the radical convention. In Pennsylvania, as in Delaware, the radical forces were weakened by the fact that most of the more ardent patriots were temporarily absent, on military assignments, unable to participate in local politics. However, a British invasion led by General Howe seemed imminent, and whenever the conservative and radical factions agreed to the calling of a new convention, the project had to be dropped because of a military emergency. This happened twice: in the fall of 1776, and the spring of 1777.

"If a regular system [had been] formed between General Howe and the friends of our Constitution," James Wilson wrote in disgust, "his motions could not have been better timed for them than they have in two different instances. When an opposition has been twice set on foot, and has twice proceeded so far as to become formidable, he has twice . . . procured a cessation." [73] One of the lessons the revolutionary leaders learned at this time, and never forgot, was that military emergencies could often be used to influence the nature of their governments.

Such emergencies, with luck, could be turned into great revolutionary opportunities.

On December 11, 1776, Congress decided that it must move to Baltimore. The British army had come to within forty miles of Philadelphia, and as Sam Adams wrote to his wife, "deliberative bodies should not sit in Places of Confusion." [74] The people of Pennsylvania and the Jerseys had shown an "unaccountable backwardness" in defending themselves, Adams thought, and their lack of spirit contrasted sadly with the conduct of Massachusetts-men, in the presence of the British, yet perhaps they were merely slower in determining their actions, and more vigorous in execution. In any case, the necessity for the move was indubitable, and Congress could carry on elsewhere as well as at Philadelphia. Even the surrender of the city, if that should occur, would not mean that the cause had been abandoned. Firmness was the order of the day; these were "the times that tried men's souls," Tom Paine wrote in the first issue of the *American Crisis* that same month.

As for McKean, he remained in Philadelphia because he was no longer (officially) a member of Congress. He stepped up his activities on behalf of the city committee, which was working now with a holding committee delegated by the departing Congress to remain in the city. There is evidence that his earliest judicial opinions in Pennsylvania were rendered to the Philadelphia city committee, in the period before the new state government had been fully established, and well before he himself had been asked to serve as Chief Justice of the Supreme Court. [75]

Meanwhile, he found time to write Caesar Rodney that the Trustees of the Newark Academy had unanimously elected Rodney a member of the board of the school, at the public visitation which had occurred on March 26th. [76] McKean's activities in the midst of the confusion were not all warlike and destructive; as he saw it, he was trying to build a better society, and educational institutions like the academy which he had attended as a youth were essential parts of the larger effort. Newark was far enough from the river, and sufficiently protected from the depredations of the British raiding parties, he thought, to be able to continue the operation of the school in spite of the disturbances of the times.

The chairman of the board was to be the Rev. Francis Alison, and the other members were all gentlemen who had been connected with the school for many years, except for His Excellency Dr. John McKinly and Colonel Samuel Patterson, who were recent additions. Little did any of them suspect that Dr. McKinly, the newly chosen President of the Delaware State, would be captured in the following fall, on board a schooner in the Christiana River, with the treasury and records of the Newark Academy as well as the records of Newcastle County in his possession. [77]

McKean, as has been noted, was not officially a member of Congress during the year 1777, but there is a distinct possibility that he continued to serve from time to time as a substitute for certain elected members who were not present, and in particular for George Read.* The records of the Delaware Council of Safety, which acted during the recess of the legislature, have not survived and perhaps were never kept, in view of the hovering British, but there is evidence that this body or some similar revolutionary cabal appointed McKean as a *pro tem* or *ex officio* member of the Congress in Philadelphia, in which he had served so long and in which Delaware was not now officially represented. In any case, he continued to be informed concerning the activities of Congress, both in Baltimore and after the return to Philadelphia in March, and served as a channel of communication between Congress and his constituents in Delaware, as always. It is even more definite that he attended meetings of Congress when that body was exiled at York. Though he lacked confidence in George Read and the conservatives, they still had confidence in him.

Several times in later years McKean made the claim that he had served as a member of Congress continuously from the beginning of the struggle against the British until the end, and he was not ordinarily inaccurate on such matters. The question was more than a technicality, for his defense of his plural officeholding, when he was criticised in 1781 for violating the constitution of Pennsylvania by serving simultaneously as a member of Congress and Chief Justice of Pennsylvania, was that he was *already* a Congressional member for Delaware, when he was appointed to the Chief Justiceship of Pennsylvania.[78] Since he was appointed to his judicial office on July 28, 1777, and sworn in on September 1 of the same year, it is clear that he was contending (without contradiction by his opponents) to have been serving in some capacity as a member of Congress during the year 1777, despite the fact that he was not reelected by the Delaware Assembly until January 30, 1778.

Apparently his failure of election in November, 1776, spared him the necessity of attending Congress in Baltimore, from December to March of that winter, without actually removing him in every respect. He had nothing to do with substantive matters, such as the establishment of the United States Lottery by Congress in November, 1776,[79] but he continued to function in a liason capacity, or as a continuing member of certain Congressional committees. His determination not to be eased out of Congress by anyone was based not only on personal ambition, but on the conviction that the success of the revolution depended on the continued presence of "firm Whigs." [80] He was not the only member of Congress who clung to office in this way, after failing of reelection; George Clymer and perhaps others made the same decision and for the same reason.[81]

The mystery as to when McKean signed the Declaration of Independence is illuminated to some extent by the fact that his name was not included on some

---

* There are many reasons for this surmise, the most important being that almost every authority on the subject insists that McKean was a member of Congress at the time he was appointed Chief Justice of the Supreme Court of Pennsylvania. McKean himself made this claim, both publicly and privately. Sanderson (Waln), Futhey and Cope, and Buchanan, as well as Peeling and other modern writers, have made this point, though all have been confused by the Delaware records indicating that McKean was not an *elected* member in 1777. The explanation, I think, lies in the fact that the Council of Safety in Delaware had authority to act during legislative recesses, and McKean was in Philadelphia and ready, as always, to perform necessary services, perhaps on an *ad hoc* basis.

of the first printed copies that were sent to the various states from Baltimore, during the Congressional exile there in January, 1777; [82] but was included in the version received by the Delaware Council, and spread upon the minutes on May 9, 1777.[83] Either he signed in late 1776, before the Congressional papers, including this Declaration, were carted from Philadelphia to Baltimore, and his name was omitted from the list given to the printer there; or, more likely, he signed shortly after the Congress had returned. In either case he had been granted access to the most important papers of the Congress at a time when he himself was not officially a member. The signature was definitely in his handwriting.

By the spring of 1777 McKean's standing was high in all three of his constituencies: in Delaware, in Pennsylvania, and in the federal union. He was still a member of the Assembly in Delaware, and although he had been removed as their delegate to Congress, he was about to be elected Speaker, in January.[84] In Pennsylvania he would soon be offered the Chief Justiceship under the new Constitution, after Joseph Reed had refused the position, and for the next twenty-two years he would dominate the politics of Pennsylvania as its circuit-riding Chief Justice. In the federal union he continued in an ill-defined but active relationship with Congress until his reelection early in 1778—after which he served continuously throughout the war, and, at the time of the Battle of Yorktown, he was serving as President of the Congress.

Chapter 13

Re-opening the Courts, 1777-80

Congress returned to Philadelphia from Baltimore early in March, 1777, and immediately set about strengthening the government of Pennsylvania.[85] After a quick look at the local scene, they resolved "that it is the indispensible duty of Congress to watch over all matters (the neglect of which, may . . . deeply affect the welfare of the United States) till such time as the Legislative and Executive Authorities of [Pennsylvania] can resume the regular exercise of their different functions." [86] At about the same time the Supreme Executive Council of the state convened, and by joint ballot with the Assembly, elected Thomas Wharton, Jr., a moderate, President, and George Bryan, a radical, Vice President.[87] A little later, early in April, they named members of a Board of War and a Navy Board to replace the Council of Safety.* As quickly as possible the new bodies began operating, although for weeks they were greatly hindered by the absence of many of the appointed leaders.

The Supreme Executive Council was supposed to have twelve members, representing each county of the state and the city of Philadelphia. However, the reluctance of most of the conservatives to support the new government until they had received assurances that there would be another constitutional convention and, above all, their unwillingness to take the prescribed oath of office, indicating loyalty to the constitution *as established by the convention,* handicapped those who were struggling to govern. Only the intervention of Congress, the aggressive

---

* The records of the War and Navy Boards have disappeared, which brings to mind the bibliographical comment of David Hawke, *In the Midst of a Revolution,* 201: "Much has been made of the vast amount of materials that survive the period without noting the equally vast amount 'lost.' . . . The pages of the journals for organizations like the American Philosophical Society and lodges of Free Masons are blank for 1776. The minutes for Philadelphia's Committee of Privates—all have been 'lost,' that is, more likely burned, probably about the time the British marched into Philadelphia in 1777."

action of the Whig Society, and the cooperation of other like-minded radicals enabled the constitutionalists to launch the new government successfully. It was in this crisis that McKean began to re-evaluate his attitude towards the Pennsylvania constitution. Unusual as this document was, he began to realize that it contained most of the features of the frames of government which had been in effect since the Charter of 1701; Pennsylvania had had a unicameral legislature, annual elections, the principle of religious freedom, and a judicial system of the same general type for a long time.[88]

To encourage reflections of this sort, and to reconcile dissidents, the Supreme Executive Council began its labors by appointing distinguished moderates to several of the most important positions. They had already elected Wharton as their President; on March 20 they appointed Joseph Reed Chief Justice of the Supreme Court for the same reason—only to have Reed hedge and delay for four months, until July 23, when he finally turned the offer down.[89] His reasons were complicated. He was expecting a military commission from General Washington at the time, he was worried about the financial security of the judicial post, and he disapproved of the oath.[90] Most of all he feared the lack of independence in the judiciary, and the subordination of that branch to the legislature. In revolutionary times, he wrote John Dickinson, a man who took such a position was exposing himself to reprisals from the "neutral trimming crowd" who would pour forth their candidates for political offices later, after they had seen which way the wind was blowing.[91] Whatever the reason, he refused—thereby joining the trimmers whom he professed to scorn.

During the spring of 1777, McKean was travelling back and forth, especially between Newark, Delaware, and Philadelphia, with side trips to New Castle and various spots in Pennsylvania. Not all of these trips were undertaken in the political cause, but some, although of a private nature, plainly demonstrated his confidence in these new governments.[92] The British forces in New York were getting ready to approach Philadelphia, first by land across New Jersey, and if that failed, by sea; no one on the American side could be certain of their route, or for that matter of their objective. Sally McKean was in Newark near her relatives expecting the birth of her second child in July. Having lost her first baby, she was understandably nervous. Her husband spent as much time with her as possible, but he was evidently in close touch with the revolutionary leaders in Philadelphia who were still attempting to inaugurate the new state government. Sarah Maria Theresa McKean was born at Newark on July 8, 1777, shortly before the crisis marked by her father's new responsibilities and the invasion of this area by the British army.

On July 28, 1777, the Supreme Executive Council offered the Chief Justiceship of Pennsylvania to McKean,[93] who forthwith accepted it, despite his previous, well publicized objections to the new constitution. By this time the Council was under considerable pressure to fill the position, and for a little while they were well satisfied with their choice. They were familiar with McKean's legal views, as well as his politics, for they had been calling on him for legal opinions for some time prior to his appointment. George Bryan, the Vice President, emerging as the strong man of the new administration because of Wharton's ill health, was the man primarily responsible for the Chief Justice's appointment [94]—and Bryan would later serve on the court under McKean for many years.

An opinion in McKean's handwriting, dated Newark, Delaware, June 23, 1777 —the Pennsylvania recipient unknown—provides an indication of the kind of service he was performing for the authorities of that state before his appointment to the Supreme Court. There is no explanation of the circumstances under which this letter was written, or the results that may have followed. Nevertheless, McKean's outline of the facts and his discussion of the questions at issue were, as ever, clear and concise, and his "answers" must have been eminently satisfactory to the officials (whoever they were) whom he was advising. It is not surprising that he was shortly afterwards offered the Chief Justiceship of the Supreme Court.

> A freeholder of Pennsylvania, in which State he was an Inhabitant, passes the river Delaware and *joins the enemies* of the said State, then being in New-Jersey, New York, & elsewhere, and adheres to them: He is arrested, tried, convicted & attainted of Treason in the State of New York.
>
> 1st Question. Can he legally allege, that he is not a subject of, nor owes allegiance to, New-York?
>
> 2d Question. How would such attainder affect his estate in Pennsylvania?
>
> 3d Question. Is there any process, that can issue by the laws of Pennsylvania, for outlawing a person, who will not appear, or by what means can a person's estate be forfeited? [95]

McKean stated in reply that since even an alien had a right to the protection of the laws of the state he happened to be in, he could not deny that he was subject to those laws. But an attainder in New York would not affect an estate in Pennsylvania, because treason "may be a different thing, and differently punished" in the two states. As for the third question, McKean was of the opinion that several statutes recently passed by the legislature of Pennsylvania, including an act "to revive and put in force such & so much of the late laws [as necessary from the colonial period]," could be said to apply to the aforesaid crime. Accordingly the freeholder "may be indicted for it in the county where the fact was inchoate, or in which he resided," and the Sheriff should make proclamation in the Quarter Sessions; then the court upon the non-appearance of the accused may proceed to attaint him, "and in consequence, his whole estate within the Commonwealth will be forfeited." [96]

McKean received his appointment on July 28 but was not sworn in until September 1. In the interval he undertook to explain his action to John Dickinson and the moderates, and negotiated a bit with the radicals, concerning the terms of his commission. To Dickinson he wrote on August 15 from Newark that the legislature had agreed again to "take the sense of the community" as to whether another convention should be called, and that when he had been in Philadelphia in June he had been asked his opinion "amongst others," and had expressed his satisfaction with the agreement. He seemed to think that Dickinson would approve of his decision, and as residence in Philadelphia was a necessary consequence, he proposed to rent one of Dickinson's houses there for his family. Although his friends had given him conflicting advice, he reported that

> the office of Chief-Justice was offered to me in the politest manner [and] upon the whole, to prevent the least suspicion that I was against any Government but such as I framed myself, and that I wanted to embroil the State and occasion disaffection to the common cause &c &c which had been liberally propagated; and to evidence that I had nothing in view but to promote the happiness of my country, I thought it my duty (tho manfestly against my interest) to imitate the Great Lord Hale, when pressed to the like by Cromwell, and was for the same and better reasons prevailed with to accept it.[97]

The comparison with Sir Matthew Hale, the Lord Chief Justice of England, was appropriate, especially with respect to the political flexibility which had enabled his great predecessor to switch allegiance from the Monarchy, to the Commonwealth, and back to the restored Monarchy without prejudice. Here indeed was a man worthy of emulation, and in line with Sir Matthew Hale's precepts McKean had no hesitation in attempting to influence the manner in which the new Court was to be established, and the terms of his own commission. A letter which he wrote to Timothy Matlack, the Secretary of the Supreme Executive Council, dated Newark, August 4, 1777, indicates that he was permitted to modify the language of his appointment, both as to form and substance:

> I have perused and examined the draught of the commission for a chief-Justice of the Supream Court of the Common-wealth of Pennsylvania, and in some places made some amendments. The 24th section of the Frame of Government occasioned the additional sentence in the 18th line of the second page. That part of the commission, that relates to the criminal jurisdiction is not so formal as it might have been, but with the additions I have made it will answer; however, what is more material, it is strictly agreeable to the present Constitution & Laws. You have the draught now returned, with my approbation of it.
>
> It will do me a favor to let me know, as soon as the other Judges are appointed. The commissions will, I suppose, be made out on parchment; there is to be no difference in them but the words "second," "third," or "fourth" instead of the word "chief." I shall conceive it to be my duty to the public to repair to Philadelphia as soon as my Associates will meet me, there to be qualified before His Excellency the President.*

Jonathan Dickinson Sergeant, Esquire, (formerly of New Jersey) was appointed Attorney General of the state on July 28, 1777—the day of McKean's appointment— but the other members of the court were not named until mid-August.[98] How much influence McKean had in selecting them cannot be determined, but from the evidence available it was substantial. Edward Burd, Esquire, of Reading, was appointed to the important and remunerative position of Prothonotary

---

* This letter found its way into the papers of Joseph Reed, of all people, because in the middle of 1778 Reed decided that he would accept office under the new constitution, after all. He became President of the Supreme Executive Council upon the expiration of the term of Thomas Wharton, Jr. Actually Wharton had died in office and George Bryan, the Vice President had filled in for him temporarily. (Reed Papers, IV, 104, New-York Hist. Soc.)

of the Supreme Court a year later, on August 12, 1778; in great joy he wrote on August 22, "I have just received a letter from Mr. McKean in which the Appointment of Prothonotary of the Supreme Court is made certain to me." [99] The Second and Third Justices, William Augustus Atlee and John Evans, were chosen on August 15, 1777. The Fourth Justice, George Bryan, was not commissioned until April 6, 1780. In the meantime Bryan had held the important position of Vice President of the Supreme Executive Council (and Acting President after Wharton's death in May 1778), and had been a leading member of the legislature in 1779–80. Unlike the other members of the Court, Bryan was a political power in his own right, and much less subject to domination by the Chief Justice.[100]

McKean's first controversy in his new position began within a few days of his appointment, while he was still the only properly accredited member of the Court; the emergency had arisen so quickly he could not wait for the other justices to join him. The Supreme Executive Council of the state had ordered the arrest of some forty persons, mostly former officers of the Proprietors or of the King, and directed that they be removed from the city as a security measure, in view of the pending invasion by the British.[101] In so doing they were following the pointed suggestion of the Congress that they should take more vigorous measures than they had yet taken, and remove potentially subversive individuals "back into the country, there to be confined or enlarged upon parole as their characters and behavior may require." [102] Congress repeated its recommendation from time to time, during the month of August, even naming those persons who should be sent away.

Included among those arrested were the Hon. John Penn, late Governor of the province, James Hamilton, Benjamin Chew, James Tilghman, Jared Ingersoll, Edward Shippen, Jr., Joseph Shippen, Jr., James Allen, Phineas Bond, Joseph Stansbury, William Smith, Richard Wister, John Drinker, Henry Drinker, *et al.* The list was long and distinguished. The Council issued a warrant to the "Gentlemen of the Board of War" for the arrest, originally, of thirty-six and eventually more than forty of the most prominent citizens of the area, and on September 2 the round-up began. Those who promised to stay in their homes or to leave the state were allowed to go free, but twenty refused to do this.[103] The event was hardly a surprise when it occurred, for there had been rumblings since the middle of June. However, most of the detainees found it difficult to believe that the state would persist in its charges against them, and openly utilized whatever political and legal machinery, or influence, was available for purposes of defense. When the blow fell, they had only the consolation of being confined in the Mason's Lodge, which was more comfortable than an ordinary jail, and more appropriate for such distinguished prisoners. Meanwhile Israel Pemberton, one of several Quaker leaders added to the original group, had had Christopher Sauer translate his protest into German on September 9th for distribution in Lebanon and Lancaster.[104]

James Tilghman's petition to the Council the day after he was taken in custody was typical of several that were submitted at that time:

Upon maturely considering the Parole . . . offered me by the honorable Board I do not find myself free to accept it. Without the least insinuation that I have been guilty of any thing which renders me suspicious, I am taken up and considered in the light of a Prisoner of War . . . Yet to avoid the horrors of a Gaol and [for the sake of my family] (altho' I think the proceeding against me is the most arbitrary that can be imagined, being imprisoned by a Precept which expresses no offence . . . and altogether contrary to the express terms of the constitution under which the Council act) . . . [I am willing to be paroled on other terms] abundantly sufficient to guard the public against any danger from a man of honor, as I am supposed to be by having a Parole offered. [If the Board refuses] I must submit to my fate . . . lamenting that the times are such that a man's innocence is not his safety.[105]

This was the beginning of a legal tangle, involving the Council, the Congress, and the newly appointed Chief Justice of Pennsylvania, which was never straightened out to the satisfaction of any of the parties. George Bryan, the Vice President of the Council, wrote to Congress asking for advice. "Few of the Quakers," he reported, "are willing to make any promise of any kind; they are therefore mostly in confinement in the Mason's Lodge . . . On this head the advice of Congress is desired, & particularly whether Augusta & Winchester in Virginia, would not be suitable places . . ."[106] The next day, September 3, 1777, Congress resolved that they approved of the Quakers' being sent to Virginia, and recommended Staunton in the County of Augusta as the most proper place—a hundred miles farther away than Winchester.[107] Council agreed and proceeded with the plans, but the imprisoned men were busily sending out petitions and remonstrances to all and sundry, and just when they were about to be herded away Congress ordered that they be "given a hearing."[108] It was too late from the Council's standpoint; furthermore, the British army was approaching, having landed at Head of Elk on August 25. If Congress wanted a hearing for the Quakers, let them conduct it.[109]

Congress refused to intervene again, and the men were finally led out of the city on September 11, with the guns at the Battle of Brandywine clearly audible. But before they left, Israel Pemberton and eight others requested writs of *habeas corpus* from Chief Justice Thomas McKean.[110] In this complicated situation, with Congress debating for hours "on one silly point," as Henry Laurens put it,[111] and the Council still wrangling, McKean made his debut. For him it was the beginning of twenty-two years of distinguished service, but at the moment it was not clear that he would last for twenty-two days. McKean had evidently decided to issue the writs on the very day the prisoners left, and by "an express" agreed to meet them at the house of Mr. Stephen Cochran in East Fallowfield, Chester County.[112] The Act of Habeas Corpus was still in effect, he said, and his action was in line with the recent suggestion of Congress. However, East Fallowfield was dangerously close to the British forces in the Brandywine area, and the Council hastened to countermand his action.

The prisoners arrived in Reading on September 15, and that same day one of the officers of the guard "left for Philadelphia to inquire whether or not they should respect the writs or other acts by the Chief Justice."[113] The Colonel in charge had already steered the caravan north of the route McKean had suggested, and had tipped off the Council, unaware till that moment that McKean had been sworn in as Chief Justice, and thus spoke with full authority. Taken aback, the Council conferred with the General Assembly, and arranged the appointment of a committee to find a legal way around the impasse. The committee met on the 14th, a Sunday, and as a result of its deliberations the Assembly passed a bill to suspend the Habeas Corpus Act until the end of the next sitting of the Assembly, providing further "that no Judge or Officer of the Supreme Court, or any inferior Court within this Commonwealth, shall issue or allow of any Writ of Habeas Corpus, or other Remedial Writ, to obstruct the Proceedings of the said Executive Council against suspected persons, in this time of imminent danger of the State." [114] Thus, by a thinly veiled *ex post facto* law, they summarily removed the issue from McKean's jurisdiction, and provided the judicial branch of the new government with an inauspicious start.

The suspension of *habeas corpus,* in the opinion of the Tories and of conservatives generally was "the very extreme of tyranny," but was deemed necessary by the embattled radicals. Unexpectedly and without cause McKean now found himself the object of much criticism from the public, and especially from the patriotic elements whom he had hitherto supported. The extremity of the emergency can be seen in the fact that the Assembly itself fled from Philadelphia to Lancaster on September 18, and was unable to return until June 25, 1778. In great distress the Chief Justice wrote to John Adams from somewhere in Chester County, also on the 18th, to convince Adams of the propriety of his action and "by your candid explanation, all others, who may not have had the same opportunities with you and me of studying & understanding the laws." As he saw it, he had had no choice:

> The writs were applied for in form, agreeable to the directions of the statute of the 31. Car. 2 ch. 2; [an English statute in this emergency!] and the only authority for the confinement, that I saw, was the copy of a letter from the Vice President [George Bryan] to Colo. Lewis Nicola. My situation was such that I had not received a Letter nor seen a News-paper from Philadelphia for a fortnight, nor could I learn any particulars respecting this affair from any one whom I met, excepting the two persons who brought the writs to me, who offered me a pamphlet written by the prisoners stating their case, which I refused to read or to accept, saying, I should determine upon the returns that should be made to the writs, and nothing else.[115]

The Habeas Corpus Act, he continued, has always "justly been esteemed the palladium of liberty," and by its terms all discretionary power had been taken away from the judges, and a penalty of £500 per prisoner had been added for refusal to allow the writ. Even if he had forgotten the oath he had taken a few days earlier, "common prudence would have prevailed upon [him] not to have incurred the forfeiture of ten thousand pounds sterling." Only if he had shown partiality to the prisoners, or favored the enemies of the revolutionary cause, which he had supported with as much sincerity and zeal "as any man in the thirteen United States," could he be deservedly criticised, and he reiterated his request that Adams would "on proper occasions explain the matter." Next to a good conscience he was most concerned to have a favorable reaction from his friends in Congress.

The Council in turn was anxious "that some account of this transaction should be given to the public as [they understand] these people mean to publish and raise a ferment." [116] In the midst of these troubles, on the 12th, the day after the Battle of Brandywine, Dr. John McKinly, the President of Delaware, was captured by the British at Wilmington and taken on board the *Roebuck,* together with the treasury and records of the Newark Academy and Newcastle County. On the 16th, following the suspension of the Habeas Corpus Act in Pennsylvania, George Bryan wrote the officer guarding the Quaker prisoners, "Sir, Council are not well informed how Mr. Chief Justice McKean came to issue writs of habeas corpus for the prisoners under your care; but are clear that you have acted right in not proceeding to East-Fallowfield; a place too near the enemy. But the Assembly has put the matter out of debate . . ." [117]

McKean now faced a crisis in two states. His position as Chief Justice of Pennsylvania had just been weakened by the action of the Assembly; at the same time he was obligated to become Acting President of Delaware, since John McKinly, the President, had been captured and George Read, the Speaker of the Council, was temporarily out of the state. [118] McKean, as Speaker of the Assembly in Delaware, was next in line as chief executive of that state, and he rushed into the breach without hesitation. The time could hardly have been worse—with the British army advancing from the head of the Chesapeake Bay towards Philadelphia, and cutting the patriots' lines of communication. As he described it in a letter to John Adams two years later;

> I too have had my full share of the anxieties cares & troubles attending the present war. For some time I was obliged to act as President of the Delaware State and as Chief Justice of this; General Howe had just landed at the head of Elk River, when I undertook to discharge those two great trusts. The consequence was to be hunted like a Fox by the enemy and envied by those, who ought to have been my friends. I was obliged to remove my family five times in a few months, and at last fixed them in a little log hut on the banks of the Susquehanna above a hundred miles from [Philadelphia]; but safety was not to be found there, for they were soon obliged to remove again, occasioned by the incursions of the Indians. In Decem[r] 1777 I was again into Congress, where for some months the United States had but nine voices and thirteen members . . .*

McKean managed to reach Delaware on September 20, immediately taking over as acting President. With the approval of two members of the Privy Council (the other two having fled to New Jersey) he issued a proclamation that the annual general election for Newcastle County would be held on October 1 at the Academy in Newark, rather than in New Castle. [119] With similar speed he called out half the militia in the county, 600 privates, but was unable to raise that number and was also disappointed in his hopes for reinforcements from General

---

* McKean to Adams, November 8, 1779, McKean Papers, I, HSP. Note the claim that he attended Congress in 1777!

Washington. He found that the British troops had carried away all the records and public papers of Newcastle County, and every shilling of the money in their treasury and loan office, as well as the funds belonging to the Academy and $25,000 in the continental loan office.[120] Accordingly he borrowed £3,000 "from Congress or any person or persons who may be willing to lend it," [121] and appointed Caesar Rodney Major General of the militia, and Messrs. Dagworthy, Dickinson, and Patterson Brigadiers: however, Dickinson refused this commission.[122] Many of the soldiers had fled from the state for safety, and others were "daily employed in supplying our enemies at Wilmington, and on board their ships of war with all kinds of provisions . . ." [123]

On September 26 McKean wrote to George Read from Lunn's Tavern, explaining that because of the captivity of President McKinly and Read's absence in Philadelphia, he felt it his duty to take emergency measures, to protect "the virtuous part of the people," but that nothing could be more distressing to his private affairs, or to his duties as Chief Justice of Pennsylvania, than to continue longer in his role as Acting President of Delaware. He begged leave to resign his command, and urged Read to return to the state as quickly as possible.[124] McKean also wrote a full report to the General Assembly of the Delaware State from Dover on October 22, 1777, with an accounting of his activities during the period of his command. By then Read had returned and the Council met at Dover on October 20. Not having a sufficient number of Councillors in attendance for a quorum, the group adjourned from day to day until the 23rd, on which date they officially met and reelected Read Speaker of the Council, hence Acting President of Delaware.[125] McKean's letter to the General Assembly was endorsed in Read's hand, "23rd Octr read 1st time, 24th, Octr read 2d time & committed." [126] Meanwhile, the British forces had passed through Delaware, on their way to Philadelphia, and were no longer a threat in this area.[127]

His duty in Delaware completed, McKean returned to Pennsylvania, moving his family five times in a few months, in order to avoid capture. On December 6 he wrote to George Read from Paxton near Harrisburg, assuring Read that Congress was determined to support the Whigs in Delaware, and was anxious to have more delegates from that state in Congress.[128] From Samuel Patterson, however, he heard in January that things were not going well in Delaware, and he received the urgent plea, "I wish you would come down and see what can be done . . ." [129] Joining Congress at York, where he found just eighteen members representing nine states, McKean was on time to welcome and, officially, "pay the necessary Compliments to" a certain Baron von Steuben, who was reputed to have been a Lieutenant General in the service of the King of Prussia, and who—regardless of rank—would soon accomplish miracles in the training and disciplining of Washington's army at Valley Forge.* Meanwhile, as a member of the Committee of Prisoners, he was receiving numerous communications about the

---

* McKean to Mrs. Sarah McKean, York, February 10, 1778, McKean Papers, VI, HSP. Von Steuben was actually an unemployed Captain. However, he proved to be a valuable acquisition at any rank. See Burnett, ed., *Letters*, III, 91. The Baron requested, and was given a brevet commission of captain "in order to guard against inconveniences which might attend him, if he should without any commission in his pocket be made a prisoner."

possibility of exchanging President McKinly—a possibility for barter which he considered no bargain.

On February 12 he wrote Read, "Who can I propose in exchange for the President? Do inform me, if you can think of any one: None occurs to me but Governor Franklin [formerly of New Jersey], and hearing a Gentleman say, that he could do more mischief than the President could do good, and for other reasons which will readily suggest themselves to you, I have little hopes for success from that proposition." [130] He went on to say that he had heard a rumor that McKinly was lodged in Philadelphia with his old friends of dubious patriotism, Robinson and Manlove, and seemed very happy with the British and the Tories.[131] To this he received a reply from Caesar Rodney in Dover, who had evidently been asked by Read to intercede with him on behalf of the unfortunate McKinly. Rodney assured McKean that Robinson and Manlove were lodging separately in Philadelphia, and that McKinly was staying with neither of them. As for the exchange, he could suggest no way in which it could be worked out, but he wished (rather lukewarmly) that something could be done, even though McKinly "Might Never Have discharged the Duty of that Station [as President of Delaware] with that Energy that you and I Could have Wished." [132]

In Pennsylvania McKean found that the court system had been dormant for almost a year, despite scattered efforts to set it in motion again.[133] The legislature under the new government had passed its first act in January, 1777,[134] which provided that all officers under the old government should be replaced, except for the trustees of the loan office. As a curious exception to the general rule, Benjamin Chew had continued to function as Register General until the legislature by act of March 14, 1777, provided for an appointment of Registers of Wills in each county, thereby replacing him. Subsequently the legislature validated and confirmed the actions that had been taken by Chew and his deputies during the interim between governments as having been necessary for the public good.[135]

The Supreme Executive Council of the state was formed in March, 1777, and in August and September proceeded to take the actions mentioned above against office-holders under the previous government. Benjamin Chew was included among those who were to be arrested, despite the fact that he had continued to function in the good graces of the revolutionaries. Chew refused to take the action of the Council seriously, at first, and thoroughly intimidated the young soldiers from the City Troop who were sent to pick him up. Eventually realizing his predicament he signed a parole that he would go to, and remain at, the Union Iron Works in New Jersey, although he insisted that there was no charge against him except that he had held office under the Proprietor. He was accompanied by Governor John Penn, and the two men remained there for ten months, until finally Congress itself resolved that they "be conveyed without delay into Pennsylvania . . . and discharged from their parole." [136] Similarly, the Quakers who had been sent by way of Reading and Carlisle to Winchester, Virginia, and eventually to Staunton, were released in April, 1778, and allowed to return to the state. Throughout the prisoners' exile, Congress and the Pennsylvania Council disagreed with each other as to their ultimate disposition, passing responsibility for their plight back and forth.[137] After a few weeks of this controversy McKean must have been relieved that the case had been removed from the jurisdiction of the Supreme Court.

The confusion in Pennsylvania during the interim period was recognized by the Supreme Court a few years later, in the case of Respublica v. Samuel Chapman in April, 1781.[138] Chapman had been born and brought up in Bucks County, and had fled to the protection of the British army on December 26, 1776. The question at issue was whether or not he had committed treason against the state of Pennsylvania by so doing. Chapman's counsel argued that at the time his client fled, there was no government established in Pennsylvania from which he could receive protection. Hence, there was none to which he could owe allegiance, "protection and allegiance being political obligations of a reciprocal nature." The doctrine of perpetual allegiance, which could be found in many books of law, applied only to established and settled governments; it was not applicable to a revolutionary situation in which a new government was being formed.[139] Chapman had never at any time owed allegiance to Pennsylvania, and therefore could not be guilty of treason to the state. The Attorney General replied that the said Samuel Chapman, the prisoner, was an inhabitant of the commonwealth and therefore subject to its jurisdiction.[140] Whereupon the issue was joined.

McKean as Chief Justice delivered a learned and historically accurate charge to the jury, in which he laid the foundation for the American concept of treason. He described the unprecedented situation in which subjects of the British Crown found themselves during the turmoil of the American Revolution. His conclusion was that there had been a suspension of all laws in Pennsylvania from May 14, 1776, until February 11, 1777, and that the legislature by act of the latter date assumed jurisdiction only over persons *then* inhabiting the state, or persons who should *thereafter* become inhabitants. Thus, each inhabitant of Pennsylvania had been free to choose sides in the political contest, without penalty, until February 11, 1777. He admitted that "a kind of government" existed in this area with sovereign powers lodged in Congress, "under whose authority a council of safety had been elected by the people." But he insisted that no express provision had been made at any time for defining treason against those temporary bodies. The case was a new one, and the Court should tread cautiously. ". . . at all events, it is better to err on the side of mercy, than of strict justice." The jury agreed with His Honor, and returned a verdict of Not Guilty.*

The Continental Congress was indeed the agency which was exercising sovereignty in the early stages of the revolution, especially in determining who should be taken prisoner and what disposition should be made of the prisoners who were held. On August 11, 1777, Elias Boudinot, the Commissary General of Prisoners, appointed William Augustus Atlee the Deputy Commissary of Prisoners for Lancaster and Reading, and shortly thereafter ordered him to remove all prisoners then in his area to Easton, since the British were coming up the

---

* It is noteworthy that February 11, 1777, was before the establishment of either the executive or the judicial branch of the new government. "This construction," McKean noted, "is favorable to traitors, and tends to the prejudice of the commonwealth. But we cannot be influenced by observations of a political nature in the exposition of the law; it is our duty to seek for, and to declare, the true intention of the legislature . . ."

Chesapeake Bay.[141] Some prisoners still remained at Lebanon, however, and on September 8, 1777, Atlee wrote to Boudinot saying that the church people there would gladly build prison barracks, in order to recover the use of their churches.[142] On December 24, as an act of reprisal against the British for a similar action, Boudinot sent orders not to let any prisoners of war "go out to work for any person whatever in Consequence of any Orders heretofore issued by the Board of War . . ." [143] Clearly the Congress was giving orders to the state.

On January 7, 1778, Boudinot enclosed a list of the Deputy Commissaries who were then serving in the different areas, as follows:

Joshua Messereau, Esq.	Massachusetts Bay
Ezekiel William, Esq.	Connecticut
Daniel Hale, Esq.	Albany, New York
John Adam, Esq.	Fishkill, New York
Robert L. Hooper, Esq.	Easton, Pennsylvania
Henry Haller, Esq.	Reading, Pennsylvania
William Atlee, Esq.	Lancaster, Pennsylvania
Thomas Peters, Esq.	York town, Pennsylvania
Joseph Holmes, Esq.	Winchester, Virginia [144]

McKean was actively engaged in this activity both as a member of the Congressional Committee on Prisoners, and also as Chief Justice of Pennsylvania.[145] On May 16, 1778, he wrote a letter from York-town (Pa.) to his wife at Paxton, which was delivered by Wm. A. Atlee, Esq., "Colo. Francis Johnston upon my recommendation, and without his sollicitation or knowledge, is appointed Commissary General of Prisoners in the stead of Mr. Boudinot, who has resigned in order to take his seat in Congress." [146] The Congress was then located temporarily at York, and most of the state government at Lancaster; this was the Valley Forge winter. The Supreme Court of Pennsylvania held its first formal meeting at Lancaster on April 7, 1778, and after concluding its business there, began its peregrinations from county seat to county seat by holding hearings at York. The move to York was a particular convenience for McKean, who was able to write to Caesar Rodney on April 28, 1778, "I have worked double tides (as the Sailors say) all last week, being every day in Court, and also in Congress . . ." [147]

Earlier in the month of April, before the Supreme Court opened, McKean had been busily corresponding with General Washington about the possibility of arranging an exchange of prisoners, in order to try some persons accused of counterfeiting the already endangered Continental currency. Washington, however, felt that Howe would never cooperate in such a scheme because the evidence would merely implicate the British.[148]

The re-opening of the Supreme Court marked the culmination of a process that had been taking place at various times throughout the state, as the radical Whigs succeeded in putting the new government into motion. Christopher Marshall reported that the Court of Quarter Sessions in Lancaster had opened the previous November, and was "conducted with great order and decorum." [149] Local offenders had been tried by a petit jury and their punishments promptly inflicted at the whipping post. A large number of reputable citizens attended and "the appearance of satisfaction was visible on their countenances."

It was generally understood that the success or failure of the new government with the common people would depend largely on the performance of the courts, and here or there the conservatives attempted to obstruct their operation, or to retain possession of the old court records. In Cumberland County as early as April, 1777, John Montgomery reported, "we shall have a blessed Set of Justices in this County . . . The Town will be full and stink[ing] with yellow w[h]iges . . . I am afraid if once they are alowd to Open the Courts it will be over with us . . ." The conservatives likewise held out against the use of paper money, continental or state, and were encouraged in their resistance by the fact that the British (in addition to counterfeiting paper money) were sometimes using hard money, and had succeeded in distributing it widely among the Quakers and other neutrals.[150]

Congress was doing everything in its power to strengthen the hand of its adherents, wherever they were in difficulty. McKean mentioned in his letter to Rodney that Congress had passed an act for arresting Charles Gordon and Thomas White "and such others as were notoriously disaffected" in the Delaware State, on a motion by the delegates from Maryland, on the charge that there was a treasonable conspiracy along the border between the two states. The intention of Congress was to have the men arrested in Maryland, in order to prevent their being rescued from the jails of Delaware by the British or the local Tories, and so released under the terms of the Habeas Corpus Act, which was still in effect in Delaware. As a delegate to Congress McKean was willing to go along with this rather high-handed proceeding, assuring Rodney at the same time—"I was called upon to name some of the most dangerous men in the State to be added to the others, but I refused, alledging the people there were now becoming good Whigs, and I hoped there would be no occasion." [151] This was the first indication he had given of disenchantment with the policies of Congress, and it is significant that it coincided with the opening of the Supreme Court of Pennsylvania, now to be his most effective vehicle. Up to this point (April, 1778) he had always supported the radical faction in Congress.

The grand opening of the Supreme Court occurred on April 7, 1778, at Lancaster. The ubiquitous Christopher Marshall was there to record the occasion in his diary: "About noon came into town Thos. McKean, Chief Judge, attended by Sheriff and sundry other gentlemen . . . When Court opened, went to Court. Stayed while the Commissions of Thos. McKean as Chief Judge [and] William Augustus Atlee as Second Judge were read, Magistrates [and] Constables called [and the] Grand Jury qualified. Then McKean delivered an elegant and spirited charge on the nature of our government, suitable to the circumstances of the times . . ." [152] The Grand Jury liked the charge so much that they had it printed by Francis Bailey, in King's-Street, Lancaster, noting that this was the first Court of the kind held in the state under the Commonwealth.[153]

In the charge McKean summed up the causes for the rebellion against British rule, and explained the difference in law between a monarchy and a government established on the authority of the people only. He defined with great precision the different types of crime, including treason against a republic, with which the Grand Jury might be expected to deal. In discussing the Constitution of 1776, he referred to the heated and unbecoming allegations with which the debate had been carried on by both sides, and concluded: "Away with these uncharitable opinions. We all mean the same thing, the happiness of the community. There cannot be perfection in this imperfect state. *Humanum est errare . . .*" [154]

In general the Court followed the circuit of the old Provincial Court of Appeal, sometimes designated the Supreme Court of the colonial period. From Lancaster and York it went to such places as Reading, Carlisle, and Chester, and thence to Philadelphia in September. The order varied from year to year in accordance with the decision of the justices as to their workload in the several counties, and eventually the circuit was greatly expanded. The docket for the first year actually began with the September sessions in Philadelphia, after the British evacuation of that city. This docket illustrated a unique feature of the Court, for in Philadelphia the justices of the Supreme Court were required by law to work in a dual capacity; they sat as a Court of Oyer and Terminer there, usually before the separate terms of the Supreme Court, and sometimes the sessions overlapped.[155] Also the justices were often obliged to retrace their steps to one or more of the county seats to sit, although not in bank, as a court of original jurisdiction, officially and specifically entitled a court of Nisi Prius.[156] In addition to the powers "usually exercised by such courts," the Supreme Court and likewise the courts of Common Pleas received from the Constitution of 1776 "the powers of a court of chancery," i.e., a court of equity as distinguished from that of common law.

The progress of the Court in the early period can best be followed in local histories, in the few cases reported by A. J. Dallas, and in such personal correspondence of the justices as may have survived, such as McKean's letters to his wife.[157] McKean noted in these letters that the Court—consisting of the justices, the attorney general, and later the prothonotary—were customarily met near the county line by the local officers, including the sheriff, the justices of the peace and constables, and sundry of the gentlemen of the law, and escorted to their lodgings or the courtroom, according to the hour of the day. The courtroom itself was often a tavern, although some of the counties had proper courthouses. From the beginning the Court was accorded great deference by the country people, and McKean was moved to report to Sally from Lancaster, "Matters have been conducted equal to my most sanguine hopes, indeed everything is as I would wish it." This was not always the case. Occasionally the formality miscarried, as when the Court came into town on one road and the would-be escort rode out to meet them on another.[158]

Each morning when the Court was in session the justices were ceremoniously escorted from their lodgings to the courtroom, and there was a tendency on the part of all concerned to dress up for the occasion. McKean wore a scarlet gown and an immense cocked hat, which he usually kept on during the entire proceedings of the Court. Occasionally he wore a sword.[159] The solemnity of the event was emphasized by the seriousness of the crimes which were tried, and the severity of the penalties inflicted; sometimes there were one or two hundred people in attendance. The statutes were later to be reformed, when the war was safely over, but in the beginning the Court was enforcing the traditional English laws with almost medieval penalties. Counterfeiting and burglary were but two of the crimes punishable by death; other crimes were expiated at the pillory by a number of lashes "well laid on." Branding and cutting off ears were also practiced, and such penalties were inflicted in addition to substantial fines. If the fine could not be paid, the culprit might be sold as a servant for periods up to seven years.[160]

Justice Atlee wrote from York on April 23, 1778, to his wife Hetty, as follows:

> We have one Man tryed here today—for Burglary—& sentence of death will be pronounced on him tomorrow morning—And to morrow morning a Woman will be tryed for killing her Husband—I fear it will go hard with her: but I heartily wish she may be acquitted, to save us the disagreeable task of ordering her to be burnt—what affects me much is that her Son, a likely young Man, of about eighteen or twenty is an Evidence against her—for the death of his Father—we shall doubtless have a tender Scene with her at the Bar & her Child giving the fatal testimony, which may bring her to the stake.

Justice Atlee's words may be somewhat misleading today. McKean also wrote to his wife from York, a few days later, and noted the sentences given in the two cases mentioned by Justice Atlee. The thief was indeed hung, but the woman who was found guilty of manslaughter was not burned in toto but branded at the stake, with a large M for manslaughter on her left hand.[161]

The Court's authority was greatly increased by the custom of rendering advisory opinions.[162] McKean moved into this role naturally; he had been advising both state and continental officials on legal matters long before he began his service on the Supreme Court. In fact, he had been busily advising the legislature on the laws they should pass in the months between his appointment as Chief Justice and the actual establishing of the Supreme Court. On April 3, 1778, he wrote George Read from York, "When I attended the general assembly of this state in December last, they obtained a promise that I would give a little assistance in draughting some bills at their adjournment in March, at which time I, accordingly, in pursuance of a letter from the speaker, went to Lancaster, and having stayed there ten days, returned to York on the 19th." [163] He was asked to advise the executives of both Pennsylvania and Delaware, and for that matter also those in the Continental Congress. The opinions were sometimes given formally in writing, and at other times in informal conferences. The attorney general occasionally joined the justices in formulating and/or signing these advisory opinions.*

Advisory opinions were normal in the revolutionary era, and it is noteworthy that when the Supreme Court of the United States was set up some years later

---

* An advisory opinion requested by officials in Delaware is cited in Burnett, ed., *Letters,* III, 300–1. In Pennsylvania, in 1780 the Council referred to McKean certain queries from the Admiralty Court. The Vice Consul of France had applied to the Judge of Admiralty of Pennsylvania for a general warrant to search vessels in the Philadelphia harbor for sailors who had deserted French ships. McKean advised that the "Jurisdiction of the Admiralty in this case might be justly called into question, even were the *thing* lawful." To Joseph Reed, July 10, 1780, Society Coll., HSP. Jonathan Dickinson Sergeant, Attorney General, also signed this opinion.

Another example, from the year 1781: "A doubt has arisen on the Construction of the nineteenth Section of the Constitution on which Council would request a Conference with the Judges of the Supreme Court for the benefit of their advice and opinion whenever the business of the Court will admit." Joseph Reed, President, In Council, Philada. April 23, 1781, to Honble the Judges of the Supreme Court, McKean Papers, I, HSP.

under the federal constitution, President Washington asked for, and expected to receive, such opinions from John Jay, the first Chief Justice. The consequences of this custom in the war years have not been fully understood. On the one hand, advisory opinions contributed to the American practice of having governmental bodies act in accordance with a received corpus of law, interpreted by experts; on the other, they threatened the federal system by providing conflicting opinions, each sponsored by an official agency, and none of them binding. In examining the advisory opinions given by McKean in his early years on the Pennsylvania Supreme Court, it is apparent that his opinions were usually asked for as a result of a conflict of interest between two or more government agencies. Not always, but frequently, the agencies were involved in intricate legal maneuvering against each other. Perhaps it is just as well that American courts later decided to avoid hypothetical matters, and to deal only with bona fide cases.

One of the most interesting disputes of the late spring of 1778 was the Hooper incident. Colonel Robert Lettis Hooper of Easton, Deputy Commissary of Prisoners, was one of those who disapproved of Pennsylvania's Constitution of 1776, though a strong patriot.[164] He refused to take the required oath of allegiance, and urged his friends to do likewise. When Jonathan Dickinson Sergeant, the Attorney General, reported him to the Supreme Executive Council, Hooper went to the next meeting of the Supreme Court at Reading, found Sergeant and thoroughly thrashed him. He also threatened other members of the Council and the Court, feeling that they had betrayed the revolution. As a result of these actions he received a writ to appear before the Court; to counter this he persuaded General Nathaniel Greene, his superior as quartermaster general at Valley Forge, to request McKean to postpone the hearing. On June 3 Greene wrote "As the Army is just upon the Wing, and part of it in all probability will march through his district, I could not without great Necessity consent to his being absent, as there is no other Person that can give the Necessary Aid upon this Occasion." [165]

The reply was vintage McKean. The Court had already achieved a position of strength which was in sharp contrast to its weakness at the time of McKean's appointment. He was aware of strong support by the state authorities against the army, and by this time was confident that Congress would not let him down. Without mincing words, and enjoying his own rhetoric, he wrote:

> I do not think, Sir, that the absence, sickness, or even death of Mr. Hooper could be attended with such a consequence, that *no other person* could be found who could give the necessary aid upon this occasion; but what attracts my attention most is your observation, that *you* cannot without great necessity *consent to his being absent.* As to that, Sir, I shall not ask *your consent,* nor that of any other person in or out of the army, whether my Precept shall be obeyed or not in Pennsylvania . . .
>
> I should be very sorry to find, that the execution of criminal laws should impede the operation of the army in any instance, but should be more so to find the latter impede the former.[166]

Conflicts of interest between governmental bodies were especially notable later in June, in the period after the British evacuation of Philadelphia. Immediately following their return the Continental Congress and the state government of Pennsylvania became involved in a dispute for control, or jurisdiction, over

Philadelphia, the chief city in the area. A ranking member of both governments, McKean increasingly favored the claims of Pennsylvania—and always he insisted on civil control over the military. The incoming American commander, Benedict Arnold, was a great fighter but temperamentally unsuited for complicated administrative engagements.[167] He antagonized the state authorities by shameless profiteering, and by fraternizing with the Tory element which had caused so much trouble before the revolutionary leaders were forced to flee to the hinterlands. Arnold proclaimed martial law on June 20, 1778, and under the terms of this proclamation assumed jurisdiction (by court martial) over purely civilian transactions.[168] In so doing he raised two distinct questions: whether he should be allowed jurisdiction in the first place, and whether he was using his official position to make personal speculations for his own profit.[169]

On August 22, 1778, the Supreme Executive Council, presided over by George Bryan, Vice President, took into consideration the case of one Frederick Verner, who was under sentence of death as a spy by one of Arnold's courts martial, on which case Council had asked for McKean's opinion. McKean advised that the said Frederick Verner should be tried (again) by the laws of Pennsylvania for treason, and that "he be detained in Safe Custody until the next Court of Oyer and Terminer and General Gaol Delivery to be holden at Philadelphia" during the September sessions. He took the high-sounding line that he was advising in favor of life. The Council thereupon ordered that this opinion be communicated to Congress, and that "the Congress be informed that the Council do approve of the same." [170] The Supreme Executive Council, supported by McKean's advisory opinion, was challenging both the Continental Congress and the Continental Army.

Arnold's most dramatic affront occurred when he married a girl half his age, the beautiful Peggy Shippen, of a socially prominent Tory family, who was supposedly on the rebound from an affair with John André, General Howe's aide-de-camp.[171] The Supreme Executive Council of Pennsylvania took a more serious view of collaborating with the enemy than Arnold apparently did, and the members were scandalized by his profiteering and arrogance. Arnold also made the mistake of treating one or two well connected enlisted men, such as Timothy Matlack's son, as if they were personal servants.[172] The Council drew up a number of charges against him, and despite the difficulty of obtaining proper legal evidence, hounded him for months. Arnold said he was "at all times ready to answer [his] public conduct to Congress or General Washington, to whom alone [he was] accountable," but he resented criticism from the state government.[173] Eventually the Council succeeded in having him reprimanded by General Washington, and reassigned. Washington, who was well aware of Arnold's fighting qualities, delivered the reprimand in such a way as to indicate that he respected Arnold, but was embarrassed by his excesses.[174] Seemingly a civil-military dispute, this was in fact a jurisdictional clash between the continental and the state governments.

In the meantime, unfortunately, Arnold had begun his treasonable correspondence with the British general in New York, aided and abetted by his high-living Tory wife.[175] The episode was significant not merely as the background for Arnold's scheme to betray West Point, but also because Congress and the Army began to lose their ascendancy over the state government while Arnold was misusing his authority in Philadelphia. McKean was not alone in shifting his stance at this time; the newly reorganized state government needed less and less help from Congress. McKean was part of an increasingly self-sufficient government that would soon be exercising effective jurisdiction over the entire state, including the city of Philadelphia, the continental as well as the state capital. Furthermore, McKean's position within this government was growing stronger; when Arnold's treachery was discovered, in the fall of 1780, it was the Chief Justice to whom the news was first brought. It was McKean who informed the Supreme Executive Council that Arnold had joined the enemy, and under him the Sheriff of the City and County of Philadelphia was "directed to make diligent search for General Arnold's papers." [176]

During the struggle between Congress and the state government, after the British evacuation of Philadelphia, McKean was as usual playing many roles simultaneously. He had already been active in rooting out the corruption and maladministration that had become rampant during the Valley Forge winter, though some of the culprits were "high in rank, and characters I did not suspect." [177] He was now assigned by Congress, with John Witherspoon and James Smith, to a Committee on Philadelphia which was to advise the army on its relations with civilians during the reoccupation. It was this committee which received the letter General Washington had written on May 31, 1778: "I should be glad to know, in case Philadelphia is evacuated, whether and what line of conduct is to be pursued respecting the goods that may be left . . . The point on which I wish direction, is with respect to goods and Merchandize, private property." [178] At the same time McKean was up to his ears in the work of the Supreme Court, which soon began to hold hearings at the College of Philadelphia, while Congress and the Supreme Executive Council moved into separate rooms at the State House.[179]

A continuing responsibility was his membership on the Committee on Prisoners. Indeed, his influence with law enforcement officers and jail administrators very likely began before he became Chief Justice; from the beginning of the war he had been exercising control over hundreds of prisoners through this Congressional committee. Prisoners could not be kept in jail indefinitely in those days without the danger of causing epidemics. Jail fever or typhus (otherwise known as ship fever or hospital fever *) made the rapid exchange of prisoners of war a practical as well as a humanitarian policy. Exchanging prisoners or releasing them on parole, with conventions or cartels to specify the conditions of their release, were really the only alternatives to slaughtering them or attempting to keep them (and their diseases) isolated on prison ships, or packed in continental mines. Both sides had an interest in exchanging prisoners; moreover, these negotiations helped the governments to retain control over their armed forces. Prisoners of war included those captured by privateers or naval vessels on the high seas, often two or three hundred at a time, as well as soldiers who surrendered on

* Caused, as we now know, by body lice.

land. The capitulation of some 5,000 troops under Burgoyne at Saratoga in the fall of 1777 was the largest single surrender to date. The Continental Congress, through its Committee on Prisoners, had a good deal of leverage by which to exercise civilian control over the military.[180]

The difficulties of exercising this control in individual cases, however, were illustrated by McKean's contretemps with General William Thompson. This dauntless soldier had been captured by the British in 1776, held in captivity for a few months, then released on parole and allowed to return to Pennsylvania. Under the terms of his release he was not allowed to fight again until he was exchanged (by proxy), and the Committee on Prisoners passed him by to exchange Governor John McKinly of Delaware for Governor William Franklin of New Jersey. Thompson complained loudly that he had been "used damned rascally" by Congress, and that McKean in particular was responsible.[181] He also pointed out that "Some who were taken sleeping in their beds [referring to General Lee, in addition to McKinly] were exchanged, whilst he who was taken fighting in the field was not exchanged."[182] On the evening of November 18, 1778, McKean and Thompson met in a Coffee House, and when the former congratulated Thompson on the fact that General Clinton had consented to his release, Thompson replied that he was obliged to Clinton, but not to Congress or to McKean. He repeated all his charges, and hot words led to an exchange of blows. McKean declared that Thompson was behaving like a bully and a brute, and vowed he would make him "repent his conduct."[183]

The next day McKean reported the incident to Congress as a breach of privilege.[184] Thompson was summoned before Congress, where he denied disrespect for that body but admitted he had called McKean a rascal and a villain. The dispute dragged on through the months of November and December, with witnesses on both sides, and Congress was caught up in a maze of personalities in which Gouverneur Morris protested that McKean's opponents never knew whether they were opposing "Mr. McKean the Delegate of Delaware" or "Mr. McKean the Chief Justice of Pennsylvania." At last Thompson was required to apologize, but on December 29 in the *Pennsylvania Packet* he accused McKean of behaving "like a Lyar, a rascal, and a coward," and challenged him to a duel. McKean's reply was printed in the same paper on December 31, and in it he noted that since Thompson was a prisoner of war he would take no further notice of the matter—"I cannot set the precedent obliging a member of Congress or a magistrate to subject himself to a duel with every person against whose opinion he gives his vote or judgment." This was to become his standard response in personal disputes arising from his official duties.*

---

* Trivial as the incident appeared, it produced more records than almost any other event in McKean's life. See Papers of the Continental Congress, No. 159, several folios, LC; Certioraries and Habeas Corpus Papers of the Supreme Court of Pennsylvania, Philadelphia; Society Misc. Coll., HSP; JCC for many dates in Nov. and Dec., 1778; letters of the members; and several newspapers.

   In his capacity as a private citizen McKean allowed no slurs or aspersions to go uncorrected; he sued Thompson for libel and in the spring of 1781 was awarded £5,700 damages, part of which sum was owed by Dunlap, in whose *Packet* the libel had appeared. To prove his point that "he only wanted to see the law and the facts settled," he then released the damages in both cases. Scharf and Westcott, *op. cit.,* I, 393.

All three branches of the Pennsylvania government exercised their powers against disaffected persons with great vigor after the return of the patriots to Philadelphia.[185] Power must be seized in revolutionary times; it is not influenced by theory, and will not follow the forms of law. The Supreme Court felt it was being generous to allow citizens who were accused of high treason "a copy of the whole indictment (but not the names of the witnesses), [in] a reasonable time, not less than one day before the trial."[186] The legislature passed acts of attainder and named persons thought to have joined the British, giving them, say, forty days to surrender and stand trial under a general treason statute. The temporary treason statutes of September, 1776, were suspended by this act of February 11, 1777, after which date allegiance to the state of Pennsylvania was to be mandatory, according to McKean's subsequent decisions.[187]

The Supreme Executive Council was given power to proclaim additional attainders in the future. Under this arrangement some 500 persons were condemned unheard, and forfeited their property to the state, approximately 400 of them in 1778, and 118 more were prosecuted in some way by the Supreme Court. There was also a form of judicial attainder, called outlawry, adopted by the Supreme Court in difficult cases, such as that of the Doan gang (Robin-Hood types) in Bucks county, whom McKean hounded persistently for many years.[188]

McKean's day-to-day activities, when he first returned to Philadelphia, and the mood of the city at that point were graphically described in a letter he wrote to Justice Atlee, dated July 7, 1778:

> My time has been taken up principally in taking the surrender of the persons proclaimed, and writing recognizances of bail. Not one has been yet committed, nor has any evidence appeared except the general charge in the proclamation, not withstanding I sit daily in the court house from 9 to 11 o'clock, and sometimes to 12, having James Goring and John Ord, Esquires, two of the Justices of the peace here, as assistants, to inform me of the abilities of the persons who offer themselves as sureties, and to hear accusers, if any should offer. The Inhabitants appear to be either afraid of one another, or the Whigs cannot yet believe that their friends have the government of the city.[189]

The power of the Supreme Court in this situation was profoundly influenced by the multiple roles of the individual justices outside of the Court. McKean, in fact, was the chief legal officer at the center of the continental government, and he was strong enough by now to withstand the clamor of the mob for blood. More than 3,000 Tories had left the city with the British, but many more remained. These people had collaborated with the enemy, and given them every possible assistance; the cry for vengeance on the part of the "furious Whigs" was almost irresistible, and countless refugees fled to Canada or to England. Under the circumstances the policy that was followed was strict, but not bloody. Those who desired to stand trial, to clear their names, were given an opportunity to appear before the Court with excellent counsel and proper procedural safeguards. Others, for reasons suspected by some but best known to themselves, fled without waiting to learn the outcome of the proceedings, but even these could leave their wives or children to try to retain or recover their property.

Taking his daughter with him—more through fear of a misalliance than fear of the Whigs—Joseph Galloway was one of those who prudently retreated with General Howe to New York, and eventually to England. His wife, Grace Growden Galloway, remained to do wordy and overconfident battle to save the family property, some of which was hers, in her own right. The Whigs returned to power in Philadelphia on June 18th; on the following day Charles Willson Peale, having laid aside palette for politics, called on Mrs. Galloway, as a member of one of the committees concerned with confiscations, and informed her that she would have to vacate her house. John Dickinson was summoned in desperation to give legal counsel, but he was not able to give her much hope that she could retain her dowry or anything else. As "no tryal would be of service," she wrote, he could only advise her "to draw up a Pet'ion to ye Chief Justice Mccean." The petition availed little, but Mrs. Galloway resisted removal until August 20, when Peale made forcible entry, and somewhat roughly escorted her to General Arnold's carriage, which had been offered her, with the General's compliments.[190]

Of all the people brought to trial in the fall of 1778, only two were actually hanged for treason. These were Abraham Carlisle, a carpenter, who was charged with having tended the gates at the northern redoubt, and John Roberts, a wealthy miller of Lower Merion, who was accused of having enlisted volunteers to serve the British army.[191] In both cases the prosecutors were the Attorney General, Jonathan Dickinson Sergeant, and Joseph Reed, his special assistant; the defense counsel were James Wilson and George Ross. The defendants were prominent Quakers, of respectable reputation, and the death sentences in these cases aroused widespread opposition and numerous appeals to the Supreme Executive Council for clemency—in which even the judges and jurymen joined.[192]

Many feared that the execution of Carlisle and Roberts would be but the precursor of widespread prosecutions, but in retrospect it would appear that the bloodlust of the mob was skillfully deflected by a government anxious to temper justice with mercy. Further, the doubts entertained concerning the execution of these two scapegoats were used to prevent further capital punishments. Indeed, only four men were hanged for treason during the war in the entire state of Pennsylvania—the others being David Dawson and Ralph Morden—in spite of the fact that the government had innumerable opportunities.[193] The British, too, were sparing in executions for treason, and the Americans did not wish to seem less civilized than their adversaries. There were plenty of atrocities on both sides during the war, but so far as actual treason cases were concerned, McKean's Court established cautious precedents which, happily, have been followed during most of American history.[194]

On November 4, 1778, Carlisle and Roberts were taken to the common with ropes around their necks and their coffins before them.[195] McKean threw himself into the sentencing of the victims with the zeal of a Calvinist clergyman; perhaps he was reminded by the religious aspects of the occasion that his mentor and good friend, Dr. Francis Alison, had died the previous fall.[196] In any case, he performed his role with a sanctimonious unction which brought down on his head all the bitterness and hostility of the disaffected elements in Philadelphia, and gave him the reputation of a hanging judge, comparable to the infamous Judge Jeffreys in English history:

> John Roberts, you have been indicted, and after a very long, a very fair and impartial trial, have been convicted of high treason . . . [the] next step is to proceed to judgment, and sorry I am that it falls to my lot to pronounce the dreadful sentence, but I must discharge my duty to my country.
>
> Treason is a crime of the most fatal and dangerous consequence to society; it is of the most malignant nature; it is of a criminal color, and of a scarlet dye. Maliciously to deprive one man of life merits the punishment of death, and blood for blood is a just restitution. What punishment, then, must he deserve, who joins the enemies of his country, and endeavours the total destruction of the lives, liberties, and property of all his fellow-citizens? . . .
>
> You will probably have but a short time to live. Before you launch into eternity, it behooves you to improve the time that may be allowed you in this world: it behooves you most seriously to reflect upon your past conduct; to repent of your evil deeds, to be incessant in prayers to the great and merciful God . . . may you, reflecting upon these things be qualified to enter into the joys of Heaven, joys unspeakable, and full of glory . . .
>
> May God be merciful unto your soul.[197]

Shortly afterwards, in New York City, the talented and popular John André read aloud at a public entertainment a *Dream,* which delighted the assembled loyalists. In this production several judges were dispensing justice in hell, and "the first person called upon was the famous Chief Justice McKean, who I found had been animated by the same spirit which formerly possessed the memorable Jeffreys. I could not but observe a flush of indignation in the eyes of the judges upon the approach of this culprit. His more than savage cruelty, his horrid disregard to the many oaths of allegiance he had taken, and the vile sacrifices he had made to justice, in the interests of rebellion, were openly rehearsed . . . He was condemned to assume the shape of a blood-hound, and the souls of Roberts and Carlisle were ordered to scourge him through the infernal regions." [198]

The Quakers and other pacifist groups generally regarded McKean as the symbol of an oppressive regime in which their pretensions to neutrality were not respected. His arrogance and susceptibility to flattery made him a natural target for the dissident elements, and by giving himself aristocratic airs and graces he played directly into their hands. The story is told of his receiving a memorial addressed to "the right Honorable Thomas M'Kean, Esq., Lord Chief Justice of Pennsylvania," upon which he remarked in open court, "These are, perhaps, more titles than I can fairly lay claim to, but at all events the petitioner has erred on the right side." [199] An anonymous loyalist poet left a long poem with the following lines:

> He who a band of ruffians keeps to kill,
> Is he not guilty of the blood they spill?
> Who guards McKean and Joseph Reed the vile,
> Help'd he not to murder Roberts and Carlisle? [200]

During the year 1779 the feud between McKean and his brother-in-law, Francis Hopkinson, was exacerbated by several acts of bitter and public conflict, which left McKean's relations with the Hopkinson and Borden families painful and strained indeed. On February 9, under the pen-name of "A. B." Hopkinson criticised McKean's conduct in the General William Thompson affair in a letter to the editor of the *Pennsylvania Packet*.[201] This controversy had divided the Continental Congress, and the Philadelphia community, into angry and mutually recriminating factions earlier that winter, and it was particularly unpleasant for McKean that a prominent member of his own circle was joining the opposition. Hopkinson then, as if to formalize his role which had been anomalous up to this point, joined in the formation of the Republican Society, organized to combat the Whig Society, in which McKean and George Bryan were the leading figures. The *Pennsylvania Gazette,* on March 24, contained a notice announcing the formation of the Republican Society, signed by eighty-two of the chief opponents of the Constitution of 1776, including Robert Morris, Benjamin Rush, James Wilson, and Francis Hopkinson.[202] For the moment the Constitutionalists and the Anti-constitutionalists, in such groups as the Whig Society and the Republican Society, were the two main factions in Pennsylvania politics.

More permanently divisive, so far as family relations were concerned, was the McKean occupancy of the confiscated home of the Rev. Jacob Duché, on the northeast corner of Third and Pine Streets, in one of the best locations in South Philadelphia.[203] Duché was the ex-pastor of St. Peter's Church, who had been called upon for prayer and preaching by the First Continental Congress. He had defected to the enemy during the British occupation of Philadelphia, prayed for the health of the King, and written an extraordinary letter to George Washington urging him to negotiate with the British at the head of his army—in defiance of Congress.* Duché was married to Francis Hopkinson's sister, and although his pathetic communication to Washington had caused intense embarrassment for Hopkinson, the latter was not at all pleased to see his sister dispossessed, and his aggressive brother-in-law moving into her house.

As for McKean, he had determined in advance that he would "not be scrupulous about buying the estate of a Traitor," [204] and had written to Sally as early as October 25, 1778, urging her to look for a house in town because "It is high time we were fixed." [205] Whatever the justice of the confiscation, the house itself was entirely satisfactory, and he kept it for the rest of his life, and willed it to his son, Joseph Borden McKean.[206] Built by Duché's father on the plan of a wing of Lambeth Palace, the residence of the Archbishop of Canterbury, the mansion at the corner of Third and Pine Streets was greatly admired. The property also included a coach house, stables, and four lots of ground.[207] McKean rented it from the state, with the permission of the Assembly at first, but eventually bought it at what was supposedly a public auction of May 28, 1781, for

---

* Duché to Washington, Phila. Oct. 8, 1777, in Hopkinson Papers, II, HSP. See also Hopkinson to Duché, Borden Town, Nov. 14, 1777, in *ibid.*, addressed to Dear Brother, "Words cannot express the Grief & Consternation that wounded my Soul at Sight of this fatal Performance." Washington, naturally, could not keep treasonable correspondence of this sort secret, no matter how embarrassing.

£7,750, with a ground-rent of 232 bushels of wheat.[208] Of this sum one-fourth was reserved by the government for the University of the State of Pennsylvania, the old College of Philadelphia, which had itself been confiscated in 1779 and turned over to a new Board of Trustees. McKean, as Chief Justice, was an *ex-officio* member of this Board.

McKean had not favored the confiscation of the College of Philadelphia, and regarded the action of the radical faction in the Assembly, which emasculated the Charter of the College,[209] as contrary to the law and unnecessary. This was encroaching on the realm of corporate property, on which McKean's views were conservative, and on educational matters he was always a staunch upholder of academic freedom. In this opinion he agreed with the Republican element in the state, and would undoubtedly have opposed the action officially, if the measure had been submitted to the Supreme Court for review, as the defenders of the College wished.* As it was, the Assembly appointed a committee to investigate the allegedly pro-Tory activities of the College officials, and later went through the formality of a hearing on College affairs, in which James Wilson and William Lewis were allowed to appear as counsel for the Trustees. The Assembly avoided a judicial determination, and used the radical majority of 33 to 16 to restructure the institution in such a way as to eliminate completely the influence of the former leaders.[210]

Having decided that the College, hereafter to be called the University of the State of Pennsylvania, was a dangerous hold-over from the old order, the Assembly appointed new Trustees in accordance with a formula which they hoped would guarantee its political reliability, under the Constitution of 1776, and at the same time prevent its being dominated by any one religious denomination. The new Trustees were to consist of three classes. "The first class consisted of persons holding offices under the government who were *ex officio* members of the board. These were, when the act was passed: 1. the president of the Supreme Executive Council, Joseph Reed; 2. the vice-president of the Council, William Moore; 3. the speaker of the General Assembly, John Bayard; 4. the chief justice of the Supreme Court, Thomas McKean; 5. the judge of the Admiralty, Francis Hopkinson; 6. the attorney general, Jonathan Dickinson Sergeant. The second class consisted of six clergymen,—the senior ministers of the Episcopal, Presbyterian, Lutheran, German Calvinist, Baptist, and Catholic Churches . . . The third class was composed of thirteen individuals,—Dr. Benjamin Franklin, then United States Minister at Paris; William Shippen, Benjamin Searle, and Frederick Muhlenberg, members of Congress from Pennsylvania; William Augustus Atlee and John Evans, judges of the Supreme Court; Timothy Matlack, secretary of the Supreme Executive Council; David Rittenhouse, state treasurer; Jonathan Bayard Smith, Samuel Morris, George Bryan, Dr. Thomas Bond, and Dr. James Hutchinson." [211]

---

* Nevins, *The American States,* 263 f, states: "All [the stated] reasons were empty, and a more dishonorable act than the repeal of the charter has seldom stained Pennsylvania's record . . . The Anti-Constitutionalists justly wrote later: [we] consider [the arguments] but as the specious coloring to a scene of predetermined injustice, which the actors therein could not safely trust to a court of law."

Unfortunately, the College or so-called University did not prosper under the new regime, and the damage wrought by the revolutionary Assembly "was not fully repaired until after the Civil War." [212] The new Trustees were chosen for their prominence, rather than their fitness for the position, and in most cases had little time for the detailed supervision of an academic institution. McKean was one of those who persevered, and on June 4, 1788, he was elected President of the Board. Shortly afterwards, the legislature of 1789 passed an act restoring the College's charter and property, reviving the institution, and declaring in its preamble that the law of the previous decade had been "repugnant to justice, a violation of the Constitution of this Commonwealth, and dangerous in its precedents to all incorporated bodies." [213] Under the circumstances this language may be considered a fair statement of McKean's views throughout the period. When the new Trustees were elected, at the union of the reestablished College and the University in 1791, McKean was chosen by the board of the University in 1791, and continued as president. How long he remained as president is not clear, but he was a member of the board until his death.[214] It is worthy of note that the secretary of the board in 1780, immediately after the revolutionary take-over, was Samuel Sterrett, who had been living with the McKeans for several years, reading law, and serving as a general factotum for the family.[215] In 1794 Joseph Borden McKean was elected a Trustee.[216]

Beginning in 1778, the Assembly had been wrestling with the still larger question of the disposition of the Penn family's land-holdings. The proprietaries were two grandsons of William Penn: John, the son of Richard, and also governor, and John, the son of Thomas.[217] The Penn family's holdings, comprising most of Pennsylvania and Delaware, were the largest complex of private land-holdings on the continent of North America (except for the Hudson's Bay Company, which remained in British hands). The Penns had, of course, been stripped of all governing authority in Pennsylvania by the Constitution of 1776; the issue to be decided by the legislature in 1779 was that of title to the soil, a separate question.[218] The disposition of the Penns' holdings in the Lower Counties (now the state of Delaware) was a matter for the Delaware legislature to decide, and was dealt with later. McKean was an influential figure in both states, and he did his utmost for the rights of private property, as he understood them, in both cases; but he was more helpful to the Penns as Chief Justice of Pennsylvania—though his advisory opinion was not followed in most respects by the Assembly [219]—than he was in Delaware, where he and Edmund Physick acted as the Penns' attorneys.[220]

The masterful leadership of Joseph Reed in the Supreme Executive Council, and George Bryan in the Assembly, enabled the state of Pennsylvania to dispose of this complicated question in a manner that was both fair to the Penns and satisfactory to the radical leaders.[221] The solution was perhaps also a tribute to the tact and wisdom of Governor John Penn, who had remained in America without giving offense to either side.[222] In Pennsylvania the process of determining the Penns' rights took most of the year 1779. There were hearings in March and again in April; the Penns were represented by George Ross, James

Wilson, Edward Tilghman, and Benjamin Chew, while the state was represented by Attorney General Sergeant.[223] Five legal questions were propounded to the Chief Justice by the Assembly, on Reed's recommendation, concerning the following points: 1. the authority of the British Crown to convey the lands; 2. the nature of the grant, as to whether it was absolute or in trust; 3. the extent of the concessions to be made to the "first purchasers;" 4. the right of the Penns to reserve land and quitrents to themselves; and 5. the effect of the Revolution on the proprietors' right of pre-emption from the Indians.[224]

McKean's opinion, delivered two days later, was not satisfactory to the Assembly, for he found against the Penns on only one point, the last, holding that the proprietors had no right of pre-emption to unsold lands in the future.[225] Nonetheless he had not hesitated to state his opinion frankly and openly, and it undoubtedly influenced the final decision, for the Assembly ordered that his opinion and their own resolutions should be published for further study. On November 27, 1779, the Divesting Act was passed, extinguishing the Penns' rights to unsold lands and quitrents, but carefully protecting the manors (laid out before July 4, 1779), and whatever could be distinguished as private property, granting as compensation the sum of £130,000, which was paid with interest within eight years of the end of the war.[226] The vote on the Divesting Act was 40 to 7. The minority were allowed to enter a protest on the record, and John Penn was permitted to address the Assembly and have his short but dignified statement printed in the Journal. In addition, the Penn family had the rare good fortune of receiving compensation from both sides; the British government later granted them an annuity of £4,000, which was paid to them and their heirs .for over a hundred years and then commuted to a lump sum payment.[227]

In Delaware the Penns did not fare so well. On July 23, 1792, about the time Pennsylvania was making its final payments to the Penn family, McKean wrote to John Dickinson explaining the proposals that he and Edmund Physick intended to make on behalf of the Penns in the case of their Delaware holdings. He observed that as agents they were embarrassed by the absence of detailed instructions, but had decided in the first instance to offer the "entierity [sic] of the Proprietary estate to the Government," and if that offer was turned down (as it was) to make proposals to individuals. He recalled that the General Assembly of 1775, of which he had been a member, would have been willing to pay the Penns seven years of quitrents, and pass a law for the easier collection of quitrents in the future, and noted that Mr. Read remembered that also.

McKean was in the habit of consulting Dickinson about many important decisions, as has been noted, but in this case there was a particular reason: ". . . my dear Sir, I have been explicit with you about this affair, as you perhaps own more land in Delaware than any other person. I have about a thousand acres myself, and my near Relations a great deal more in Newcastle county, subject to the same terms." [228] Unfortunately, the climate of opinion had changed greatly in the intervening years, and McKean was no longer a member of the Delaware Assembly, or active in Delaware politics. The former Whigs were in disrepute at the time, and the transaction was too big a coup for out-of-state lawyers to negotiate successfully; the Delaware Assembly simply ignored the claims of the Penns. If the offer had been made during the war, it might have been more successful.

The fairness and reasonableness of the Divesting Act of 1779 in Pennsylvania were all the more remarkable in that the passage of the act came less than eight weeks after the "Fort Wilson Riot"—the high-water mark of revolutionary violence in Philadelphia, during which a couple of Signers of the Declaration almost lost their lives.[229] The affair took its name from the bloodshed that occurred at the home of James Wilson, at Third and Walnut Streets, and resulted from a number of causes, including agitation against the merchants of the city for the high prices of consumer goods, anxiety caused by the devaluation of the currency, the unpopularity of lawyers who defended the former Tories, and the general instability of the supporters of the Constitution of 1776. On October 5, 1779, a mob of disgruntled militiamen held a meeting at Mrs. Burns' Tavern at the edge of the common to protest the activities of alleged monopolists and forestallers; soon they were joined by a motley group of waterfront toughs and hangers-on. About thirty conservatives, headed by Robert Morris, Thomas Mifflin, General William Thompson, and a one-armed veteran named Colonel Campbell gathered at James Wilson's house to defend themselves and prevent trouble. A feeling of alarm swept the city.

The radical mob armed with muskets and bayonets, gathering strength as it moved, proceeded up Walnut Street, dragging two field-pieces and beating drums. Arriving at Wilson's house, the mob surged towards the gate. Fortunately, someone had sent to warn President Reed, then confined by illness, of the impending violence. Colonel Campbell threatened the mob, and General Mifflin tried to harangue them, but shots were fired, and at least one man was killed on each side, including Colonel Campbell. At the critical moment Reed galloped up with his coattails flying, a detachment of city militia behind him, and dispersed the mob, but not before General Arnold, who had also hastened to the rescue single-handed, had been insulted and required to beat an undignified retreat.[230] The next day Reed called a meeting in the Supreme Court room of the State House; both sides aired their griveances, and began to cool off. The revolution at that moment had almost begun to devour its children.

At the time of the incident, McKean and Atlee were in York, holding court, and although McKean was sent for, he displayed a peculiar reluctance to return to Philadelphia. Justice Atlee wrote to his wife, "Dear Hetty," from York on October 12th:

> The return of an Express who brought Letters for Mr. McKean gives me the opportunity to telling you [sic] that we arrived here all well & continue so—tho' we are very uneasy about the troubles in Philadelphia—The Chief Justice is again sent for—but is not yet determined whether 'tis best to go down or not—the President [Reed] is very unwell & some bad People seem taking advantage of his situation to cause disturbances & distress him more.[231]

McKean was not avoiding the dilemma: keeping the courts open in all counties of the state was an overriding consideration, of the utmost importance. At this time executive functions were performed by the Court as well as by the Supreme Executive Council; in the various localities the Court not only appointed the constables and justices of the peace, but had additional personnel to enforce its decrees.[232] The Court also directed intelligence and counter-intelligence operations, and a little later an act was passed enabling *both the Supreme Executive Council and the Justices of the Supreme Court* to "apprehend suspected persons, and to increase the fines to which persons are liable for neglecting to perform their militia duty." [233] In July, 1779, Samuel R. Fisher, a Quaker, was convicted of misprision of treason for writing a letter to his brother Jabez in New York City, and McKean casually mentioned to Sally, "on account of [this letter] I sent a warrant for him some months ago, and committed him as he refused to give bail; his sentence is to forfeit half his estate, & to remain in prison during the war."[234] Actually, the obstinate Friend was the victor in a sense; he was released by the Supreme Executive Council in February, 1781, still stubbornly refusing to give recognizance for good behavior.[235] The classic situation was here reversed: a soft-hearted executive was releasing the prisoner of a tough court—instead of the other way around.

In 1779 the Court travelled from Philadelphia to Chester, Reading, Easton, Lancaster, York, and Carlisle,[236] and in each county dispensed justice for those held in jail, besides making certain that the law-enforcement apparatus was fully manned. The next March the Court started in again with hearings at Philadelphia, followed by more hearings at Chester, Lancaster, York, Carlisle, Chester, Philadelphia, Easton, Reading, and Chester.[237] McKean did not hesitate to impanel juries, and compel reluctant citizens to serve as constables—and require all concerned to attend Court. The entry in the Court's docket for April 5, 1779, listed justices of the peace and constables for the City and County of Philadelphia (over a hundred names), concluding with an off-hand note: "Ordered that an attachment issue against the constables of Germantown, the Northern and Passyunk Township for their contempt in not attending this court—which having accordingly issued—the said Constables were taken by the Sheriff and brought before this Court—and upon the reason rendered by them were discharged by the Court upon payment of costs." [238] At other times the absentees were less fortunate, and were fined £10 each.*

In his capacity as a member of Congress, McKean laid before Congress various resolutions adopted by the government of Delaware in January, 1779, concerning the Articles of Confederation and Perpetual Union, which had been under consideration by the states since 1777.[239] The gist of these resolutions was that while the state of Delaware generally approved of the plan, there were doubts and reservations concerning the 8th and 9th Articles, and in particular the provisions for supplying the common treasury "in proportion to the value of land," and for depriving a state of territory "for the benefit of the United States." [240] Delaware was a small state located on the eastern seaboard, and was concerned about

---

* Oyer and Terminer Docket, 351. For other offenses punishments of branding and whipping were handed out freely. A certain Anne Winters, for stealing the goods of the Chief Justice, was punished as follows: 50 lashes, restoring the goods or paying the value thereof, paying a fine equal to the value, and two years of hard labor. *Ibid.*, 55.

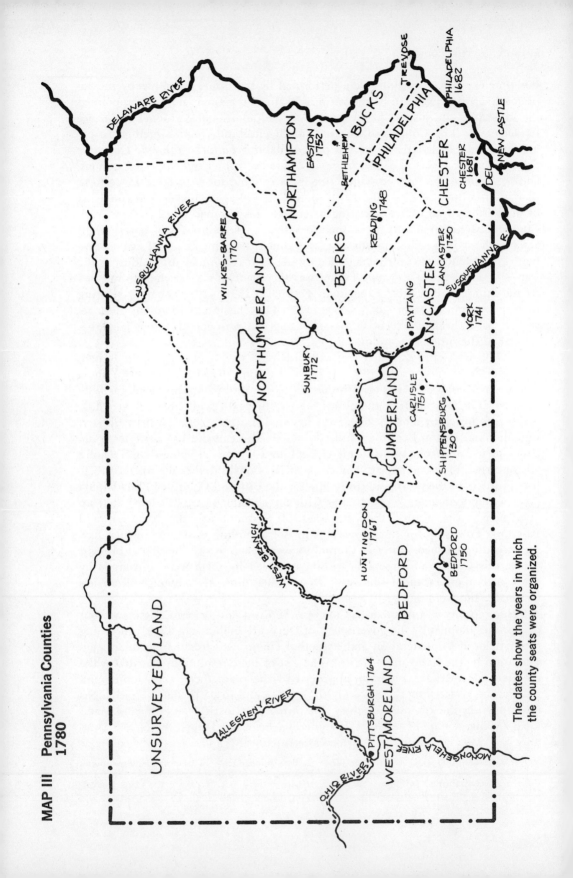

MAP III   Pennsylvania Counties 1780

DELAWARE RIVER

TREVOSE

PHILADELPHIA 1682

NEW CASTLE

NORTHAMPTON

BUCKS

EASTON 1752

BETHLEHEM

PHILADELPHIA

CHESTER

CHESTER 1681

DEL

SUSQUEHANNA RIVER

WILKES-BARRE 1770

NORTHUMBERLAND

BERKS

READING 1748

LANCASTER 1750

LAN·CASTER

SUSQUEHANNA R.

PAXTANG

SUNBURY 1772

YORK 1741

CUMBERLAND

CARLISLE 1751

SHIPPENSBURG 1750

WEST BRANCH

HUNTINGDON 1767

BEDFORD

BEDFORD 1750

UNSURVEYED LAND

ALLEGHENY RIVER

PITTSBURGH 1764

WEST MORELAND

MONONGAHELA RIVER

OHIO RIVER

The dates show the years in which the county seats were organized.

GEORGE BRYAN, by A. Rosenthal.
(Courtesy: Independence Hall Collection.)

JOSEPH REED, by Charles Willson Peale, ca. 1785. *(Courtesy: Historical Society of Pennsylvania.)*

TIMOTHY MATLACK, by Rembrandt Peale (?). *(Courtesy: National Gallery of Art.)* -

STATE HOUSE, ca. 1776, by Charles Willson Peale.
(Courtesy: Independence National Historical Park Collection.)

THOMAS McKEAN, by Charles Willson Peale.
(Courtesy: Independence Hall Collection.)

the claims of some states to territory all the way west to the Mississippi or to the presumptive but vague South Sea. The United States in Congress assembled "should and ought to have the power of fixing their western limits," and these limits should be near the present line of settlement, while all ungranted land beyond that point should be regarded as a common estate, won from the British and the Indians by the blood and treasure of all.[241] This was essentially the same position as that taken by the state of Maryland, but Delaware did not insist on a general acceptance of this point, as Maryland did, authorizing McKean to sign and ratify the Articles in February, 1779, in view of the great disadvantage of further delay. His two colleagues signed on May 5 following.[242]

On October 1, 1779, the day of the general election in Delaware, McKean attended at New Castle, and asked his constituents to release him from the position he had held for seventeen years as a member of the Assembly of Delaware. He was willing to continue as Delaware's delegate to Congress (in fact, he was to become President of Congress in 1781), but his duties in Congress and as Chief Justice of Pennsylvania took so much of his time that it was no longer advisable for him to continue to serve in the legislature at New Castle.[243] Whereupon his constituents paid him the signal compliment of asking him to list seven persons suitable for election to the Assembly. He replied that he knew not only seven, but seventy, whom he considered worthy of their votes, and asked that he be excused from listing a few on the ground that he might give offense to many of his friends. His constituents persisted, however, and he wrote down seven names; according to the Autobiographical Sketch written in his old age, all seven were immediately elected to the legislature. The satisfaction he had evidently given his Delaware supporters was one of his proudest memories.[244]

Nevertheless, McKean's primary contribution in this period was his service as Chief Justice of the Supreme Court of Pennsylvania, a position which he held for twenty-two years, from 1777 to 1799. There was as yet no Court of Appeals in this state to review the decisions reached by the Supreme Court, when acting as a court of original jurisdiction, and there was no federal judiciary whatsoever. Because of his experience in the state Supreme Court, McKean was aware of these needs, and in both instances was among the leaders in supplying the missing governmental machinery. The High Court of Errors and Appeals was established by act of February 28, 1780, and McKean and several others were commissioned on November 20.[245] The function of this court was to hear appeals from the Supreme Court, the Register's Court, and the Court of Admiralty.[246] The members were: the President of the Supreme Executive Council, Joseph Reed; the Justices of the Supreme Court, Justices McKean, Atlee, Evans, and Bryan; the new Judge of Admiralty, Francis Hopkinson; and "three persons of known integrity and ability," who were not immediately named.[247]

The need for the court was not as great as had been anticipated, and in the first two years only one case was heard. Eventually distinguished jurists, such as the former Chief Justice, Benjamin Chew, were appointed and the court performed useful service; McKean continued as a member as long as the court existed, serving until 1806, after he had become Governor. From the beginning there were jurisdictional problems—Francis Hopkinson complaining in March, 1780: "under the existing laws, the jurisdiction of the Court of Admiralty and the Supreme Court overlapped to such an extent that the First and Second Judges of the Supreme Court [could] hold a Court of Admiralty Sessions in Philadelphia, and the Third and Fourth Judges [after Bryan's anticipated appointment in April] hold a like court at the same time in Lancaster, and the Judge of Admiralty be present at neither."[248] He went on to say that the legislature by the creation of the new court of Errors and Appeals did nothing to remove the confusion.

Unfortunately for Hopkinson, he was badly outnumbered by the judges of the Supreme Court, and despite his known integrity, and the purity of his public and private life, he eventually suffered the humiliation of an impeachment before the Supreme Executive Council on charges of embezzlement and extortion—charges for which he always blamed McKean. Samuel Sterrett, McKean's protegé, had become Clerk of the General Assembly and was one of the prime instigators of the proceedings. Hopkinson was represented by James Wilson and Jared Ingersoll. The trial, which lasted for three days, was probably intended as a tacit warning or chastisement in itself. The questions raised were petty matters, such as whether or not he had received a present of a suit of clothes, and if he had, was it a gift or a bribe? At worst, he was guilty of political naiveté. His unanimous acquittal by the Council was but small consolation to a man of Hopkinson's sensitivity.[249]

Even earlier McKean had been maneuvering toward the establishment of a federal court of appeals; in this case he was acting as a member of Congress anxious to remove such difficulties as the Congressional Commissioners of Appeals had suffered in the case of the sloop *Active,* in which Benedict Arnold had been involved. On January 8, 1780, McKean was appointed a member of a committee, consisting of Oliver Ellsworth, Thomas Houston, Robert Livingstone, and himself, to plan for the formation of a federal Court of Appeals, and on the 27th he was elected chairman of the committee which prepared a draft of a commission for the judges of this new court.[250] Later he was nominated in Congress, on three separate occasions, as a candidate for judge of the court, but each time failed of election.[251] He made a significant contribution, however, by insisting repeatedly on the formation of an independent judiciary, and upholding the principle that judges should hold their commissions during good behavior—and not be held on a short leash, as they were in Pennsylvania.

Plainly, from the formation and the composition of these various courts, the principle of separation of powers had not yet been clearly worked out. The Congress, the Executive Council, and the courts were all jealous of their prerogatives, but puzzled as to what these prerogatives were. The perennial disputes were illustrated by the Griswold case in 1780, which was a repetition of the use or abuse of *habeas corpus* which had agitated the authorities in 1778, over the Quakers who were exiled to Virginia.[252] The Council vehemently protested an act of the Assembly which they considered "degrading" to the Council, in that it implied a "superior confidence" in the Court. Led by Joseph Reed, the Council had ordered a certain Joseph Griswold apprehended as a treason suspect; lo and behold, Chief Justice McKean released him on a writ of *habeas corpus* without consulting, or even informing, Council. McKean remonstrated that his action had been "strictly conformable to law and [his] duty," insisting that commitments by Council were of no more validity than those of a justice of the peace. Even in England, he pointed out, commitments by the King or the Privy Council were subject to examination by the judges.

Council responded in kind. Employing language one might hear today on the lips of an embattled police chief, mayor, or governor, they said: "It has been the policy of all other States, and even of the enemy, at this juncture, to repose a confidence in the Executive powers to guard the publick safety by commitments not subject to the examination of any other, and much less an inferior authority, for such we deem the Justices of the Supreme Court on this occasion . . ." [253] The Chief Justice did not concur with this opinion, and the dispute was not settled. By the time a new state constitution was established, ten years later, he appeared to have won his point.

*   *   *   *   *   *

In 1780 the future seemed to brighten for both his public and private affairs. The war was pretty well stabilized in the middle states by that time. Thomas McKean, Jr. was born November 20, 1779. Sally and the family joined him permanently in Philadelphia, so that he was able to enjoy a normal family life for the first time in years, and Sally was properly aware of her social standing and obligations—such as working on Mrs. (Esther de Berdt) Reed's committee to solicit contributions towards supplies urgently needed by the soldiers. The Bank of Philadelphia was founded at the same time, to contribute to the common cause, and McKean was one of the first subscribers, in the amount of £2000 —clear proof of prosperity as well as patriotism.*

He could begin to contemplate with assurance the ancient phrases with which petitions to judges conclude:

> And we as in duty bound shall ever pray for yo'r
> Honors health and happiness,
> That Age may crowne your Snowy hairs with
> Caesar's Honors and with Nestor's years.[254]

---

* The Bank of North America was formed in 1780, chartered on Dec. 31, 1781, and for three years was the only bank in the new republic. The Massachusetts Bank was charteded Feb. 7, 1784. Scharf and Westcott, *op. cit.*, I, 409; John Bach McMaster, *A History of the People of the United States* (New York, 1885), II, 29–30.

Textnotes

Chapter 1. Ancestors

[1] Thomas McKean to Andrew Buchanan, Philadelphia, June 2, 1804, Dreer Coll., Signers, Historical Society of Pennsylvania (HSP).

[2] See Chap. 7.

[3] *Two Hundredth Anniversay of the New London Presbyterian Church . . . Celebrated June 13, 14, and 15, 1926, Historical Sketch with Illustrations.*

[4] See esp. Roberdeau Buchanan, *Genealogy of the McKean Family,* and *The Life of the Hon. Thomas McKean* (Inquirer Printing Co., Lancaster, Pa., 1890). Roberdeau Buchanan was a great-grandson of Thomas McKean, the Signer.

[5] See esp. Gregory B. Keen, *The Descendants of Jöran Kyn of New Sweden* (Swedish Colonial Society, Philadelphia, 1913), 92 ff, 253 ff. Kyn was the founder of Upland, which became the city of Chester, Pa.

[6] The clan had other branches, such as the McIvors, McNabs, and McIntires, but it was the McIans who were the ancestors of the McKeans.

[7] Fred G. McKean, comp., *McKean Historical Notes* (Washington, 1906).

[8] James Logan in 1729, quoted in Lewis R. Harley, *The Life of Charles Thomson* (Philadelphia, 1900), 17. Many reasons have been given for the Scotch-Irish exodus: esp. the penal laws, the decline of the wool trade following Parliamentary legislation in 1699, the expiration of long-term leases and the raising of rents, ca. 1717–1720. Also see *Journal of the American Irish Hist. Soc.,* IX (1912), 110.

[9] Quoted in Buchanan, *op. cit.,* 10.

[10] Harry Wilson to Charles W. Heathcote, West Chester, Pa., Jan. 1, 1939, obtained from the Historical Society of York County.

[11] *Ibid.* Mr. Wilson describes his interest in these matters as follows: "As there seems to be a difference of opinion as to the locations of McKean's Birthplace, for my own information as well as yours, I have decided to go into this matter as fully as I can and settle if possible the right location. I [checked] Dr. H. T. C. Heagey's statement that Gov. McKean was born in West Fallowfield Twp [Cochranville] instead of New London Twp, as Judge J. Smith Futhey states. (Gilbert Cope is

242

my authority that Futhey was the author of that part of the Chester County History relating to western & southern part of the County printed by them in 1881.)"

[12] *Two Hundredth Anniversary of the New London Presbyterian Church . . . 1926,* and Harry Wilson's letter, Jan. 1, 1939.

[13] If Susannah was a widow during part of this migration, she probably travelled with a group of families. See Henry Jones Ford, *The Scotch-Irish in America* (Princeton, 1915), 236–9.

[14] William Cobbett, *Porcupine's Works* (12 vols., London, 1801), VII, 333, *Gazette Selections,* quoted in Buchanan, *op. cit.,* 86.

[15] Harry Wilson's 1939 letter, cited above, mentions these on-the-spot investigations: "During the winter of 1888–89 I lived in the village of New London, being employed by the board of Trustees of the New London Academy to conduct the school under the care of the New London Presbyterian Church. . . . Three members of my Board of Trustees . . . were interested in historical matters. Especially so was Jesse C. Dickey . . . a member of the state assembly, then a member of Congress, served in the Civil War, and was a most live little man. . . . Part of Mr. Dickey's land had been occupied by Susannah McCain, the Grandmother of Governor Thomas McKean, and he told me that an adjoining farm to his, then owned by Joseph Pierce, was the birthplace of the Governor." Wilson also cites the 1845 and the 1876 editions of the Rev. Robt. P. DuBois' *History of the New London Presbyterian Church* in support of his conclusion.

[16] Part of the time the Land Office was closed. See *Proceedings of the Scotch-Irish Society of America* (10 vols., 1889–1901), VIII, 75; Albert S. Bolles, *Pennsylvania, Province and State . . . 1609–1790* (2 vols., Philadelphia, 1899), II, 130 f.

[17] Cited in Futhey and Cope, *History of Chester County, Pennsylvania* (Philadelphia, 1881), 193.

[18] *Ibid.,* 643 f. The seemingly arbitrary choice of "Y" as a shorthand symbol or abbreviation for "th" is actually logical; as first used, before Gutenberg, it was a symbol of the Greek alphabet, written something like the Greek γ, which lapsed into "Y." Similar abbreviations or symbols persisted for several centuries, even into the early twentieth—e. g. § for "ss." These peculiarities should be kept in mind when deciphering MSS of the period.

[19] Harry Wilson's letter, Jan. 1, 1939, notes: "Dated December 28, 1730."

Chapter 2. His Father's Failure

[20] *Ibid.,* "Recorded in Will Book #1, page 342."

[21] Her gravestone reads: "Letitia McKean, died August 1742, in the 33rd year of her age."

[22] Information about Dr. Alison's school may be found at the University of Delaware, Newark, Delaware, and at the Presbyterian Ministers' Fund, Alison Bldg., Rittenhouse Square, Philadelphia.

[23] Cited in Harry Wilson's letter, Jan. 1, 1939. "Woodsbe" may be a transcriber's error for "needs be."

[24] For legal action involving Andrew Caldwell, see Thomas McKean to James Abel, Newcastle, March 24, 1760, in Etting Papers, Signers, V, 57, HSP.

[25] Harry Wilson's letter, Jan. 1, 1939.

[26] *Ibid.* Buchanan, *op. cit.,* quotes a letter from a Miss Philena McKeen, who obtained information from her father, the Rev. Silas McKeen and Judge Levi McKeen, of the New England branch of the family, with this statement, originally written in

1842: "After the death of his wife Letitia, who died in 1742, he removed to the State of Delaware, New Castle county, where he died. . . ."

[27] There is a letter from Caesar Rodney to "Thomas McKean of the Borough of Wilmington," dated July 10, 1779, appointing him Captain in the militia. *Delaware History*, XII (1966–67), 158.

[28] Receipt to Caesar Rodney, H. F. Brown Coll., Historical Society of Delaware (HSD). This curious document, in the handwriting of the twenty-three year old McKean, reads: "Whereas Caesar Rodeney Esq hath this day given me an Order on the Gaoler of Chester County for three pounds for his taking up a certain James Fulton, who escaped from him, it being for the use of Mr. Wm. McKean; Now if ever the said Sum is hereafter recovered by any other person for taking up sd Fulton from sd Casar Rodeney, I do promise to reimburse him. Fbry 17th, 1758. Thos. McKean."

[29] In the Logan Papers, HSP, there is a long and complicated agreement between "Thomas McKane of the township of Tredyffrin" and Thomas Harrison of Lower Merion, dated July 10, 1750, concerning the rental for a ten year period of some land in Easttown.

[30] The inscriptions on the tombs of the nearby graveyards are included in *Two Hundredth Anniversay of the New London Presbyterian Church . . . 1926.*

Chapter 3. Education under the Rev. Francis Alison

[31] McKean Papers, HSP. IV, 43.

[32] George H. Ryden, "The Newark Academy of Delaware in Colonial Days," *Pennsylvania History*, II (1935), 205–224. The dates 1741 and 1743 have both been given for the founding of Dr. Alison's school, but the Rev. Thomas Clinton Pears, Jr., in his biographical essay, "Francis Alison, Colonial Educator," *Delaware Notes*, Seventeenth Series, 1944, Univ. of Delaware, says that it actually became a school in November, 1743, though Dr. Alison may have had a few pupils earlier.

[33] *Ibid.*, also Benjamin Franklin's *Pennsylvania Gazette*, Nov. 24, 1743: "We are informed that there is a Free-School opened at the House of a Mr. Alison in Chester County, for the Promotion of Learning, where all Persons may be instructed in the Languages and some other Parts of Polite Literature, without any Expenses for their Education."

[34] Biographical information on Francis Alison in the Files of the Presbyterian Ministers' Fund; esp. George V. Gardner to Rev. Alexander Mackie, the Manse, New London, Pa., July 11, 1950, on the occasion of the dedication of the Alison Bldg. in Philadelphia.

[35] *Two Hundredth Anniversary of the New London Presbyterian Church . . . 1926.* See also Benjamin J. Lossing, *Eminent Americans* (New York, 1855).

[36] Armitage information in Genealogical Section, HSD. See also Frederick A. Virkus, *The Abridged Compendium of American Genealogy, First Families of America*, III (1928), Chicago, Ill.

[37] Enoch Armitage bond to Mary Watson, Aug. 15, 1757, in H. F. Brown Coll. of Rodney Material, HSD. Endorsed: "Received of Mr. Casar Rodeney, late Sheriff, Twenty-three pounds fourteen shillings, the Principal, Interest, and Attorney's Fee on the within Bond. Novemr 15th, 1759. Tho. McKean."

[38] Bible belonging to Thomas McKean, printed 1752, with entries concerning births, deaths, etc., connected with his second marriage, which lasted from 1774 to his death in 1817. McKean Papers, HSP, IV, 50.

[39] According to Univ. of Penna., *Biographical Catalogue of the Matriculates of the College . . . 1749–1893* (Philadelphia, 1894), Benjamin Alison was born to Francis and Hannah Alison at New London in 1745, and Francis Alison, Jr. was born there in 1751; Hannah Armitage Alison was undoubtedly living at New London during those years.

[40] William Nelson, *New Jersey Biographical and Genealogical Notes,* New Jersey Historical Society, Newark, N. J., IX (1916), 166–7.

[41] Originally printed in the *Pennsylvania Journal* shortly after Dr. Alison's death, and quoted in Pears, *op. cit.*

[42] In 1755, Dr. Alison made a journey to New England with John Bartram, the naturalist, in the course of which he met Dr. Stiles. Benjamin Franklin wrote a letter of introduction for them, addressed to his friend, Jared Eliot: "I wrote to you yesterday, and now I write again. You will say, It can't rain, but it pours; for I not only send you manuscript, but living letters. The former may be short, but the latter will be longer and yet more agreeable. Mr. Bartram I believe you will find to be at least twenty folio pages, large paper well filled, on the subjects of botany, fossils, husbandry, and the first creation. This Mr. Alison is as many or more on agriculture, philosophy, your own Catholic divinity, and various other points of learning equally useful and engaging. Read them both. It will take you at least a week; and then answer by sending me two of the little kind, or by coming yourself." Quoted by Thomas H. Montgomery, *A History of the University of Pennsylvania* (Philadelphia, 1900).

[43] Quoted in Pears, *op. cit.* Altogether the Synod of Philadelphia contributed £157 10 0 in the first four and a half years of the school's existence.

[44] George W. Corner, ed. *The Autobiography of Benjamin Rush* (Princeton, 1948), 289, 294. Also "Alison" in DAB.

[45] Francis Alison to Ezra Stiles, Oct. 22, 1773, quoted in Pears, *op. cit.*

[46] See William Warren Sweet, *Religion in the Development of American Culture, 1765–1840* (New York, 1952), 3–13, and George V. Gardner's letter, July 11, 1950.

[47] V. Lansing Collins, *Princeton: Past and Present* (Princeton, 1931, 1945), 1 ff.

[48] Ryden, *op. cit.* Also John A. Munroe, *Federalist Delaware, 1775–1815* (New Brunswick, 1954), 58 f. For the text of the charter and a bibliography, see *Delaware History,* IV, 149–156. There were seven Presbyterian clergymen and six laymen on the board of trustees:

Rev. Francis Alison	William Allen
Rev. Alexander McDowell	Charles Thomson
Rev. John Ewing	Andrew Allen
Rev. William McKennan	Thomas McKean
Rev. Patrick Alison	James Mease
Rev. Matthew Wilson	John Evans
Rev. Hugh Williamson	

[49] To Ezra Stiles, Oct. 30, 1766, Presbyterian Historical Society, 425 Lombard St., Philadelphia (MS, A1 4c, 14a).

[50] Lawrence H. Gipson points out that the question whether the Three Lower Counties belonged to the Crown or to the Penn family was never clearly settled. For his further discussion of their peculiar position, see Lawrence H. Gipson, "An Anomalous Colony," *Pennsylvania History,* XXVII (1960), 144–164, subsequently incorporated in *The British Empire Before the American Revolution,* Vol. III (Revised), Chap. VIII, 189–93.

[51] "Circular Letter," Philadelphia, March 30, 1764, in Jared Sparks, ed., *The Works of Benjamin Franklin* (10 vols., Boston, 1840), VII, 281 f.

[52] Dr. Alison's formulation of his fear of Anglicanism was: "How shall ye Colonies have security that Bishops when sent among us shall become . . . peaceable harmless

Creatures? . . . for they have power by ye common & statute law of England to erect courts, to plague & torment us; & these privileges they will claim, & what way can we prevent their claims from taking place? I am now reading Gibson's Codex of Ecclesiastical Laws, to know ye extent to their power." To Ezra Stiles, Dec. 4, 1766, Presbyterian Historical Society (MS A1 4c 15a).

53 George Bryan's well-known Almanac Diary (now in the Library of Congress) contains much skillful propaganda on this subject: for example, (1) "our fellow subjects on the borders are in great measure abandoned to a relentless enemy, and many, when they lie down have great cause to dread that they shall not rise in safety. Some think the Quakers are not displeased at this, as it reduces other people not of their society to the same proportion with them." (2) "During many years past our Quaker Assembly have made a bustle of defending theirs and the people's privileges against the Proprietaries, merely to keep up a dust, that their own unfitness for Government, in time of war, might be the less attended to." (3) "Dr. Benjamin Franklin hath gone deep with the Quakers into this business . . . as it is well known that he proposed this scheme of a change of Government, & is perhaps the only man that is serious in it."

54 "Remarks on a Late Protest Against the Appointment of Mr. Franklin as Agent for this Province," in Albert Henry Smyth, ed., *The Writings of Benjamin Franklin* (10 vols., New York, 1905–07), IV.

55 Presbyterian Historical Society (MS A1 4c 15a).

56 "Witherspoon's preaching, scholarship, and capacity for securing funds soon satisfied even the meticulous requirements of the foremost of American Presbyterians, Francis Alison." Carl and Jessica Bridenbaugh, *Rebels and Gentlemen, Philadelphia in the Age of Franklin* (New York, 1965), 63.

57 See *Collections of the New York Historical Society* (1878), 102, 284.

58 Presbyterian Historical Society (MS A1 4, Folder No. 2).

59 *Ibid.*

60 *Ibid.* (MS A1 4c 14a).

61 Italics supplied.

62 *Ibid.* (MS A1 4c 15a).

Chapter 4. Early Career in New Castle

63 The most complete and detailed history of early Delaware is J. Thomas Scharf's *History of Delaware* (2 vols., Phila., 1888), reissued in the Kernikat Press, Port Washington, N.Y., 1972.

64 *New Castle on the Delaware*, 133.

65 Munroe, *op. cit.*, 68, says: "The Crown had never vetoed local legislation; indeed it appears that the acts of the colonial assembly were not even sent to England." Joseph Henry Smith, *Appeals to the Privy Council from the American Plantations* (New York, 1950), 251, says, "Since no act from the Lower Counties was ever submitted for royal approbation, these acts escaped the fate of the Pennsylvania prototype."

66 *The Papers of Benjamin Franklin*, Leonard W. Labaree, ed. (New Haven, 1968), XII, 207, Franklin to Charles Thomson, 1765. See also *ibid.*, XI, 465–6, 474–5; William R. Shepherd, *History of Proprietary Government in Pennsylvania* (New York, 1896), 345.

67 John A. Munroe, *op. cit.*, 22 ff.

68 William G. Armor, *Lives of the Governors of Pennsylvania* (Philadelphia, 1872), 306,

taken from *Sanderson's Biography of the Signers* . . . , VI (Philadelphia, 1824), "Thomas M'Kean," Robert Waln, Jr., 349–50.

69 Society Coll., HSP. Also see Certificate signed by Wm Till, Oct. 9, 1754, of being admitted a Practitioner at Law in the Supream [*sic*] Court for the Lower Counties, in Hampton L. Carson Coll., HSP.

70 Gregory B. Keen, *The Descendants of Jöran Kyn of New Sweden* (Swedish Colonial Society, Philadelphia, 1913), 93.

71 *Ibid.* 253 ff. Dr. John Finney's will, dated September 6, 1770, with a Codicil, dated March 21, 1774 (the day before he died), can be found in the office of the Register of Wills, Newcastle County, Wilmington, Delaware. David Finney's will is there also, and is dated February 1, 1805. It was probated May 20, 1806.

72 Thomas McKean Thompson, "The Thompson Register," 1848, 2 f, obtained in typescript from the Delaware State Archives, Dover. This account is also printed, in slightly different form, in PMHB, LII, 59, f, 111 f.

73 For the history of the provincial bar, see David Paul Brown, *The Forum* . . . (Philadelphia, 1856), I, Ch. II; John Hill Martin, *Martin's Bench and Bar of Philadelphia* (Philadelphia, 1883).

74 *Martin's Bench and Bar* . . . , 17–21.

75 *New Castle on the Delaware,* 84–85 and 102.

76 "The Thompson Register," 3–5. The property was otherwise known as Mussel Cripple —meaning low or swampy land for shellfish.

77 Keen, *op. cit.,* 93.

78 *Ibid.,* 93 ff.

79 "The Thompson Register," 31.

80 In Pennsylvania, a few years later, "James Allen, a graduate of the College of Philadelphia (1759) and a student at the Middle Temple (he also studied law with Edward Shippen in Philadelphia), estimated that he earned between £300 and £400 in 1773, the first year he practiced law." Anton-Herman Chroust, *The Rise of the Legal Profession in America* (2 vols., Norman, Oklahoma, 1965), I, 179–180 and 40.

81 Letter from Mrs. R. A. Bankert, 28 the Strand, New Castle, to the author, Oct. 8, 1969.

82 "The Thompson Register," 33.

83 An autobiographical letter to George Washington, April 27, 1789, Hampton C. Carson Coll., HSP.

84 "The Thompson Register," 31–32.

85 Kenneth Umbreit, *Founding Fathers,* New York: Harper & Brothers, 1941, pp. 204, 206, or any standard biography.

86 Leonard W. Levy, *Origins of the Fifth Amendment,* New York: Oxford University Press, 1968 (paper ed., 1971), 369. Ch. XII contains an excellent account of the status of law and lawyers in colonial America.

87 For lists of law books, etc. in use in colonies, and through the Revolutionary era, see Leonard W. Levy, *op. cit.,* 520–544, and Bernhard Knollenberg, *Origin of the American Revolution: 1759–1766,* New York: Collier-Macmillan, 1960–61 (paperback, rev. ed., 1968), 277–319.

88 Autobiographical Sketch, Society Coll., HSP. Also see appointment by John Ross, Attorney General, approved at Lewes, Aug. 2, 1757, in Hampton L. Carson Coll., HSP.

89 Autobiographical Sketch. A true copy of Assembly's Minutes can be found in the McKean Folder, Hampton L. Carson Coll., HSP.

90 McKean Papers, I, 1, HSP. See Thomas McKean to Thomas Sergeant, May 22, 1814, Society Coll., HSP.

91 Docket, "Supreme Court—General Motions, 1750; Divorce, 1800," (Philadelphia City Hall), lists kept by Edward Burd. See also *Martin's Bench and Bar,* 243–326.

92 Dickinson's name appears in the list of attorneys admitted to the Philadelphia bar, 1682 to 1883, compiled by John Hill Martin from several sources (other than the Burd lists), with comparisons, errors and omissions noted; the oft-quoted R. F. Williams' catalogue seems particularly prone to inaccuracies. This list, in addition to another, also notes those attorneys admitted to the Supreme Court of Pennsylvania; yet Dickinson is not noted on either list. Martin states that "admissions in Deed Book B [which given] are to the Supreme Court of the Province [only]. . . . As a practice of two years in the lower courts was necessary before admission to the Supreme Court, reference must [also] be had to the separate list of admissions in Sheriff's Deed Book B . . ." *Martin's Bench and Bar*, 234–35, 237–38, 243, 263.

93 Autobiographical Sketch, Society Coll., HSP.

94 Keen, *op. cit.*, 235 ff.

95 *Ibid.*, 94. See George H. Ryden, *Delaware, the First State of the Union* (Wilmington, 1938), 45. Following the enactment of the 1756 militia law, William Armstrong became Colonel; John Finney, Lt. Col.; John McKinly, Maj.; and Richard McWilliam, one of the Captains for New Castle.

96 A number of writers, apparently misled by the Latin certificate in the Hampton L. Carson Coll., HSP, have said that McKean studied law in London at the Middle Temple. The Latin is in an old-fashioned script and is difficult to read, but properly translated states that McKean was a special student, who paid the fees mentioned above. As additional evidence, there is a campaign pamphlet, written in Philadelphia, Aug. 7, 1799, "To the Republicans of Pennsylvania," when McKean was running for Governor, which makes the categorical statement: "Mr. M'Kean is *charged* with being an Irishman; but the truth is, that he is a *native of Chester County* in the State of Pennsylvania, and never was out of the United States since the hour of his birth." This pamphlet was signed by Peter Muhlenberg, Samuel Miles, A. J. Dallas, Michael Leib, William Penrose, and Tench Coxe. Widener Library, Harvard Univ. (U.S. 16674.5).

97 For a discussion of admission *per favor*, see John H. Powell, *General Washington and the Jack Ass* (Thomas Yoseloff, South Brunswick, New York, London, 1969), 24, 53. Andrew Hamilton and a number of other Pennsylvania lawyers had been admitted in this way. See Charles P. Keith, *The Provincial Councillors* (Philadelphia, 1883), 121–2.

98 Keen, *op. cit.*, 95.

99 David Finney to Benjamin Franklin, Newcastle, Feb. 27, 1774, Franklin Papers, American Philosophical Society (Vol. 4, part 1, 10), and David Finney & others *v.* James Byrne, represented by John Moland, 13 pp., *ibid.* (Vol. 53, part 1, 13).

100 On July 10, 1781, Finney wrote to Franklin in Paris, asking if it was still within his power to obtain information from London concerning this appeal (*Ibid.*, Vol. 22, 76). Also see Joseph Henry Smith, *Appeals to the Privy Council from the American Plantations* (New York, 1950), 653.

101 Autobiographical Sketch, Society Coll., HSP.

102 *Ibid.*

103 Autobiographical Sketch, Society Coll., HSP. They were published as *The Laws of the Government of New-Castle, Kent and Sussex Upon Delaware* (2 vols., Wilmington, 1763).

104 June 8, 1762. McKean Papers, HSP, I, 2.

105 "The Thompson Register," 32–33.

Chapter 5. Family Beginnings

[1] Autobiographical Sketch, Society Coll., HSP.

[2] D. A. B. and Parke Godwin's *Cyclopedia of Biography* (New York, 1865, with *Supplement*, 1872). See also Fred B. Rogers and A. Reasoner Sayer, *The Healing Art: A History of the Medical Society of New Jersey* (Trenton, 1966).

[3] Charles P. Keith, *The Provincial Councillors,* etc. (Philadelphia, 1883), 53 f. Philemon Dickinson's marriage, although unusual in that he married his first cousin, provides a typical name-trap for the unwary: he married his mother's namesake and niece, Mary, daughter of Dr. Thomas Cadwalader.

[4] McKean Papers, HSP VI, 65.

[5] McKean Papers, HSP, I, 1–2. Also Thomas McKean to Thomas Sergeant, May 22, 1814, Society Coll., HSP.

[6] John A. Munroe, "The Philadelawareans: A Study in the Relations Between Philadelphia and Delaware in the Late Eighteenth Century," PMHB, LXIX, 128–149.

[7] *New Jersey Archives,* 1st. Ser., XXVII, 514–515.

[8] Appointment by John Ross, Atty. Gen., approved at Lewes, Aug. 2, 1757, in Hampton L. Carson Coll., HSP.

[9] D.A.B., PMHB, I, 207; and Ellis Paxson Oberholtzer, *Philadelphia, A History of the City and Its People* (4 vols., Phila., no date), I 217–8. Also Burton Alva Konkle, *Benjamin Chew, 1722–1810* (Phila., 1932), esp. 86–90. An ancestor, John Chew, had come to Virginia as early as 1624. J. H. Martin, *Martin's Bench and Bar, 27.*

[10] George Everett Hastings, *The Life and Works of Francis Hopkinson* (Univ. of Chicago, 1926), and Moses Coit Tyler, *The Literary History of the American Revolution* (2 vols., New York, 1897); also Carl Bode, *et. al.,* eds., *American Literature* (New York, 1966); also Carl and Jessica Bridenbaugh, *Rebels and Gentlemen* (New York, 1965), Keith, *op. cit.,* Burton Alva Konkle, *George Bryan . . .* (Philadelphia, 1902), and *Benjamin Chew . . .* (Philadelphia, 1932). Chew trained William and Edward Tilghman in the study of the law.

[11] Benjamin Chew to Caesar Rodney [Dover], Decr. 25, 1758, in *Delaware History,* I, 100.

[12] PMHB, XVIII, 265–6.

[13] The best biographical study, complete with bibliography, is Fred B. Rogers, M.D., "Robert McKean, First President of the Medical Society of New Jersey," *Jour. Med. Soc. of N.J.* Sept., 1953.

[14] Benjamin Rush to John Morgan, Oct. 21, 1768, *Letters of Benjamin Rush, 1761–1792* (2 vols., Princeton, 1951), I, 65. Betsy Copping Corner, *William Shippen, Jr., Pioneer in American Medical Education . . .* (Philadelphia, Am. Phil. Soc., 1954) 69, 70. Stephen Wickes, *History of Medicine in New Jersey and of its Medical Men* (Newark, N.J., 1879), 57.

[15] *New Jersey Archives,* 1st. Ser., XXV, 472–3. Also Penn MSS, 1684–1772, HSP, VII, 111.

[16] *Ibid.*

[17] Arthur Foley, *The Early English Colonies: A Summary of the Lecture by the Right Hon. and Right Rev. Arthur Foley, Lord Bishop of London, with Additional Notes and Illustrations, Delivered at the Richmond Auditorium, Virginia, October 4, 1907* (Milwaukee, 1908). 76–7.

[18] *Ibid.*

[19] *New Jersey Archives,* 1st Ser., XX, 407–8.

[20] *Ibid.*

[21] William Stevens Perry, D.D., *The History of the American Episcopal Church, 1587–1883* (2 vols., Boston, 1885), I, 241–3. Also *New Jersey Archives,* 1st Ser., XXV, 472–3.

[22] Penn MSS, 1684–1772, HSP, VII, 111.

[23] *New Jersey Archives,* 1st. Ser., XX, 434.

[24] Rogers, "Robert McKean, First President. . . ." There has been some confusion as to the date of Robert McKean's marriage; I agree with the date that Rogers gives here.

[25] William Nelson, *New Jersey Biographical and Genealogical Notes,* New Jersey Historical Society, Newark, IX (1916), 166–7. Gouverneur Morris, the diarist, was a grandson of Gov. Lewis Morris. Robert Morris, the financier, was not related to this family.

[26] *CDAB,* 703.

[27] *New Jersey Archives,* 1st Ser., IX, 338–340 n. Also *Proceedings of the New Jersey Historical Society,* New Ser., VII (1922), 23.

[28] Nelson, *op. cit. New Jersey Archives,* 1st Ser., XXV, 472–3.

[29] Nelson, *op. cit.*

[30] Rogers, "Robert McKean, First President . . ."

[31] *Ibid.*

[32] *Ibid.* Also SPG, Original Letters B, Vol. 24, Library of Congress.

[33] "The Thompson Register," 11, 35.

[34] Several legal records identify William McKean's daughter as "Letitia" or "Latitia"; her first cousin and brother-in-law, Thomas McKean Thompson, refers to her consistently as "Elizabeth" in the printed versions or copies of his "Thompson Register." Possibly her full name was Letitia Elizabeth (as used here in text), and to avoid confusion among other Letitias, a family name almost as frequent as "Thomas," she was known as "Elizabeth." But an equally likely possibility is that the family called her "Letty," a very common diminuitive for "Letitia," which could have been misread as "Betty" by the first copyist, and hence, unfortunately, over-corrected to "Elizabeth."

[35] *Ibid., passim.*

[36] The *Aurora,* July, 1806, quoted in R. Buchanan, *McKean,* 97; Scharf & Westcott, *History of Philadelphia,* I, 520.

[37] "The Thompson Register," 12–13.

[38] *Ibid.,* 7, 9.

[39] August 31, September 2, 1776, from Redlion Hundred, Del., McKean to Sally Armitage McKean, in Philadelphia. McKean Papers, HSP, VI, 5.

[40] "The Thompson Register," 36–7.

[41] George Bryan to Wm. Augustus Atlee, Dec. 31, 1781, Atlee Papers, Library of Congress. Information about William is almost non-existent, except for glancing references of this sort.

[42] The will of William McKean, of St. George's Hundred, was admitted to probate, Jan. 2, 1782, in Newcastle Co., Delaware. His wife, Mary, and brother-in-law, John Thompson were named executors; his presumptive widow, however, had died on Dec. 29, 1781. On Aug. 17, 1785, the will of Veronica Peterson was admitted to probate, in which her "dau. Mary (dec'd) and her husband William McKean (dec'd.);" are named. *A Calendar of Delaware Wills, New Castle County, 1682–1800* (New York, 1911), 97, 108–109.

William McKean was a Mason, belonging to Lodge No. 2, in Philadelphia, whose membership included several prominent residents of the Lower Counties, as well as prominent Philadelphians—a Lodge notable also for its revolutionary patriotism. On Sept. 22, 1779, McKean was "raised to the degree of a Master Mason" and paid his "Dues 64 Dollars," *Freemasonry in Pennsylvania, 1727–1907* . . . Vol. I (Philadelphia, 1908). 353–355.

[43] McKean Papers, HSP, VI, 23. Also letter in the Henry E. Huntington Library from Thomas McKean to Matthew Irwin, dated Philadelphia, Janry. 14, 1782, begin-

ning: "Mrs. McKean, Tommy's mother, died on Saturday the 29th of last month at Newcastle, where he yet remains."

44 "The Thompson Register," 31. Thompson's recollections concerning these two children were contradicted in some details by an indenture between Letitia Elizabeth (McKean) Clark, widow, and Thomas McKean, dated Feb. 24, 1812, in the files of the Recorder of Deeds, Newcastle County. The Register of Wills in Newcastle County has the will of William McKean, "intending a voyage to the West Indies" [1779?], and the will of Thomas B[irmingham] McKean of Bordentown, Burlington County, New Jersey, dated April 3, 1788.

45 Some records of his early cases are still preserved: for example, Enoch Armitage, Cordwainer, bond to Mary Watson for £23.14.0 Aug. 15, 1757, H. F. Brown Coll. of Rodney Material, HSD; Thomas McKean to Richard Peters, Aug. 5, 1760, Peters Papers, V, 88, HSP; and Fallow v. Justis, Narr. & Plea, May 1761, Chas. Roberts Autograph Letters Coll., Haverford College.

46 Skidmore v. Vanables, Kent County, Nov. term, 1766, Thomas McKean Folder, Hampton L. Carson Coll., HSP.

47 R. Buchanan, McKean, 19, 20. Other incidents and anecdotes, some of which may be apocryphal, can be found in Dudley Cammett Lunt, Tales of the Delaware Bench and Bar (University of Delaware, 1961); David Paul Brown, The Forum (2 vols., Philadelphia, 1856).

48 McKean Papers, HSP, I, 3.

49 The New Jersey Almanac, Tercentenary Edition (Trenton, 1963), 422, 556.

50 See Inventory of the Goods, Chattels, and Personal Estate of Joseph Borden, late of the County of Burlington, Esquire, deceased . . . , May 8–16, 1791, Archives and History Bureau, New Jersey State Library, Trenton.

51 For biographical information see Hattie Borden Weld, Historical and Genealogical Record . . . Richard and Joan Borden [and] Some of their Descendants, 1899, and John W. Jordan, Colonial Families of Philadelphia (2 vols., N.Y. Chicago, 1911), I, 906–917. Also New Jersey Archives, 1st Ser., XXW, 654–5 n. Also William Nelson, ed., "New Jersey Biographical and Genealogical Notes . . ." The Colls. of the New Jersey Historical Society, IX (1916), 46–9.

52 The appointment as Attorney at Law was dated June 1765, and was signed by Chas. Read; the certificate appointing McKean Solicitor and Counsellor at Law was dated Oct. 31, 1766, and was signed by Wm. Franklin. Both documents in Hampton L. Carson Coll., HSP.

53 New Jersey Archives, 1st Ser., X, 426–8 n.

54 Also Nelson, op. cit., 47–49, and New Jersey Archives, 1st Ser., XXIV, 654–5 n.

55 Tombstone in graveyard of Emmanuel Episcopal Church, New Castle.

56 Univ. of Penna., Biographical Catalogue of the Matriculates of the College, together with Lists of the Members of the College Faculty, and the Trustees, Officers, and Recipients of Honorary Degrees, 1749–1893. (Phila., 1894).

57 A number of writers have made this observation. For example, Philip Davidson, Propaganda and the American Revolution, 199, refers to McKean and Mifflin as "primarily speakers rather than writers."

58 Wm. Nelson, op. cit.

59 Wm. Nelson, Edward Antill and his Descendants (Paterson, N.J., 1899); also, Proceedings of the New Jersey Hist. Soc., New Ser., VII (1922), 23.

60 For the land in West Fallowfield township, see Property Map in Harry Wilson's letter, Jan. 1, 1939, Historical Society of York County.

61 "The laws of what came to be described as the 'Government of New Castle, Kent and Sussex upon Delaware,' were first printed . . . in 1741 and again in 1752 by Benjamin Franklin. In 1763 they were yet again collected and published by Thomas McKean and Caesar Rodney. The acts passed from the time of the first

Delaware assembly in October, 1704, that appear in these now excessively rare volumes, were all collected and collated by George Read in his revision of the *Laws of the State of Delaware* . . . printed in two volumes at New Castle by Samuel and John Adams [coincidence, no kin to the famous cousins] in 1797 . . . there is in these acts but a single reference to a court of law prior to the year 1719, . . ." Dudley Cammett Lunt, *Tales of the Delaware Bench and Bar,* 41.

[62] Buchanan, *op. cit.,* 17.

[63] *New Castle on the Delaware,* 50–52. New England towns also had outlying lands that were held "in common" in addition to *the* Common, but they did not have this kind of trusteeship. In Old England, there had been comparable arrangements, but so far as America was concerned, the New Castle Common was unusual.

[64] *Ibid.*

[65] See James Hedley Peeling, "The Public Life of Thomas McKean, 1734–1817," unpublished Ph.D. thesis, Univ. of Chicago (1929), 13. On Oct. 7, 1765, McKean was paid £30, "his first year's salary," and on Oct. 25, 1766, the same amount, "his second year's salary," etc. See *Minutes of the House of Representatives of the Government of the Counties of New Castle, Kent and Sussex upon Delaware at Sessions held at New Castle in the Years, 1765–1766–1767–1768–1769–1770,* 21, 102, 136, 173.

[66] Hampton L. Carson Coll., HSP. In his Autobiographical Sketch McKean stated: "On the tenth of July 1765 the Governor appointed him Notary and Tabellion publick (there was no other) within the Government of the Lower Counties of Delaware. . . ." In the Feinstein Coll., APS, there is a memorandum, dated May 23, 1770, in McKean's handwriting, in which he was exercising his function as "notary & Tabellion Publick. . . ." He had been reappointed in 1769.

[67] Buchanan, *op. cit.,* 17.

Chapter 6. Interruption—The Stamp Act Congress

[68] See James Miller Leake, *The Virginia Committee System and the American Revolution* (Baltimore, 1917). Leake concentrates on committees of correspondence from 1759 to 1770.

[69] Merrill, Jensen, *The Founding of a Nation: A History of the American Revolution, 1763–1776* (New York, 1968), 85.

[70] *Ibid.,* 85, 105, 135. Jaspar Maudit had not been very vigorous, and was soon replaced by Denneys de Berdt. In 1770 de Berdt's daughter married Joseph Reed, who was to be President of Pennsylvania during the war years, 1778–1781.

[71] *Ibid.,* 84.

[72] Merrill Jensen, "The American People and the American Revolution," *Jour. of Amer. Hist.* (June, 1970), 19.

[73] *Ibid.* For a detailed discussion, see James H. Hutson, "The Campaign to Make Pennsylvania a Royal Province, 1764–1770," PMHB, XCIV, No. 4 (Oct., 1970), and XCV (Jan., 1971).

[74] Thomas McKean, John Caton, and Benjamin Burton to Henry Wilmot, Esq., Oct. 30, 1764, Papers Relating to the Lower Counties, Vol. 15, 283, Penn MSS, HSP.

[75] "To the King's Most Excellent Majesty in Council," in *ibid.,* 281.

[76] See James Gardner's Lessee *v.* Benjamin Chew, Esquire, in McKean's handwriting, in which McKean represented Chew in connection with some land in Kent County. Morse Coll., HSD.

[77] Penn MSS, HSP, quoted in Burton Alva Konkle, *Benjamin Chew, 1722–1810* (Philadelphia, 1932), 104.

[78] Edmund S. Morgan and Helen M. Morgan, *The Stamp Act Crisis: Prologue to Revolution* (Chapel Hill, 1953), 29.

[79] *Ibid.*, quoting from William Allen to D. Barclay & Sons, Nov. 20, 1764, in Lewis B. Walker, ed., *The Burd Papers: Extracts from Chief Justice William Allen's Letter Book.* (n.p. 1897), 65.

[80] See chap. entitled "The Logic of Rebellion" in Bernard Bailyn, *The Ideological Origins of the American Revolution* (Cambridge, 1967).

[81] John Shy, *Towards Lexington: The Role of the British Army in the Coming of the American Revolution,* chap. entitled "The Problems of Peace."

[82] Morgan and Morgan, *op. cit.,* 53 f.

[83] *Ibid.,* 16 f.

[84] *Ibid.,* 53.

[85] *Records of the Colony of Rhode Island,* IV, 404.

[86] *The Papers of Benjamin Franklin* (New Haven, 1968), XII, 65 ff.

[87] Bernard Knollenberg, *Origin of the American Revolution* (rev. ed. Collier Macmillan, 1960), 208–9.

[88] "The Stamp Act, notwithstanding all the Opposition we have been able to give it, will pass. Every Step in the Law, every Newspaper, Advertisement is severely tax'd. If this should, as I imagine it will, occasion less Law, and less Printing, 'twill fall particularly hard on us Lawyers and Printers." Franklin to John Ross, from London, Feb. 14, 1765. *The Papers of Benjamin Franklin* (New Haven, 1968), 68.

[89] William Gordon, *History of the Rise, Progress, and Establishment of the Independence of the United States of America* (New York, 1794), I, 119. (Also 4 vols., London, 1788.)

[90] John J. Waters, Jr., *The Otis Family in Provincial and Revolutionary Massachusetts* (Chapel Hill, 1968), 155, quoting from Gordon.

[91] The legislators of the Three Lower Counties, acting as individuals, appointed delegates to the Stamp Act Congress on Sept. 21, 1765, "being of Opinion that the method proposed by the Honorable House of Assembly of the province of Massachusetts-Bay is the most likely to obtain a Redress of these Grievances, and taking into Consideration the Misfortune we at present Labour under, in not having it in our Power to Convene, as a House, and in a Regular Manner to appoint a Committee . . ." From Stewart Coll., Library, Glassboro State College (N.J.), in material turned over to *Niles' Weekly Register,* June 25, 1812, by Caesar A. Rodney, available in *Delaware History,* XII, 57–8.

[92] Morgan and Morgan, *op. cit.,* 103.

[93] *Delaware History,* XII, 57–8. By prearrangement the five leading men in each of the three counties nominated the same slate. Kent County acted on Sept. 13th, Sussex on the 17th, and Newcastle on the 21st. Hezekiah Niles, *Principles and Acts of the Revolution* (Baltimore, 1822), 454. Also John A. Munroe, *Federalist Delaware, 1775–1815* (New Brunswick, 1954), 72.

[94] Quoted in Henry C. Conrad, *History of the State of Delaware* (3 vols., Wilmington, 1908), I, 90 f. Also see George H. Ryden, ed., *Letters to and from Caesar Rodney, 1756–1784* (Philadelphia, 1933), 55–6.

[95] Note also that John Rodney informed Caesar Rodney on March 13, 1764, that Kollock had become Chief Justice in place of Ryves Holt, who had died earlier in 1764. *Delaware History,* I, 101. This must have been an interim appointment, however, until the next scheduled elections: John Vining was elected, and commissioned Chief Justice, Nov. 27, 1764. John H. Martin, *Bench and Bar,* 20.

[96] Caesar Rodney to Thomas Rodney, Oct. 20, 1765, in Ryden, ed., *Letters,* 26.

[97] Thomas McKean to John Adams, Aug. 20, 1813, McKean Papers, HSP, IV, 25.

98 The "Journal of the Stamp-Act Congress" including list of members attending, can be found in Hezekiah Niles, *Principles and Acts of the Revolution in America,* (New York, 1876), 155–169.

99 Morgan and Morgan, *op. cit.,* 103–4. "Otis was always unpredictable, and the insanity that clouded his later years may already have been affecting him, but it would seem that his role at the congress was as subdued as [Gov. Bernard of Mass.] could have wished." It was Thomas Hutchinson who called Otis the "great incendiary." *Papers of Benjamin Franklin,* XIII, 3.

100 John Watts to Governor Monckton, October 12, 1765, Massachusetts Historical Society, *Collections,* 4th Ser., X, 579–580.

101 Lawrence H. Gipson, *The Coming of the Revolution* (New York, 1954), 98.

102 January 13, 1804. McKean Papers, HSP, III, 84.

103 October 20, 1765. Ryden, *Letters,* 25–6.

104 June 21, 1812. McKean Papers, HSP, IV, 24.

105 Niles, *Principles and Acts,* 456–7. The Journal of the Stamp Act Congress was given to Niles by Caesar A. Rodney, the nephew of Caesar Rodney. Also note: "We had Seven fair copies taken of each of those addresses. . . Signed by the Committees of all the Colonies, except South Carolina, Connectcut [sic] and New York, who were not impowered." Caesar Rodney to Mr. Wilmer, December, 1765, Brown Coll., HSD, available in *Delaware History,* XII, 58–9.

106 McKean Papers, HSP, IV, 25.

107 Autobiographical Sketch, Society Coll., HSP. On June 9, 1766, McKean and Rodney were paid £140 "for their Expenses attending the Congress at New-York." See *Minutes of the House of Representatives . . . [of Delaware], 1765–1766–1767–1768–1769–1770,* 73.

108 McKean to John Adams, Aug. 20, 1813. McKean Papers, IV.

109 Morgan and Morgan, *op. cit.,* 160–161.

110 John Hughes, stamp distributor for Pennsylvania, also refused to resign, but since he was "ill to the point of death," he was allowed to go free when he promised not to execute his commission.

111 Ogden suffered the humiliation of being rebuked by the Assembly. *New Jersey Archives,* 1st Ser., IX, 525.

112 Entry of May 28, 1766, *Diary and Autobiography of John Adams,* ed. L. H. Butterfield, (Cambridge, 1961), I, 313.

113 William Franklin to Benjamin Franklin, from N.J., July 13, 1766. *The Papers of Benjamin Franklin,* XII, 334.

114 *Pa. Gazette* and *Pa. Journal,* Dec. 19, 1765; I *N.J. Archives,* XXXIV, 680–2, quoted in *The Papers of Benjamin Franklin,* XII, 369 n 7.

115 Jensen, *The Founding of a Nation,* 140–1. Morgan and Morgan, *op. cit.,* 175–176, say that all courts were open in several colonies (including Delaware) before the news of repeal was received.

116 The resistance of the commercial groups probably had more influence on Parliament than that of the lawyers, since it was supported by similar groups in England. J. Thomas Scharf and Thompson Westcott, *History of Philadelphia* (3 vols., 1884) distinguish between merchants, traders, and retailers in their discussion. Also Morgan and Morgan, *op. cit.,* 160–161.

117 Reporting a long conversation with Lord Dartmouth on the colonial reaction to the Stamp Act, Franklin noted that "His Lordship heard all with great Attention and Patience. As to the Address expected from the Congress, he doubted some Difficulty would arise about receiving it, as it was an irregular Meeting, unauthoriz'd by any American Constitution. I said, I hoped Government here would not be too nice on that Head; That the Mode was indeed new, but to the People there it seem'd necessary, their separate Petitions last Year being rejected. And to refuse hearing Complaints and Redressing Grievances, from Punctilios about Form,

had always an ill Effect . . ." Benjamin Franklin to William Franklin, London, Nov. 9, 1765. *The Papers of Benjamin Franklin*, XII, 364. The Stamp Act Congress' petitions and memorials are printed in Edmund S. Morgan, ed., *Prologue to Revolution Sources and Documents on the Stamp Act Crisis, 1764–1766* (Chapel Hill, 1959).

[118] Lawrence H. Gipson, "The Great Debate in the Committee of the Whole House of Commons on the Stamp Act, 1766, as Reported by Nathaniel Ryder," PMHB, LXXXVI, 10 ff. Only a fragment was ever reported from one of Pitt's most effective speeches, an off-hand remark that the greatest defect he saw in the reports of the Stamp Act Congress was that one of the Petitioners was named "Oliver." Dennys de Berdt to Joseph Reed, March 18, 1766, quoted in William Reed, *The Life of Esther de Berdt, afterwards Esther Reed* (Philadelphia, 1853), 78.

[119] Benson J. Lossing, *The Pictorial Field-Book of the American Revolution* (2 vols., New York, 1850), II, 53. Captain Wise's brig *Minerva* had been chartered by Dennys de Berdt, agent for the Stamp Act Congress.

[120] *Ibid.*

[121] Watson's *Annals*, 678, and Francis Hopkinson, "My dear Mama," Derry, July 2, 1766, Hopkinson Coll., HSP.

[122] Leake, *op. cit.*, 57, states it was "probable that the intercolonial committee of correspondence was an adaption to colonial revolutionary needs of a committee appointed to communicate with the colonial agent—a committee that was well-known in the southern and middle colonies."

Chapter 7. Robert McKean and the New Jersey Medical Society

[123] Fred B. Rogers, M.D., "The Last Illness of Robert McKean (1732–1767)," *The Journal of the Medical Society of New Jersey*, LIV, 11 (Nov., 1957), 541, quoting Robert McKean to the Secretary, SPG, April 17, 1767. (Letters to the SPG can be located in *The Fulham Papers in the Lambeth Palace Library, American Colonial Section, Calendar and Indexes*, compiled by William Wilson Manross (Oxford, 1965), Index No. 2, Names appearing in the Documents. Microfilms in L.C.)

[124] A longer passage of the same letter, quoted in Fred B. Rogers, M.D. "Robert McKean, First President of the Medical Society of New Jersey," *ibid.*, L, 9 (Sept., 1953), 434.

[125] Rogers, "The Last Illness of Robert McKean . . .", 540, states: "For want of fifty cents' worth of isoniazid and for lack of a small supply of para-aminoalicylic acid, the career of Robert McKean was cut short at the age of 35."

[126] Quoted in Rogers, "Robert McKean, First President . . .", 433.

[127] Sketch of Robert McKean in *New Jersey Archives*, 1st Ser., XXV, 472–3. His former parish had referred to him as "a gentleman whose Simplicity of Manners, whose gentle, mild & charitable Disposition & whose innocent life have rendered him dear to us, & amiable to men of all denominations . . ." SPG, Original Letters B, Vol. 24, L.C.

[128] Fred B. Rogers and A. Reasoner Sayre, *The Healing Art: A History of the Medical Society of New Jersey* (Trenton, 1966), 26, mention a transient medical society in Boston in 1735. Then came the New Jersey Society in 1766, the Massachusetts Medical Society in 1781, the Medical and Chirurgical Faculty of Maryland in 1784, and the College of Physicians of Philadelphia in 1787.

[129] "There seems to have been little objection from the [medical] profession about clerical competition; the clergy needed other means of support, just as the physicians [did]. Indeed the complaints about the joining of the two professions came from

another direction entirely—the parishioner-patients. They felt embarrassed in settling accounts with their own minister and believed that the practice of physic interfered with the duty of a clergyman." David L. Cowen, *Medicine and Health in New Jersey: A History* (Vol. 16 in *The New Jersey Historical Series,* Princeton, 1964), 6–7.

[130] Rogers and Sayre, *The Healing Art,* 19.

[131] The *New York Mercury,* June 27 and July 14, 1766, in the New-York Historical Society, New York City. The membership was soon afterwards extended to include both Jerseys.

[132] Rogers and Sayre, *The Healing Art,* 19.

[133] It is interesting that "the 'greatest part of the congregation' of the Anglican Church at Perth Amboy rejected the Rev. Isaac Brown in 1769 on these grounds [combining the two professions]," Cowen, *op. cit.,* 6–7. The congregation was not expressing its disrespect for its previous pastor; more likely they had come to feel that combining these roles was too much for one man.

[134] Rogers and Sayre, *The Healing Art,* 19.

[135] The full text is given as an Appendix to Rogers and Syre, *The Healing Art,* 309–311. In this document "there was no suggestion of their asking any protection for themselves." See "Address on McKean Tablet Presentation" by Wells P. Eagleton, M.D., on the occasion of the 225 Anniversary of the establishment of St. Peter's Church, in *Journal of the Medical Society of New Jersey,* December, 1923, 445–7.

[136] Abstracted from Rogers and Sayre, *The Healing Art,* 28.

[137] Unfortunately, the Table of Fees and Rates, signed by Robert McKean as President of the Society, was made public before the more idealistic Instruments of Association.

[138] Rogers and Syre, *The Healing Art,* 29–30.

[139] In late May, 1767, a convention of Anglicans from New York and New Jersey had deputed Dr. Myles Cooper, President of King's College, and Dr. McKean "to visit the southern part of the continent, for the purpose of securing the cooperation of their brethren in procuring an American episcopate." Arthur Lyon Cross, *The Anglican Episcopate and the American Colonies* (Harvard Historical Studies, IX, 1902, reprinted Hamden, Conn., 1964), 231. On May 23, 1767 Sir John St. Clair, QMG in America, wrote from Elizabeth to His Excellency Horatio Sharpe in Maryland a letter which he expected that Cooper and McKean would carry to the Governor. PMHB, IX, (1885), 12–13. I do not know if McKean was able to make this trip.

[140] This letter was apparently copied by Jonathan Elmer, who was Dr. Morgan's apprentice, and survived unknown and unread for two centuries in Elmer's notebook. It was printed for the first time in Rogers, "The Last Illness of Robert McKean . . ." in 1957, through the courtesy of Mrs. Robert P. Elmer of Wayne, Pa.

[141] *Ibid.*

[142] See William Nelson, *Edward Antill and His Descendants* (Paterson, N.J., 1899); also *Proceedings of the New Jersey Historical Society,* New Ser., VII (1922), 23.

[143] John Antill, a brother, married first one, then another of the daughters of Cadwallader Colden, Royal Governor of New York. In the Revolutionary War he became a Lt. Col. of a loyalist regiment of New Jersey volunteers, commanded by Courtlandt Skinner, and another brother, Edward, became a Lt. Col. in Moses Hazen's American regiment in Canada. John had a chance meeting with his brother Edward, then a prisoner of war, and thus had an unusual opportunity to help him. *New Jersey Archives,* 1st Ser., IX, 338–340 n.

[144] Isabella Antill McKean remarried in 1772, a Mr. McNeil.

[145] Thomas McKean's second son, Robert McKean, who was undoubtedly named for his uncle, seems to have grown up in Bordentown, New Jersey, and to have gone into business there. In later years he took over his grandfather's stage-boat, stage-coach

line, but failed to make the agreed-upon annual payments. In some way this difficulty embroiled Thomas McKean in a dispute with his father-in-law, Joseph Borden, that lasted until Borden's death. See Joseph Borden and Elizabeth Borden to Robert McKean, Apr. 29, 1786, and the wills of Joseph and Elizabeth Borden, State Library, Trenton, N.J.

[146] McKean Papers, III, HSP.

Chapter 8. Hare or Hound?

[147] From Thomas Balch, ed. *Examination of Joseph Galloway, Esq., by . . . The House of Commons* (Phila., 1855).

[148] Julian P. Boyd, *Anglo-American Union: Joseph Galloway's Plans to Preserve the British Empire, 1774–1788* (Phila., 1941), 19.

[149] John M. Coleman, "Joseph Galloway and the British Occupation of Philadelphia," *Pennsylvania History*, XXX, 3 (July, 1963).

[150] See Philip Davidson, *Propaganda and the American Revolution, passim.* Note also the disappearance of the correspondence between Franklin and Foxcroft, the two deputy postmasters general from November, 1764, to February, 1769. *The Papers of Benjamin Franklin*, XIII, 14.

[151] Hampton L. Carson Coll., HSP.

[152] *Ibid.*

[153] *Ibid.*

[154] *Ibid.*

[155] Society Coll. and Cadwalader Coll., HSP.

[156] Hampton L. Carson Coll., HSP.

[157] *Ibid.*

[158] *Ibid.*

[159] Public Archives Commission, Dover, Del.

[160] Joseph Shippen Letterbooks, APS.

[161] McKean Papers, IV, 43, and Society Coll., HSP.

[162] Benson J. Lossing, *Field-Book of the American Revolution*, I, 466.

[163] Henry Alonzo Cushing, ed., *The Writings of Samuel Adams* (3 vols., New York, 1907), III, 2, 67, etc.

[164] *Minutes of the House of Representatives . . . 1765 . . . 1770*, 39.

[165] *Ibid.*, 40–50. De Berdt was agent for the Assembly of Massachusetts-Bay, but not for the Governor's party, which had another agent.

[166] *Minutes of the House of Representatives . . . 1765 . . . 1770*, 53, 72.

[167] *Ibid.*, 70–71.

[168] *Ibid.*, 106–108.

[169] Rodney's facial cancer was troubling him and was several times to require surgery. On June 23, 1768, he wrote from Philadelphia that Dr. Thomas Bond had "extracted the hard Crusted Matter which had risen so high—and it has left a hole I believe quite to the Bone, and extends for the Length from the corner of my Eye above half way down my Nose—such a Sore must take considerable time to Cure up—if it ever does; However . . . I am perfectly easy as to any pain." Ryden, ed., *op. cit.*, 30.

[170] On Sept. 23, 1766, Dennys de Berdt wrote from London, "You have done me great Honor by Vote of the House, in my Favour, which I have also had from two other assemblies, but as yet no other Symbol or Token of Respect but from you, which when ever I look on I shall a fresh remember your grateful Esteem, and

my Obligation to serve your Province whenever it lies in my Power." *Minutes of the House of Representatives,* 121.

171 *Minutes of the House of Representatives,* 119–120.

172 Merrill Jensen, *The Founding of a Nation: A History of the American Revolution, 1763–1776* (New York, 1968), 211–214.

173 The Quartering Act of 1765 was a mild one containing provisions suggested by Franklin and Pownall forbidding the billeting of troops in private homes; instead the colonial governors with the advice of their councils "were to hire vacant buildings and fit them up as temporary barracks." *The Papers of Benjamin Franklin,* XII, 106. See also J. Alan Rogers, "Opposition to the Quartering of Troops During the French and Indian War," *Military Affairs,* XXIV, No. 1 (Feb., 1970). The problem was that the Quartering Acts required the colonies to provide such things as firewood, bedding, candles, salt, vinegar, cooking utensils, and rations of beer, cider, or rum.

174 Jensen, *op. cit.,* 213.

175 *Ibid.,* 215–220.

176 See Chap. VII, "The Aftermath of the Stamp Act in Britain: the Townshend Program," in *ibid.*

177 The records "in 1903 were printed under the title of *Original Land Titles in Delaware, commonly known as the Duke of York Record . . . 1646 to 1679.*" This printed form ends on a torn manuscript page, numbered 267, leaving fifteen pages missing from the total given in the Act of 1770 (*Laws of Delaware,* I, 455–9)—lost when the British troops carried the records away from New Castle in 1777, See *Delaware History,* VI, 160.

178 *Proceedings of the New Jersey Historical Society,* New Ser., VII (1922), 23.

179 Autobiographical Sketch, Society Coll., HSP.

180 Francis Bernard to Henry S. Conway, Boston, Jan. 19, 1766, *Collections of the Connecticut Historical Society,* XVIII.

181 *Ibid.*

182 Jensen, *op. cit.,* 244.

183 *Ibid.,* 244–5.

184 By 1765 there were twenty-three newspapers in steady publication in the colonies, including the *Philadelphische Staatsbote,* which exploded over the "Stämpfel-Acte," calling it "das unlandsverfassungsmässigste [unconstitutional] Gesetz so diese Colonie sich je hätten vorstellen können." There were none in the Lower Counties or New Jersey; those colonies depended on those of their neighbors. By 1775, the number had increased to thirty-eight, seven of which were published in Philadelphia. Arthur M. Schlesinger, *Prelude to Independence, The Newspaper War on Britain, 1764–1766* (New York, 1965), 52, 74, 86, 215–16.

185 *Biography of the Signers of the Declaration of Independence, by John Sanderson* (Philadelphia, 1823), IIII [*sic*], 29–35, biography of George Read, "written by William Read of Newcastle."

186 See Watson's *Annals,* 680. Also *Memoirs of a Life, Chiefly Passed in Pennsylvania, within the Last Sixty Years, with Occasional Remarks upon the General Occurrences, Character and Spirit of that Eventful Period* (Harrisburg, 1811), reprinted in Phila. in 1846 with John Stockton Littel, ed., Alexander Graydon, *Memoirs, of His Own Time . . .* 117–120. Graydon stated (p. 122): "As to the genuine sons of Hibernia, it was enough for them to know that England was the antagonist. Stimulants here were wholly superfluous; and the sequel has constantly shown, that in a contest with Englishmen, Irishmen, like the mettlesome coursers of Phaeton, only require reining in."

187 There had been a spate of correspondence between John Wilkes and the Boston Sons of Liberty in 1768–9, which is published in part in the Mass. Hist. Soc. *Proceedings,* XLVII (1913–4), 190–214, and can be found in full in the Brit. Museum,

Add. MSS, No. 30870. Wilkes had also been in contact with radical leaders in other colonies, most notably in South Carolina.

For the continuing connection between the New England and the Philadelphia radicals, see H. James Henderson, "Constitutionalists and Republicans in the Continental Congress, 1778–1786," *Pennsylvania History,* XXXVI, 2 (April, 1969). Henderson makes extensive use of William B. Reed, ed., *Life and Correspondence of Joseph Reed* (Phila., 1847) and *Extracts from the Diary of Christopher Marshall, 1774–1781,* William Duane, ed. (Albany, 1877). Reed had shared quarters in London with a number of American fellow students, including John Morgan, Samuel Powell, Stephen Sayre, Richard Stockton, and Arthur Lee. Reed, *Life of Esther de Berdt,* 24–5.

188 Roche, *op. cit.,* 32, and Dennys de Berdt to the Committee of the House of Assembly of the Lower Counties on Delaware (London, no date, Richard S. Rodney Papers, HSD.) Reed and other Pennsylvanians were well known in New England. On July 6, 1775, Joseph Trumbull wrote to Silas Deane, "Colᵒ Reed is [Washington's] Secretary. I was acquainted with Majʳ Mifflin before and shall . . . do him every favʳ in my Power." (*Colls. of the Conn. State Historical Society,* XXIII (1930), 6–7.

189 Reed's correspondence with Lord Dartmouth consisted of twelve letters from him between December, 1773, and February, 1775, and several letters from Lord Dartmouth in return. His wife, his brother-in-law in England, Dennis de Berdt, and his brother-in-law in Philadelphia, Charles Pettit, were probably the only people who knew about the correspondence until later, when rumors began to circulate in England that Reed had been a paid informer. In the nineteenth century George Bancroft, an American historian of the nationalist school, wrote, "I regard him as shuffling, pusillanimous, and irresolute," but Bancroft apparently had some of this correspondence confused with letters by Charles Read. See Bancroft's *Joseph Reed, a Historical Essay* (New York, 1867). Roche, *op. cit.,* tells the story in a chapter entitled, "The Patriot Who Would be Peacemaker."

190 Sam Adams to Joseph Warren, Philadelphia, Sept. 25, 1774, in Cushing, *op. cit.,* III, 157–8.

191 Sam Adams to Richard Henry Lee, Boston, April 10, 1773, in *ibid.,* III, 25.

192 Geo. Clymer and Thomas Mifflin to Sam Adams, Philadelphia, Dec. 27, 1773, in Samuel Adams Papers, MSS Div., NYPL. Mifflin had visited Adams in July, 1773. See *Pennsylvania History,* XV (July, 1948), 9–23.

193 Sam Adams to John Dickinson, Boston, March 27, 1773, in Cushing, *op. cit.,* III, 14, wrote: "Mr. J[osiah] Q[uincy] a young Gent. but eminent here in the profession of the law is soon expected to arrive at Philadelphia from South Carolina. Could he be introduced into the Company of Mr. Dickinson & Mr. Reed he would esteem himself honord and his Conversation mt not be unentertaining even to them."

194 Sam Adams to Thomas Young, Philadelphia, Oct. 17, 1774, in *ibid.,* III, 162–3.

195 Davidson, *op. cit.,* 57, lists James Otis, Sam Adams, and Joseph Warren as the most influential members of the committee, and Dr. Benjamin Church, Dr. Thomas Young, William Molineaux, William and Joseph Greenleaf, and Josiah Quincy as among the most active. All of these people were listed as proscribed in the *Boston Gazette* in 1774. See Hezekian Niles, *Principles and Acts of the Revolution in America* (New York, Chicago, 1876—originally Baltimore, 1822), 111.

196 Carl and Jessica Bridenbaugh, *Rebels and Gentlemen; Philadelphia in the Age of Franklin* (New York, 1965), 298.

197 James Miller Leake, *The Virginia Committee System and the American Revolution* (Baltimore, 1917), 56, says, "New England seems to have played little part in the development of the colonial system of standing legislative committees; this system was worked out in the middle and southern colonies . . . As it did not figure to any large extent in the colonial legislatures of New England, those American his-

torical writers who were New Englanders (perhaps a majority of all our contributors to American history) have overlooked the fact that the system existed [earlier]. With an imperfect understanding of this committee system, which played so important a part in the legislative life of the middle and southern colonies, it is not hard to understand why the historians of New England . . . attached an undue amount of importance to the local revolutionary committees of Massachusetts."

198 *Ibid., passim.* The interpretation given here is greatly influenced by Bernard Knollenberg's *Origin of the American Revolution, 1759–1766* (1960), which emphasizes the political disagreements of the early period.

199 Leake, *op. cit.*, 65.

200 Leake felt that legislative correspondence with an agent in London should be associated primarily with Virginia in the early period. The Proprietors of Pennsylvania (and Delaware) were required by charter to have an agent in London, so this correspondence was originally conducted by the executive. When Benjamin Franklin was sent to London by the legislature in 1757, it was by an antiproprietary faction with which the Lower Counties (Delaware) did not wish to be associated.

201 *Minutes of the House of Representatives . . . 1765 . . . 1770,* 156.

202 *Ibid.,* 159.

203 *Minutes of the House of Representatives . . . 1765 . . . 1770,* 167–8.

204 *Ibid.,* 182.

205 *Ibid.,* 181.

206 *Ibid.,* 127–8. Thomas Rodney, unlike his brother Caesar, took a strong pro-slavery line. In an undated essay (Brown Coll., HSD) he wrote: "You may ask perhaps why the Negroes were born Slaves . . . more than others? And may you not as well ask why the Buzzards are obliged to eat nothing but Carrion, & the Tumble Bugs to work continually among Excrements. Nature answers by saying It was necessary & therefore she has fiitted them for it & made it their delight." (The disgusting nature of these images may cast light on the delusions from which Thomas Rodney frequently suffered.)

207 *Ibid.,* 232.

208 *Ibid.,* 229–230.

209 *Ibid.,* 218. "How truly deplorable must be the Case of a wretched America[n] who, having incurred the Displeasure of any one in Power, is dragged from his native Home, and his dearest domestic Connections, thrown into a Prison, not to await his Trial before a Court, Jury or Judges, from a Knowledge of whom he is encouraged to hope for speedy Justice, but to exchange his Imprisonment in his own country for Fetters among Strangers: Conveyed to a distant Land, where no Friend, no Relation, will alleviate his Distresses, or minister to his Necessities; and where no Witness can be found to testify his Innocence, shunned by the Reputable and Honest, and consigned to the Society and Converse of the Wretched and the Abandoned, he can only pray that he may soon end his Misery with his Life."

210 *Ibid.,* 245–7.

211 *Ibid.,* 231.

212 *Ibid.*

213 Leake, *op. cit.*, 143–6.

214 Text of the charter and bibliography can be found in *Delaware History*, IV, 149–156.

215 The Academy was built in 1773, and the charter was issued by John and Thomas Penn, April 10, 1773. The first trustees were Bishop William White, Thomas McKean, Dr. Robert Smith, Thomas Gilpin, Dr. Nicholas Way, Joseph Shallcross, and the Rev. Lawrence Girelius, who was President of the Board. *Delaware History*, III, 181.

216 See esp. Univ. of Penna., *Biographical Catalogue of the Matriculates of the College, Together with Lists of the Members of the College Faculty, and the Trustees, Officers, and Recipients of Honorary Degrees, 1749–1893* (Phila., 1894).

217 *Early Proceedings of the American Philosophical Society . . . 1744 to 1838* (Phila., 1884), 12. The transit of Venus across the sun occurred on June 3, 1769, and the Society was very active in organizing teams of astronomical observers. See also Brooks Hindle, "The Rise of the American Philosophical Society, 1766–1787," unpublished Ph.D. dissertation (Univ. of Pennsylvania, 1949), 26.

218 *Miscellaneous Essays and Occasional Writings of Francis Hopkinson* (Phila., 1792) located in Franklin Coll., Sterling Library, Yale.

219 Documents in Hampton L. Carson Coll., HPS.

220 Hopkinson was not yet publicly identified with the revolutionary cause; he had earlier written one of *Four Dissertations on the Reciprocal Advantages of a Perpetual Union between Great Britain and Her Colonies* (Printed by William and Thomas Bradford, Philadelphia, 1766).

221 The town of Boston, in Nov. 1772, was complaining bitterly against the Collectors of His Majesty's Customs, and their deputies. See Cushing, *op. cit.*, II, 361.

222 *To the Electors of Pennsylvania;* by A Pennsylvanian, 1799, John Carter Brown Library, Providence.

223 *Aurora,* Nov. 12, 1799, cited in G. S. Rowe, unpublished dissertation, "Power, Politics and Public Service: The Life of Thomas McKean, 1734–1817" (Stanford, 1969), 38 n.

Chapter 9. The First Continental Congress

1 Cushing, *op. cit.*, II, 46 f.

2 Christopher Gadsden to Samuel Adams, Charles Town, June 5, 1774, in Richard Walsh, ed., *The Writings of Christopher Gadsden, 1746–1805* (Columbia, S. C., 1966), 94 f. indicates that South Carolinians in 1774 still remembered the bitterness they had felt when Massachusetts merchants broke their "first resolutions" in 1770.

3 Reed, *The Life of Esther de Berdt,* 135.

4 *Ibid.,* 75.

5 In the papers of the Virginia committee in the *Journals of the House of Burgesses, 1773–1776,* 53 f., quoted in Leake, *op. cit.,* 141–2.

6 "The ground which was covered by the people, on Monday last, in the State-House Square, being measured, it was calculated, by two different persons, unknown to each other, that there was near 8,000 people collected there; and many hundreds, who were on the way, were disappointed reaching the place of meeting, before the business was over, owing to the short notice that was given." *The Pennsylvania Journal and The Weekly Advertiser,* No. 1621, Dec. 29, 1773, in *New Jersey Colonial Documents,* 1st Ser., XXIX, 174.

7 Sam Adams Papers, MSS Div., NYPL.

8 The article of Dec. 29, 1773, continues: "Yesterday, at three quarters of an hour after two o'clock, Capt. Ayres of the Tea-Ship *Polly,* with Mr. Barclay, late one of the Consignees, left Arch-street wharf, on board a pilot boat (having been 46 hours in town) to follow the ship to Reedy-Island, and from thence transport the East-India Company's *Adventure* to its *old rotting place* in Leading-Hall-street, Lon-

don . . . He was attended to the wharf by a concourse of people, who wished him a good voyage."

9 Peter Force, ed., *American Archives*, Ser. IV, I, 406–7. Clymer added, "I expect in a few weeks to see you at Boston, with a brother of Mr. Dickinson's [Philemon Dickinson]."

10 This epitaph can be found in three places: 1) on Mary Borden McKean's tombstone in the graveyard of Emmanuel Church, New Castle; 2) in *Miscellaneous Essays and Occasional Writings of Francis Hopkinson*, published in 1792, the year after his death; and 3) in Thomas McKean's handwriting in the Collections of the Huntington Library, San Marino, California.

11 McKean to Sally McKean, July 20, 1779; July 30, 1779, McKean Papers, VI, HSP. Sally owned land in the Christiana Bridge area, which McKean was in the process of selling.

12 McKean to Sally McKean, Aug. 1, 1776, McKean Papers, VI.

13 *Ibid.*, Aug. 7, 1776.

14 *Ibid.*, May 27, 1778.

15 *Ibid.*, April 20, 1778.

16 *Ibid.*, June 9, 1778.

17 *Ibid.*, July 12, 1779.

18 *Ibid.*, July 30, 1779.

19 Caesar Rodney to Thomas Rodney, March 14, 1770, in Ryden, ed., *op. cit.*, 35–6.

20 McKean to Sally McKean, Aug. 7, 1776, McKean Papers, VI.

21 *Ibid.*, April 20, 1778.

22 *Ibid.*, Feb. 10, 1778.

23 It is noteworthy that McKean was soon to be cooperating in military matters with Dr. Alison. In the Society Coll., HSP, there is a petition to the Council of Safety by a certain Thos. Wallace, dated Oct. 19, 1776, requesting a military commission. It was signed on his behalf by Thomas McKean (Colonel, 4th Bn Phila. Assn), Wm Bradford, Andw. Hodge, Wm Hodge, and Francis Alison.

24 John A. Munroe, *Federalist Delaware*, 47–8.

25 McKean to Sally Mckean, July 26, 1776.

26 *Ibid.*, Aug. 7, 1776.

27 *Ibid.*, June 17, 1778.

28 Agreement, Joseph and Elizabeth Borden with Robert McKean, dated April 17, 1786, recorded April 29, 1789. Archives and History Bureau, New Jersey State Library, Trenton.

29 William Franklin recommended Hopkinson for membership in the Governor's Council on Feb. 28, 1774. See *Archives of the State of New Jersey*, X, 425–6. He was still serving on the Council in 1775. This group included a few men who would subsequently become patriots, but it was primarily pro-British. William Franklin listed the members of His Majesty's Council of New Jersey in March, 1775, as follows:

1. Peter Kemble
2. David Ogden
3. William Alexander,
   claiming to be Earl of Stirling
4. John Stevens
5. Samuel Smith
6. James Parker
7. Frederick Smyth
8. Stephen Skinner
10. Daniel Coxe
11. John Lawrence
12. Francis Hopkinson

30 *New Jersey Colonial Documents, Newspaper Extracts,* XXIX, 308 ff. This controversy began in March, 1774.

31 *Ibid.,* 345.

32 E. Miriam Lewis, "The Minutes of the Wilmington Academy," *Delaware History,* III, 181.

33 H. B. Weld, *The Borden Family,* 101–2, and J. W. Jordan, *Colonial Families of Philadelphia,* 914. The latter refers to it as a committee of observation, but this was the term used *after* the Association of October, 1774. See also *New Jersey Colonial Documents,* 1st Ser., X, 432 f.

34 Benson J. Lossing, *The Pictorial Field-Book of the Revolution,* II, 186.

35 G. Keen, "Descendants of Jöran Kyn," PMHB, IV, 234–7. Finney's will was dated Sept. 6, 1770; a codicil dated March 21, 1774 (the day before he died) refers to the recent death of his wife. Register of Wills, Newcastle County.

36 See "Part of Old Philadelphia, a Map Showing Historic Buildings & Sites from the Founding until the Early Nineteenth Century," compiled by Grant Miles Simon, F. A. I. A., included in *Historic Philadelphia,* Vol. 43, Part I, *Transactions of the American Philosophical Society,* 1953.

37 John Adams, *Diary,* Tues., Oct. 11, 1774. The Clarke's Inn location would explain the presence of McKean's name in 1775 on a list of associators for the Middle Ward, "west of Fourth Street and between Market and Chestnut Streets." Watson's *Annals,* 350, has this interesting description of their cuisine: "They trained little bow-legged dogs, called spit-dogs, to run in a hollow cylinder, like a squirrel, by which impulse was given to a turnjack, which kept the meat in motion, suspended before the kitchen fire . . . As cooking time approached, it was no uncommon thing to see the cooks running about the streets looking up their truant labourers."

38 Jonathan Dickinson Sergeant had been Clerk of the meeting at New Brunswick on July 21, 1774, which had sent delegates from New Jersey to the First Continental Congress. A twelve-man committee of correspondence for the province, including Joseph Borden and Elias Boudinot, was also named at their meeting. *New Jersey Colonial Documents,* 1st Ser., X, 432 f.

39 John A. Munroe, *Federalist Delaware,* 80 f.; Philip Davidson, *Propaganda and the American Revolution,* 199; and Lawrence H. Gipson, *The British Empire Before the American Revolution,* XII, 190–2.

40 *Collections of the New-York Historical Society for the Year 1878,* 269 f., 282 f.

41 *Ibid.,* 269.

42 Full text, printed, in Judge Richard S. Rodney Coll. of the George Read Papers, HSD. George Read wrote to Caesar Rodney that same day, "When the People [500 and more] had convened Mr. McKean as Chairman of the Meeting opened the Occasion thereof, by pointing out the Matters complained of as done by the Parliament of Great Britain for the Oppression of America . . . and the Apprehensions the Colonies in General are under of an increase of that Oppression from the Conduct toward the Town of Boston . . . & there was the greatest unanimity, not a Sign of dissent appeared." Leon de Valinger, Jr., ed., "Rodney Letters," *Delaware History,* I, 102.

43 Harold Hancock, ed., "The Kent County Loyalists: Documents," *Delaware History,* VI, 92 ff., esp. 96.

44 Gipson, Vol., XXI, 192 n. writes, "This address is printed in *American Archives,* 4th Ser., I, 658–61, where it is simply stated that it was by a 'gentleman [who] introduced the business of the Assembly . . .' but the date is given as July 28 instead of July 23, the date of the Lewes meeting . . ." Gipson also cites the *Pennsylvania Gazette,* Aug. 3, 1774, but the speech is not there.

45 The Kent County Committee to Thomas Robinson in Sussex County, July 21, 1774, *Delaware History,* IV, 98.

46 *Rhode Island Colonial Records, 1770–1776,* VII, 302. The letter, dated Aug. 2, 1774, and signed by Rodney, Read, McKean, McKinly, and Robinson, was addressed "To the Honorable, the Speaker of the House of Assembly, of the Colony of Rhode Island and Providence Plantations, to be communicated to the Committee of Correspondence." (The original is in the Rhode Island State Archives, Misc. Letters, 1770–1779, Folder II, Item #46.)

47 Yale University, MSS.

48 JCC, I, 15–30, contains the credentials of the delegates. See also Leake, *op. cit.,* 147–8.

49 Gipson, Vol. XII, 183–190, summarizes the maneuvering in Pennsylvania prior to the convening of Congress.

50 E. C. Burnett, *The Continental Congress,* 21.

51 JCC, I, 21.

52 Benjamin J. Lossing, *The Pictorial Field-Book of the Revolution,* II, 59, lists all delegates, except Boerum and Haring of New York; information concerning the latter can be found in Mark M. Boatner, *Encyclopedia of the American Revolution,* 269–273, who cites JCC and Burnett's *Letters, passim.* Note that John Dickinson was added to the delegation on Oct. 15, 1774.

53 Harper's *Encyclopedia, U.S. History,* II, 315.

54 E. C. Burnett, *Continental Congress,* 29.

55 *The Pennsylvania Gazette* for Aug. 24, 1774, contained a brief notice, signed by Charles Thomson, "The Trustees of the Academy of Newark are desired to attend their half-yearly visitation at the said Academy on Tuesday, the 13th of September next." Soon there was another notice, "The public visitation of the Academy of Newark is postponed . . ." *New Jersey Documents,* 1st Ser., XXIX, 455, 479.

56 Catherine Drinker Bowen, *John Adams and the American Revolution* (Boston, 1950), 464, cites this passage and notes Adams' surprise at hearing some very plain-spoken revolutionary talk. "Was this the cautious attitude they had been led to expect outside of New England? In Boston's Green Dragon Tavern, one could not hear worse!"

57 There are several editions of John Adams' *Diary,* and many passages from it are quoted in Burnett's *Letters of the Members of the Continental Congress* (8 vols.). Quotations can easily be located by the date of the entry.

58 Julian P. Boyd, *Anglo-American Union: Joseph Galloway's Plans to Preserve the British Empire, 1774–1788* (Philadelphia, 1941), 28–9.

59 *Ibid.*

60 *Sanderson's Biography* . . . VI, 278; Boatner, *Encyclopedia of the American Revolution; DAB.* Samuel Adams's record of attendance almost equalled that of McKean.

61 Jensen, *The Founding of a Nation,* 490, says, "The delegates went first to Carpenters Hall whereupon Thomas Lynch of South Carolina proposed that Congress meet there. James Duane of New York objected that they should at least look at the State House out of courtesy to Galloway, but there was a 'general cry' that this was a good room and a 'great majority' voted to stay where they were. Lynch then proposed Peyton Randolph, speaker of the Virginia House of Burgesses, for presiding officer."

62 The Indian Conference, Easton, 1756. Watson, *Annals,* 546.

63 *The Pennsylvania Gazette,* No. 2385, Sept. 7, 1774.

64 Watson, *Annals,* 546. Thomson held the job for fifteen years, for the entire duration of the Continental Congresses.

65 John Adams' *Diary,* Sept. 7, 1774. The "Collect" was the thirty-fifth psalm.

66 From Galloway's pamphlet *Historical and Political Reflections,* 66 cited in Boyd, *op. cit.,* 30–1.

67 Hezekiah Niles, *Principles and Acts of the Revolution in America* (New York, Chicago, 1876—originally Baltimore, 1822), 107. Adams wrote Niles, Feb. 5, 1819,

"This is the original paper that I read to Patrick Henry in the fall of the year 1774, which produced his rapturous burst of approbation, and solemn asseveration 'I AM OF THAT MAN'S MIND.' I pray you to send it back to me. I would not exchange this original for the show book of Harvard College . . ."

[68] *Ibid.*

[69] Adams to Warren, July 24, 1775. Unfortunately, the British intercepted the letter and gleefully published it in Draper's *Massachusetts Gazette.*

[70] Burnett, *The Continental Congress,* Chap. III, "The First Congress," contains the best summary of the committees. See also Burnett, *Letters.*

[71] *Ibid.*

[72] Jensen, *The Founding of a Nation,* 499, says, "It is unknown how individual delegates voted then or on 22 October when Congress 'met, dismissed the plan for a union, etc.,' but it is significant that even the Rhode Island delegates split, with Samuel Ward opposing and Stephen Hopkins favoring the plan. However narrow the victory, the opponents of the plan went ahead and provided a striking example of what a later generation would call 'managed news.' When the journals of Congress were published in November, all mention of the plan and the votes upon it were omitted. It was left for an outraged Joseph Galloway to present his plan of union to the American people in a pamphlet he published shortly thereafter." *A Candid Examination of the Mutual Claims of Great Britain and the Colonies* (New York, 1775).

[73] Friday, Oct. 21, 1774, JCC, I, 101.

[74] Patrick Henry's phrase, from speech in a Virginia convention shortly after the First Continental Congress.

[75] Henry Steele Commager, ed., *Documents of American History* (New York, 1940), 84.

[76] *Ibid.,* 86.

[77] Long passages from this speech are quoted in Basil Williams, *The Life of William Pitt, Earl of Chatham* (2 vols., New York, 1966—first edition, London, 1913), 305. Williams gives as his source Hugh M. Boyd, *Genuine Abstract from two Speeches of the late Earl of Chatham,* 1799, and notes that the text of the speeches had to be reconstructed from several accounts.

Chapter 10. The War Begins, 1775

[78] *The New-York Journal, or The General Advertiser,* No. 1663, Nov. 17, 1774, in *New Jersey Colonial Documents,* 1st Ser., XXIX, 529–531.

[79] *Ibid.*

[80] Shy, *op. cit.,* 412–3.

[81] Peter Oliver, *Peter Oliver's Origin & Progress of the American Rebellion, A Tory View,* eds. Douglass Adair & John A. Schutz (Stanford, 1961), 114–115. Oliver gives the correct dates for Gage's arrival, and Hutchinson's departure.

[82] *Gage Correspondence,* I, 371, cited in Shy, *op. cit.,* 411.

[83] "Merchant John Andrews was pleased to hear that a recaptured deserter was not to be executed; 'but when we find that a thousand lashes is the substitute, we are equally shock'd . . . Early this morning a poor culprit received 250 lashes, which number he is to receive four successive weeks . . .' But any number of lashes, and even an occasional execution on the Common, could not stop desertion." Letters of John Andrews to William Barrell, MHSP for 1864–1865. 341, cited in Shy, *op. cit.,* 413.

84 Shy, *op. cit.,* 415, summed up his plight, "Gage had won nothing but faint praise for his efforts to scrupulously perform the office of Governor, and in so doing was on the brink of failure as Commander in Chief."

85 Walpole, *Journal,* I, 447. Items in Horace Walpole's *Journal* can easily be located by date. In his biographical sketch of Chatham, Walpole said that "it is well known that his last speech relating to the independence of America was the knell of his own decease . . . on the 11th of May, 1778." Horatio Walpole, *A Catalogue of the Royal and Noble Authors of England, Scotland, and Ireland* (London, 1806) Vol. IV, 315 [This *Catalogue* being written after Walpole succeeded as Earl of Orford, is signed "Horatio" not "Horace."]

86 Gov. William Franklin had sent Lord Dartmouth copies of Galloway's secret letters of Sept. 3d and 5th shortly after they were written. On Dec. 6, 1774, he sent Galloway's "Plan," dated Sept. 6th, and certain other information. *New Jersey Colonial Documents,* 1st Ser., X, 473–8, 503–4.

87 Horace Walpole, *Memoirs of the Reign of King George the Third,* IV (London, 1845), 84.

88 *The Papers of Benjamin Franklin,* XII, 362–65.

89 *Extracts from the Diary of Christopher Marshall, 1774–1781* (Albany, 1877), 13.

90 *Ibid.* Also see Force, *American Archives,* 4th Ser., I, 1169–72, for proceedings of the convention. Jensen, *The Founding of a Nation,* 529, says: "The Philadelphia committee, whose most prominent members were also members of the legislature, did not use the authority [to call another convention] until May 1776. Thus the legal assembly, unlike all other colonies except Delaware, remained the focal point in the struggle over policy until the very eve of independence, and remained opposed to independence until within days of its declaration."

91 Alexander Graydon, *Memoirs of His Own Time,* John Stockton Littell, ed., (Philadelphia, 1846) 124.

92 A letter by James Read to his brother George Read, Jan. 2, 1775 (Richard S. Rodney Papers, HSD) contains this reference: "Mrs. Correy had a great opinion of Mr. McKean's abilities & inclinations to serve her [concerning property on 3rd St., Philadelphia] therefore she took the Papers to him for his opinion & I imagine she has been a good deal disappointed, though she does not chuse to say much about it, but her son Samuel tells me that he does not think Mr. McKean understands the matter at all . . . that he is not a Person to be depended on in this affair." Whereupon, with this letter, "the Papers" in question were sent to George Read, "All tied up in A Handkerchief."

93 McKean Papers, HSP, VI, 1.

94 McKean Papers, HSP, III, 84.

95 Rodney and Read also used the word "Government" to refer to the three-man delegation. For example, see *Delaware History,* XII, 64.

96 Cushing, III, 207–9.

97 *Diary of Christopher Marshall,* 15. The complete official dispatch arrived two days later.

98 Scharf & Westcott, *Hist. of Philadelphia,* I, 295–97.

99 PMHB, IX, 186. In November the Association was made compulsory.

100 Scharf and Westcott, *op. cit.,* I, 298. Also *Historic Philadelphia* (Vol. 43, Part I, *Transactions of the American Philosophical Society,* 1953), 156

101 *Colonial Records,* X, 279 ff.

102 *Pa. Archives,* III, 4th ser., Ch. V, "The Committee of Safety . . . The Council of Safety," 545–625.

103 Scharf and Westcott, *op. cit.,* I, 293.

104 JCC, II, 18.

105 *Diary of Christopher Marshall,* 37. For the location of "Philosophical Hall" see APS Mins., March 16, 1770, II, 95–6, and Brooke Hindle, "The Rise of the American

Philosophical Society, 1766–1787," unpublished doctoral dissertation (University of Pennsylvania, 1949), 52.

106 Theodore Thayer, *Pennsylvania Politics and the Growth of Democracy, 1740–1776* (Harrisburg, 1953), 166.

107 Charles H. Lincoln, *The Revolutionary Movement in Pennsylvania, 1760–1776* (Philadelphia, 1901), 190.

108 Scharf & Westcott agree concerning the appointment of the sub-committee by the committee of correspondence, and its members: Thomas McKean, George Clymer, Jonathan B. Smith, Benjamin Jones, Sharpe Delany, John Wilcox, and Timothy Matlack. Scharf & Westcott, *History of Philadelphia*, I, p. 302.

109 *Diary of Christopher Marshall,* 50. John Hancock of Massachusetts subsequently became President of the Congress.

110 *Ibid.*

111 See John M. Coleman, "How 'Continental' was the Continental Congress?" in *History Today,* Aug., 1968. Canada included the Hudson Bay Region and Nova Scotia, as well as Quebec. Still British at this time, the garrisons in East Florida and West Florida outweighed the civilian populations there; thus these colonies were never represented in the Congress.

112 Dated July 24, 1775. The original is in the Yeates Coll., HSP.

113 John Adams to John M. Jackson, Dec. 30, 1817. Adams continued: "Mr. Henry was in Congress in 1774, and a small part of 1775. He was called home by his state to take a military command. McKean and Rodney continued members, and, I believe I never voted in opposition to them in any instance." This statement, and others like it, can be given too sweeping an interpretation, so far as McKean was concerned. As we will see, in the period after the beginning of the French Revolution, and during the Federalist era, McKean and Adams were frequently at odds.

114 Ryden, *op. cit.,* 57.

115 *Ibid.,* 60.

116 *Ibid.,* 58.

117 *Ibid.,* 60.

118 *Ibid.,* 62.

119 John C. Fitzpatrick, ed., *Writings of Washington,* III, 456–7.

120 Nov. 24, 1775. *Diary of Christopher Marshall,* 52.

121 Buchanan, *op. cit.,* 124.

122 *New Jersey Archives,* 1st Ser., IX, 338–340 n. Also see Christopher Ward, *The War of the Revolution* (John Richard Alden, ed., 2 vols., New York, 1952), 1956. Another of Arnold's right-hand men at Quebec was Eleazer Oswald, who was to have many a run-in with McKean in later years. (Lossing, *op. cit.,* II, 151 n.)

123 Sept. 30, 1775, JCC, III, 321; JCC, I, 211.

124 A committee appointed by Congress, gave a decision in Dec., 1782, in favor of Pennsylvania, theoretically ending the "Pennamite Wars." Actual settlement of complicated land-claims, taxes, etc. dragged on past 1800.

125 Sam Adams wrote George Read about the subscription on Feb. 24, 1775, adding as a postscript, "The Committee have a prospect of negotiating this matter with a friend in Philadelphia." This postscript was not included by Cushing, and was apparently written only on the letter received by George Read, and available to his biographer, ("Wm. Read of New Castle," Sanderson, *Biography of the Signers to the Declaration of Independence,* (Philadelphia, 1823).) There is no proof that the "friend in Philadelphia" was McKean; I have made the inference that McKean might have been the man, because of his official responsibility for transmitting money and goods from Philadelphia at that time. Cushing noted (III, 223) a receipt to Sam Adams for a thousand dollars which Read had sent him as "being the Donation of the County of Newcastle on Delaware."

126 JCC, II, 85.

127 *Ibid.*, II, 212, 224, 252. Also V, 460, 603, and VI, 810 and 1068.
128 *Ibid.*, IV, 49, 58, 63.
129 *Ibid.*, II, 253–5.
130 Burnett, ed., *Letters*, I, 274, from the Richard Smith *Diary*.
131 Butterfield, ed., *The Adams Papers*, III, 339.
132 Jennings B. Sanders, *Evolution of the Executive Departments of the Continental Congress, 1774–1789* (Chapel Hill, 1935), 51 ff. Also Lossing, *op. cit.*, II, 647, summarizes the development of the other committee as follows: "On the twenty-ninth of November, 1775, Congress appointed Benjamin Harrison, Dr. Franklin, Thomas Johnson (the nominator of George Washington), John Dickinson, and John Jay, a committee for the purpose of carrying on foreign correspondence, through friends of America in Europe, and endeavor to ascertain the views of foreign governments respecting American affairs. This committee, though changed in persons, conducted all the foreign correspondence of the United States until 1781, when a 'Department of Foreign Affairs' was established. On the seventeenth of April, 1777, Congress changed the name of the 'Committee of Secret Correspondence' to 'Committee of Foreign Affairs,' and at the same time appointed Thomas Paine . . . secretary to the committee, with a salary of seventy dollars a month . . . a position of great trust and responsibility, and Paine appears to have conducted the business satisfactorily until he [quarrelled] with Silas Deane, and imprudently revealed state secrets."
133 15 George III, 10, 18.
134 John Adams took copious notes. See Butterfield, ed., *The Adams Papers*, II, 188, ff.
135 *Ibid.*, 206.
136 16 George III, c. 5.
137 Burnett, ed., *Letters*, I, 205. Available also in any of the several editions of John Adams' *Diary*.
138 Oct. 21, 1775, JCC, III, 304.
139 Jasper Yeates to Edward Burd, Aug. 2, 1775, in Lewis Burd Walker, ed., *The Burd Papers, 1763–1828* (Philadelphia, 1899), 23. Yeates was later to become a Justice of the Supreme Court of Pennsylvania, and Burd was to be Prothonotary. They were both considered active patriots in 1775, but were not yet in favor of independence.
140 Peeling, *op. cit.*, 41.
141 Charles H. Lincoln, *The Revolutionary Movement in Pennsylvania* (Philadelphia, 1901), 257–8 n.
142 Quoted in David Hawke, *In the Midst of a Revolution* (Philadelphia, 1961), 109.
143 Burnett, ed. *Letters*, I, 275, 348. The point was that Congress was assuming control.
144 Burnett, ed., *Letters*, I, 275.
145 PMHB, XXXIX, 143–169; JCC, IV, 246.
146 As an example, Richard Cary wrote to Joseph Reed in May, 1775, "[General Gage's] conduct to encourage the Negroes to leave their masters and come into his service, which many have done, is astonishing." Wm. B. Reed, *The Life of Esther de Berdt, afterwards Esther Reed*, 214.
147 Ryden, *op. cit.*, 66–7. Christopher Marshall fills in some of the details, in his entry for Sept 6, "Between eleven and twelve this forenoon, about thirty of our associators waited upon and conducted Isaac Hunt [father of Leigh Hunt, the poet and essayist] from his dwelling to the Coffee House, where having placed him in a cart, he very politely acknowledged he had said and acted wrong, for which he asked pardon of the public and committed himself under the protection of the associators, to defend him from any gross insults from the populace. This, his behavior, they approved him, and conducted him in that situation, with drum beating, through the principal streets, he acknowledging his misconduct in divers places. But as they were coming down town, stopping at the corner where Dr.

[K]earsley lives, to make his declaration, it's said the Dr. threw open his window, snapped a pistol twice amongst the crowd, upon which they seized him, took his pistol, with another in his pocket from him, both of which were loaded with swan shot. In the scuffle, he got wounded in the hand. They then took Hunt out of the cart, conducted him safe home, put [K]earsley in, brought him to [the] Coffee House, where persuasions were used to cause him to make concessions, but to no effect. They then, with drum beating paraded the streets round the town, then took him back to his house and left him there, but as the mob were prevented by the associators, who guarded him, from tarring and feathering, yet after the associators were gone, they then broke the windows and abused the house, &c."

Isaac Hunt was a lawyer who had defended the right of one of his clients to trade in defiance of the edict of the committee. His particular offense was that he "requested to have the minutes of the meeting in writing, with leave to give his answer in writing the which was looked upon to be only evasive . . ." (Marshall, entry for Aug. 22.)

[148] R. B. Nye and J. E. Morpurgo, *A History of the United States* (2 vols., Middlesex, England, 1955, revised 1964), I, 198–9.

[149] The activities of the city committee were likewise kept secret, except from those who needed to know.

[150] In 1793 Galloway wrote to McKean, "My life, during several months, was in perpetual jeopardy. Every night I expected would be my last. Men were excited by some persons from the northward, by falsehoods fabricated for the purpose, to put me to death. Several attempts were made, but providentially prevented before the execution. I declared my innocence in the public papers in vain." (McKean Papers, HSP, II, 108.) Also *M'Fingal: An Epic Poem*, John Trumbull, New York: American Book Exchange, 1881. With Introduction & Notes by Benson J. Lossing. "Canto Third. The Liberty Pole," p. 99.

> Did you [Satan] not in as vile and shallow way,
> Fright our poor Philadelphian, Galloway,
> Your Congress when the daring ribald
> Belied, berated and bescribbled?
> What ropes and halters did you send,
> Terrific emblems of his end,
> Till least [sic] he'd hang in more than effigy,
> Fled in a fog the trembling refugee?

Chapter 11. Independence, 1776

[151] Instructions dated March 29, 1775, in Ryden, ed., *op. cit.,* 56. The delegates received similar instructions as late as March 22, 1776, in *ibid.,* 72–3.

[152] John Adams to Samuel Chase, June 24, 1776, Charles Francis Adams, ed., *The Life and Works of John Adams* (10 vols., Boston, 1850–56), IX, 413.

[153] H. J. Henderson, Jr., "Political Factions in the Continental Congress: 1774–1783," unpublished doctoral dissertation (Columbia Univ., 1962), 92, 68.

[154] John Adams' motion in Congress, May 10, 1776. This resolution together with its more radical preamble of May 15, 1776, precipitated a revolutionary take-over in Pennsylvania and greatly strengthened the hand of the radicals in Delaware and the other reluctant colonies.

[155] Ryden, *op. cit.,* 91–2.

156 *Martin's Bench and Bar* (Phila., 1883), 167–68, under "Speakers of the Assembly, of Pennsylvania," 1682–1789, lists: "1769–73, Joseph Galloway; 1773, Thomas McKean *; 1773–4, Joseph Galloway . . . * Part of session only." This may refer to McKean as Speaker of the Lower Counties at this time, but McKean is the only Speaker of that Assembly thus included. Under the anomalous relations of the Lower Counties to the Province, it is possible that visiting Philadelphia as frequently as he did, McKean was given the privilege of that Assembly's chair briefly, as Speaker *pro tem.*

157 JCC, II, 109–110. James Thomas Flexner. *The Traitor and the Spy, Benedict Arnold and John André* (N.Y., 1953) 46.

158 JCC, IV, 40.

159 Antill's exploits are set forth in some detail in John Richard Alden, ed., Christopher Ward, *The War of the Revolution* (2 vols., New York, 1952), I, 195–6.

160 Burnett, *Letters*, I, 319.

161 The Provincial Congress of Massachusetts to Paul Revere, Robert Morris to Oswald Eve, quoted in Esther Forbes, *Paul Revere & the World He Lived In* (Boston, 1942), 302–03; Scharf & Westcott, *History of Philadelphia*, I, 387.

162 Burnett, *Letters*, I, 331, 451; also John Adams' *Works*, III, 46.

163 Burnett, *Letters*, I, 335–340.

164 *Ibid.*, 411.

165 JCC, IV, 261–2.

166 Schuyler Papers, 1441, NYPL.

167 "Narrative Journal of Captain Smythe, Queen's Rangers," PMHB, XXXIX, 143–169.

168 Report of Committee on Prisoners, April 6, 1776, in McKean's handwriting. Papers of the Continental Congress, No. 28, Folio 33.

169 Smyth's Tory activities had caused Congress much trouble. See JCC, IV, 239, 246, 262, and 408.

170 JCC, III, 442.

171 Peeling, *op. cit.*, 37, citing JCC, III, 419, 436, 459; IV, 108. There is also a letter from McKean, Dickinson, and Wilson to Gen. Schuyler, dated July 18, 1775. (Misc. Schuyler Papers, New-York Historical Society.)

172 Jennings B. Sanders, *Evolution of Executive Departments of the Continental Congress, 1774–1789* (Chapel Hill, 1935), contains the best general discussion of the subject.

173 Peeling, *op. cit.*, 31.

174 Roberdeau Buchanan, *op. cit.*, 25. Also Clymer MSS, HSP, 4, 7–8.

175 Note, however, that as late as April 14, 1777, Thomas McKean's name headed a list of subscribers of White Clay-Creek Hundred, New Castle County, enrolling themselves in a company of militia which was part of a battalion commanded by Col. Samuel Patterson. McKean enclosed the list to Patterson, certifying that on the previous day "upwards of fifty of the within-named Inrollers met at the Academy in the town of Newark [Dr. Alison's old school] in pursuance . . . [etc.]," and Patterson certified "on Enquiry that the above return is Just and true," and forwarded it to His Excellency, John McKinly, then President of Delaware. (H. F. Brown Coll. of Rodney Material, HSD.)

176 Buchanan, *op. cit.*, 26.

177 Edward Tilghman to his father, Feb. 4, 1776, quoted in Charles J. Stillé, *The Life and Times of John Dickinson, 1732–1808* (Philadelphia, 1891), 173–4.

178 David Hawke, *In the Midst of a Revolution*, 18–20.

179 Joseph Shippen, Jr., in Philadelphia, wrote to Edward Shippen, on Feb. 29, "Tim. Matlack & a number of other violent wrongheaded people of the inferior Class have been the chief Promoters of the wild Scheme; and it was opposed by the few *Gentlemen* belonging to the Committee—but they were outvoted by a great Majority." (Shippen Papers, Vol. 12, HSP.)

[180] *Diary of Christopher Marshall,* March 4, says "five o'clock [it met] in order to take into consideration the Report of the Committee of Correspondence respecting the propriety of suspending the calling of the Provincial Convention for a few days in order to see the event of sundry petitions now before the House of Assembly. Accordingly, the suspension was agreed to." The committee here appears to be a larger and more representative body than the committee of correspondence.

[181] Niles, *Principles and Acts,* 243–4, contains the Petition and Remonstrance of the light infantry company of Dover, to the Honorable House of Representatives, for the government of the counties of New Castle, Kent, and Sussex, on Delaware, now sitting at New Castle, March 1776, as follows: "That T. R. of Sussex county, esq. having for a long time past been of ill fame, and published by diverse committees in several newspapers as an enemy to his country, and the said T. R. presuming to pass through our county, and at a critical conjuncture to sit in your honorable house, as one of our representatives, we thought ourselves bound in duty, as we regarded the honor of your honorable house, and the true interest and safety of the public, to take said T. R. into custody until your honorable house could take order in the matter. Thereupon as attempt being made to arrest Mr. R. col. M. of Sussex county also, drew his sword, and tho' he was made well acquainted with the reasons and principles upon which it was thought necessary to arrest Mr. R. he swore he would defend him at the risk of his life. Upon this, he was immediately disarmed, and his violent conduct, together with the well known connection between the two men, inducing the company to consider Mr. M. as in the same predicament with Mr. R."

[182] A pamphlet printed in Philadelphia in 1788, probably by Dr. James Tilton, entitled *The Biographical History of Dionysius, Tyrant of Delaware, addressed to the People of the United States of America, by Timoleon,* in which George Read was compared with Dionysius, the infamous tyrant of ancient Syracuse, included these charges: "Instead of regarding the iniquities of this culprit, *Dionysius* talked in a high strain of the breach of privilege of the house. An order issued, summoning the infantry to attend the house, which they instantly obeyed. Mention was even made of imprisoning them for so daring an offence. But the spirit of New Castle county did not at that time, favor this measure . . . For many days after the examination of the witnesses, which went chiefly to an enquiry into the offence of the infantry, there was no open discussion as usual in the house. At the ringing of the bell, a minority of patriotic members met regularly; but *Dionysius,* in secret cabal, threatened some members, and allured others with promises, until he brought his measure to bear. Finally it was resolved, that R. and his associate (who had also been arrested for standing in his defence) should take their seats; and the light infantry was dismissed." John A. Munroe brought out a new edition of this pamphlet (Univ. of Delaware Press, 1958) with editorial comments by Thomas Rodney, which included the reference to McKean.

[183] In May 1776 John Haslet wrote to Caesar Rodney, "the County is now unguarded, & a large tract of Marsh covered with stock from one end of it to the other is Open to the Depredations of the Enemy! . . . [I] fear Congress must either disarm a large part of Kent & Sussex, or see their Recommendations treated to Contempt." (Ryden, *op. cit.,* 87.) The raiding parties were in the habit of paying their friends and robbing their enemies.

[184] Jensen, *The Founding of a Nation,* 665.

[185] 16 Geo. III, c. 5. The text of the American Prohibitory Act, Dec. 22, 1775, can be found in Jensen, ed., *English Historical Documents,* IX, 853.

[186] Jensen, *The Founding of a Nation,* 650, citing *Parliamentary History of England,* XVIII, 1059.

[187] *Ibid.,* 659.

[188] Ryden, *op. cit.*, 72–3.

[189] *South Carolina Provincial Congress Journals,* 184, 227, 248, 254. Also see John Drayton, *Memoirs of the American Revolution* (2 vols., Charleston, 1821), II, 172 ff. The latter work was based, without acknowledgment, on the writings of the author's father, William Henry Drayton.

[190] David Hawke, *In the Midst of a Revolution,* chap. entitled "The Election."

[191] Christopher Marshall recorded in his *Diary,* on May 1, "This has been one of the sharpest contests, yet peaceable, that has been for a number of years, except some small disturbance among the Dutch, occasioned by some unwarrantable expressions of Joseph Swift, viz., that except they were naturalized, they had no more right to a vote than a Negro or Indian . . ."

Distressed at the victory of the moderates, Marshall continued, "I think it may be said with propriety that the Quakers, Papists, Church, Allen family, with all the Proprietary party, were never seemingly so happily united as at this election . . ."

[192] Cushing, *op. cit.*, III, 284–5. To Samuel Cooper, April 30, 1776.

[193] Hawke, *op. cit.*, 113.

[194] *Diary of Christopher Marshall,* May 3, 10.

[195] George Read wrote to Rodney and McKean from Wilmington on Friday, May 10, 1776, "The committee of safety have thought it highly necessary that you should be acquainted with the situation of the magazine at Lewistown, to exert your influence for an immediate supply of powder and lead, which, I suppose, must be by land, as the Roebuck and Liverpool will probably continue as high up the river as Reedy Island; this morning they are in the bite below Newcastle, and though the row-gallies have proceeded down from Christiana creek's mouth, about two hours ago, I am apprehensive the high wind now blowing, will not permit their acting to advantage in that cove.

"We have had warm cannonading between the ships and gallies these two days past, all within our view. Great intrepidity was shown on the part of our people, who compelled the two ships to retire, not much to their credit; but it appeared to me the ships were afraid the gallies would get below them . . . As to other particulars, I must refer you to some of the very many spectators from your city, who will have returned before this time." (Quoted in Sanderson's *Biography of the Signers,* IIII, [sic] 41–2.)

[196] John Adams to John Winthrop, May 12, *Massachusetts Historical Society Collections,* Ser. 5, Vol. 4, 301–2.

[197] Thomas Rodney had a conversation with Dickinson in Dover, and wrote his brother a letter on May 19, which revealed that Dickinson's understanding of "reconciliation" and Rodney's were not at all the same: "as I was walking Down Town with Mr. John Dickinson when I recd [your letter] I mentioned to him the Resolution of Congress; and he answer'd it was made before he Left there; upon which I observed to him many advantages that would follow our assuming Government to which he agreed & observed many others 'And that it would not prevent but perhaps promote a more speedy reconciliation, because the longer they let Government exist before they offer Terms the more firm the Government would be, & therefore the more difficult to effect a reconciliation.' I should apprehend from the above sentiments that Mr. D—has some glimmering hopes of reconciliation yet, or that he ment thereby, to flatter those who have such hopes, to acquiese in the resolution of Congress—Peace, and reconciliation will henceforth be my ardent wish but never to mix our Government with Britains any more." (Ryden, *op. cit.*, 82.)

[198] Butterfield, ed., *The Adams Papers,* II, 238.

[199] *Ibid.*, 239. McKean's idea was similar to that of Thomas Rodney—reconciliation on American terms.

200 *Ibid.,* "Our Petitions have not been heard—[we] are to be answered with Mirmidons from abroad."

201 *Ibid.,* 240, 239.

202 I agree with David Hawke's comment (*op. cit.,* 215) in his Bibliographical Note: "Charles Page Smith's *James Wilson—Founding Father, 1742–1798* (Chapel Hill, N.C., 1956) has misinterpreted his role during the Revolution in order to make him fit the picture of an early liberal." Wilson was farther away from the patriotic element in his thinking than his mentor, John Dickinson, was.

203 Carter Braxton to Landon Carter, May 17, in Burnett, *Letters,* I, 454. However, James Allen gave the result as seven colonies to four (PMHB, IX, 187). If Allen was correct, Pennsylvania voted with the majority.

204 *Diary of Christopher Marshall,* May 15.

205 *Ibid.,* May 16.

206 Broadside Coll. for 1776, HSP.

207 "The Alarm," *ibid.,* Item 18, HSP. A New Hampshire delegate wrote to a friend, on May 19, "What will be the consequence [of the meeting of the city] I know not, but think the Assembly will be dissolved, and a Convention called." Josiah Bartlett to John Langdon, Bartlett Papers, No. 92, New Hampshire Historical Society.

208 On May 21 Josiah Bartlett continued the letter above: "Yesterday the city met, agreeable to notification, in the field before the State House a Stage being erected for the Moderator (Col. Roberdeau) and the chief speakers Mr. McKean &c. I am told they unanimously voted that the present House of Assembly are not competent to changing the form of Government, and have given orders for calling a Convention. The Pennsylvania Assembly was to meet yesterday. I fear some convulsions in the Colony."

209 John Adams to James Warren, May 20, in Massachusetts Historical Society, *The Warren-Adams Letters* (2 vols., 1917, 1925).

210 Clitherall, Diary, PMHB, XXII, 470.

211 In this particular passage I am following what purports to be a verbatim quotation from PMHB, XLVIII, 320–1.

212 Watson, *Annals,* 421; Force, *Archives,* 4th Ser., VI, 520–21. This communication, unsigned but cited as the Philadelphia Committee to the Several Counties in the Province, may be assumed to have been sent by McKean, the Chairman.

213 Hawke, *op. cit.,* 137, says, "For Roberdeau the Assembly was not a discredited body. It would continue to function while the source of power was transferred from the Crown to the people. The transfer would be orderly. Roberdeau and those he spoke for failed to see in their political innocence what a politician like [Caesar] Rodney knew from instinct—you cannot destroy confidence in an institution and expect it to continue functioning with public support."

214 PMHB, XLVIII, 325.

215 Rush to Julia Stockton Rush, May 29. Butterfield, ed., *Letters,* (2 vols., Princeton, 1951), I, 99. Julia Stockton was the daughter of Richard Stockton, soon to be elected a delegate to the Continental Congress for New Jersey, and a Signer of the Declaration. They were married January 11, 1776. (*The Autobiography of Benjamin Rush . . .* ed. George W. Corner (Princeton, 1948), 18.)

216 *Diary of Christopher Marshall,* May 24.

217 Ryden, *op. cit.,* 82–3.

218 *Ibid.,* 85.

219 On May 29 [sic] George Read wrote, "I take an opportunity by Mr. McKean of writing . . ." (Shippen Papers, Vol. 7, HSP.)

220 Thomas McKean, President, to the Associators of Pennsylvania, June 25, 1776, in Martin L. Montgomery, *History of Berks County, Pennsylvania, from 1774 to 1783* (Reading, Pa., Chas. F. Hange, Printer, 1894), 48.

221 Force, *Archives,* 4th Ser., VI, 951 ff.

222 May 23, 1776, Yeates Papers, HSP.

223 Quoted in Thayer, *Pennsylvania Politics* (Harrisburg, 1953), 189–190. It is hardly surprising that he was dismissed—or resigned—from his position of tutor at the College of Philadelphia; more remarkable, perhaps, was his re-appointment, indeed, promotion, as professor of mathematics when the institution was re-organized in 1779 as the University of Pennsylvania, with a new board of trustees—including Thomas McKean. George B. Wood, *Early History of the University of Pennsylvania . . .* Philadelphia, 1896 (3rd ed.) 85–89; Scharf & Westcott, *History of Philadelphia,* I, 322–23.

224 Joseph Hawley to Sam Adams, April 1, 1776, Adams Papers, NYPL.

225 Charles Lee to Robert Morris, April 16, 1776 *Lee Papers* (NYHSC, 1871), I, 426.

226 See Julian Boyd, ed., *The Papers of Thomas Jefferson,* I, 229 f.

227 John H. Powell, *General Washington and the Jack Ass,* 98, says: "Dickinson had the delicate problem of a massive, articulate urban public opinion in Philadelphia to sway behind him, he had a care for the New York situation, and he was entirely committed to those policies which would bring about a union of the colonies— all the colonies."

228 Nor did matters of such import free him from those of detail. In May Joseph Borden, father of his first wife, sent "a sample of Sulphurious Stones . . . Ritcher than any before discovered," which discovery was soon followed by the gentleman himself, waiting upon the committee. *Penna. Archives,* IV, 753.

229 Bonvouloir to Vergennes, 28 Dec., 1775, quoted in Cecil B. Currey, *Code Number 72 Ben Franklin: Patriot or Spy?* (Englewood Cliffs, N.J., 1972), 64, from Henri Doniol, ed., *Histoire de la participation de la France à l'établissement des Etats-Unis d'Amérique,* (Paris, 1884–92), I, 377; also see Robert C. Alberts, *The Golden Voyage: The Life and Times of William Bingham, 1752–1804* (Boston, 1969), 16 f.

230 Franklin Papers, APS, Committee of Secret Correspondence, 85–287.

231 Currey, *op. cit.,* 64–66; the contract is found in Force, *Archives,* 4th Ser., VI, 771–82. Currey considers that although no connection with the French government has been found, the firm had its "tacit backing," and that Franklin was personally responsible for the firm's obtaining the contract.

232 Force, *Archives,* 4th Ser., IV, 689–90.

233 *Warren-Adams Letters,* I, 256.

234 *Diary of Christopher Marshall,* 76.

235 Burnett, *The Continental Congress,* 177.

236 *Diary of Christopher Marshall,* 76 f.

237 *Ibid.,* also Theodore Thayer, *Pennsylvania Politics and the Growth of Democracy,* 183.

238 *Pennsylvania Evening Post,* June 11.

239 PMHB, XXV, 368.

240 Force, *Archives,* 4th Ser., VI, 784–5.

241 The chronology of the Declaration is summarized in Caroll Frey, *The Independence Square Neighborhood* (1926), 119 f.

242 Burnett, *Letters,* I, 476–7.

243 Burnett, *The Continental Congress,* 173. Also see JCC, V, 428–432.

244 Buchanan, *Life of the Hon. Thomas McKean,* 24. Also Butterfield, ed., *The Adams Papers,* III, 393.

245 *Pennsylvania Archives,* IV, 773, includes a letter from Robert Morris, Chairman of the Secret Committee, to the Pennsylvania Committee of Safety, Philia., June 13, 1776: "The Congress having recd information of a dangerous Insurrection of Tories in the Lower Counties, have directed me to send down immediately One Ton of Powder & a suitable quantity of Lead if to be obtained. The powder I have issued orders for, but Lead I have not, nor do I know where to get it, unless upon this occasion you shou'd think proper to spare a quantity for this service."

246 *Diary of Christopher Marshall,* 77–8.

247 *Archives of the State of New Jersey,* First Ser., X, Frederick W. Ricord and William Nelson, eds. (New Jersey Hist. Soc., 1886), 710.

248 *Ibid.* The Provincial Congress asked the Continental Congress for advice as to how to handle Gov. Franklin, who had demonstrated a high order of ability in negotiating with them. Eventually they ordered him transported to Hartford, Conn., under guard. On June 22 Gov. Franklin argued that since the Assembly of Delaware "under the authority derived from the Crown" had considered the resolves of the Continental Congress, presented to them by Thomas McKean, and "so far from considering such meeting as a contempt or violation of the Resolve of the Continental Congress, they resolved they were the *only* proper persons to take that Resolve into consideration," therefore the legislature of New Jersey should behave in like manner, and prevent illegal activities. (*Ibid.,* 728.) Impatient with Franklin's delaying tactics, Congress removed him from the scene.

249 Force, *Archives,* 4th Ser., VI, 884.

250 Ryden, *op. cit.,* 92.

251 Burnett, *Letters,* I, 491.

252 John A. Munroe, *Federalist Delaware, 1775–1815,* "The Delaware State."

253 Ryden, *op. cit.,* 93 n. Rodney wrote from Lewes on June 23, "The first step taken when we arrived at Lewes was to send Subpena's for all those persons said to be concerned in the insurrection, in consequence of which they appeared verry fully." (*Delaware History,* XII, 66.)

254 *Diary of Christopher Marshall,* June 18.

255 See Force, *Archives,* 4th Ser., VI, 951–966, for a complete record of the entire conference. Scharf and Westcott's account is based on this.

256 *Ibid.*

257 *Diary of Christopher Marshall,* June 18.

258 Force, *Archives,* 4th Ser., VI, 951 f (for June 22).

259 *Diary of Christopher Marshall,* June 28. The text of the oath is given in a footnote in William Duane's edition of the *Diary,* and in Force's *Archives.*

260 Force, *Archives,* 4th Ser., VI, 951 f. It is not known how the Conference obtained possession of this minute.

261 Penna. Historical and Museum Commission, Information Leaflet No. 3, "The Military System of Pennsylvania During the Revolutionary War."

262 These detailed plans and orders can be followed in the JCC.

263 Sanderson's *Biography of the Signers* (first ed., 1824), Futhey & Cope, *History of Chester County* (1881), Buchanan, *op. cit.,* (1890), etc.

264 Franklin wrote Washington on June 21, "I am just recovering from a severe fit of the Gout, which has kept me from Congress and Company almost ever since you left us, so that I know little of what has pass'd there, except that a Declaration of Independence is preparing . . ."

McKean wrote to A. J. Dallas, on Sept. 26, 1796 (McKean Papers, HSP, III, 10) that he "was one of the committee, with Doctor Benjamin Rush, & two others who drafted [the Pennsylvania] declaration . . ." Thus, Franklin probably was active on the committee, though not in the Conference.

265 Jefferson wrote to Franklin, on the 21st, and Julian P. Boyd suggests that he was sending Franklin a draft copy of the Declaration, since that was the only document "concerning which we know indisputably that TJ consulted Franklin privately." (*The Papers of Thomas Jefferson,* I, 405.)

A letter from Franklin to Benjamin Rush, dated June 26, has recently been found, indicating that Franklin was confined to the house of Edward Duffield on the Bristol Pike, during June. Rush was a member of the committee which drafted Pennsylvania's declaration of independence. (Malone, *Jefferson,* I, 230n.) I have not seen this letter.

[266] We have already cited (No. 207) "The Alarm," which was sent out on May 19 even though it had been prepared and printed *before* the decision to hold a mass meeting on May 20.

[267] An early draft of the Declaration of Independence (JCC, V, 489 f.) contained the following language, all of it struck out by Congress: "he has waged cruel war against human nature itself, violating it's most sacred rights of life & liberty in the persons of a distant people, who never offended him, captivating them & carrying them into slavery in another hemisphere, or to incur miserable death in their transportation thither. This piratical warfare, the opprobrium of *infidel* powers is the warfare of the CHRISTIAN king of Great Britain determined to keep open a market where MEN should be bought and sold, he has prostituted his negative for suppressing every legislative attempt to prohibit or to restrain this execrable commerce: and that this assemblage of horrors might want no fact of distinguished dye, he is now exciting those very people to rise in arms among us, and to purchase that liberty of which *he* had deprived them, by murdering the people among whom *he* also obtruded them: thus paying off former crimes committeed against the *liberties* of the people, with crimes which he urged them to commit against the *lives* of another."

[268] The text can be found in Niles, *Principles and Acts,* 223, as well as in Force's *Archives.*

[269] There was no sectional or local requirement for the prejudice expressed in this document. Pennsylvania actually outlawed slavery (by gradual emancipation) during the Revolution. McKean obviously was unable to see beyond his own rather narrow formulation of the legal aspects of the question; Jefferson, as always, was more subtle and complex. But *neither* of them could accept the possibility that they themselves were guilty of a sin.

[270] Thomas McKean to Caesar A. Rodney, Aug. 22, 1813, Stauffer Coll., NYPL. McKean was here speaking of the Declaration of Independence. John Adams, who always insisted that the Declaration was originally signed on July 4, 1776, nevertheless felt that it was absurd to require everyone to sign it, even those who became members after the event. John Adams to Caesar A. Rodney, April 30, 1823. This letter, and several others pertaining to the signing, can be found in Burnett, *Letters,* I, 528, f.

[271] The Committee of Safety's moderate and radical membership included: Thomas Wharton, Jr., George Clymer, James Mease, John Nixon, George Ross, Samuel Miles, and David Rittenhouse.

[272] *Colonial Records,* X, 623–5. Some additional communications from the Committee of Safety can be found in *Pennsylvania Archives,* IV, 778.

[273] Scharf and Westcott, *op. cit.,* I, 312.

[274] *Pennsylvania Archives,* IV, 779.

[275] James McSherry, *A History of Maryland* (Baltimore, 1850), 194 f.; Jensen, *The Founding of a Nation,* 699; Butterfield, ed., *Diary and Autobiography of John Adams,* III, 395.

[276] The Congressional committee which visited Quebec, March to June, 1776, under the leadership of Benjamin Franklin, included three prominent Marylanders: Samuel Chase, Charles Carroll, and his brother, Father John Carroll. The latter two were carefully chosen as prominent Catholics—John Carroll was a Jesuit priest and Charles Carroll was to be the only Catholic to sign the Declaration.

[277] Burnett, *The Continental Congress,* 180.

[278] Boyd, ed., *The Papers of Thomas Jefferson,* I, 313 f.

[279] John H. Powell, *General Washington and the Jack Ass,* 161–2. "What [the Congress] had witnessed was one of those small, subtle strokes in George Clinton's twisting, turning dance through public life, at the outset of his forty years of artful straddling, which would lead him to permanent domination of New York's rambunctious mobs in democratical revolution . . . This morning he had revealed, in his

ordinary way, how well he already knew the secret of eating his cake and having it, too."

280 Butterfield, ed., *op. cit.*, III, 396. "Dickinson's very able speech of 1 July, long unknown to historians, survives . . . in a partial rough draft extended by notes . . ." John H. Powell has reconstructed it in PMHB, LXV (Oct., 1941), 458 f., and in "The Day of American Independence" in *General Washington and the Jack Ass.* Also see Stillé, *Dickinson, 367 f.*

281 Dumas Malone, *The Story of the Declaration of Independence* (New York, 1954), 61.

282 John Adams to "Govr. Mackean," Quincy, July 30, 1815 (McKean Papers, HSP, IV, 46). Adams' description of Congressional oratory was this: "Dr. Witherspoon has published Speeches, which he wrote beforehand and delivered Memoriter as he did his Sermons. But these I believe are the only Speeches ever committed to writing. The orators, while I was in Congress from 1774 to 1778 appeared to me very universally extemporaneous, and I have never heard of any committed to writing, before or after delivery."

283 Scharf and Westcott, *History of Philadelphia*, I, 316–7.

284 Thomas McKean to Alexander James Dallas, Philadelphia, Sept. 26, 1796 (McKean Papers, HSP, III, 10).

285 Ryden, *op. cit.,* 95 n.

286 Thomas McKean to Caesar A. Rodney, Philadelphia, Aug. 22, 1813 (Stauffer Coll., NYPL). Ryden in *Letters* states, "In this connection it is necessary to state that we have only McKean's word for it that he sent an 'express' to Rodney, as there is no reference by the latter to this fact in any of his known letters. It is quite certain that Rodney reached Philadelphia on July 2 (probably late in the afternoon) and that he joined McKean in placing Delaware with the majority when Lee's resolution was voted for in a formal manner upon its being referred from the Committee of the Whole House."

287 *Diary of Christopher Marshall,* July 1.

288 *Ibid.*

289 Burnett, *The Continental Congress,* 182, and Boyd, ed., *The Papers of Thomas Jefferson,* I, 314.

290 Facsimile of the document, Manuscript Div., Library of Congress.

291 Dumas Malone, *The Story of the Declaration of Independence,* 72.

292 Lossing, *The Pictorial Field-Book of the Revolution,* II, 74.

293 Burnett, *The Continental Congress,* 187.

294 Scharf and Westcott, *History of Philadelphia,* I, 329 f.

295 *Diary of Christopher Marshall,* July 3.

296 *Ibid.*

297 Dumas Malone, *Jefferson,* I, 229 adds this sardonic note; "On July 4, 1776, at Oxford, where Lord North was chancellor, honorary degrees were conferred by that ancient and honorable university on Thomas Hutchinson, late Governor of Massachusetts Bay, and Peter Oliver, late Deputy Governor."

298 *Ibid.* "On July 4 this thoughtful and observant man arose at dawn according to his custom, noting in the back of his Account Book that the temperature was 68° Fahrenheit at 6 a.m. On his way to or from the State House that very day he paid for a thermometer, but undoubtedly he had used this or another one already. His record of the temperature from this time forward, wherever he happened to be was practically unbroken . . . To one of his upbringing this day must have been quite comfortable. His highest reading of the thermometer, 76°, was at one o'clock. His thoughts were not wholly of the place and season, however, for on that day he also paid for seven pairs of women's gloves, destined for Monticello."

299 *Diary of Christopher Marshall,* July 4.

300 *Ibid.*

301 McKean's rapid disappearances and reappearances had such dizzying effect on wit-

nesses that their accounts understandably vary. See the bemusement of John Adams, below, in Note 304.

302 Scharf and Westcott, *History of Philadelphia,* I, 330.

303 *Ibid.*

304 Adams's error in referring to McKean as Attorney General in Pennsylvania was not an indication of impaired memory. McKean was, in a sense, an attorney general, since the city committee in Philadelphia (which McKean headed) was constantly prosecuting people for alleged offenses "against America." The significant point was Adams' impression that McKean had many duties outside of Congress, and was permitted to attend to them without formal permission.

The quotation comes from a letter to Caesar A. Rodney, dated April 30, 1823. Adams was commenting on McKean's letter to Caesar A. Rodney of Aug. 22, 1813; the entire exchange is included in Burnett's *Letters,* I. Adams' explicit statement was, "Congress chose to sleep another night, and ordered the signature for the next day. Accordingly on the next day the 4th July 1776 the Declaration of Independence was then signed by all the members then present. Mr. McKean was not then present for he had so many avocations in Delaware, and as Attorney General in Pennsylvania that he could not constantly attend in Congress. I have no doubt that he voted for independence in the Committee of the whole, on the 2d, and for the resolutions in Congress on the 3d but he was not present and did not sign on the 4th."

McKean's letter stated, "I was not in Congress *after* the 4th for some months, having marched with my regiment of associators of this city, as Colonel, to support General Washington . . ." [Italics supplied.]

305 Sanderson's *Biography of the Signers of the Declaration of Independence,* article on Thomas McKean by Robert Waln, Jr., in the first edition, 1823–4. Sanderson is a group *nom de plume* for many authors, and the book has appeared in many forms; the later editors (cf. Robert T. Conrad, Philadelphia, 1848) often seem to have been unaware that they were using abridged versions. Original in Beineke Library, Yale University.

306 The New York delegates were bound by instructions dated June 11, JCC, V, 505 n.

307 Boyd, ed., *The Papers of Thomas Jefferson,* I, 306 ". . . a copy of the *Journals of Congress* (Philadelphia: Aitken, 1777) in the New York Public Library contains a marginal note in the handwriting of Charles Thomson listing the names of four New York delegates, and opposite these names is the following: 'signed July 15.' This marginal note was obviously written late in Thomson's life (Hazleton, p. 207–8) but it was the considered statement of the usually reliable Secretary of Congress." To this fragment of information, I can only add the query: if there had not been a preliminary signing on July 4, what sort of paper would there have been for the New York delegates to add their names to? The document had not yet been engrossed on parchment.

308 Ryden, *op. cit.,* 94–5.

309 The President and the Secretary could authenticate, but not ratify, a document. Complete ratification required the signatures of all members and, to be legally binding, the seals of the states or that of the United States. Such seals had not yet been designed. Meanwhile, an authenticated copy of the Declaration was delivered in the evening to John Dunlap, printer, at his shop on the southeast corner of High (Market) and Seventh Streets, opposite the home of J. Graff, whose second floor had been rented since the end of May to Thomas Jefferson. Luther P. Eisenhart, ed., *Historic Philadelphia* (APS, 1953), 284.

310 John Adams' only entry for July 4 in his Autobiography (Butterfield, *op. cit.,* III, 398) had to do with the seal. The device which the committee presented to Congress on Aug. 20, 1776, was not considered satisfactory, and was put aside until 1782, when a new one was brought forward in time for the peace treaty. This

was just one among many indications that the revolutionary leaders, although aware of legal formalities, were more interested in getting on with the revolution.

311 The traditional story is told in Lossing's *Pictorial Field-Book of the Revolution,* II, 78–9, and in many other places. However, the Rev. Jacob Duché wrote in 1774, "In the hall is a handsome staircase which leads up to the third story of the steeple . . . [thence] to the fourth story by another flight of stairs . . . [The part with the bell] is in such a ruinous condition that they are afraid to ring the bell, lest by so doing the steeple should fall down." (PMHB, XXIII, 1889, 417 f.) Perhaps this discrepancy can be resolved by the explanation in Watson's *Annals* (1st ed., 1830), 343 f. that since the steeple was found to be in a state of decay about 1774, "it was deemed advisable to take it down, leaving only a small belfry to cover the bell." Watson goes on to say that it was "not a little singular that the bell, when first set up, should, in its colonial character, have been inscribed as its motto—'Proclaim liberty throughout the land, and to all the people thereof.' "

312 Boyd, ed., *The Papers of Thomas Jefferson,* I, 299–308, contains the clearest and most concise review of the very complicated question of the signing. Jefferson, like Adams, believed that the Declaration was first signed on the 4th. On May 12, 1819, he wrote to Samuel Adams Wells "it was not till the 2d. of July that the Declaration itself was taken up; nor till the 4th. that it was decided; and it was signed by every member present, except Mr. Dickinson."

On Aug. 6, 1822, he added a historical memorandum as a P.S. as follows: "since the date of this letter, to wit this day Aug. 6, 22 I receive a new publication of the Secret Journals of Congress, wherein is stated a Resoln of July 19, 1776 that the Declaration passed on the 4th. be fairly engrossed on parchment, and when engrossed, be signed by every member, and another of Aug. 2 that being engrossed and compared at the table was signed by the members. that is to say the copy engrossed on parchment (for durability) was signed by the members after being compared at the table with the original one signed on paper as before stated. I add this P. S. to the copy of my letter to mr. Wells to prevent confounding the signature of the original with that of the copy engrossed on parchment."

313 *Diary of Christopher Marshall,* July 4. (William Duane's edition, entitled *Passages from the Rememberancer of Christopher Marshall,* omits details at certain critical points, and therefore in this passage and others I have used the original manuscript in HSP.)

314 Burnett, ed., *Letters,* I, 532, analyzes the chief source of the confusion as follows: "Touching the question of the date when McKean himself signed the Declaration his own statements lack something in definiteness . . . In his draft of August 4, 1796, he says: 'I had not heard that the Instrument had been engrossed on parchment and signed until some weeks after I returned from camp, and (I believe) until I returned from Newcastle . . . but I subscribed my name to it in the presence of the Congress sometime in the 1776.' In the finished draft of September 26 this statement reads: 'but I must have subscribed my name to it not long after.' This change in the form of a statement seems to indicate that McKean was not quite positive in his recollection of the time and circumstances of his signing.

"In 1796 McKean also seemed to be in some doubt whether he signed the Declaration before going to Newcastle to take part in the constitutional convention or after his return. In the letter to Rodney in 1813 he is positive upon this point: 'When the associators were discharged I returned to Philadelphia, took my seat in Congress and then signed the declaration parchment. Two days later I went to Newcastle,' etc. It will be observed that in the letter of September 26, 1796, McKean speaks of his return from Newcastle in October. The Delaware convention opened August 27 and closed September 21. The journals of Congress indicate that McKean was present at the end of September, and was appointed to comittees on September 25 and 27. There is no other record of his attendance in the autumn of 1776, and from December 2, 1776, to January 30, 1778, he was not a member of Congress. If he actually signed the declaration in the autumn of 1776, a point on which he seems to be positive, it is still unaccountable why his name should not have appeared on the signed Declaration distributed in January, 1777, since all the other names appear there, even that of Matthew Thornton, who signed in November."

The dispute over the signing continued in later years, as a result of McKean's letters and the publication of the journals of the Congress, and it will be time enough to continue this discussion when we get to the proper point. McKean's final statement on the subject, based on research by his son and grandson, was written just eight days before his death in 1817. He may have been right at that time, or he may have been wrong, but his mind was still clear.

The best we can do here is suggest that the parchment which was signed by most members on Aug. 2, and by all the other Signers (except McKean) between that date and November, was taken to the printer for distribution with names in January, 1777, without McKean's signature. McKean himself was not certain that he signed before the end of the year 1776. It is a logical possibility that the publication of the document without his name in January, 1777, called his attention to this omission, and that he signed shortly thereafter—on the parchment. As for the original paper, signed on July 4 according to Adams, Jefferson, and others, it has never been found. Perhaps it was destroyed by Charles Thomson in order to prevent confusion, since the signatures on that document would have differed considerably from what had become the official list.

315 Other declarations of independence had been issued in 1774 and 1775. On June 10, 1774, the Scotch-Irish of Londonderry Township, Lancaster County, and on June 11, 1774, the Pennsylvania Germans of East and West Hanover Townships, Dauphin County, had issued such declarations. (Levi Hummel, "Notes on the Hummel Family," in *The Penn Germania*, cont. as *The Pennsylvania-German*, II, 2 (Feb., 1913), 148). There was also the famous Mecklenburg Declaration that was issued in Charlotte, N. C., in 1775.

316 *The Journals of Henry Melchoir Muhlenberg*, trans. T. G. Tapper & J. W. Doberstein (Philadelphia, 1945), II, 721–2.

317 Scharf and Westcott, *History of Philadelphia*, I, 321 and n. 1.

318 *Ibid.*

319 *Diary of Christopher Marshall*, July 5.

320 John W. Jordan, *Colonial Families of Philadelphia*, I, 909 f.

321 Scharf and Westcott, *History of Philadelphia*, I, 329 f.

322 *Ibid.*, 320.

323 *Diary of Christopher Marshall*, July 5.

324 Scharf and Westcott, *History of Philadelphia*, I, 330 f.; *Colonial Records*, X, 639, 648.

325 *Diary of Christopher Marshall*, July 8. Many historians have said that John Nixon read the Declaration while standing on "the platform of the observatory erected by the American Philosophical Society to observe the Transit of Venus in 1769." This has become part of the folklore of American history. However, it is more likely that he was standing on the platform erected for Colonel Roberdeau and the other Colonels (including McKean) in time for the mass meeting on May 20, 1776. If the earlier platform had still been there, why the need to build one for Col. Roberdeau? (See Josiah Barlett to John Langdon, Bartlett Papers, No. 92, New Hampshire Historical Society.)

326 Dumas Malone, *Jefferson*, I, 230, writes: "Jefferson must have been present but he was not in the spotlight; nobody announced that he was the author of this paper or led him forward upon the stage to take a bow. Cheers mounted to the sky; battalions paraded on the Common; and the bells rang all day and most of the night. This was in celebration not of a document but of an event."

327 Dumas Malone, *The Story of the Declaration of Independence,* 82.
328 Cited in F. Moore, *Diary of the American Revolution,* 131–2.
329 Lossing, *The Pictorial Field-Book of the Revolution,* II, 595; Malone, *The Story* . . . 129.
330 Watson, *Annals,* Appendix, p. 30.
331 See Boyd, ed., *The Papers of Thomas Jefferson,* I, 456–8.
332 From July 11 to 25 *The Diary of Christopher Marshall* notes almost daily departures of troops for the Jerseys.
333 Boyd, ed., *The Papers of Thomas Jefferson,* I, 323–4. Also JCC for the membership of the Committee appointed June 12.
334 *Ibid.* Congress sent the Articles to the states in 1777, but they were not finally ratified until 1781. See Burnett, *The Continental Congress,* 219 ff.
335 McKean had evidently left Philadelphia no later than July 18, because the resolution of July 19, about the engrossing of the Declaration, was news to him later. His wife wrote her first letter to him on Sunday, July 21. Unfortunately, none of *her* letters has been saved.
336 McKean Papers, HSP, VI.
337 *The Burd Papers: Selections from Letters Written by Edward Burd, 1763–1828,* ed. by Lewis Burd Walker (1899), 89.

Chapter 12. Revolutionary Governments, 1776–77

1 Quoted in Basil Williams, *The Life of William Pitt, Earl of Chatham* (2 vols., New New York, 1966—first edition, London, 1913), II, 317.
2 *Ibid.,* 321. As early as Feb. 1775, Chatham had scolded his colleagues in no uncertain terms: "The whole of your political conduct has been one continued series of weakness, temerity, despotism, ignorance, futility, negligence, and the most notorious servility, incapacity, and corruption. On reconsideration I must allow you one merit, a strict attention to your own interests: in that view you appear sound statesmen and politicians." (*Ibid.,* 311.)
3 McKean Papers, HSP, VI, 4.
4 *Pennsylvania Archives,* V, 121–3. Sept. 5, 1776.
5 *Ibid.*
6 *The Burd Papers: Selections from Letters Written by Edward Burd, 1763–1828,* ed. by Lewis Burd Walker (1899), 91.
7 Quoted in Washington's letter to McKean, Headquarters, New York, Aug. 13, 1776 (McKean Papers, HSP, I, 7).
8 *Ibid.* Washington had also written to McKean on Aug. 6, concerning a French baron who was in New York complaining of having been denied an appointment in the American army, and "having his papers and Credentials kept from him" by McKean. (*Writings of George Washington,* V, 375.)
9 There are several detailed lists of McKean's papers in a handwriting which I think is Sally's in the McKean Folder Hampton L. Carson Coll., HSP. Also many of the letters in the main collection have been endorsed in the same, or a similar, hand. Sally's handwriting, in her old age, can be found in the family Bible (McKean Papers, HSP) and in the inventory attached to McKean's will (filed with the Register of Wills, Philadelphia, July 17, 1818).
10 McKean Papers, HSP, VI, 3.
11 John A. Munroe, *Federalist Delaware, 1775–1815* (New Brunswick, 1954), 87.

[12] *Ibid.*

[13] McKean Papers, HSP, VI, 3.

[14] McKean to Joseph Reed, Aug. 29, 1780, cited in William B. Reed, *Life and Correspondence of Joseph Reed* (2 vols., Philadelphia, 1847), I, 250.

[15] *Porcupine's Works,* XI, 46. Also see Mary Elizabeth Clark, *Peter Porcupine in America: The Career of William Cobbett, 1792–1800* (Philadelphia, 1939), 151.

[16] McKean Papers, HSP, VI, 3 (Aug. 1, 1776)

[17] *Ibid.,* 4. (Aug. 7, 1776) On Aug. 3, it is of interest to note, Caesar Rodney wrote to his brother from Philadelphia, "Yesterday Came to Town a Ship belonging to the Congress from France with ten Tunns of Powder, about forty Tunns of Lead, one thousand Stand of Arms, &c. &c." (Ryden, *op. cit.,* 100.)

[18] McKean Papers, HSP, VI, 3.

[19] *Ibid.*

[20] The Assembly had been called together by Caesar Rodney, as Speaker, and had decided that each of the three counties would elect ten delegates to the Constitutional Convention. If the conservatives who were elected had all been "Tories," as the radicals sometimes called them, this election would have been a far greater disaster for the radical cause than it actually was.

[21] *The Pennsylvania Evening Post* reported on Aug. 13 that the Constitutional Convention at Philadelphia had resolved that such battalions as had supplied their quotas of the flying camp could return, if this was deemed expedient by the Generals and Field Officers.

[22] John A. Munroe, *Federalist Delaware,* 83–6, contains an excellent discussion of the Convention, complete with bibliography.

[23] On Sept. 12, 1776, Rodney wrote to John Haslet, "When Read went to Newcastle he prevailed on me to Stay in Congress, and that he would get the convention to give a power to one Member to Act, so that our Government might be Represented by me alone till the Convention Should Rise—I mentioned this to Mr. McKean who directly declared they Should make no appointment to Delegates, nor even alter the powers Given them, least they (meaning the Convention) Should plead that as a president [precedent] for going into some other appointments—Which they were not Authorized to do by their Choice—Therefore Upon the Whole I don't imagine they will Attempt any change." (Ryden, *op cit.,* 116.)

[24] Rodney to Thomas Rodney, Aug. 28, 1776. (*Ibid.,* 105–6.)

[25] *Ibid.*

[26] Buchanan, *op. cit.,* 51–4. The 1813 letter is in McKean Papers, HSP IV, 26.

[27] Buchanan, *op. cit.,* 51. McKean's letter was quoted by both Sanderson and Buchanan. Buchanan contradicted himself, however, because while he accepted Sanderson's mythical account of McKean's writing the constitution single-handed, he also cited *The Proceedings of the Convention of the Delaware State held at New-Castle in 1776* (New-Castle, 1776), which clearly indicated that the procedure was more complicated.

[28] Buchanan, *op. cit.,* 54. A paragraph on this page of Buchanan's book, which seems to have been inserted after the rest of the section was written, proves that Buchanan was aware of the above chronology of events, set forth in the *Proceedings.* However, he allowed the mythical account to stand.

[29] William T. Read, *Life and Correspondence of George Read* (Philadelphia, 1870).

[30] John A. Munroe, *Federalist Delaware,* 85.

[31] Peeling, *op. cit.,* 67.

[32] Ryden, *op. cit.,* 108.

[33] *Ibid.,* 116.

[34] McKean Papers, HSP, VI, 6. McKean's nephew, Thomas McKean Thompson, was also ill at this time.

[35] *Proceedings of the Convention of the Delaware State held at New Castle in 1776*

(New-Castle, 1776, and reprinted at Wilmington, 1927). Also see "The Thompson Register."

[36] Peeling, *op. cit.*, 62 f., following the *Proceedings*.

[37] Ryden, *op. cit.*, 114.

[38] *Ibid.*, 119. Also Robert Allen Rutland, *The Birth of the Bill of Rights, 1776–1791*. (New York, London, 1955, 1962), Chap. 4, "The New Republic Acts." The Delaware bill of rights may not have been very original, certainly not by Virginia standards, but the process by which the states imitated each other was highly significant as a means of developing a consensus. During the revolutionary war the American states were held together by consensus, and nothing else. The Articles of Confederation were discussed and agreed to in Congress, and again a consensus was developed, but they were not fully ratified by the states and were not binding until 1781.

Writing in 1898, Professor Max Ferrand noted the similarities between the Maryland and the Delaware bills of rights, and expressed the view that Maryland had borrowed from Delaware. Read's letter, which was published in the 1930's, indicated that the borrowing was the other way around. McKean was well acquainted with the Carrolls, Chase, Paca, and others in Maryland, and two of his daughters were to marry the sons of General Andrew Buchanan, of Baltimore, but there is no direct evidence that McKean was the channel of communication from Maryland to Delaware, except for the inferences that can be drawn from his membership in Congress, and his having stopped off at Philadelphia on his way to the Convention at New Castle.

[39] Peeling, *op. cit.*, 65, following the *Proceedings*.

[40] Ryden, *op. cit.*, 123–4.

[41] *Ibid.*

[42] *Ibid.*

[43] *Ibid.*

[44] Munroe, *Federalist Delaware*, 85–6. John Haslet thought that it was "astonishing . . . the hand of McK[ea]n was in it."

[45] Francis N. Thorp, *Federal and State Constitutions* (7 vols., Washington, 1909), *passim.*

[46] George Read wrote a letter to Rodney with a brilliant summary of the provisions of the constitution then agreed upon, complete to the last detail in two pages, on September 17, 1776. (Ryden, *op. cit.*, 119–120.)

[47] Buchanan, *op. cit.*, 47 and JCC, V, 818–821.

[48] Merrill Jensen, *The New Nation: A History of the United States During the Confederation, 1781–1789* (New York, 1950), 25 ff.

[49] Charles H. Stillé, *The Life and Writings of John Dickinson* (Philadelphia, 1891), I, 200 f.

[50] Ryden, *op. cit.*, 135 n; Buchanan, 22; Munroe, 90.

[51] Stillé, *op. cit.*, 204–5.

[52] Quoted in Stillé, *op. cit.*, 210.

[53] JCC, V, 846.

[54] Samuel Eliot Morison, *John Paul Jones: A Sailor's Biography* (Boston, 1959), 120 f. "It was understood by Jones that the American Commissioners in Paris were to build or buy a new frigate for him in Paris."

[55] Ryden, *op. cit.*, 143.

[56] David Hawke, *In the Midst of a Revolution* (Philadelphia, 1961), 192 f. "Christopher Marshall's deep feeling against the document emerged solely out of his religious quarrel with James Cannon . . . Benjamin Rush reacted against the Constitution, too, but for more complicated reasons . . ." He later wrote to John Adams, "From you I learned to discover the danger of the Constitution of Pennsylvania . . ." (Butterfield, ed., *Rush Letters*, I, 114–5.)

[57] *Diary of Christopher Marshall*, Oct. 17, 1776.

[58] *Ibid.*

[59] Hawke, *op. cit.,* 92. "The backcountry delegates no doubt headed home pleased with a job well done. They had preserved the basic form of the old government. They had made certain that only God-fearing men would get elected to office. And their work had won the approval of the eminent Dr. Franklin. These men were probably as shocked and astonished as any when their handiwork met with instant and loud howls of protest."

[60] *Diary of Christopher Marshall,* Oct. 21–22.

[61] *Pennsylvania Gazette,* Oct. 23, 1776. Also see J. Paul Selsam, *The Pennsylvania Constitution of 1776: A Study of Revolutionary Democracy* (Philadelphia, 1936).

[62] After he had had a decade of experience as Chief Justice under the new constitution, McKean wrote an incisive summary of his objections in a letter to John Adams, but it must not be assumed that he understood the question so clearly during the debates, before the constitution had gone into effect. McKean Papers, HSP, III. April 30, 1787.

[63] Scharf and Westcott, I, 324.

[64] McKean Papers, HSP, VI.

[65] Henry Fisher to Council, Lewes, Oct. 25, 1776, endorsed "Received at Newcastle, Oct. 30th, and forwarded by their most humble servant, Tho. M'Kean." *Pennsylvania Archives,* V, 53–5.

[66] Dr. Benjamin Rush to Council, Nov. 1, 1776, *ibid.,* 58.

[67] *Minutes of the Council of the Delaware State, from 1776 to 1792* (Dover, published by authority of the General Assembly, 1886), 13.

[68] *Ibid.,* 14.

[69] *Ibid.,* 22 f.

[70] "Minutes of a Meeting at the Indian Queen, 1776," *Pennsylvania Archives,* V, 73–4.

[71] *Ibid.,* V, 94–5, 98–9. Stansbury had been tried in absentia at the Indian Queen Tavern, at the southeast corner of Fourth and Market Streets. He later turned out to be a loyalist, as well as a musician of parts, and carried the first messages from Benedict Arnold to John André which led to the attempted betrayal of West Point. Many years after his death, in 1860, *The Loyal Verses of Joseph Stansbury and Dr. Jonathan Odell,* edited by Winthrop Sargent, was printed in Albany.

[72] Robert L. Brunhouse, *The Counter-Revolution in Pennsylvania, 1776–1790* (Harrisburg, 1942), Chap. II, "The Rise of the Radicals."

[73] James Wilson to Arthur St. Clair, July 3, 1777, in William Henry Smith, *St. Clair Papers: the Life and Public Service of Arthur St. Clair* (2 vols., Cincinnati, 1882), I, 417.

[74] Cushing, *op. cit.,* III, 322–8.

[75] See esp. opinion of June 23, 1777, MSS Div., NYPL. The Constitutional Convention, earlier, had appointed commissioners to hear and determine the cases of persons held in prison. George Bryan and James Young had been appointed commissioners for this purpose in Philadelphia. (Scharf and Westcott, I, 323–4) The Congressional holding committee was headed by Robert Morris.

[76] Newark, April 7, 1777, Harold B. Hancock, ed., "Letters to and from Caesar Rodney," *Delaware History,* XII, 75.

[77] McKinly had been chosen President in February, and was captured in September, 1777; he was taken on board the *Roebuck,* which had been in the area for a long time. (Ryden, *op. cit.,* 236–7; Munroe, *op. cit.,* 91.)

[78] See esp. "An Answer to Tenax abt. Presidsy of the Congress," August 6, 1781, addressed "To the Printer." McKean Papers, I, HSP.

[79] Lucius Wilmerding, Jr., "The United States Lottery," *The New-York Hist. Quat.,* January 1963. The lottery was a money-making scheme that dragged on into the 1780's with dubious results. McKean was to be Chairman of the Lottery Committee of Congress in 1781.

80 The Assembly delayed its decision in Read's case, several times, while Congress urged them to replace him; eventually Congressional requests to Delaware for a representative ceased, and it may be surmised that McKean was accepted as Read's stand-in.

81 *Sanderson's Biography,* article by Robert Waln, Jr. (1st. ed., 1823–4), IV, 188–9, notes that Clymer was reelected to Congress on March 12, 1777, and served until May, when ill health compelled him to resign. On Sept. 14, 1777, he was not reelected but served for awhile after that time. Christopher Marshall's *Diary* gives Feb. 23 as the date for Clymer's election, but confirms the fact that he continued to serve in the fall of 1777.

82 Dumas Malone, *The Story of the Declaration of Independence,* 249, 292. Donald Cooke, *Fathers of America's Freedom* (1969), 20. Buchanan, *op. cit.,* 46–7, concluded that McKean did not sign until after January 1777. Matthew Thornton, on the other hand, signed before that date—and in time for the Baltimore printing, although he was not elected to Congress until September —— in November 1776.

83 *Minutes of the Council of the Delaware State,* 109–114.

84 *Ibid.,* 10, 35.

Chapter 13. Re-opening the Courts, 1777–80

85 Burnett, *The Continental Congress,* 237.

86 *Pennsylvania Archives,* V, 310.

87 On March 4, 1777, the Supreme Executive Council under the new constitution met, and their minutes begin in *Col. Rec.,* XI, 173. Also see *Penna. Archives,* V, 252–3.

88 Susan Hicks, "The Pennsylvania Constitution of 1776," Valley Forge Historical Society, *The Picket Post,* Jan.–April, 1966.

89 Roche, Brunhouse, Peeling, Meehan, and Rowe all have discussions of Reed's appointment, complete with bibliographies.

90 See esp. Reed to Supreme Executive Council, July 22, 1777, Reed MSS, IV, New-York Hist. Soc. and discussion in Roche, *Joseph Reed,* 244–5 n. Also *Col. Rec.,* XI, 186, 202, 249, and 289.

91 Reed to Dickinson, Logan Papers, VIII, 93, HSP. Also A. S. Bolles, *Pennsylvania, Province and State,* II, 108–9, and Roche, *op. cit.,* 120–1.

92 See indenture to land in Newark purchased by Thomas McKean, from Samuel Patterson and Charles Thomson for £150, May, 1777, Morris Library, Univ. of Delaware, Newark.

93 Extract from the Minutes of the Council by Timothy Matlack, Secretary, Philadelphia, July 28, 1777, in Hampton L. Carson Coll., HSP. Young Lafayette had arrived in Philadelphia the day before.

94 Meehan, *op. cit.,* 83.

95 Manuscript Division, NYPL.

96 *Ibid.* See also Thos. McKean to Vice President George Bryan, Yorktown, May 27, 1777, concerning persons who should be tried, etc. in *Pennsylvania Archives,* VI, 555.

97 McKean Papers, I, HSP.

98 Dallas, *Pennsylvania Reports,* I, 32. Also *Col. Rec.,* XI, 253 f.

99 Edward Burd to E. Shippen of Lancaster, Reading, Aug. 22, 1778, cited in J. Bennett Nolan, ed., *Neddie Burd's Reading Letters* (1927), 97.

100 Thomas R. Meehan, "The Pennsylvania Supreme Court in the Law and Politics of

the Commonwealth, 1776–1790," unpub. doctoral dissertation (Wisconsin, 1960), 1, ff.

[101] *Pennsylvania Archives*, V, 478–81. Also Keith, *Provincial Councillors,* 330.

[102] *Pennsylvania Archives*, V, 469 f. *Colonial Records,* XI, 264, 267, 283–290.

[103] Bibliographies available in Peeling, Meehan, and Rowe.

[104] See Theodore Thayer, *Israel Pemberton,* 218–233.

[105] *Pennsylvania Archives*, V, 502–3. Also see p. 484 and *Col. Rec.,* XI, 285.

[106] *Pennsylvania Archives*, V, 574.

[107] *Colonial Records*, XI, 290.

[108] *Pennsylvania Archives*, V, 596.

[109] Theodore Thayer, *Israel Pemberton,* 214 f.

[110] *Ibid.* Pemberton Papers, XXXI, *passim,* HPS.

[111] Henry Laurens, as quoted in Burnett, ed., *Letters,* II, 80.

[112] Thayer, *Israel Pemberton,* 222. The Quakers (as the prisoners were always referred to) left Philadelphia on September 11, with the guns at Brandywine Creek sounding in the distance. Not until the 13th did Council receive word that McKean had qualified as Chief Justice, by taking the oath of office administered to him by Joseph Gardner of Chester County. (*Col. Rec.,* X, 270 and XI, 254, 303–4; *Penna. Archives,* V, 621; and *Diary of Christopher Marshall,* 127.) Marshall had now moved to Lancaster.

[113] Thayer, *op. cit.,* 223, from Pemberton Papers, XXX, 113, HSP. McKean had also ordered that "the body of Samuel Pleasants" be brought before him at East Fallowfield, Chester Co. (McKean Papers, I, HSP.)

[114] Broadside printed by Styner and Cist, Second near Arch Street, copy in The Library Company, Philadelphia.

[115] McKean to Adams, September 18 (or 19), 1777, McKean Papers, I, HSP.

[110] *Pennsylvania Archives*, V, 586.

[117] George Bryan, Vice President, to Alexander Nesbutt [Nesbitt], presumably the officer who had left the prisoners at Reading, September 16, 1777, *Col. Rec.,* XI, 308, and *Penna. Archives,* V, 628.

[118] McKean probably became Speaker of the Assembly in October, 1776, though the records are not clear. For the general situation see Munroe, *Federalist Delaware,* 92–3.

[119] McKean to the General Assembly of the Delaware State, Dover, October 22, 1777, H. F. Brown Coll. of Rodney Material, HSD. The Newark Academy was closed as an academic institution from September, 1777, until ca. 1780. During part of this time it served as a shoe factory for the continental forces. See Munroe, *op. cit.,* 63–4.

[120] McKean to the General Assembly, October 22, 1777.

[121] McKean to Read, Lunn's Tavern, September 26, 1777, Richard S. Rodney Coll. of George Read Papers, HSD.

[122] *Ibid.*

[123] McKean to the General Assembly, October 22, 1777.

[124] McKean to Read, September 26, 1777. Read with his family returned to Delaware by way of southern New Jersey, almost getting captured in the process.

[125] *Minutes of the Council of the Delaware State,* 141–2. Although McKean was presumably replaced by Read at this time, Congress continued to deal with McKean on Delaware matters, at least into November.

[126] McKean to the General Assembly, October 22, 1777.

[127] The British had occupied Wilmington briefly, and had controlled New Castle and the shore of the Delaware River and Bay. On the 16th of October they withdrew to the north.

[128] McKean to Read, Paxton, December 6, 1777, Richard S. Rodney Coll. of George Read Papers, HSD.

[129] Patterson to McKean, Wilmington, January 8, 1778, McKean Papers, I, HSP.

[130] McKean to Read, York, February 12, 1778, Richard S. Rodney Coll. of the George Read Papers, HSD.

[131] *Ibid.*

[132] Rodney to McKean, Dover, March 9, 1778, McKean Papers, I, HSP. Read also wrote to McKean, March 4, 1778, quoted in Sanderson, IV, 58 f.

[133] Albert S. Bolles, *Pennsylvania, Province and State,* II, ch. 11, 31. See also William H. Loyd, *The Early Courts of Pennsylvania,* 124 f.

[134] Several acts were passed by the Assembly in January, 1777, before the Supreme Executive Council was organized, and therefore before the new members of the judiciary were appointed. IX *Statutes at Large,* 29, put "such and so much of the laws of the province as were necessary in the commonwealth" into effect, and provided that the courts of quarter sessions and gaol delivery, petty sessions, common pleas, orphans' courts, the supreme court, and courts of oyer and terminer and general gaol delivery be held with all the powers previously exercised. It took several months, however, for this directive to be implemented. The first session of common pleas was held in Philadelphia in September, 1777, but was immediately suspended by the British occupation.

[135] Charles P. Keith, *Provincial Councillors,* 329 f.

[136] *Ibid.,* 315, 330.

[137] Theodore Thayer, *Israel Pemberton,* 218, 233.

[138] A. J. Dallas, *Reports of Cases . . . in the Courts of Pennsylvania* (Philadelphia, 1790), 53–60. McKean's Court was here confirming an advisory opinion which they had delivered to the legislature in 1779. See *Penna. Archives,* VII, 644–6.

[139] The counsel for the prisoner cited such sources as Puffendorff, Locke, Burlamaqui, and Blackstone.

[140] The Attorney General took the position that the Declaration of Independence caused every state in the union to be free and independent, and that Congress had recommended that new governments should be framed adequate to the exigencies of their affairs; thus, the councils of safety and other temporary bodies discharged the functions of the state. He cited the Journals of Congress for various dates in May, June, and July, 1776.

[141] Elias Boudinot to William Augustus Atlee, Philadelphia, August 11, 1777, Wm. A. Atlee Papers, LC.

[142] Atlee to Boudinot, September 8, 1777, in *ibid.*

[143] Boudinot to Atlee, Lancaster, December 24, 1777, in *ibid.*

[144] Boudinot to Atlee, Camp, January 7, 1778, in *ibid.* See also Charles H. Metzger, S. J. *The Prisoner in the American Revolution,* chap. on "The Commissary."

[145] McKean had been in the backcountry as early as September, 1777. When the trouble with the Quakers first broke out, and McKean wrote to John Adams by way of explanation, he said, "My situation was such that I had not received a letter nor seen a News-paper from Philadelphia for a fortnight." It has been speculated that he was already busy organizing the court system at that time, but it is more likely that he was working for Congress, and perhaps looking for places where his family might stay.

[146] McKean Papers, VI, HSP.

[147] Burnett, ed., *Letters,* III, 198.

[148] McKean Papers, VI, HSP.

[149] *Diary of Christopher Marshall,* 141.

[150] *Penna. Archives,* V, 505–6; also Brunhouse, *op. cit.,* 37. George W. Greene, *Historical View of the American Revolution,* 151 f., says the British referred scornfully to the "pasteboard money of the rebels."

[151] McKean to Rodney, York-town, April 28, 1778, Feinstone Coll., APS, cited as above in Burnett, ed., *Letters,* III, 198.

152 *Diary of Christopher Marshall,* 176.
153 Charge Delivered to the Grand-Jury by the Honourable Thomas M'Kean, Esquire, Chief Justice of Pennsylvania, at a Court of Oyer and Terminer, and General Gaol Delivery, held at Lancaster, for the County of Lancaster, on the Seventh Day of April, 1778, being the first Court of the Kind held in the State under the Common-wealth, and published at the special Request of the said Grand Jury. Lancaster, Printed by FRANCIS BAILEY, in King's Street, M, DCC, LXXVIII. (APS copy is inscribed to John Dickinson, Esquire, in McKean's hand.)
154 *Ibid.*
155 Oyer and Terminer Docket, Sept. 1778 to Dec. 1786, Prothonotary, Pennsylvania Supreme Court, Philadelphia. Upon occasion they sat as a Court of Oyer and Terminer for Bucks and Chester as well. McKean to Atlee, July 7, 1778, Atlee Papers, L.C.
156 Although various attempts were made over the years to abolish the court of Nisi Prius, this specific duty of the Supreme Court was not done away with until the Constitution of 1874. *The Pennsylvania Manual* (Harrisburg, 1948), 43.
157 These letters can all be found in McKean Papers, VI, HSP.
158 McKean to Mrs. Sarah McKean, per Negro Sam, April 9, 1778 in *ibid.*
159 Buchanan, *op. cit.,* 61 f.
160 These sentences may be found in the earlier cases referred to in Dallas, also in McKean's and Atlee's letters. Catherine S. Crary in *The Price of Loyalty: Tory Writings From the Revolutionary Era* (New York, 1973), 383 f. describes the corporal and capital punishments in common use in the colonies, or the new states.
161 Atlee to his wife Hetty (Esther), York, April 23, 1778, Wm. A. Atlee Papers, LC. McKean to Sally McKean, York, April 28, 1778, McKean Papers, VI, HSP.
162 Peeling, *op. cit.,* 166–169, and Roche, *op. cit.,* 153–4 deal with the disposition of the Proprietary estates, one of the most important of the advisory opinions—though it was not followed in detail. There were many other examples.
163 McKean to Read, York Town, April 3, 1778, quoted in Sanderson, IV, 165. This invitation was confirmed in a letter: Jno. Bayard, Lancaster, Feb. 28, 1778, to McKean that "there are several Bills proposed which will require your Advice and Assistance," McKean Papers, I, HSP.
164 Brunhouse, *op. cit.,* 48 f. See also collection of Hooper correspondence in the Northampton County Historical and Genealogical Society, which includes letters to and from Elias Boudinot concerning prisoners of war held at Easton, who were mostly Hessians captured at Red Bank and Mud Island. Hooper was greatly affected by the "wretched state" of his charges, and was willing to hire them out to the local farmers—an arrangement that pleased the Pennsylvania Germans of Northampton County, and was literally a life-saver for the Hessians. When he was ordered to keep them in close confinement, to "retaliate against the British," they got jail fever and many of them died.
165 Nathanael Greene, QMG, to the Hon. Thomas McKean, Camp Valley Forge, June 3, 1778, McKean Papers, I. HSP. In this discussion I am borrowing the ideas and in some places the language of my article, "Thomas McKean and the Origin of an Independent Judiciary," *Pennsylvania History,* April 1967, 111–130.
166 McKean to Major General Green, QMG, June 9, 1778, McKean Papers, I, HSP. Also see *Penna. Archives,* VI, 266–8.
167 Willard M. Wallace, *Traitorous Hero, the Life and Fortunes of Benedict Arnold* (New York, 1954), 162 f. Also James Thomas Flexner, *The Traitor and the Spy* (New York, 1953), 221 f.
168 Proclamation by the hon. maj. gen. Arnold in the *Pennsylvania Evening Post,* issue of June 20, 1778, Bound Vol. IV, 210, HSP.
169 Among the charges against Arnold were these: that he used government wagons for

his private purposes and that he speculated in cargoes of ships, such as the *Active.*

[170] McKean to the Supreme Exec. Council, Philadelphia, Aug. 22, 1778, *Col. Rec.,* XI, 561–2.

[171] Much has been written concerning the innocence of Peggy Shippen Arnold, but Carl Van Doren, *Secret History of the American Revolution* (New York, 1941), 183 f. successfully implicates her in her husband's treasonable schemes.

[172] The story is told in Flexner, *op. cit.,* 239 f. Brunhouse, *op. cit.,* 65 f. Wallace, *op. cit.,* 171 f. Matlack was Secretary of the Council.

[173] Cited in Van Doren, *op. cit.,* 188.

[174] Burnhouse, *op. cit.,* 67.

[175] The correspondence can be found in the Clinton Papers, Wm. L Clements Library, Ann Arbor. Some of it was in code, some of it written left-handed. The man in charge of the correspondence in the British headquarters was John André, now aide-de-camp to General Clinton.

[176] *Colonial Records,* XII, 490. Peggy Shippen Arnold was the sister of Betsy Shippen Burd, the wife of Edward Burd, Prothonotary of the Supreme Court. Burd was greatly distressed by his brother-in-law's treason, and anxious to prove his own patriotism.

[177] JCC, X, 140 discusses efforts in February, 1778. On April 3, 1778, he wrote to George Read, "Peculation, neglect of duty, avarice, and insolence in most departments abound, but with the favor of God, I shall contribute my part to drag forth and punish the culprits." Burnett, ed., *Letters,* III, 149–50. Also W. T. Read, *op. cit.,* 309. McKean had thought there was sufficient clothing for the whole army for a year, but "I am told most of the troops are naked."

[178] John C. Fitzpatrick, ed., *Writings of Washington,* II, 499–500.

[179] Scharf and Westcott, *op. cit.,* I, 394 f.

[180] The Committee on Prisoners made recommendations to Congress and supervised the arrangements which Congress decreed, but Congress normally confirmed the recommendations of the committee. Benson J. Lossing, *Field-Book of the Revolution,* II, 646 n, states "A *sergeant,* was reckoned equal to two privates . . . *captain,* sixteen; *major,* twenty-eight; *lieutenant colonel,* seventy-two; *colonel,* one hundred; *brigadier general,* two hundred; *major general,* three hundred and seventy-two; *lieutenant-general,* a thousand and forty-four; *adjutant* and *quartermaster,* six; *surgeon,* six . . ." Note the low rating of the medical profession.

[181] McKean had in fact recommended the exchange of McKinly for Franklin. See Henry Laurens to Rawlins Lowndes, December 16, 1778, Burnett, ed., *Letters,* III, 537. It might be noted in passing that Thompson was married to the sister of George Read's wife.

[182] Quoted in Thompson Westcott, *Historic Mansions of Philadelphia,* 77–8. Also see *Col. Records,* XI, 659–660, and Robert Sears, *The Pictorial History of the American Revolution* (New York, 1846), 232.

[183] Papers of the Continental Congress, No. 159, folio 292, LC.

[184] *Ibid.,* also JCC, XII, 1146, 1149.

[185] See Henry J. Young, "The Treatment of the Loyalists in Pennsylvania," unpub. doctoral dissertation at Johns Hopkins University, 1955, esp. Chap. V, "The Punishment of the Dynamic Loyalists."

[186] *Respublica v. Molder et al.,* in A. J. Dallas, *Pennsylvania Reports,* I, 32.

[187] Thomas R. Meehan, "The Pennsylvania Supreme Court in the Law and Politics of the Commonwealth, 1776–1790," unpub. doctoral dissertation (Wisconsin, 1960), 130 f.

[188] Oyer and Terminer Docket, Sept., 1778 to Dec. 1786, pp. 142, 146–7, 193, 239; Appearance Docket, 226–230, Supreme Court of Pennsylvania, *Respublica v. Aaron Doan,* I Dallas 86. Also see postscript in letter McKean wrote to his wife from Bedford

as late as October 29, 1783, that Joseph Doan, senior, was in jail there, Mahlon Doan and another member of the gang were confined in Pittsburgh, and three others at York, as of that date.

[189] McKean to Atlee, Philadelphia, July 7, 1778, Wm. A. Atlee Papers, LC.

[190] See "Diary of Grace Growden Galloway," with Introduction by Raymond C. Werner, PMHB, XV, 32 ff. Also see my article, "Joseph Galloway and the British Occupation of Philadelphia," in *Pennsylvania History*, XXX, 272 ff., and Charles Coleman Sellers, *Charles Willson Peale* (New York, 1969), 164–5, 170.

[191] Scharf and Westcott, *op. cit.*, I, 394 f. Allan Nevins, *The American States During and After the Revolution*, 255 f. Also I Dallas 34 f. and 39 f. McKean's notes on the Roberts trial can be found in the Morristown National Historical Park, Morristion, N.J., but parts of them are quite illegible, unlike most of McKean's papers. Also see *Penna. Archives*, 6th Ser., XII, 793.

[192] *Pennsylvania Archives*, VII, 25–58.

[193] David Dawson and Ralph Morden were both executed in 1780. I know relatively little about the former, but have done two articles on the latter: "The Treason of Ralph Morden and Robert Land," PMHB, LXXXIX, 4, and "Robert Land and Some Frontier Skirmishes," *Ontario History*, XLVIII, 2.

[194] See Bradley Chapin, "The Law of Treason during the American Revolution," unpub. doctoral dissertation (Cornell, 1952), subsequently published as *The American Law of Treason: Revolutionary and Early National Origins* (Seattle, 1954), esp. chap. 4, "The Times that Tried Men's Souls."

[195] *Colonial Records*, VII, 21; Isaac Sharpless, *Quaker Government in Pennsylvania*, II, 194. It may be pertinent to note that one of those cited with Roberts and Carlisle was the former Sheriff of Bucks County, Samuel Biles, Esq., whose daughter Mary married Joseph Borden III in November, 1778. This connection may have had a bearing on McKean's strained relations with the Bordens. (*Penna. Archives*, 4th Ser., III, 669 f.)

[196] Benson J. Lossing, *Eminent Americans*, 47.

[197] *Pennsylvania Packet*, November 7, 1778; W. B. Read, *op. cit.*, II, 35–6.

[198] Frank Moore, *Diary of the American Revolution* (New York, 1860), II, 120 f.

[199] David P. Brown, *The Forum* (Philadelphia, 1856), II, 327.

[200] Cited in Buchanan, *op. cit.*, 63, from Winthrop Sargent, *Loyalist Poetry of the Revolution*. (Probably written by Jos. Stansbury.)

[201] Hastings, *Francis Hopkinson*, 478.

[202] *Ibid.*, 371–2.

[203] Buchanan, *op. cit.*, 69; Scharf and Westcott, *op. cit.*, I, 397, n. 3.

[204] McKean to Sally McKean, July 12, 1779, in McKean Papers, VI, HSP.

[205] McKean to Sally McKean, Oct. 25, 1778, in McKean Papers, VI, HSP.

[206] The Last Will and Testament of Thomas McKean, Aug. 13, 1814, filed with Inventory, July 17, 1818, Recorder of Deeds, Court of Common Pleas, County of Philadelphia.

[207] Watson, *Annals*, 359; Scharf and Westcott, *op. cit.*, I, 420.

[208] "Account of Forfeited Estates," May 28, 1781, RG-4, and Certificate of Duché's Estate, June 28, 1781, RG-27, Div. of Archives and Manuscripts, PHMC, Harrisburg.

[209] Brunhouse, *op. cit.*, 78, says, "Technically the old charter was not voided; the amendments and alterations were so sweeping that actually it amounted to revocation."

[210] Brunhouse, *op. cit.*, 78.

[211] Scharf and Westcott, *op. cit.*, I, 406.

[212] Nevins, *op. cit.*, 261.

[213] Cited in *ibid.* For McKean's appointment see Notice of Thomas McKean's Election as President of the University of the State of Pennsylvania, Thomas McKean Folder, Hampton L. Carson Coll., HSP.

[214] University of Pennsylvania, *Biographical Catalogue of the Matriculates of the College, together with a List of the Members of the College Faculty, and the Trustees, Officers, and Recipients of Honorary Degrees, 1749–1893*, xiv.

[215] *Ibid.*, xviii.

[216] *Ibid.*, xiv.

[217] A. Bolles, *Pennsylvania, Province and State*, II, 154.

[218] Roche, *op. cit.*, 153; Brunhouse, *op. cit.*, 79.

[219] See Samuel Hazard's *Register of Pennsylvania*, X, 113–5 for McKean's opinion.

[220] Thomas McKean and Edmund Physick, *A Calm Appeal to the People of the State of Delaware*, Sept. 3, 1793, reprinted by Zachariah Poulson, junr., No. 8, Chestnut Street, Philadelphia, contains a detailed statement of the Penns' proposals for the state of Delaware.

[221] Roche, *op. cit.*, 153–4.

[222] Bolles, *op. cit.*, II, 154–5.

[223] Brunhouse, *op. cit.*, 79.

[224] *Journals of the House of Representatives of the Commonwealth of Pennsylvania, 1776–1781* (Philadelphia, 1782), 347.

[225] The King had power to grant the Charter, he said, since no other European power claimed the lands in question. The grant was absolute, like those made to Lord Baltimore and Lord Berkeley. The concessions were limited to the adventurers and purchasers at the time the grant was made. The quitrents resulted from the nature of the estate, and there was no requirement (as the Assembly had hinted) that the monies received should be used entirely for government purposes. (See Peeling, *op. cit.*, 167.)

[226] James T. Mitchell and Henry Flanders, eds., *The Statutes at Large of Pennsylvania from 1682 to 1801* (Harrisburg, 1896–1908), X, 33–39; and Wm. B. Reed, *Life and Correspondence of Joseph Reed* (Philadelphia, 1847), II, 168.

[227] Wayland F. Dunaway, *A History of Pennsylvania*, 184.

[228] McKean to Dickinson, Philadelphia, July 23, 1792, Robt. R. Logan Family Papers, HSP.

[229] Burton Alva Konkle, *The Life and Times of Thomas Smith, 1745–1809* (Philadelphia, 1904), 119–120; also discussions in Brunhouse, Nevins, Peeling, Wallace, *et al.*

[230] Wallace, *op. cit.*, 207–8, cites Van Doren, *Secret History of the American Revolution*, who in turn used the Clinton Papers, Wm. L. Clements Library, Ann Arbor. Brunhouse, Nevins, and Konkle do not mention the discomfiture of Benedict Arnold. Scharf and Westcott, *op. cit.*, I, 401–2, give an explicit eye-witness account.

[231] Atlee to Mrs. Atlee, York, Oct. 12, 1779, Wm. A. Atlee Papers, LC.

[232] For a summary see John M. Coleman, "Thomas McKean and the Origin of an Independent Judiciary," *Pennsylvania History*, April, 1967. A great deal of relevant information can be found in the Dreer, Gratz, Provincial Delegates, and Society Colls., HSP.

[233] *Colonial Records*, XII, 495.

[234] McKean to Sally McKean, Philadelphia, July 26, 1779, McKean Papers, VI, 26, HSP. See also "Journal of Samuel Rowland Fisher, of Philadelphia, 1779–1781," contrib. by Anna Wharton Morris, PMHB, XLI, 145.

[235] Scharf and Westcott, *op. cit.*, I, 400.

[236] Extract from Oyer and Terminer Docket, Sept. 1778 to Dec. 1786, Prothonotary, Pennsylvania Supreme Court, Philadelphia.

[237] *Ibid.*

[238] *Ibid.*, The practice of making innocent people pay costs is still an issue in Pennsylvania. McKean started it in 1779, and it became law in 1805, when he was Governor. *Civil Liberties Record*, Greater Phila. A.C.L.U., February 1963, Vol. 12, No. 1.

239 Burnett, *The Continental Congress,* 219 ff.

240 Sanderson's biog. of George Read, IIII, 69 f.

241 *Minutes of the Council of the Delaware State,* 371 f.

242 *Ibid.,* 379–397, 400, 404. Also Burnett, *op. cit.,* Chap. XXV, "Confederation Ratified."
    JCC, xiii, 186, 236; xiv, 548.

243 Buchanan, *op. cit.,* borrowing from Sanderson IIII, 267–9.

244 Autobiographical Sketch, Society Coll., HSP.

245 Buchanan, *op. cit.,* 68, following Martin's *Bench and Bar.*

246 Peeling, *op. cit.,* 189, following Loyd's *Early Courts of Pennsylvania.*

247 Burton Alva Konkle, *George Bryan,* 221; *Benjamin Chew,* 200; and *Thomas Smith,*
    220.

248 Quoted in Hastings, *Francis Hopkinson,* 237 f.

249 Edward Burd to Jasper Yeates, Philadelphia, December 27, 1780, in Lewis Burd
    Walker, ed., *The Burd Papers: Selections from Letters Written by Edward Burd,*
    1763–1828 (1899), 120. Also see *The Pennsylvania State Trials; Containing the*
    Impeachment, Trial, and Acquittal of Francis Hopkinson, and John Nicholson,
    Esquires (Edmund Hogen, ed., Philadelphia, 1794.) and Scharf and Westcott, *op.*
    cit., I, 413.

250 JCC, XVI, 32 f.

251 *Ibid.,* XVI, 77; 357; XVII, 397.

252 Brunhouse, *op. cit.,* 101. Also see exchange of letters in *Penna. Archives,* VIII, 649 f.

253 Peeling, *op. cit.,* 156–8, following *Colonial Records,* XII, 564–6. Also see McKean to
    Reed, December 12, 1780, Gratz Coll., Case 1, Box 20, HSP.

254 This completes the form with which most petitions end, "And we as in duty bound
    shall ever pray, etc.," according to Dundley C. Lunt, *Tales of the Delaware Bench*
    and Bar (New York, 1963), 23.

Bibliography

I. LIBRARIES: MANUSCRIPTS AND COLLECTIONS

CANADA

HAMILTON
  Hamilton Public Library
    Loyalist records and local publications:
      The Caduceus, pub. by the Hamilton Public Library
      New Dominion Monthly Magazine
      Grimsby Hist. Soc., *Annals of the Forty*
      Hamilton Spectator
      Head of the Lake Hist. Soc., *Publications*
      Ontario Hist. Soc., *Papers and Records*
      Niagara Hist. Soc., *Publications*
      United Empire Loyalists (U.E.L.) Ass'n., *Transactions*
      Wentworth Hist. Soc., *Journal and Transactions*

OTTAWA
  Public Archives of Canada
    Bouquet Coll.
    Daniel Claus Papers
    Haldimand Papers
    Misc. Indian Papers

TORONTO
  Ontario Archives
    Land records, Loyalist petitions

ENGLAND

LONDON
British Museum
  Additional MSS
  Auckland Papers (William Eden)
  Haldimand Papers
Lambeth Palace
  Society for the Propagation of the Gospel (SPG) Papers
Public Records Office (PRO)
  Records of the British Ministries

UNITED STATES

CALIFORNIA

SAN MARINO
Henry E. Huntington Library and Art Gallery
  Benedict Arnold items
  Francis Hopkinson items
  T. McKean items

CONNECTICUT

HARTFORD
Connecticut State Library
Chas. Thomson and T. McKean items
  The Trumbull Papers
  Trumbull Family Papers

NEW HAVEN
Yale University, Beineke Library
Yale University, Sterling Library
  Benjamin Franklin Colls.
  T. McKean items
  Francis Hopkinson items
  Yale Univ. MSS

DELAWARE

DOVER
Public Archives Commission
  Executive Correspondence
  Gen. Ref., 69
  Read, Rodney and McKean items
  Ridgely Papers

GREENVILLE
  The Hagley Museum
    T. McKean items

NEW CASTLE
  The Amstel House
  Emmanuel Episcopal Church
  New Castle Presbyterian Church
  New Castle Public Library

NEWARK
  Morris Library, University of Delaware
    T. McKean items

WILMINGTON
  Historical Society of Delaware (HSD)
    H. F. Brown Coll. of Rodney Material
    Fisher Coll.
    Genealogical Section
    General Reference No. 69
    McKean Coll.
    Morse Coll.
    Richard S. Rodney Coll. of Read Materials
    Society Coll.
  Newcastle County Courthouse
    Recorder of Deeds
    Register of Wills

MASSACHUSETTS

BOSTON
  Massachusetts Historical Society
    The Adams Letter Book
    The Adams Papers
    W. Eustis Coll.
    G. E. French Coll.
    Wm. Heath Coll.
    Jefferson Coll.
    Misc. Coll.
    Otis Papers
    Pickering Papers
    Waterston Coll.

CAMBRIDGE
  Harvard University
    Langdell Library, T. McKean items
    Widener Library, T. McKean items

The Treasure Room
Wm. Cobbett (Porcupine) items

MICHIGAN

ANN ARBOR
Wm. L. Clements Library
Sir Henry Clinton Papers
Nathaniel Greene Papers
Misc. MSS Coll.
Stopford-Sackville MSS
U. S. Congress Papers

NEW HAMPSHIRE

CONCORD
New Hampshire Historical Society
Bartlett Papers

NEW JERSEY

BORDENTOWN
Bordentown Library Association
Borden family items
GLASSBORO
Glassboro State College Library
Stewart Coll.
MORRISTOWN
Morristown National Historical Park
Half a dozen McKean letters
Trial of John Roberts, 11 pp.
NEWARK
New Jersey Historical Society
Antill items
Borden items
Hopkinson items
Robert McKean items
PRINCETON
Princeton University Library
Adams Papers (microfilm from Mass. Hist. Soc.)
Papers of Thomas Jefferson
TRENTON
New Jersey State Library, Archives and History Bureau
Borden items
Indentures, wills, etc.

NEW YORK

NEW YORK
  Columbia University Library
    T. McKean items from Evans
  The New-York Historical Society
    Gallatin Papers
    Gates Papers
    John Jay Papers
    Livingston Papers
    McDougall Papers
    McLane Papers
    T. McKean items
    Misc. Schuyler MSS
    Misc. Wallace Coll.
    R. H. Morris Coll.
    Newspaper file
    Joseph Reed Papers, Vail Coll.
    U. S. Military Philosophical Society
  New York Public Library (NYPL)
    Samuel Adams Papers, MSS Div.
    Balch's Loyalist Letters
    Bancroft Coll.
    British Hqs. Papers in America
    Loyalist Transcripts
    T. McKean items in Misc. Papers
    Newspaper Cuttings Collected by James Riker
    Schuyler Papers
    Stauffer Coll.

PENNSYLVANIA

EAST STROUDSBURG
  East Stroudsburg State College
    Kemp Library
      Pickering Papers (microfilm from Mass. Hist. Soc.)
EASTON
  Lafayette College, Kirby Library
    Minutes, Northampton Co. Committee of Correspondence, 1774
  Lafayette College, David Skillman Library
    American Friends of Lafayette Coll.
  Northampton County Courthouse
    18th Cent. records
    Quarter Sessions, Dockets

Northampton Co. Historical and Genealogical Society
  A. D. Chidsey Colls.
  Wm. L. Hooper Papers
  Papers Read Before the N. C. Hist. & Gen. Soc.

HARRISBURG
  Div. of Public Records (Bureau of Archives and History), PHMC
    Records of the Supreme Executive Council
      Conviction and Clemency Papers
      Forfeited Estates file, RG-4
    Executive Correspondence, RG-26
    General Correspondence
    Letter Books, RG-26
    Resolves of the General Assembly, RG-27
    Revolutionary Papers
    Original Tax lists, etc. in *Penna. Archives*

HAVERFORD
  Haverford College
    Philips Coll.
    Chas. Roberts Autograph Letters Coll.

LANCASTER
  Lancaster County Historical Society
    T. McKean items

PHILADELPHIA
  Alison Bldg., Rittenhouse Square
    Presbyterian Ministers' Fund Colls.
  American Philosophical Society (APS)
    APS Archives and Minutes
    Franklin Papers
    Franklin Papers, Com. of Secret Correspondence
    Franklin Papers, Corresp. of R. H. Lee
    Feinstein Coll.
    Joseph Shippen Letterbooks
    Early Proceedings of the APS . . . 1744 to 1838 (Philadelphia, 1884)
  City Hall
    Recorder of Deeds
    Register of Wills
  Free Library
    Hampton L. Carson Coll. of law books
    Rare Book Dept.
  Library of the College of Physicians of Philadelphia
    Robert McKean items
  The Library Company
    Broadsides, flyers
    Numerous statutes, printed as separate publications

Historical Society of Pennsylvania (HSP)
  Balch Papers
  Cadwalader Coll.
  Hampton L. Carson Coll.
  Clymer MSS
  Tench Coxe Papers
  Delaware MSS (on the Lower Counties)
  Dreer Coll.
  Etting Papers: Signers
  Gratz Coll.
  Hopkinson Papers
  Logan Papers
  Robert R. Logan Family Papers
  McKean Papers, 6 vols.
  Diary of Christopher Marshall (original)
  Pemberton Papers
  Penn MSS, Papers Relating to Lower Counties
  Penn MSS, 1684–1772
  Peters Papers
  Provincial Delegates Coll.
  Read Documents
  Shippen Papers
  Society Coll.
  Sprague Coll.: Lives of the Signers
  Supreme Court Notes
  Yeates Papers
  Broadside Coll. for 1776
Independence National Park
  Coll. of references in other libraries to activities in Independence Park area
Jenkins Law Library, Philadelphia Bar Association
Library of the Philadelphia Bar Association
  Many bound pamphlets
Presbyterian Historical Society
  Francis Alison MSS
  Ezra Stiles MSS
Prothonotary, Supreme Court, City Hall
  Appearance Docket
  Papers in Attainder
  Writs of Certiorari and Habeas Corpus
  Doan Gang #32
  Forfeited Estates files
  Oyer and Terminer Dockets:
    Sept. 1778 to Dec. 1786, 1787 to 1828
  Edward Shippen file
  Supreme Court: General Motions, 1750;
    Divorce, 1800 (docket with list of lawyers)

Special historical files of the Prothonotary
University of Pennsylvania Library
  Archives
University of Pennsylvania Law School
  (McKean lecture hall, and law club)
SWARTHMORE
  Friends Historical Library of Swarthmore
    Unpub. MSS of Burton Alva Konkle:
      "David Lloyd and the First Half Century of Pennsylvania"
      "Life and Writings of James Wilson, 1742–1798"
VALLEY FORGE
  The Picket Post
WEST CHESTER
  Chester County Historical Society
    T. McKean items
WILKES-BARRE
  Wyoming Historical and Geological Society
    (See Susquehanna Company Papers)
    T. McKean items
YORK
  Historical Society of York County
    T. McKean items

RHODE ISLAND

PROVIDENCE
  John Carter Brown Library
    Pennsylvania Pamphlets and MSS

VIRGINIA

WILLIAMSBURG
  Institute of Early American History and Culture
    Carleton (or Dorchester) Papers

WASHINGTON, D. C.

Library of Congress (L.C.)
  Wm. L. Atlee Papers
  George Bryan's Almanac Diary
  Papers of the Continental Congress
  Peter Force Papers
  T. McKean items
  Pennsylvania Papers
  Society for the Propagation of the Gospel (SPG) original Letters
  Charles Thomson MSS
  Rare Book Room
    Tench Coxe items

National Archives
   Continental Congress, Misc. Papers
   T. McKean items
   Tim. Pickering Letter Books
   W. D. Coll., Revolutionary War Records

WISCONSIN

MADISON
   The Historical Society of Wisconsin
   25 vols. Draper MSS, incl. Loyalist and Indian materials

II. CONTEMPORARY PRINTED ACCOUNTS

AUTOBIOGRAPHY, CORRESPONDENCE & PAPERS

Adair, Douglass and Schutz, John A., ed., *Peter Oliver's Origin and Progress of the American Rebellion* (N. Y., 1936; re-issued, Stanford, Calif., 1961)

Adams, Charles Francis, ed., *The Life and Works of John Adams* (10 vols., Boston, 1850–56)

Boyd, Julian P., ed., *The Papers of Thomas Jefferson* (17 vols. to date, Princeton, 1950–   )

Boyd, Julian P., ed., *The Susquehanna Company Papers* (11 vols., Ithaca, 1930–71; Vol. V–XI edited by Robert J. Taylor)

Boyer, Melville, J., ed., *The Letter Book of Jacob Weiss, Deputy Quartermaster General of the Revolution* (Allentown, Pa., 1951) [Vol. 21 of the Proceedings of the Lehigh County Hist. Soc.]

The Burd Papers: Extracts from Chief Justice William Allen's Letter Book (n.p., 1897)

Burnett, Edmund Cody, ed., *Letters of the Members of the Continental Congress* (8 vols., Washington, 1921–36)

Butterfield, Lyman H., ed., *et al., The Adams Papers* (4 vols., Cambridge, 1961–   )

Butterfield, Lyman H., ed., *Letters of Benjamin Rush, 1761–1792* (2 vols., Princeton, 1951)

Corner, George W., ed., *The Autobiography of Benjamin Rush* (Princeton, 1948)

Crary, Catherine S., ed., *The Price of Loyalty: Tory Writings from the Revolutionary Era* (N. Y., 1973)

Cushing, Henry Alonzo, ed., *The Writings of Samuel Adams* (3 vols., N. Y., 1907)

Dorson, Richard M., ed., *America Rebels: Narratives of the Patriots* (N. Y., 1953)

Drayton, John, *Memoirs of the American Revolution* (2 vols., Charleston, 1821, based on the notes of the author's father, William Henry Drayton)

Duane, William, ed., *Extracts from the Diary of Christopher Marshall, 1774–1781* Albany, N. Y., 1877 (original in HSP)

Graydon, Alexander, *Memoirs of a Life Chiefly Passed in Pennsylvania within the Last Sixty years, with Occasional Remarks upon the General Occurrences, Character and Spirit of that Eventful Period* (Harrisburg, 1811; reprinted Phila., 1846, John Stockton Littel, ed., as *Memoirs of His Own Time*)

Hart, A. B., ed., *American History Told by Contemporaries* (2 vols., N. Y., 1934)

Hastings, George Everett, *The Life and Works of Francis Hopkinson* (Chicago, 1926)

Fitzpatrick, John C., ed., *Writings of Washington* (39 vols., Washington, 1931–44)

Labaree, Leonard W., ed., *The Papers of Benjamin Franklin* (17 vols. to 1973, New Haven; vols. 16, 17, ed. William B. Willcox)

Lewis, John Frederick, ed., *Thomas Spry, Lawyer and Physician: The First Attorney Admitted to Practise under English Law in the Delaware River Settlements now . . . Pennsylvania, New Jersey and Delaware* (Phila., 1932)

Mass. Hist. Soc., comp., *The Warren-Adams Letters* (2 vols., Boston, 1917, 1925)

Nolan, J. Bennet, ed., *Neddie Burd's Reading Letters* (Reading, Pa., 1927)

Read, William Thompson, ed., *Life and Correspondence of George Read* (Phila., 1870)

Reed, William B., ed., *Life and Correspondence of Joseph Reed* (2 vols., Phila., 1847)

Ryden, George H., ed., *Letters to and from Caesar Rodney, 1756–1784* (Phila., 1933; reprinted Dover, Del., 1943)

Smith, William Henry, ed., *St. Clair Papers: The Life and Public Service of Arthur St. Clair* (2 vols., Cincinnati, 1882)

Sparks, Jared, ed., *Diplomatic Correspondence of the American Revolution* (12 vols., Boston, 1829–30)

Sparks, Jared, ed., *The Works of Benjamin Franklin* (10 vols., Boston, 1840)

Stillé, Charles J., *The Life and Times of John Dickinson, 1732–1808* (Phila., 1891)

Tappert, T. G. and Doberstein, J. W., trans. & ed., *The Journals of Henry Melchoir Muhlenberg* (2 vols., Phila., 1945)

Tatum, Edward H., Jr., ed., *The American Journal of Ambrose Serle, Secretary to Lord Howe, 1776–1778* (San Marino, Calif., 1940)

Thompson, Thomas McKean, "The Thompson Register," in Delaware State Archives, Dover, and in slightly different form in PMHB, LII, No. 1

Vaughan, Alden T., ed., *America Before the Revolution, 1725–1775* [Contemporary accounts] (Englewood Cliffs, N. J., 1967)

Walker, Lewis Burd, ed., *The Burd Papers, Selections from Letters Written by Edward Burd, 1763–1828* (Phila., 1899)

Walpole, Horace, *The Letters . . .* [var. ed]; *The Letters of Horace Walpole,* selected by William Hadley (1 vol., London, 1926)

Walpole, Horace, *Memoirs of the Reign of King George III* (4 vols., London, 1845)

Walsh, Richard, ed., *The Writings of Christopher Gadsden, 1746–1805* (Columbia, S. C., 1966)

Wharton, Francis, ed., *The Revolutionary Diplomatic Correspondence of the United States* (6 vols., Washington, 1889)

Willcox, William B., ed., *The American Rebellion, Sir Henry Clinton's Narrative of his Campaigns, 1775–1782* (New Haven, 1954)

BROADSIDES & PAMPHLETS

To the Electors of Pennsylvania, by a Pennsylvanian, 1799 (John Carter Brown Library, Providence) [Anon.]

"To the Republicans of Pennsylvania," [Anon.] Aug. 7, 1799

Balch, Thomas, ed., *Examination of Joseph Galloway, Esq. . . . by . . . The House of Commons* (Phila., 1855)

Boyd, Hugh M., *Genuine Abstract from Two Speeches of the late Earl of Chatham* (1799)

College of Philadelphia, *Four Dissertations on the Reciprocal Advantages of a Perpetual Union Between Great Britain and Her Colonies* (Phila., 1766)— Beineke Library, Yale University

Galloway, Joseph, *A Candid Examination of the Mutual Claims of Great Britain and the Colonies* (N. Y., 1775)

McKean, Thomas, *Charge Delivered to the Grand Jury by the Honorable Thomas McKean, Esquire* (Lancaster, printed by Francis Bailey, 1778), The Library Company, Phila.

McKean, Thomas, and Physick, Edmund, *A Calm Appeal to the People of the State of Delaware,* Sept. 3, 1793 (Printed by Zachariah Poulson, Jun'r., No. 8 Chestnut Street, Phila.)—Widener Library, Harvard University

Rush, Benjamin, *An Account of the Bilious Remitting Yellow Fever . . .* (Phila., 1794)

Henry Wilson of West Chester, letter to Prof. Charles W. Heathcote, Jan. 1, 1939: maps and data from land records in Chester County pertaining to Thomas McKean, in Hist. Soc. of York County

Wöchentliche Philadelphische Staatsbote (Phila., Jan. 6, 1766)

NEWSPAPERS

Boston Gazette (1719–1798)

Draper's *Massachusetts Gazette: and the Boston Weekly News-letter* (1704–1776)

Moore, Frank, ed., *Diary of the American Revolution* [newspapers, broadsides, extracts] (2 vols., N. Y., 1860)

The New-York Gazette: and the Weekly Mercury (1752–1783)

The New-York Journal; or, the General Advertiser (1766–1783)

Niles' Weekly Register (Baltimore, 1811–1849)

The Aurora (Phila., 1794–1829, 1834–35) [see the Philadelphia *General Advertiser*]

The Pennsylvania Chronicle (Phila., 1767–1774)

The Pennsylvania Evening Post (Phila., 1776–1783)

Pennsylvania Gazette (Phila., 1728–1815)

The General Advertiser (Phila., 1790–94) [In 1794, *The General Advertiser* became the *Aurora*. See also the *Pennsylvania Journal*]

Pennsylvania Journal and Weekly Advertiser (Phila., 1742–93) [in 1793, the *Journal* merged with the *General Advertiser*]

Philadelphische Staatsbote (Phila., ca. 1761–1777)

Tory Newspapers Printed in Philadelphia during the British Occupation (HSP)
 Pennsylvania Ledger or the Philadelphia Market Day Advertiser
 The Pennsylvania Evening Post
 Royal Pennsylvania Gazette

BOOKS

Cobbett, William, *Porcupine's Works* (12 vols., London, 1801)

Dickinson, John, *The Political Writings of John Dickinson, Esq.* (2 vols., Wilmington, Del., 1801) in Franklin Coll., Yale University

Gordon, William, *History of the Rise, Progress and Establishment of the Independence of the United States of America* (N. Y., 1794)

Hopkinson, Francis, *Miscellaneous Essays and Occasional Writings of Francis Hopkinson* (Phila., 1792)

Sargent, Winthrop, ed., *The Loyal Verses of Joseph Stansbury and Dr. Jonathan Odell* (Albany, N. Y., 1860)

[Tilton, Dr. James?] Munroe, John A., ed., *The Biographical History of Dionysius, Tyrant of Delaware, addressed to the People of the United States of America by Timoleon* (Newark, Del., 1958)

Trumbull, John, *M'Fingal: An Epic Poem* (with notes by Benson J. Lossing, N. Y., 1881)

Walople, Horace, *A Catalogue of the Royal and Noble Authors of England, Scotland and Ireland* (5 vols., London, 1806)

Watson, John F., *Annals of Philadelphia* (Phila., 1830)

III. OFFICIAL RECORDS AND DOCUMENTS

(See also I, MSS & Collections)

DELAWARE

Delaware Archives (5 vols., Wilmington, 1911–16)

Original Land Titles in Delaware, commonly known as the Duke of York Record . . . 1646 to 1679 (1903)

A Calendar of Delaware Wills, New Castle County, 1682–1800 (N. Y., 1911)

The Laws of the Government of New-Castle, Kent and Sussex upon Delaware, 1753–62 (2 vols., Wilmington, 1763, pub. by authority of the General Assembly, by Thomas McKean and Caesar Rodney.) [Believed to be first book printed in Del.] The Library Company of Phila.

Read, George, ed., *Laws of the State of Delaware, 1700–1797* (2 vols., New Castle, printed by Samuel and John Adams [no kin to the famous cousins], 1797)

Minutes of the Council of the Delaware State, from 1776 to 1792 (Dover, pub. by authority of the General Assembly, 1886)

Votes and Proceedings of the House of Representatives of the Government of the Counties of New Castle, Kent, and Sussex, upon Delaware, at a Session of Assembly Held at New Castle the Twenty-First Day of October (the Twentieth Being Sunday) 1765. Published by George Read and Thomas McKean, Esquires, by Order of the Assembly (Wilmington, Printed and Sold by James Adams, in Market Street, 1770)

Minutes of the House of Representatives of the Government of the Counties of New Castle, Kent and Sussex upon Delaware at Sessions held at New Castle in the Years, 1765–1766–1767–1768–1769–1770 (Dover, 1931)

Proceedings of the Convention of the Delaware State held at New Castle in 1776 (New Castle, 1776, reprinted Wilmington, 1927)

Corrections and Addenda to the Printed Volume Published by the State of Delaware, 1886, under the title "Minutes of the Council of the Delaware State from 1776 to 1792" (Dover, 1928)

MICHIGAN

Michigan Pioneer and Historical Collections, 1892

NEW JERSEY

The New Jersey Almanac, Tercentenary Edition (Trenton, 1963)

Archives of the State of New Jersey, First Series, Documents Relating to the Colonial History, 1631–1800.

Proceedings of the New Jersey Historical Society, then *New Jersey History*

Minutes of the Provincial Congress and the Council of Safety of the State of New Jersey [1775–1776] (Trenton, 1879)

NEW YORK

New-York Historical Society Collections [esp.] *for the Years 1871–5, 1878, 1883, 1916*

New York Genealogical and Biographical Record

PENNSYLVANIA

Pennsylvania Archives
1. *Colonial Records, 1683–1790,* 16 vols., Phila., 1852–53
2. 9 Series, 1852–1937
   (See *Guide to the Published Archives of Pennsylvania, Covering 138 vols.,* by Henry Howard Eddy, 1949)

Acts of the General Assembly . . . of Pennsylvania (Phila., 1812)

Journals of the House of Representatives of the Commonwealth of Pennsylvania 1776–1781 (Phila., 1782)

The Statutes at Large of Pennsylvania from 1682–1801 (Harrisburg, 1896–1908, James T. Mitchell and Henry Flanders, eds.)

Votes and Proceedings of the House of Representatives of the Province of Pennsylvania, 1682–1776 (6 vols., Phila., 1752–76)

Hazard's Register of Pennsylvania, Samuel Hazard, ed. (16 vols., Phila., 1828–1836)

McKean, Thomas, ed., *The Acts of the General Assembly of the Commonwealth of Pennsylvania* (Phila., 1782) [Referred to as "McKean's Laws"]

Pennsylvania Constitutional Conventions: Proceedings Relative to the Calling of the Conventions of 1776 and 1790 (Harrisburg, 1825)

Minutes of the Convention of the State of Pennsylvania from Monday, September 2, to Saturday, September 7, 1776 [The Library Company] (Phila., 1776)

Votes of the Pennsylvania Assembly, Oct. 1775–Sept. 1776 [The Library Company]

RHODE ISLAND

J. B. Bartlett, ed., *Records of the Colony of Rhode Island and Providence Plantation in New England (1636–1792)* (10 vols. Providence, 1856–65)

SOUTH CAROLINA

Journals of Provincial Congress of 1775 and 1776

VIRGINA

Kennedy, J. P., ed., *Journals of the House of Burgesses* [1761–1776] (4 vols., Williamsburg, 1905–1907)

WISCONSIN

Collections of the State Historical Society of Wisconsin, 1888, "Papers from the Canadian Archives, 1778–1783"

NATIONAL

Commager, Henry Steele, ed., *Documents of American History* (N. Y., 1940)

Force, Peter, ed., *American Achives,* Ser. IV and V (9 vols., Washington, 1837–1853)

Jensen, Merrill, ed., *English Historical Documents, IX, American Colonial Documents to 1776* (N. Y., 1955)

Ford, W. C. and Hunt, Gaillard, eds., *Journals of the Continental Congress, 1774–1789* (JCC) (34 vols., Washington, 1904–1937)

Morgan, Edmund S., ed., *Prologue to Revolution, Sources and Documents on the Stamp Act Crisis, 1774–1776* (Chapel Hill, 1959)

Niles, Hezekiah, *Principles and Acts of the Revolution* (Baltimore, 1822, also N. Y., 1876)

Stevens, Benjamin Franklin, comp., *Facsimilies of Manuscripts in European Archives Relating to America, 1773–1783* (24 vols., London, 1889–95)

Thorp, Francis H., *Federal and State Constitutions* (7 vols., Washington, 1909)

The Charlemagne Tower Collection of American Colonial Laws (privately printed for the HSP, Phila., 1890)

CANADIAN

Ontario Public Archives

Report of the Bureau of Archives for the Province of Ontario (esp. 1904–05, for "Proceedings of the Loyalist Commissioners, U. E. L. Inquiry" . . .)

Papers and Records of the Ontario Historical Society

Proceedings Transactions of the Royal Society of Canada (esp. Siebert, Wilbur H., "The Loyalists and Six Nations in the Niagara Peninsula," Third Ser., IX)

IV. COURT RECORDS, LAW REPORTS AND STUDIES

(See also entries I, MSS and Collections, and III, Official
Records and Documents)

PENNSYLVANIA: MSS & Collections:

Easton, Northampton County Courthouse

Harrisburg, Div. of Public Records (Bureau of Archives and History)

Philadelphia, City Hall, Office of the Prothonotary of the Supreme Court, Court Records

Philadelphia, HSP, Supreme Court Notes

Archbold, John Frederick, comp., ed., *The Practice of the Court of the King's Bench* (2 vols., 2nd American edition, N. Y., 1838)

Binney, Horace, ed., *Reports of Cases Adjudged in the Supreme Court of Pennsylvania* (Phila., 1809–1815, reprinted, 6 vols., 1890–1891)

Blackstone's Commentaries . . . , var. editions; *Erlich's Blackstone* (2 vols., N. Y., ed. 1959)

Brown, David Paul, *The Forum* (2 vols., Phila., 1856)

Chapin, Bradley, *The American Law of Treason: Revolutionary and Early National Origins* (Seattle, 1964)

Chroust, Anton-Hermann, *The Rise of the Legal Profession in America* (2 vols., Norman, Okla., 1965)

Dallas, A. J., Esq., *Reports of Cases Ruled and Adjudged in the Courts of Pennsylvania* (Phila., 1790)

Dallas, A. J., Esq., [The Above] *Continued as Reports of Cases . . . in the Several Courts of the United States and of Pennsylvania.* Vol. II, 1798; Vol. III, 1799; Vol. IV, 1807. The series dedicated to Thomas McKean. (Also the 4 vols., Phila., 1830, which are more complete.)

Eastman, Frank M., *Courts and Lawyers of Pennsylvania* (3 vols., N. Y., 1922)

Fleming, Donald and Bailyn, Bernard, ed., *Law in American History* (Cambridge, 1971)

Harding, Alan, *A Social History of English Law* (London, 1966)

Hogan, Edmund, ed., *The Pennsylvania State Trials: Containing the Impeachment, Trial, and Acquittal of Francis Hopkinson, and John Nicholson, Esquires* (Phila., 1794)

The Law Association of Philadelphia, *Addresses Delivered March 13, 1902 . . . To Commemorate the Centennial . . . of the Law Association* (Phila., 1906)

Levy, Leonard W., *Origins of the Fifth Amendment* (N. Y., 1968)

Loyd, William H., *The Early Courts of Pennsylvania* (Boston, 1910)

Lunt, Dudley Cammett, *Tales of the Delaware Bench and Bar* (Newark, Del., 1961)

Martin, John Hill, *Martin's Bench and Bar of Philadelphia* (Phila., 1883)

Miller, Helen Hill, *The Case for Liberty,* [Colonial court cases 1676–1773] (Chapel Hill, 1965)

Oberholtzer, Ellis Paxson, *The Referendum in America . . .* (Phila., 1893) [Vol. IV in *Political Economy and Public Law Series,* Univ. of Pa.]

Rutland, Robert Allen, *The Birth of the Bill of Rights, 1776–1791* (N. Y., London, 1955, 1962)

Smith, Joseph Henry, *Appeals to the Privy Council from the American Plantations* (N. Y., 1950)

V. BOOKS, GENERAL

BIOGRAPHIES

Alberts, Robert C., *The Golden Voyage: The Life and Times of William Bingham, 1752–1804* (Boston, 1969)

Allan, H. S., *John Hancock, Patriot in Purple* (N. Y., 1948)

Anderson, Troyer Steele, *The Command of the Howe Brothers During the American Revolution* (N. Y., 1936)

Armor, William G., *Lives of the Governors of Pennsylvania* (Phila., 1872)

Bancroft, George, *Joseph Reed, a Historical Essay* (N. Y., 1967)

Bowen, Catherine Drinker, *John Adams and the American Revolution* (Boston, 1950)

Bridenbaugh, Carl & Jessica, *Rebels and Gentlemen, Philadelphia in the Age of Franklin* (N. Y., 1965)

Buchanan, Roberdeau, *Genealogy of the McKean Family and* [the] *Life of the Hon. Thomas McKean* (Lancaster, Pa., 1890)

Clark, Mary Elizabeth, *Peter Porcupine in America; the Career of William Cobbett, 1792–1800* (Phila., 1939)

Corner, Betsy Copping, *William Shippen, Jr., Pioneer in American Medical Education* (Phila., APS, 1954)

Currey, Cecil B., *Code Number 72 Ben Franklin: Patriot or Spy?* (Englewood Cliffs, N. J., 1972)

Davids, Richard Wistar, *The Wistar Family: A Genealogy of the Descendants of Caspar Wistar* (Phila., 1898)

Finney, J. M. T., *A Surgeon's Life, the Autobiography of J. M. T. Finney* (N. Y., 1940)

Flexner, James T., *The Traitor and the Spy* (N. Y., 1953)

Forbes, Esther, *Paul Revere and the World He Lived In* (Boston, 1942)

Gruber, Ira D., *The Howe Brothers and the American Revolution* (N. Y., 1972)

Hamilton, William B., *Thomas Rodney: Revolutionary and Builder of the West* (Durham, N. C., 1953)

Harley, Lewis R., *The Life of Charles Thomson* (Phila., 1900)

Jordan, John W., *Colonial Families of Philadelphia* (2 vols., N. Y., & Chicago, 1911)

Keen, Gregory B., *The Descendants of Jöran Kyn of New Sweden* (Phila., 1913); also see *PMHB*.

Keith, Charles P., *The Provincial Councillors of Pennsylvania, Who Held Office Between 1733 and 1776, and Those Earlier Councillors, Who Were Some Time Chief Magistrates of the Province, and Their Descendants* (Phila., & Trenton, 1883)

Konkle, Burton Alva, *George Bryan and the Constitution of Pennsylvania, 1731–1791* (Phila., 1922)

Konkle, Burton Alva, *Benjamin Chew, 1722–1810* (Phila., 1932)

Konkle, Burton Alva, *The Life and Times of Thomas Smith, 1745–1809* (Phila., 1904)

Lossing, Benson J., *Eminent Americans* (N. Y., 1855, with additions, 1886)

McGee, Dorothy Horton, *Famous Signers of the Declaration* (N. Y., 1955)

Malone, Dumas, *Jefferson and his Time* (4 vols. to date, Boston, 1948–70)

Miller, John C., *Sam Adams: Pioneer in Propaganda* (Boston, 1936)

Morison, Samuel Eliot, *John Paul Jones: A Sailor's Biography* (Boston, 1959)

Nelson, William, *Edward Antill and His Descendants* (Patterson, N. J., 1899)

Nelson, William, *New Jersey Biographical and Genealogical Notes* (Newark, N. J., 1916)

Powell, John H., *General Washington and the Jack Ass* (South Brunswick, N. J., 1969)

Reed, William B., *The Life of Esther de Berdt, afterwards Esther Reed of Pennsylvania* (Phila., 1853)

Roche, John F., *Joseph Reed, a Moderate in the American Revolution* (N. Y., 1957)

Rogers, Thomas J., *Lives of the Departed Heroes, Sages and Statesmen . . .* [of the Revolution], (N. Y., 1834)

Ross, George E., *Know Your Declaration of Independence and the 56 Signers* (N. Y., 1963)

Rossman, Kenneth R., *Thomas Mifflin and the Politics of the American Revolution* (Chapel Hill, 1952)

Sabine, Lorenzo, *The American Loyalists, Biographical Sketches* (Springfield, Mass., 1847, 1864, and 1957)

"Sanderson, John," *Biography of the Signers of Independence by John Sanderson* (Phila., 1823, 1st ed., 8 vols. . . . various later editions, incl. abridged single vol. Many authors, group non de plume)

Sellers, Charles Coleman, *Charles Willson Peale* (N. Y., 1969)

Smith, Charles Page, *James Wilson, Founding Father* (Chapel Hill, 1956)

Springer, Ruth L., *John Morton in Contemporary Records* (Harrisburg, PHMC, 1967)

Stone, William L., *Life of Joseph Brant* (2 vols., Albany, N. Y., 1864)

Thayer, Theodore, *Israel Pemberton, King of the Quakers* (Phila., 1943)

Umbreit, Kenneth, *Founding Fathers: Men Who Shaped Our Tradition* (N. Y., 1941)

Van Doren, Carl, *Benjamin Franklin* (N. Y., 1938)

Wallace, Willard M., *Traitorous Hero, the Life and Fortunes of Benedict Arnold* (N. Y., 1954)

Waters, John V., *The Otis Family in Provincial and Revolutionary Massachusetts* (Chapel Hill, 1968)

Weld, Hattie Borden, *Historical and Genealogical Record . . . Richard and Joan Borden* [and] *Some of their Descendants* (n. p., 1899)

Williams, Basil, *The Life of William Pitt, Earl of Chatham* (2 vols., London, 1913, later N. Y., 1966)

HISTORY AND OTHER STUDIES

Alden, John Richard, *The American Revolution, 1775–1783* (N. Y., 1954)

Bailyn, Bernard, *The Ideological Origins of the American Revolution* (Cambridge, 1967)

Becker, Carl L., *The Declaration of Independence* (N. Y., 1922)

Bode, Carl et al., eds., *American Literature* (N. Y., 1966)

Bolles, Albert S., *Pennsylvania, Province and State . . . 1609–1790* (2 vols., Phila., 1899)

Boorstin, Daniel J., *The Americans: The Colonial Experience* (N. Y., 1958)

Boyd, Julian P., ed., *Anglo-American Union, Joseph Galloway's Plans to Preserve the British Empire 1774–1788* (Phila., 1941)

Brunhouse, Robert L., *The Counter-Revolution in Pennsylvania, 1766–1790* (Harrisburg, 1942)

Burnett, Edmund Cody, *The Continental Congress* (N. Y., 1941)

Burt, A. L., *The United States, Great Britain, and British North America* (New Haven, 1940)

Chidsey, A. D., Jr., *A Frontier Village, Pre-Revolutionary Easton* (Easton, Pa., 1940)

Collins, V. Lansing, *Princeton, Past and Present* (Princeton, 1931, 1945)

Conrad, Henry C., *History of the State of Delaware* (3 vols., Wilmington, 1908)

Cooke, Donald E., *Fathers of America's Freedom* (n. p., copyright Hammond, Inc., 1969)

Cowen, David L., *Medicine and Health in New Jersey: A History* (vol. 16 in the New Jersey Historical Series, Princeton, 1964)

Cross, Arthur Lyon, *The Anglican Episcopate and the American Colonies* (Harvard Hist. Studies, IX, 1902, reprinted Hamden, Conn., 1964)

Davidson, Philip, *Propaganda and the American Revolution, 1763–1783* (Chapel Hill, 1941)

Doniol, Henri, ed., *Histoire de la participation de la France à l'établissement des Etats-Unis d'Amérique* (5 vols., Paris, 1884–90)

Dunaway, Wayland F., *A History of Pennsylvania* (N. Y., 1935–1948)

Eisenhart, Luther P., *Historic Philadelphia* (Phila., APS, 1953)

Flick, Alexander C., ed., *History of the State of New York* (10 vols., N. Y., 1933–37)

Foley, Arthur, *The Early English Colonies: A Summary of the Lecture by the Right Hon. and Right Rev. Arthur Foley, Lord Bishop of London, with Additional Notes and Illustrations, Delivered at the Richmond Auditorium, Virginia, October 4, 1907* (Milwaukee, 1908)

Ford, Henry Jones, *The Scotch-Irish in America* (Princeton, 1915)

Frey, Caroll, *The Independence Square Neighborhood* (Phila., 1926)

Futhey, J. Smith and Cope, Gilbert, *History of Chester County, Pennsylvania* (Phila., 1881)

Gipson, Lawrence H., *The British Empire Before the American Revolution* (15 vols., N. Y.)

Goodrich, Phineas G., *History of Wayne County* (Honesdale, Pa., 1880)

Grattan, Thomas Colley, *Civilised America* (2 vols., London, 1859)

Greene, Evarts Boutell, *The Foundations of American Nationality* (N. Y., 1922)

Greene, George W., *Historical View of the American Revolution* (N. Y., 1865)

Haverstick, John, *The Progress of the Protestant* (N. Y., 1968)

Hawke, David, *In the Midst of a Revolution* (Phila., 1961)

Heller, William J., *History of Northampton County* (2 vols., 1920)

Higginbotham, Sanford W., *The Keystone in the Democratic Arch, 1800–1816* (Harrisburg, 1952)

Hindle, Brooke, *The Pursuit of Science in Revolutionary America, 1735–1785* (Chapel Hill, 1956)

Hofstadter, Richard, *America at 1750: A Social Portrait* (N. Y., 1971)

Horner, William S., *This Old Monmouth of Ours* (Freehold, N. Y., 1932)

Jenkins, H. M., *Pennsylvania, Colonial and Federal; a History, 1608–1903* (3 vols., Phila., 1903)

Jensen, Merrill, *The New Nation: A History of the United States During the Confederation, 1708–1789* (N. Y., 1950)

Jensen, Merrill, *The Founding of a Nation: A History of the American Revolution, 1763–1776* (N. Y., 1968)

Jones, Rufus, *The Quaker in the American Colonies* (N. Y., 1966)

Klein, Philip S., and Hoogenboom, Ari, *A History of Pennsylvania* (N. Y., 1973)

Knollenberg, Bernard, *Origin of the American Revolution* (N. Y., 1960)

Labaree, Benjamin Woods, *The Boston Tea Party* (N. Y., 1964)

Lanctot, Gustave, *Canada and the American Revolution, 1774–1783* (Toronto, Canada, 1967)

Leake, James Miller, *The Virginia Committee System and the American Revolution* (Baltimore, 1917)

Lincoln, Charles H., *The Revolutionary Movement in Pennsylvania* (Phila., 1901)

Lossing, Benson J., *The Pictorial Field-Book of the American Revolution* (2 vols., N. Y., 1850)

McMaster, John Bach, *A History of the People of the United States . . .* [1783–1861] (8 vols., N. Y., 1883–1913)

McSherry, James, *A History of Maryland* (Baltimore, 1850)

Malone, Dumas, *The Story of the Declaration of Independence* (N. Y., 1954)

Mathews, Alfred, *History of Wayne, Pike, and Monroe Counties* (Phila., 1886)

Metzger, Charles H., S. J., *The Prisoner in the American Revolution* (Chicago, 1971)

Montgomery, Martin L., *History of Berks County, Pennsylvania, from 1774 to 1783* (Reading, Pa., 1894)

Montgomery, Thomas H., *A History of the University of Pennsylvania* (Phila., 1900)

Morgan, Edmund and Helen M., *The Stamp Act Crisis: Prologue to Revolution* (Chapel Hill, 1953)

Morris, Richard B., *Government and Labor in Early America* (N. Y., 1946)

Munroe, John A., *Federalist Delaware, 1775–1815* (New Brunswick, N. Y., 1954)

Nevins, Allan, *The American States During and After the Revolution* (N. Y., 1924)

Nye, R. B., and Morpurgo, J. E., *A History of the United States* (2 vols., Middlesex, England, 1955, revised, 1964)

Oberholtzer, Ellis Paxson, *Philadelphia, A History of the City and People* (4 vols., Phila., no date)

Pennypacker, Hon. Samuel W., *Pennsylvania the Keystone* (Phila., 1914)

Perry, William Steven, *The History of the American Episcopal Church, 1587–1883* (2 vols., Boston, 1885)

Rogers, Fred B. and Sayer, A. Reasoner, *The Healing Art: a History of the Medical Society of New Jersey* (Trenton, 1966)

Rossiter, Clinton, *The Political Thought of the American Revolution* (N. Y., 1953)

Ruik, Ewald, *Printing in Delaware, 1761–1800* (Wilmington, Del., 1969)

Ryden, George H., *Delaware, the First State of the Union* (Wilmington, Del., 1938)

Ryerson, Egerton, *The Loyalists of America and Their Times* (2 vols., Montreal, Canada, 1880)

Sachse, Julius F., *Old Masonic Lodges of Pennsylvania . . . 1730–1800* (2 vols., Phila., 1912–13)

Sanders, Jennings B., *Evolution of Executive Departments of the Continental Congress* (Chapel Hill, 1935)

Scharf, J. Thomas, *History of Delaware* (2 vols., Phila., 1888), reissued by the Kernikat Press, Port Washington, N. Y., 1972.

Scharf, J. Thomas and Westcott, Thompson, *History of Philadelphia* (3 vols., Phila., 1884)

Schlesinger, Arthur M., *Prelude to Independence, the Newspaper War on Britain, 1764–1776* (N. Y., 1965)

Sears, Robert, *The Pictorial History of the American Revolution: with a Sketch of the Early History of the Country* . . . (N. Y., 1846)

Selsam, J. Paul, *The Pennsylvania Constitution of 1776: a Study of Revolutionary Democracy* (Phila., 1936)

Severance, Frank H., *Old Trails on the Niagara Frontier* (Cleveland, 1903)

Sharpless, Isaac, *A History of Quaker Government in Pennsylvania* (2 vols., Phila., 1899)

Shepherd, William R., *History of Proprietary Government in Pennsylvania* (N. Y., 1896)

Shy, John, *Towards Lexington: the Role of the British Army in the Coming of the American Revolution* (Princeton, 1965)

Siebert, Wilbur H., *The Loyalists of Pennsylvania* (Columbus, Ohio, 1894)

Smith, Paul H., *Loyalists and Redcoats: A Study in British Revolutionary Policy* (N. Y., copyright Univ. of N. C. Chapel Hill, 1964)

Stevens, Sylvester K., *Pennsylvania, Birthplace of a Nation* (N. Y., 1964)

Sweet, William Warren, *Religion in the Development of American Culture 1765–1840* (N. Y., 1952)

Swigett, Howard, *War out of Niagara* (N. Y., 1933)

Thayer, Theodore, *Pennsylvania Politics and the Growth of Democracy, 1740–1776* (Harrisburg, 1953)

Tyler, Moses Coit, *The Literary History of the American Revolution* (2 vols., N. Y., 1897)

Wallace, Paul A. W., *Indian Paths of Pennsylvania* (Harrisburg, 1965)

Ward, Christopher, *The War of the Revolution* (John Richard Alden, ed., 2 vols., N. Y., 1952)

Westcott, Thompson, *Historic Mansions of Philadelphia* (Phila., 1877, revised ed., 1895)

Wickes, Stephen, *History of Medicine in New Jersey and of its Medical Men* (Newark, N. J., 1879)

Wood, George B., *Early History of the University of Pennsylvania* . . . (Phila., 1896, 3rd ed.)

Woodward, E. M. and Hageman, John, *History of Burlington and Mercer Counties, with Biographical Sketches of Many of their Pioneer and Prominent Men* (Phila., 1883)

Wright, Louis B., *The Atlantic Frontier, Colonial American Civilization* (Ithaca, N. Y., 1947)

VI. PUBLICATIONS

ARTICLES

Coleman, John M., "The Treason of Ralph Morden and Robert Land," *PMHB,* Oct., 1955

Coleman, John M., "Robert Land and Some Frontier Skirmishes," *Ontario History,* 1956, No. 2

Coleman, John M., "Joseph Galloway and the British Occupation of Philadelphia," *Penna. History,* July, 1963

Coleman, John M., "Thomas McKean and the Origin of an Independent Judiciary," *Penna. History,* April, 1967

Coleman, John M., "How 'Continental' was the Continental Congress?" *History Today,* Aug., 1968

Cunningham, Mary E., "The Case of the 'Active'," *Penna. History,* XII 1946

Cunningham, Noble E., Jr., "Early Political Handbills in the United States," *William and Mary Quarterly,* Third Ser., XIV

De Valinger, Leon Jr., "Rodney Letters," *Delaware History,* I, No. 1

Gipson, Lawrence H., "An Anomalous Colony" *Penna. History,* 1960, No. 2

Gipson, Lawrence H., "The Great Debate in the Committee of the Whole House of Commons on the Stamp Act, 1766, as Reported by Nathaniel Ryder," *PMHB,* LXXXVI, No. 1

Hancock, Harold B., "Letters to and from Caesar Rodney," *Delaware History,* XII, No. 1

Hancock, Harold, ed., "The Kent County Loyalists: Documents," *Delaware History,* VI, No. 1

Henderson, H. James, "Constitutionalists and Republicans in the Continental Congress, 1778–1786," *Penna. History,* XXXVI, No. 2

Hicks, Susan, "The Pennsylvania Constitution of 1776," Valley Forge Hist. Soc., *The Picket Post.* Jan.–Apr., 1966

Hummel, Levi, "Notes on the Hummel Family," *The Penn-Germania,* continued as *The Pennsylvania-German,* II, 1913, No. 2

Hurst, Willard, "Treason in the United States," *Harvard Law Review,* Dec., 1944, Feb., 1945, July, 1945

Hurst, Willard, "English Sources of the American Law of Treason," *Wisconsin Law Review,* May, 1945

Hutson, James H., "The Campaign to Make Pennsylvania a Royal Province, 1764–1770," *PMHB,* XCIV, No. 4 and XCV, No. 1

Jensen, Merrill, "The American People and the American Revolution," *Jour. of Amer. History,* June, 1970

Lewis, E. Miriam, "The Minutes of the Wilmington Academy," *Delaware History,* III, No. 2

Thomas McKean, letter to George Washington, 1789, *American History Review,* II, No. 1

Meehan, Thomas R., "Courts, Cases, and Counselors in Revolutionary and Post-Revolutionary Pennsylvania," *PMHB,* 1967, No. 1

Meehan, Thomas R., "Divorce in Early Pennsylvania," *PMHB,* 507

Morris, Anna Wharton, ed., "Journal of Samuel Rowland Fisher of Philadelphia 1779–1781," *PMHB,* 1917, No. 2

Munroe, John A., "The Philadelawareans: A Study in the Relations Between Philadelphia and Delaware in the Late Eighteenth Century," *PMHB,* LXIX, No. 2

Pears, Thomas Clinton, "Francis Alison, Colonial Educator," *Delaware Notes,* Seventeenth Ser., 1944

Rogers, Fred B., "The Last Illness of Robert McKean (1732–1767)," *Journal of the Medical Society of New Jersey*

Rogers, Fred B., "Robert McKean, First President of the Medical Society of New Jersey," *Journal of the Medical Society of New Jersey,* Sept., 1953

Rogers, J. Alan, "Colonial Opposition to the Quartering of Troops during the French and Indian War," *Military Affairs,* Feb., 1970

Rowe, Gail S., "Thomas McKean and the Coming of the Revolution," *PMHB,* XCVI, No. 1

Rowe, Gail S., "The Legal Career of Thomas McKean, 1750–1775," *Delaware History,* XVI, 1 (pub. after this book went to press)

Smythe, John, "Narrative Journal of Captain Smythe, Queen's Rangers," *PMHB,* XXXIX, No. 2

Walker, Lewis Burd, "Life of Margaret Shippen, Wife of Benedict Arnold," *PMHB,* 1901, No. 1

Wilmerding, Lucius, Jr., "The United States Lottery," *The New-York Hist. Quart*[erly] Jan., 1963

Young, Henry J., "Treason and its Punishment," *PMHB,* XC

PAMPHLETS AND OCCASIONAL PUBLICATIONS

Conrad, Henry Clay, "The Three Signers . . . an Address . . . before the Sons of Delaware, of Philadelphia, Pennsylvania, Saturday evening, Jan. 30, 1897" (Wilmington, 1897)—Widener Library, Harvard University

Delaware Federal Writers' Project, *New Castle on the Delaware* (1950)

Munroe, John A., *Delaware Becomes a State* (Newark, Del., 1953)

Penna. Hist. and Museum Commission (PHMC), Information Leaflet No. 3, "The Military System of Pennsylvania During the Revolutionary War"

Two Hundredth Anniversary of the New London Presbyterian Church . . . Celebrated June 13, 14, and 15, 1926, Historical Sketch with Illustrations

JOURNALS

American Historical Review (AHR)

Transactions of the Moravian Historical Society [Bethlehem, Pa.]

Transactions of the American Philosophical Society

Greater Philadelphia Am. Civ. Lib. Union [ACLU], *Civil Liberties Record,* Feb., 1963, Vol. 12, No. 1

Collections of the Connecticut Historical Society

Delaware History
Delaware Notes
Harvard Law Review
History Today (pub. by *Financial Times,* London)
Journal of American History (see *Miss. Valley Hist. Rev.*)
Journal of the American Irish Historical Society
Massachusetts Historical Society Collections
Massachusetts Historical Society Proceedings
Journal of the Medical Society of New Jersey
Military Affairs
Mississippi Valley Historical Review, which became the *Journal of American History* (June, 1964)
Proceedings of the New Jersey Historical Society
New-York Historical Quarterly
Ontario History
The Penn-Germania, continued as *The Pennsylvania-German*
The Pennsylvania Docket
Pennsylvania Library Notes
Pennsylvania History
Pennsylvania Magazine of History and Biography (PMHB)
The Picket Post [Valley Forge, Pa.]
Proceedings of the Scotch-Irish Society of America
William and Mary Quarterly
Wisconsin Law Review

VII. UNPUBLISHED MONOGRAPHS

Chapin, Bradley, "The Law of Treason During the American Revolution," Ph.D. dissertation (Cornell, 1952), subsequently published as *The American Law of Treason* (Seattle, 1964)

Di Bacco, Thomas Victor, "Thomas McKean, Revolutionary Leader, 1774–1781" MA thesis (The American University, 1962)

Henderson, H. J., Jr., "Political Factions in the Continental Congress, 1774–1783," Ph.D. dissertation (Columbia, 1962)

Hindle, Brooke, "The Rise of the American Philosophical Society, 1766–1787," Ph.D. dissertation (University of Pennsylvania, 1949)

Kuntzleman, Oliver C., "Joseph Galloway, Loyalist," Ph.D. dissertation (Temple, 1941)

Meehan, Thomas R., "The Pennsylvania Supreme Court in the Law and Politics of the Commonwealth, 1776–1790," Ph.D. dissertation (Wisconsin, 1960)

Peeling, James H., "The Public Life of Thomas McKean, 1734–1817," Ph.D. dissertation (Chicago, 1929)

Rossie, Jonathan G., "The Politics of Command: the Continental Congress and Its Generals," Ph.D. dissertation (Wisconsin, 1966)

Rowe, Gail S., "Power, Politics and Public Service: the Life of Thomas McKean, 1734–1817," Ph.D. dissertation (Stanford, 1969)

Young, Henry J., "The Treatment of the Loyalists in Pennsylvania," Ph.D. dissertation (Johns Hopkins, 1955)

VIII. BIBLIOGRAPHIES AND REFERENCES

(in addition to in-house lists published by most of the large libraries visited)

Boatner, Mark M., III, *Encyclopedia of the American Revolution* (N. Y., 1966)

Beers, Henry P., "Bibliographies of Pennsylvania History," *Penna. Hist.,* I & II

Bining, Arthur C., comp., "A Selected Bibliography of Secondary Works on Pennsylvania History," *Penna. Lib. Notes,* Oct. 1933

County Government and Archives in Pennsylvania (Penna. Hist. & Mus. Comm., Harrisburg, 1947)

Dictionary of American Biography (DAB) (23 vols., N. Y., 1945)

Dictionary of National Biography (DNB) (63 vols., London, 1885–1901)

Evans, Charles, *American Bibliography* (14 vols., Chicago, 1903–1959) and *Supplement* (1970)

Goodwin, Parke, *Cyclopedia of Biography* (N. Y., 1865, with Supplement, 1872)

Harper's Encyclopedia of United States History (10 vols., N. Y., 1901)

The Pennsylvania Manual, Vol. 88, 1947–1948 (until 1922 pub. as *Smull's Legislative Hand-Book*) (Harrisburg, 1948)

Reed, Henry Clay and Marion, *Bibliography of Delaware through 1960* (1965)

Scribner's *Concise Dictionary of American Biography* (N. Y., 1964)

Manross, William Wilson, *The Fulham Papers in the Lambeth Palace Library, American Colonial Section, Calendar and Indexes* (Oxford, 1965)

University of Pennsylvania, *Biographical Catalogue of the Matriculates of the College, together with Lists of the Members of the College Faculty, and the Trustees, Officers, and Recipients of Honorary Degrees, 1749–1893* (Phila., 1894)

Virkus, Frederick A., *The Abridged Compendium of American Genealogy, First Families of America* (Chicago, 1928)

References for Maps

Map I, S. E. Pennsylvania & N. Delaware

Base map—U. S. Geodetic Survey Quadrangles, corrected to period 1730–1791.

"A Plan of the City and Environs of Philadelphia," 1777 survey by M. Scull and G. Heap, London. Possession of Author. Magazine, 1777.

"Chester County, 1820," prepared by John Hindman, Philadelphia, Pa., 1822. Chester County Hist. Society Collection.

"Delaware and Eastern Shore, Md., with Soundings of Delaware Bay, 1801," Public Archives Commission, Hall of Records, Dover, Del.

Howell, Reading, "Pennsylvania in 1791," copied from his Larger Map, HSP.

Wallace, Paul A. W., *Indian Paths of Pennsylvania, passim,* Commonwealth of Pennsylvania, Pennsylvania Historical and Museum Commission, Harrisburg, Pa. 1965.

Map II, New Jersey 1730–1780

Base Map—Geologic Map of New Jersey, 1959, by the Department of Conservation and Economic Development, Bureau of Geology and Topography.

U. S. Geologic Survey, NK 18-11, Series V501.

"Province of New Jersey," 2nd Edition, 1778, by the King's Surveyors *et. al.,* Engraved and published by Wm. Faden, Charing Cross, England.

Paxson, Henry D., "1776 Sesqui-Centenial Map, Bucks County Pa.," for Washington Crossing Park Commission of Pa., 1926, in N.J. State Library, Historical Section.

Map III, Pennsylvania Counties, 1780

Based on a map by Harold Faye in Stevens, Cordier, and Benjamin, *Exploring Pennsylvania,* Harcourt, Brace and Co. 1953, 57.

INDEX

Asterisks denote legal and judicial matters with which TMcK was concerned, as attorney or judge. Maps, tables, and textnotes have not been indexed. Daggers denote places whose locations have varied on paper, through divisions or sub-divisions of counties. Space considerations have caused the omission of states other than Delaware and Pennsylvania.